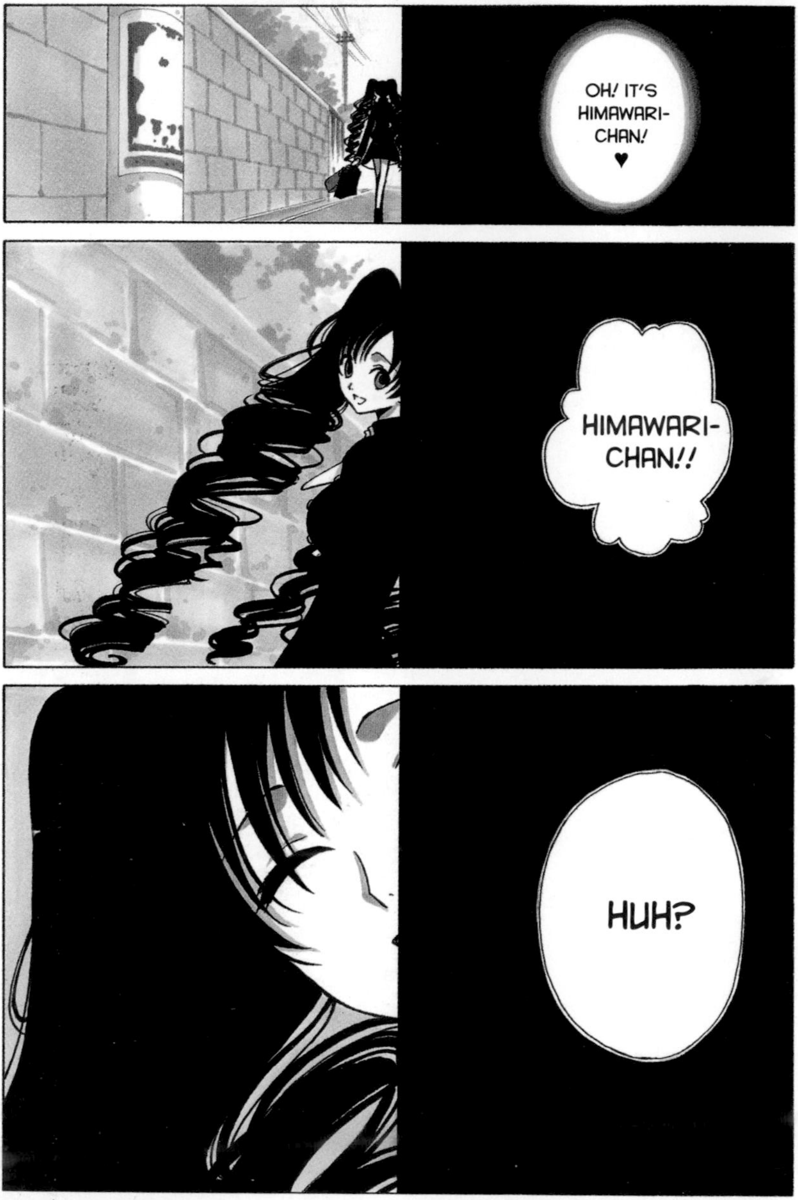
OH! IT'S HIMAWARI-CHAN! ♥
HIMAWARI-CHAN!!
HUH?

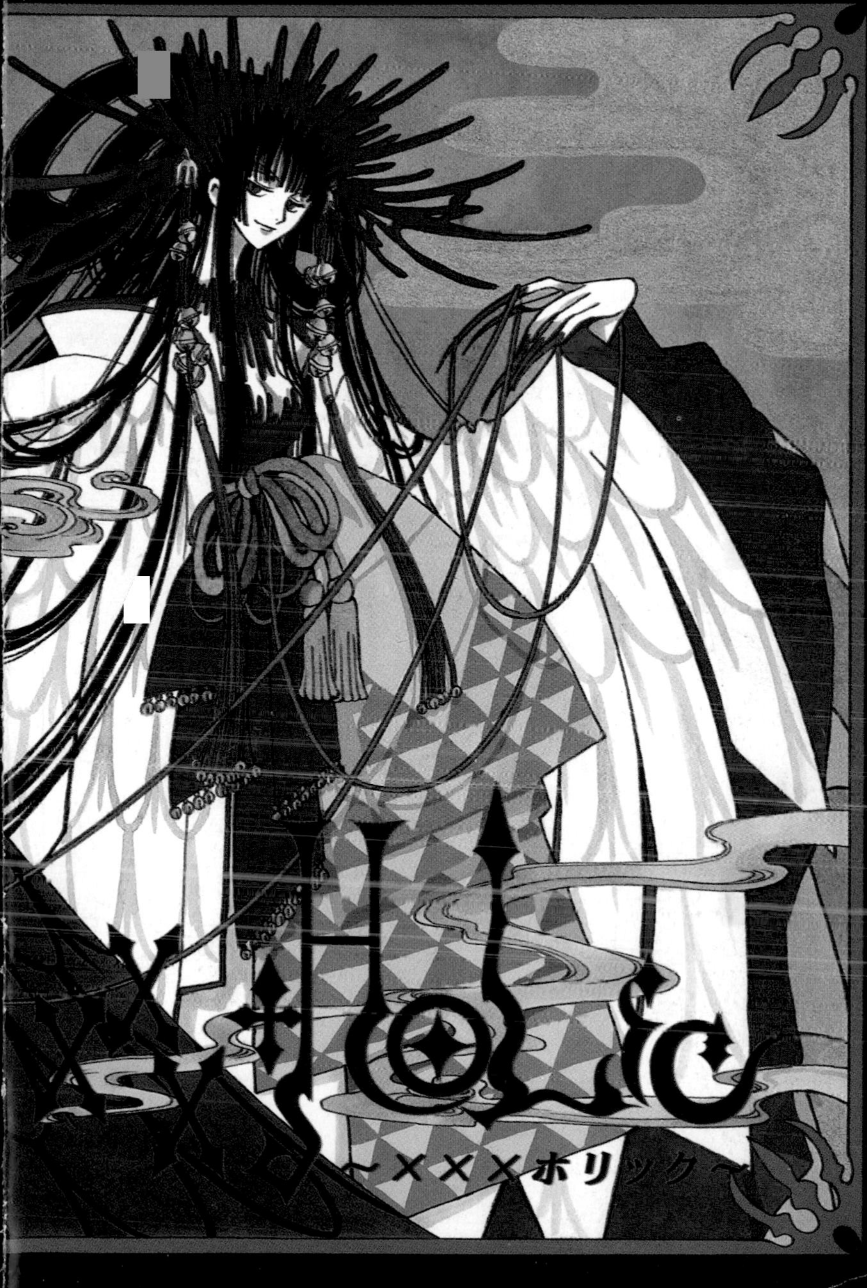
xxxHOLiC
〜×××ホリック〜

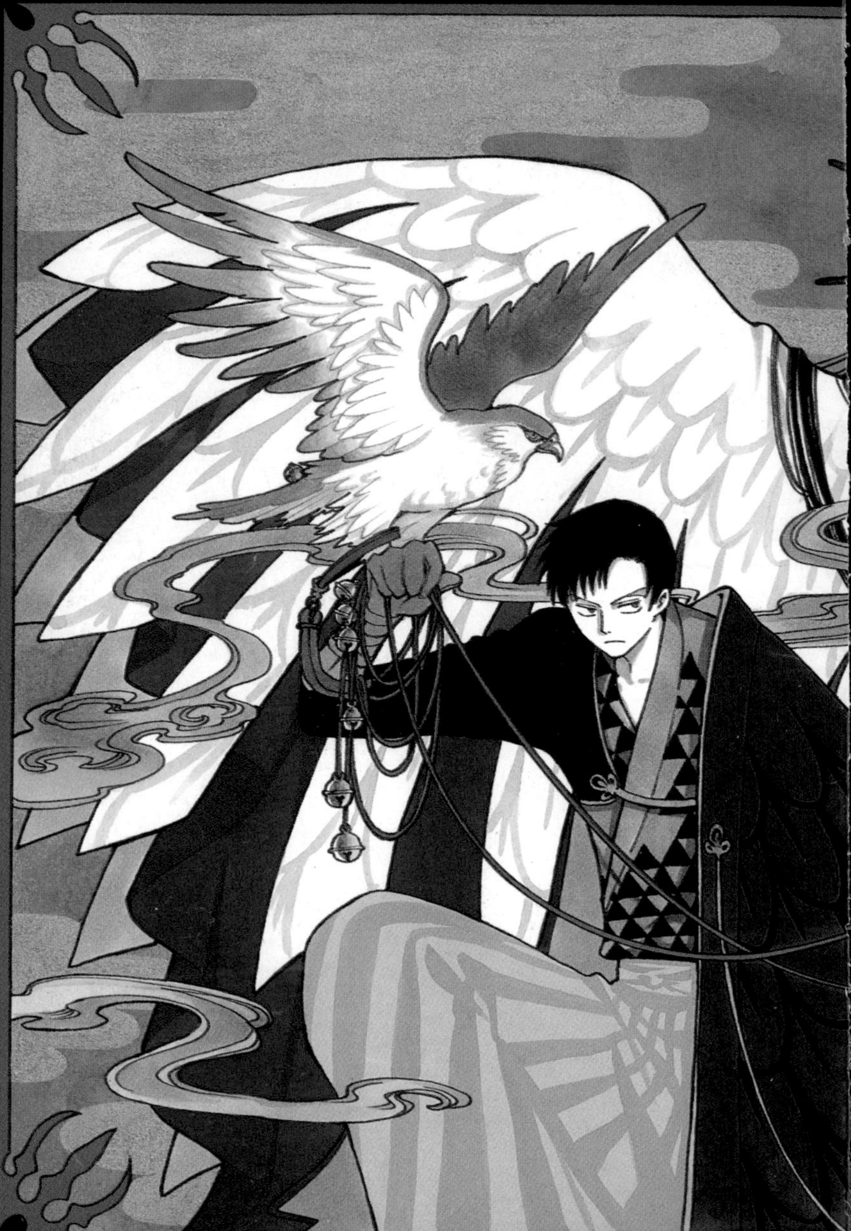

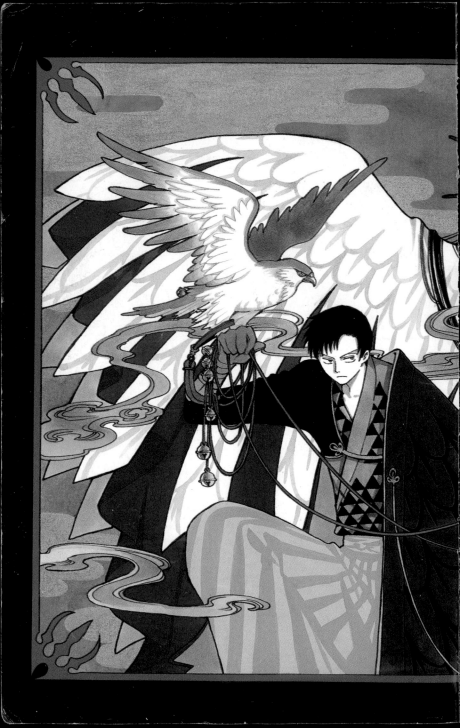

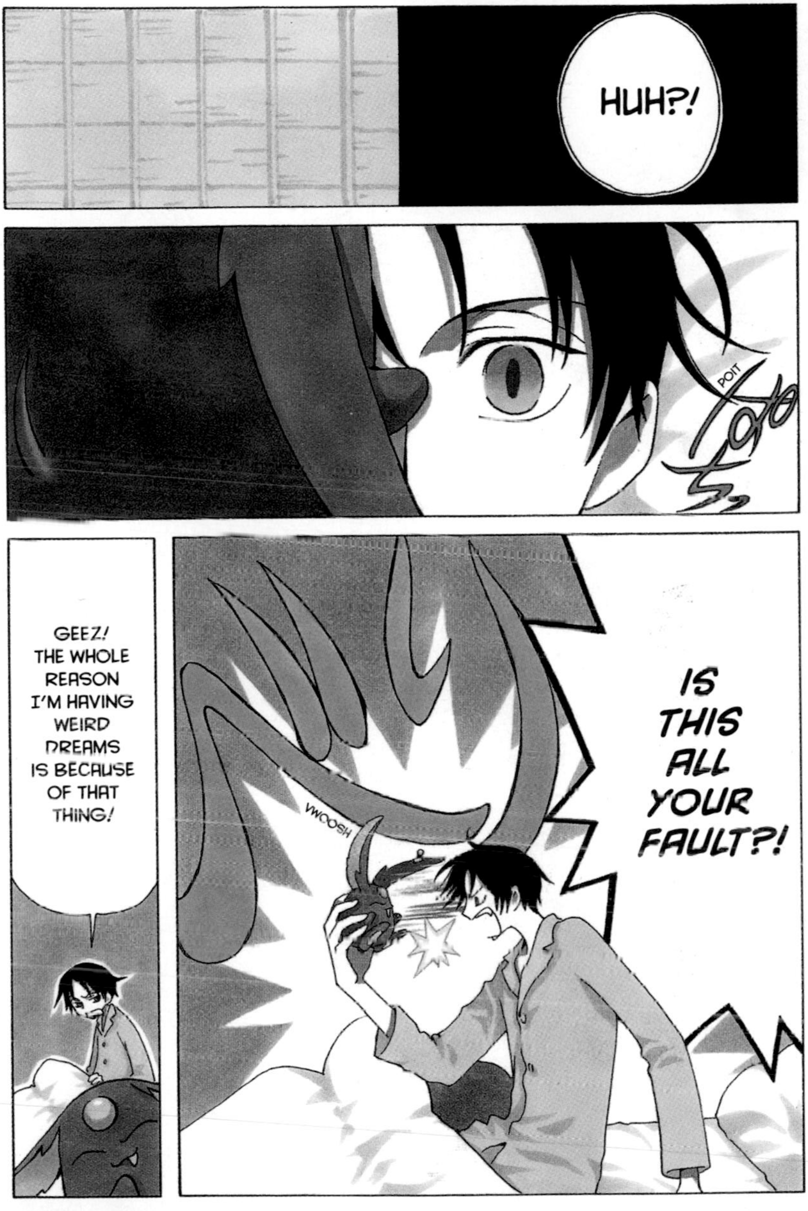
HUH?!
POIT
IS THIS ALL YOUR FAULT?!
VWOOSH
GEEZ! THE WHOLE REASON I'M HAVING WEIRD DREAMS IS BECAUSE OF THAT THING!

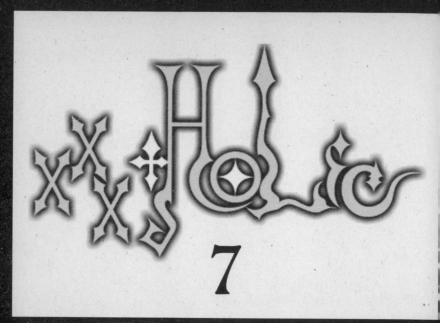

7

CLAMP

TRANSLATED AND ADAPTED BY
William Flanagan

LETTERED BY
Dana Hayward

BALLANTINE BOOKS · NEW YORK

2-07
11-

A Del Rey Trade Paperback Original

xxxHOLiC copyright © 2005 by CLAMP
English translation copyright © 2006 by CLAMP

Published in the United States by Del Rey Books, an imprint of The Random House Publishing Group, a division of Random House, Inc., New York.

Del Rey is a registered trademark and the Del Rey colophon is a trademark of Random House, Inc.

Publication rights arranged through Kodansha Ltd.

First published in Japan in 2005 by Kodansha Ltd., Tokyo.

ISBN 0-345-48335-9

Printed in the United States of America

www.delreymanga.com

9 8 7 6 5 4 3 2

Translator and Adaptor—William Flanagan
Lettering—Dana Hayward
Cover Design—David Stevenson

xxxHOLiC crosses over with *Tsubasa*. Although it isn't necessary to read *Tsubasa* to understand the events in *xxxHOLiC,* you'll get to see the same events from different perspectives if you read both series!

Contents

Honorifics Explained

Throughout the Del Rey Manga books, you will find Japanese honorifics left intact in the translations. For those not familiar with how the Japanese use honorifics and, more important, how they differ from American honorifics, we present this brief overview.

Politeness has always been a critical facet of Japanese culture. Ever since the feudal era, when Japan was a highly stratified society, use of honorifics—which can be defined as polite speech that indicates relationship or status—has played an essential role in the Japanese language. When addressing someone in Japanese, an honorific usually takes the form of a suffix attached to one's name (example: "Asuna-san"), or as a title at the end of one's name or in place of the name itself (example: "Negi-sensei," or simply "Sensei!").

Honorifics can be expressions of respect or endearment. In the context of manga and anime, honorifics give insight into the nature of the relationship between characters. Many translations into English leave out these important honorifics, and therefore distort the "feel" of the original Japanese. Because Japanese honorifics contain nuances that English honorifics lack, it is our policy at Del Rey not to translate them. Here, instead, is a guide to some of the honorifics you may encounter in Del Rey Manga.

-san: This is the most common honorific, and is equivalent to Mr., Miss, Ms., Mrs., etc. It is the all-purpose honorific and can be used in any situation where politeness is required.

-sama: This is one level higher than "-san." It is used to confer great respect.

-dono: This comes from the word "tono," which means "lord." It is an even higher level than "-sama," and confers utmost respect.

-kun: This suffix is used at the end of boys' names to express familiarity or endearment. It is also sometimes used by men among friends, or when addressing someone younger or of a lower station.

-chan: This is used to express endearment, mostly toward girls. It is also used for little boys, pets, and even among lovers. It gives a sense of childish cuteness.

Bozu: This is an informal way to refer to a boy, similar to the English term "kid" or "squirt."

Sempai/Senpai: This title suggests that the addressee is one's senior in a group or organization. It is most often used in a school setting, where underclassmen refer to their upperclassmen as "sempai." It can also be used in the workplace, such as when a newer employee addresses an employee who has seniority in the company.

Kohai: This is the opposite of "sempai," and is used toward underclassmen in school or newcomers in the workplace. It connotes that the addressee is of a lower station.

Sensei: Literally meaning "one who has come before," this title is used for teachers, doctors, or masters of any profession or art.

-[blank]: Usually forgotten in these lists, but perhaps the most significant difference between Japanese and English. The lack of honorific means that the speaker has permission to address the person in a very intimate way. Usually, only family, spouses, or very close friends have this kind of permission. Known as *yobisute*, it can be gratifying when someone who has earned the intimacy starts to call one by one's name without an honorific. But when that intimacy hasn't been earned, it can also be very insulting.

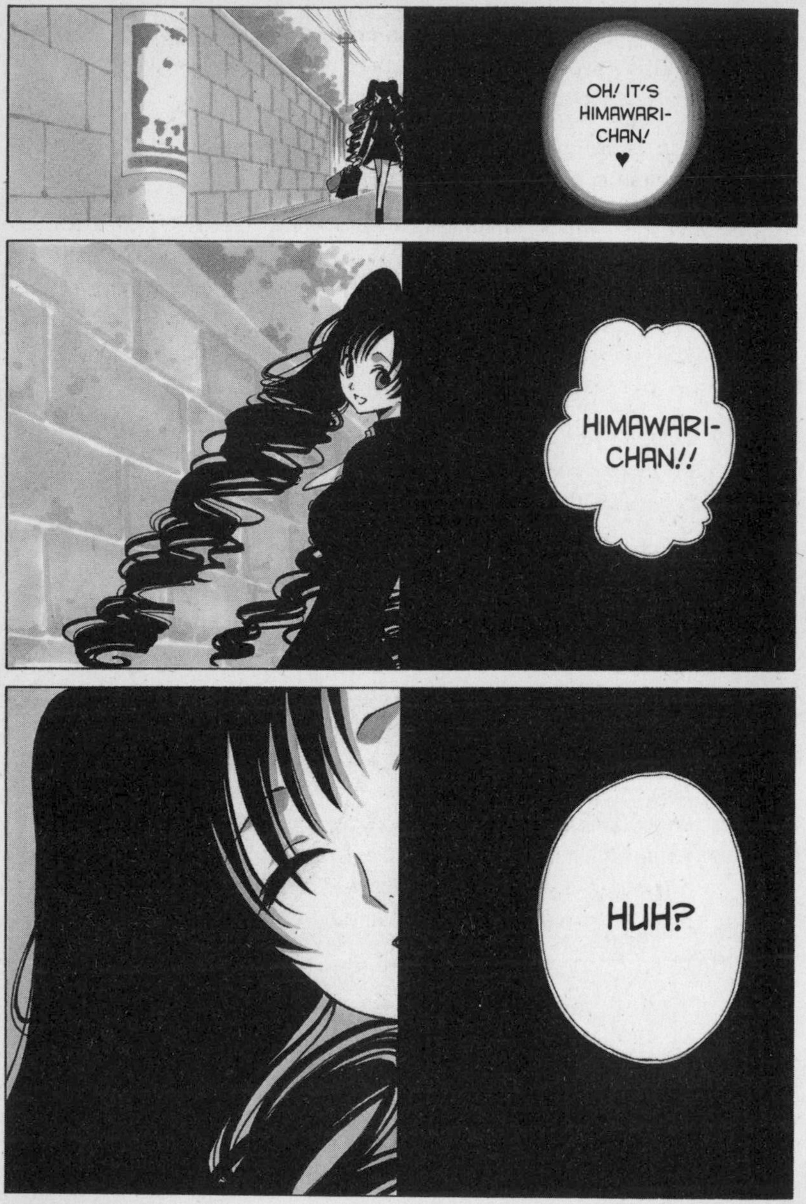
OH! IT'S HIMAWARI-CHAN! ♥
HIMAWARI-CHAN!!
HUH?

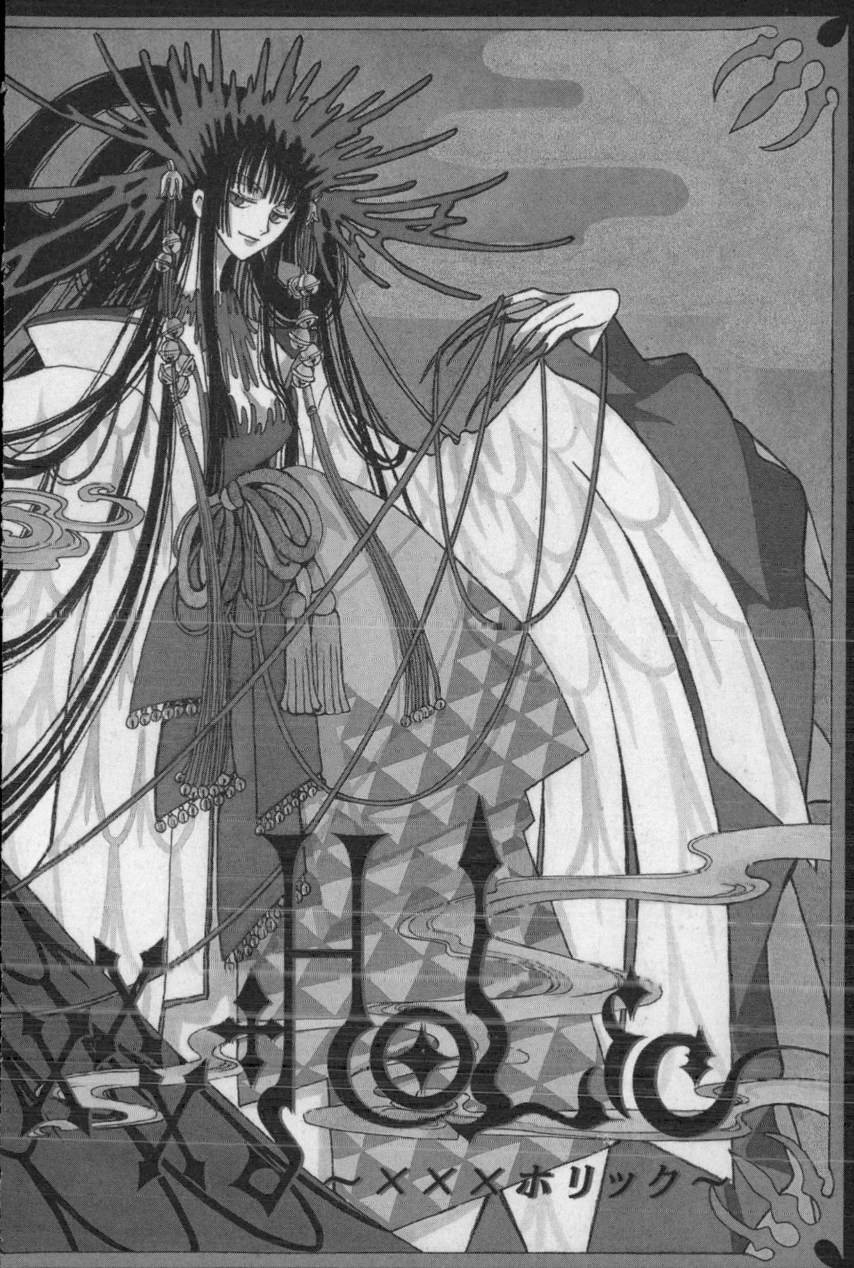
xxxHOLiC
〜×××ホリック〜

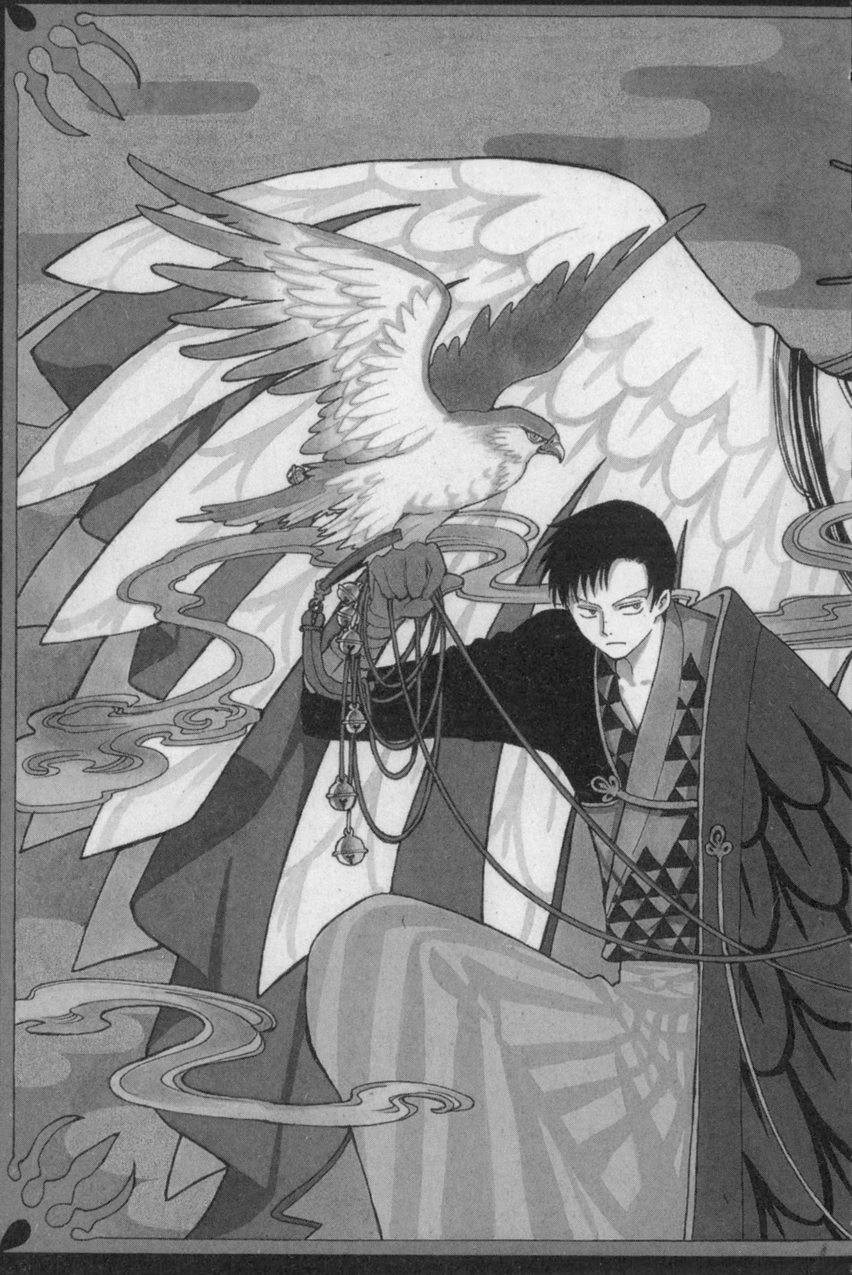

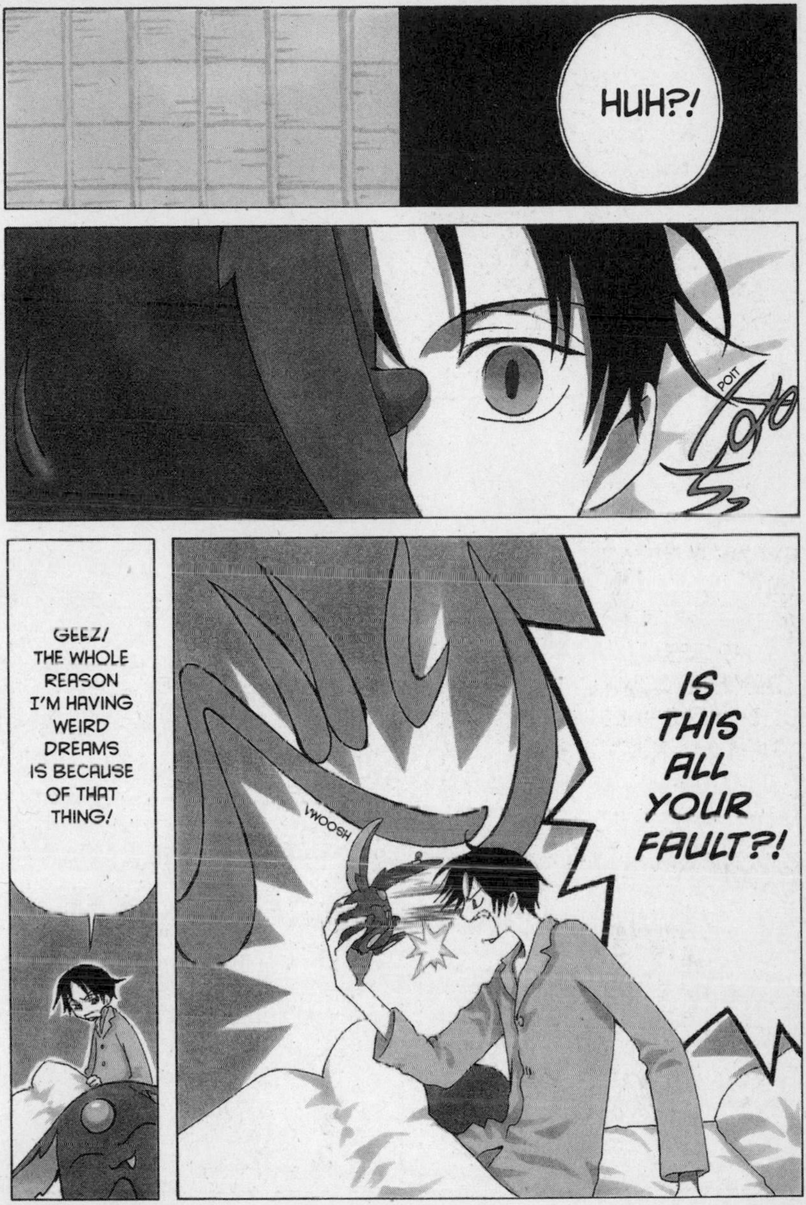
HUH?!
POIT
IS THIS ALL YOUR FAULT?!
WOOSH!
GEEZ! THE WHOLE REASON I'M HAVING WEIRD DREAMS IS BECAUSE OF THAT THING!

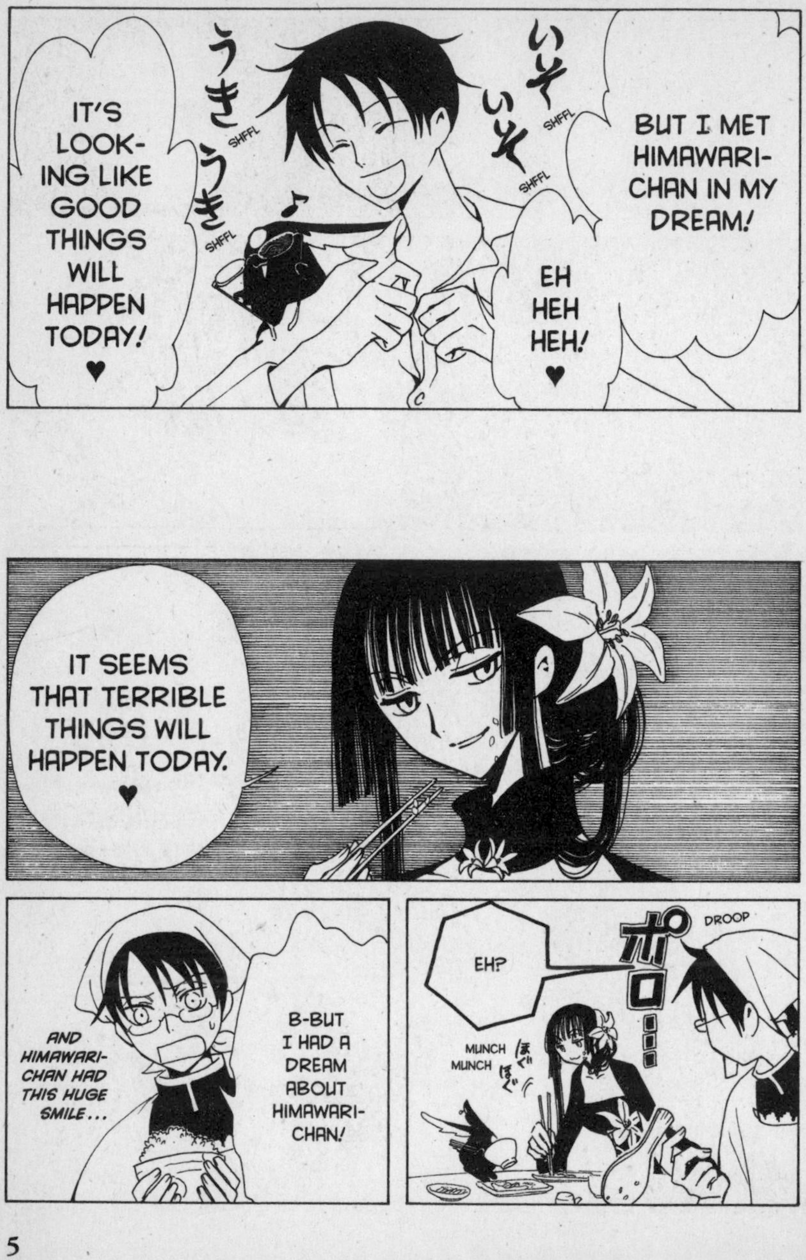
BUT I MET HIMAWARI-CHAN IN MY DREAM!
EH HEH HEH! ♥
いそいそ
SHFFL SHFFL
うきうき
SHFFL SHFFL
IT'S LOOKING LIKE GOOD THINGS WILL HAPPEN TODAY! ♥
IT SEEMS THAT TERRIBLE THINGS WILL HAPPEN TODAY. ♥
DROOP
ポロ…
EH?
MUNCH MUNCH
B-BUT I HAD A DREAM ABOUT HIMAWARI-CHAN!
AND HIMAWARI-CHAN HAD THIS HUGE SMILE...

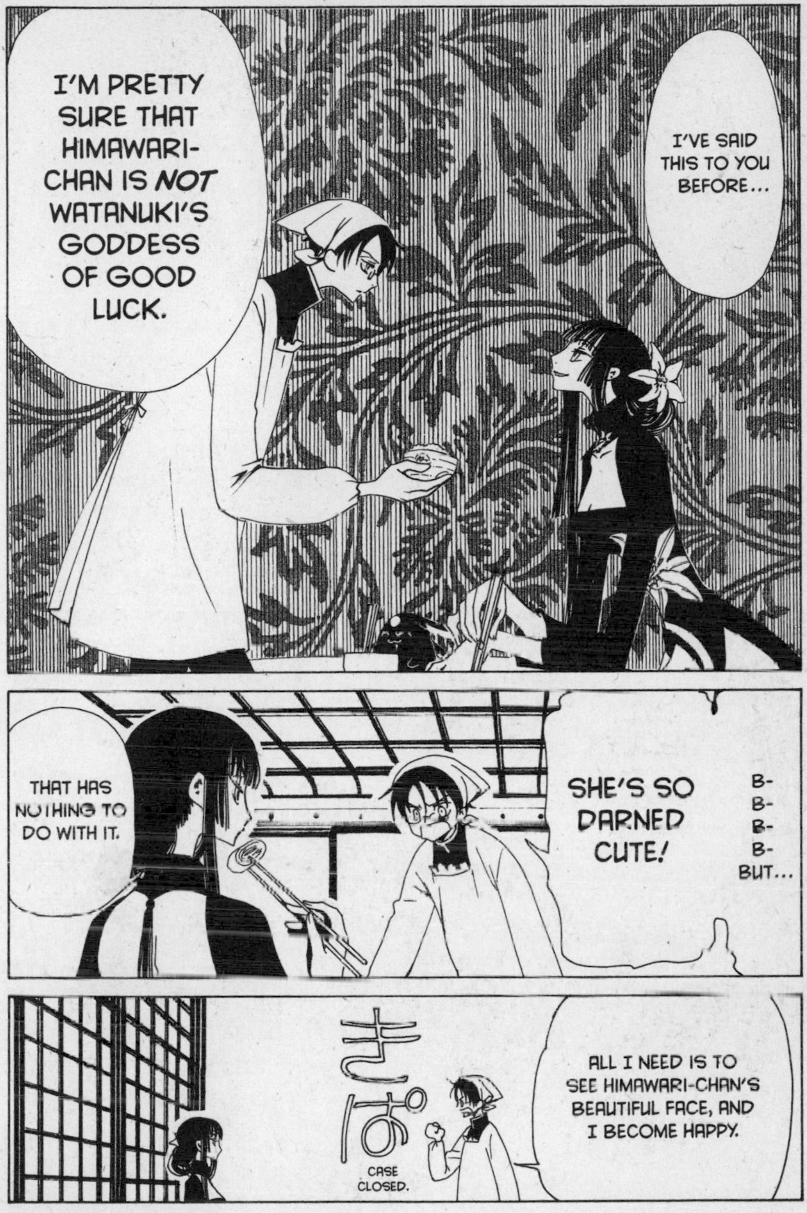
I'VE SAID THIS TO YOU BEFORE...
I'M PRETTY SURE THAT HIMAWARI-CHAN IS *NOT* WATANUKI'S GODDESS OF GOOD LUCK.
B-B-B-B-BUT...
SHE'S SO DARNED CUTE!
THAT HAS NOTHING TO DO WITH IT.
ALL I NEED IS TO SEE HIMAWARI-CHAN'S BEAUTIFUL FACE, AND I BECOME HAPPY.
きぱ
CASE CLOSED.

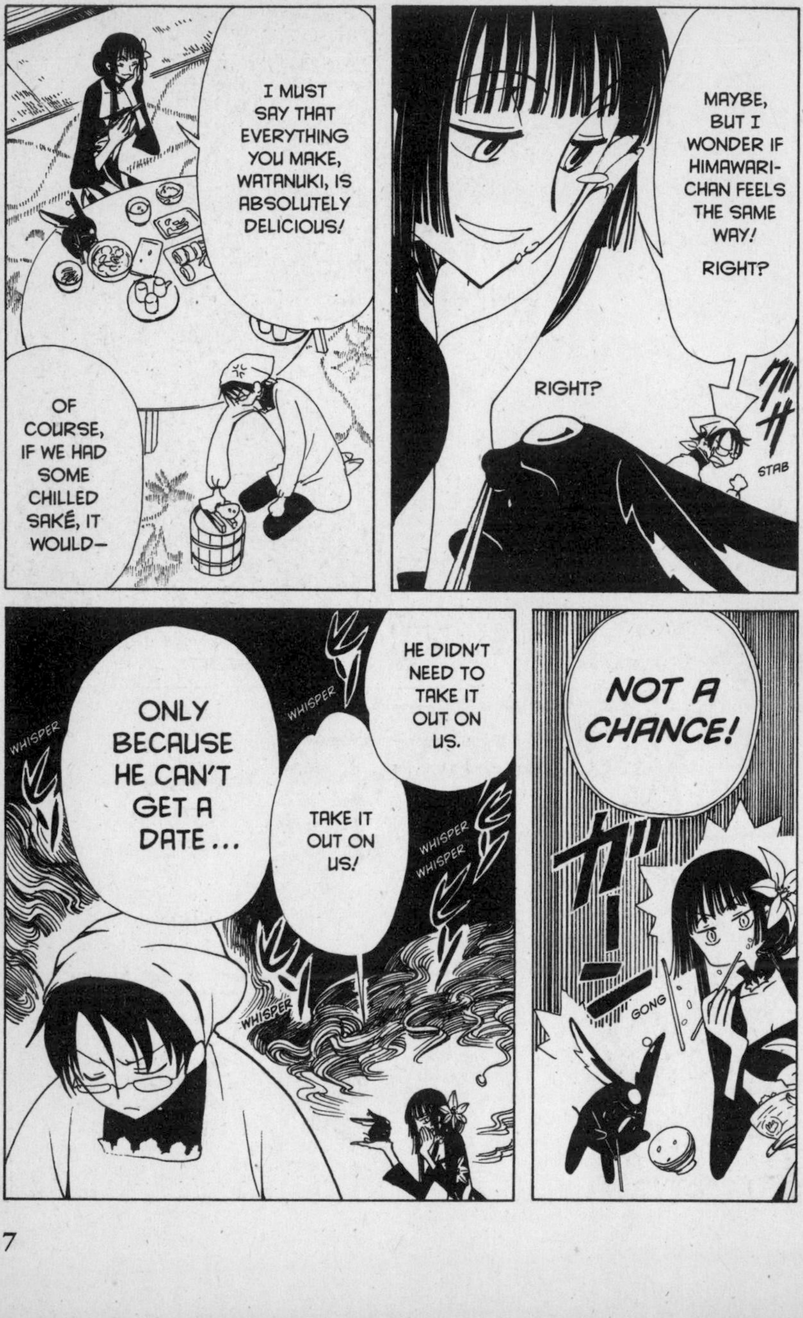
MAYBE, BUT I WONDER IF HIMAWARI-CHAN FEELS THE SAME WAY!
RIGHT?
RIGHT?
STAB
I MUST SAY THAT EVERYTHING YOU MAKE, WATANUKI, IS ABSOLUTELY DELICIOUS!
OF COURSE, IF WE HAD SOME CHILLED SAKÉ, IT WOULD—
NOT A CHANCE!
GONG
HE DIDN'T NEED TO TAKE IT OUT ON US.
WHISPER
ONLY BECAUSE HE CAN'T GET A DATE...
WHISPER
TAKE IT OUT ON US!
WHISPER
WHISPER
WHISPER

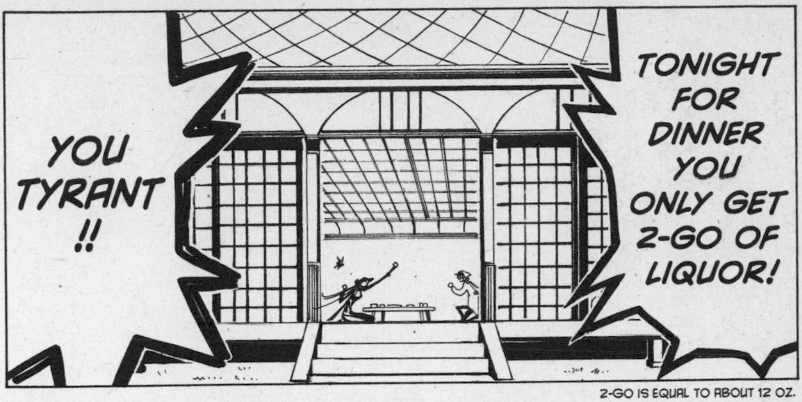
TONIGHT FOR DINNER YOU ONLY GET 2-GO OF LIQUOR!
YOU TYRANT !!

2-GO IS EQUAL TO ABOUT 12 OZ.

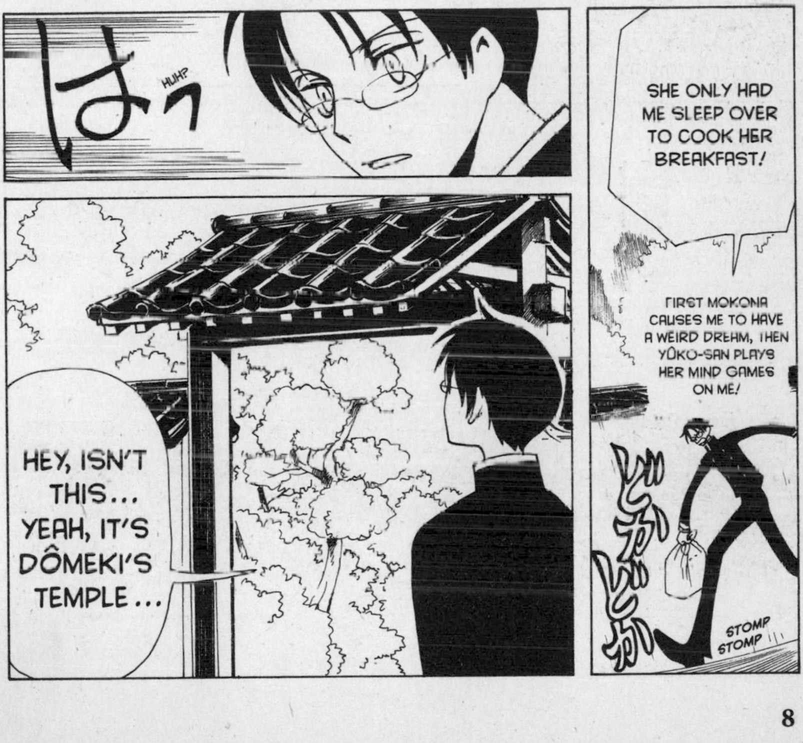
SHE ONLY HAD ME SLEEP OVER TO COOK HER BREAKFAST!
FIRST MOKONA CAUSES ME TO HAVE A WEIRD DREAM, THEN YÛKO-SAN PLAYS HER MIND GAMES ON ME!
STOMP STOMP
はっ
HUH?
HEY, ISN'T THIS... YEAH, IT'S DÔMEKI'S TEMPLE...

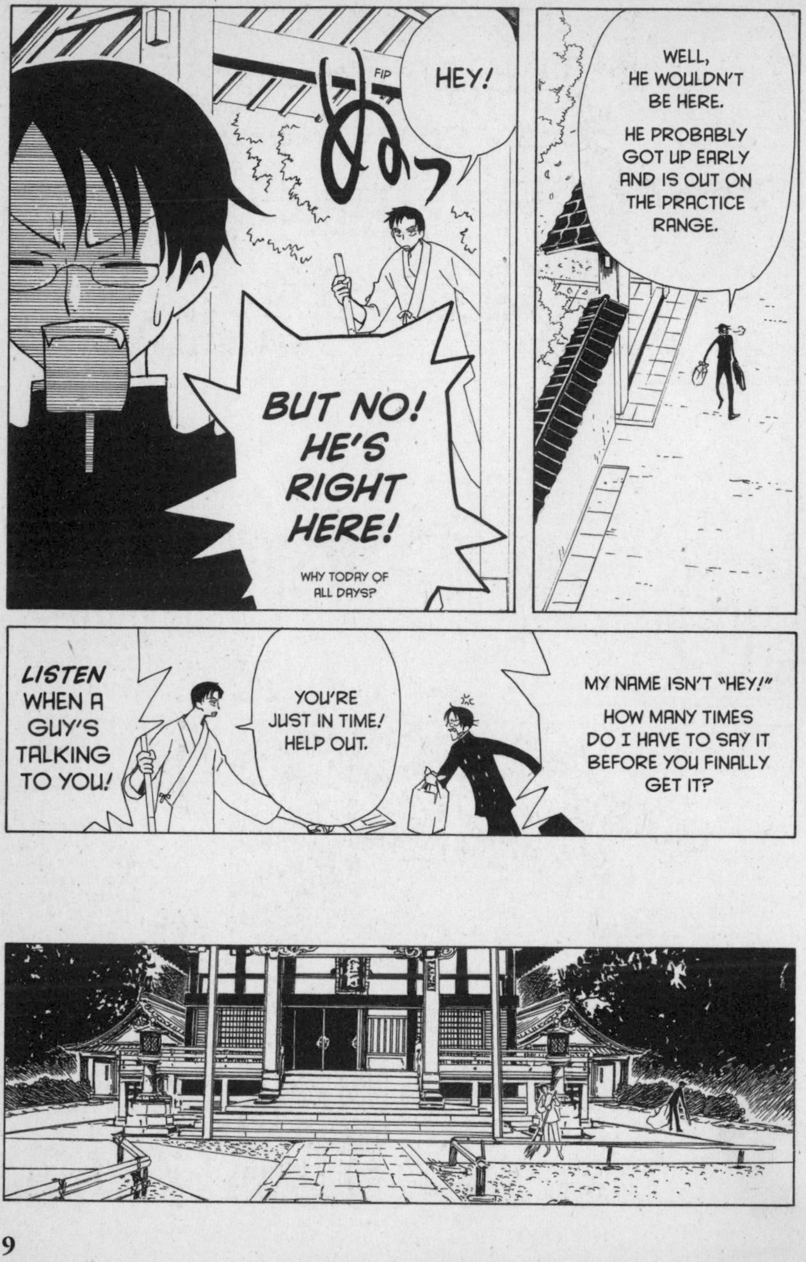
WELL, HE WOULDN'T BE HERE.
HE PROBABLY GOT UP EARLY AND IS OUT ON THE PRACTICE RANGE.
HEY!
ぬっ
FIP
BUT NO! HE'S RIGHT HERE!
WHY TODAY OF ALL DAYS?
MY NAME ISN'T "HEY!"
HOW MANY TIMES DO I HAVE TO SAY IT BEFORE YOU FINALLY GET IT?
YOU'RE JUST IN TIME! HELP OUT.
LISTEN WHEN A GUY'S TALKING TO YOU!

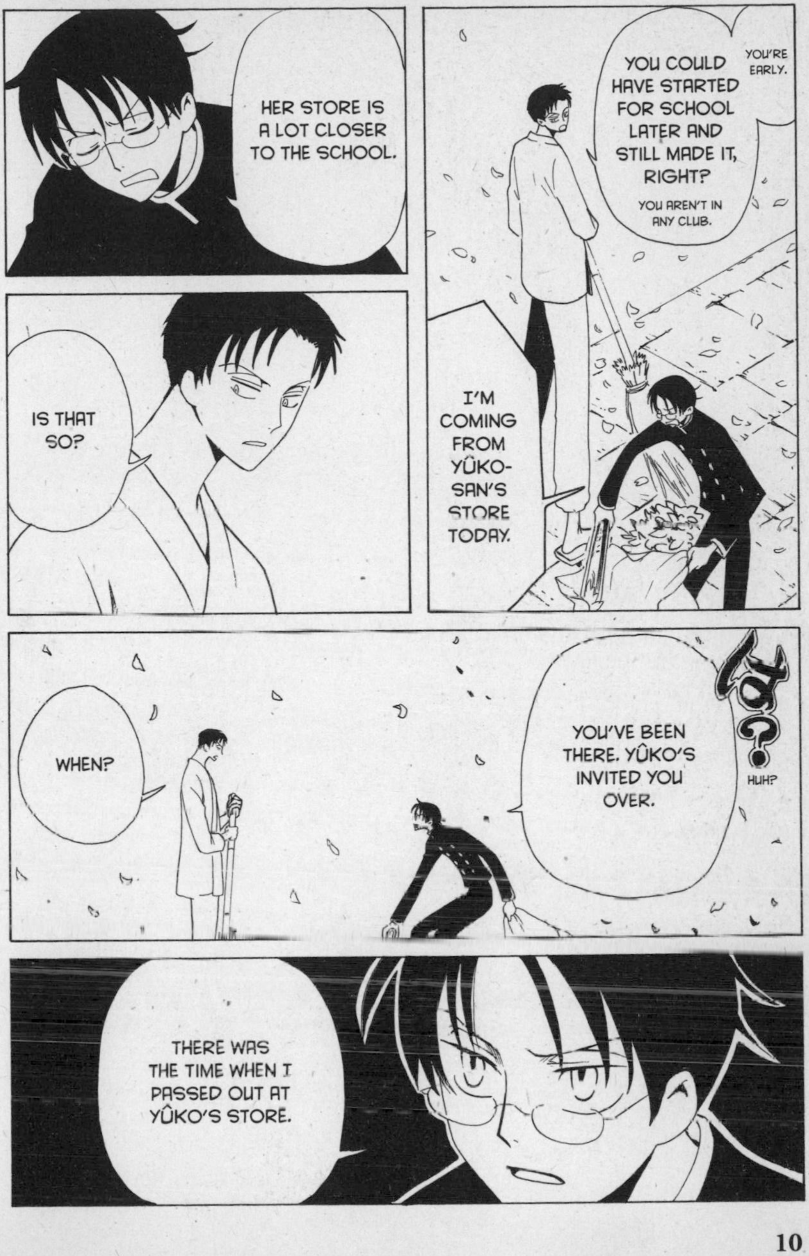
YOU'RE EARLY.
YOU COULD HAVE STARTED FOR SCHOOL LATER AND STILL MADE IT, RIGHT?
YOU AREN'T IN ANY CLUB.
I'M COMING FROM YÛKO-SAN'S STORE TODAY.
HER STORE IS A LOT CLOSER TO THE SCHOOL.
IS THAT SO?
は?
HUH?
YOU'VE BEEN THERE. YÛKO'S INVITED YOU OVER.
WHEN?
THERE WAS THE TIME WHEN I PASSED OUT AT YÛKO'S STORE.

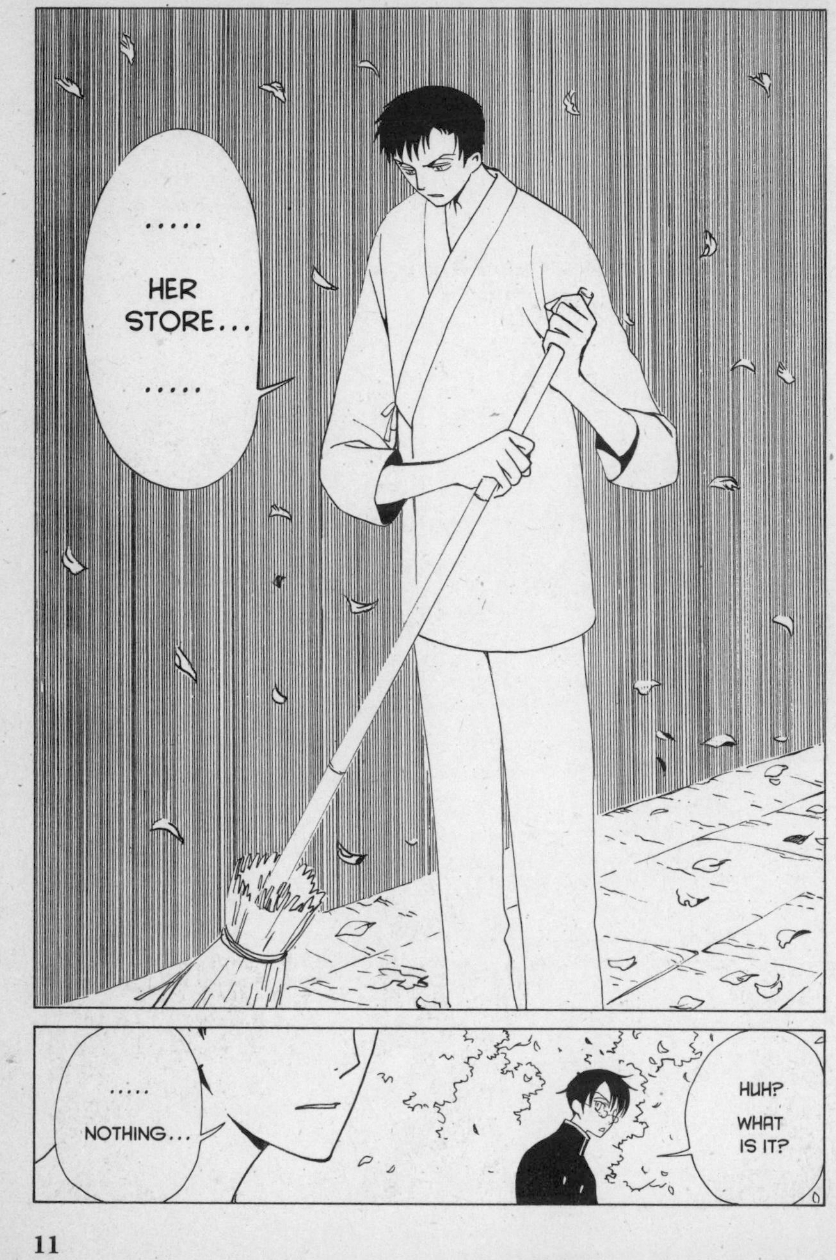
..... HER STORE... .....
HUH? WHAT IS IT?
..... NOTHING...

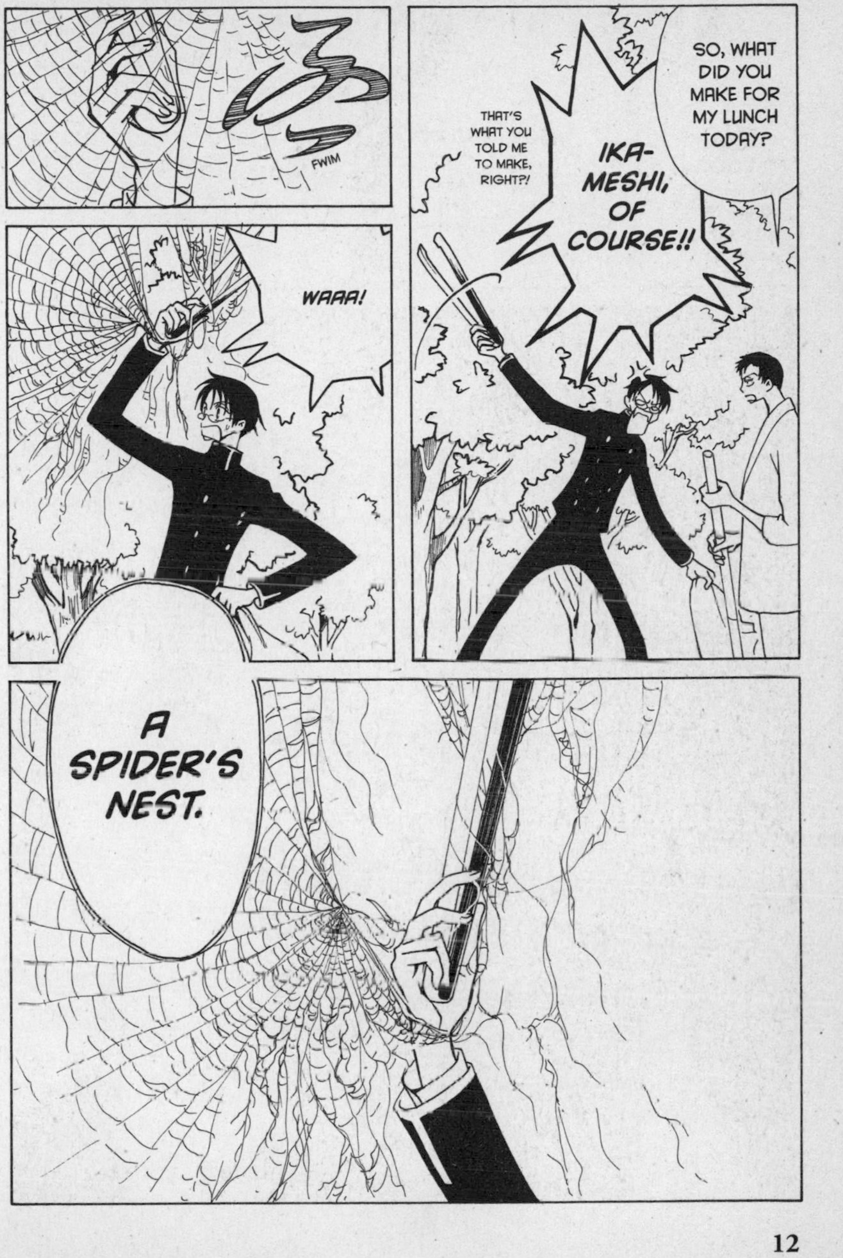
SO, WHAT DID YOU MAKE FOR MY LUNCH TODAY?
IKA-MESHI, OF COURSE!!
THAT'S WHAT YOU TOLD ME TO MAKE, RIGHT?!
FWIM
WAAA!
A SPIDER'S NEST.

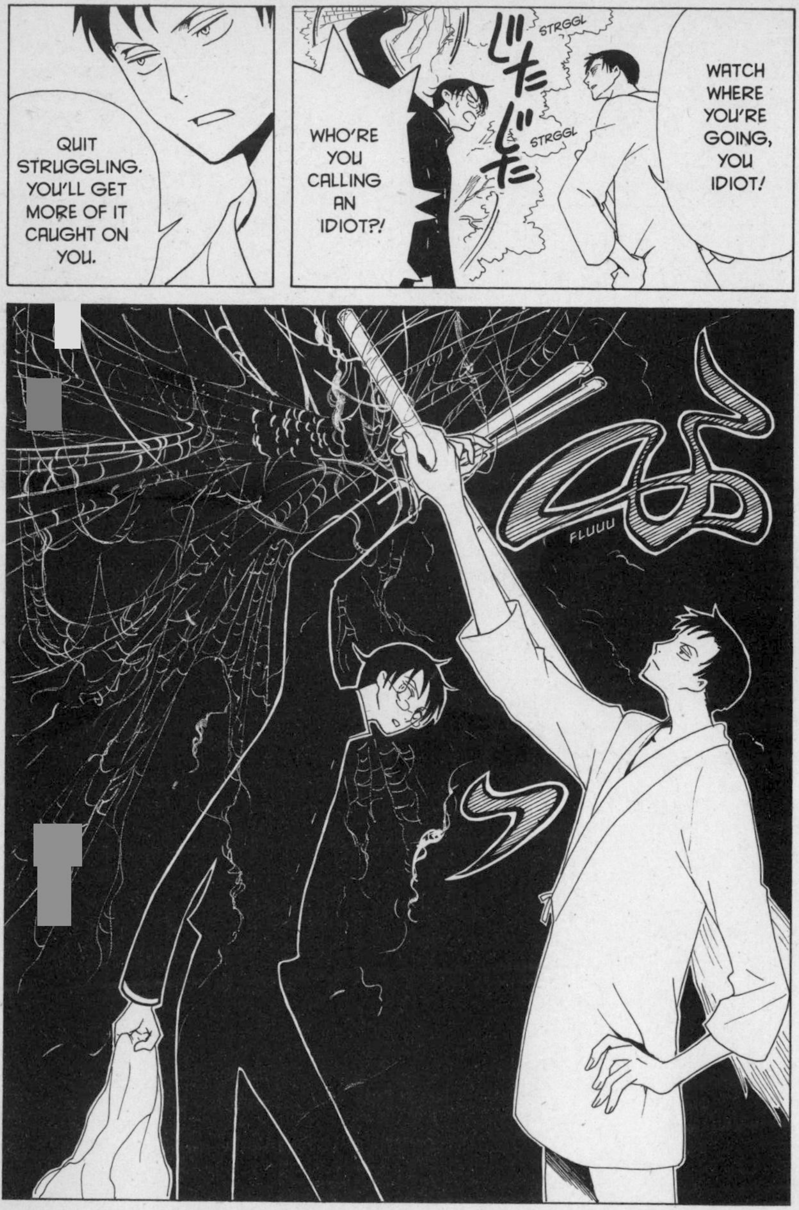
WATCH WHERE YOU'RE GOING, YOU IDIOT!
じたじた
STRGGL
STRGGL
WHO'RE YOU CALLING AN IDIOT?!
QUIT STRUGGLING. YOU'LL GET MORE OF IT CAUGHT ON YOU.
FLUUU

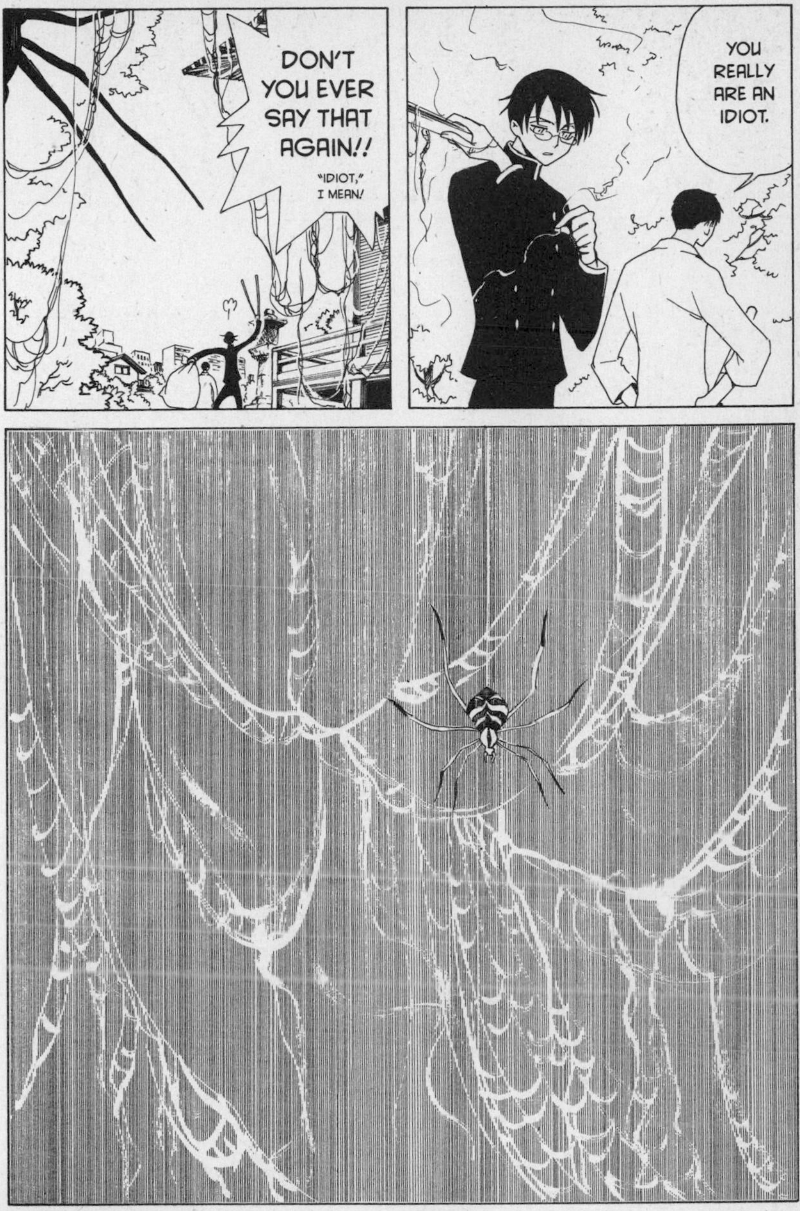
YOU REALLY ARE AN IDIOT.
DON'T YOU EVER SAY THAT AGAIN!!
"IDIOT," I MEAN!

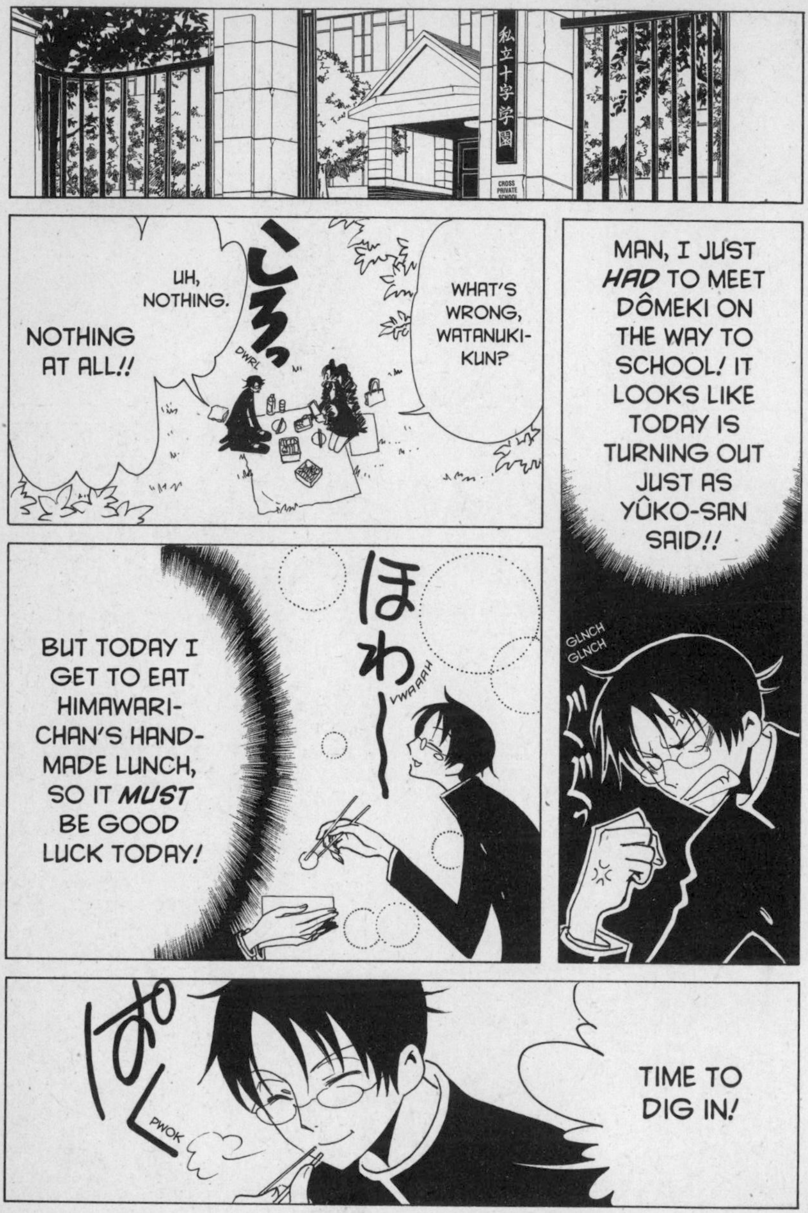
私立十字学園
CROSS PRIVATE SCHOOL
MAN, I JUST *HAD* TO MEET DÔMEKI ON THE WAY TO SCHOOL! IT LOOKS LIKE TODAY IS TURNING OUT JUST AS YÛKO-SAN SAID!!
GLNCH GLNCH
WHAT'S WRONG, WATANUKI-KUN?
ころっ
DWRL
UH, NOTHING.
NOTHING AT ALL!!
ほわ～
VWAAAH
BUT TODAY I GET TO EAT HIMAWARI-CHAN'S HAND-MADE LUNCH, SO IT *MUST* BE GOOD LUCK TODAY!
TIME TO DIG IN!
ぱく
PWOK

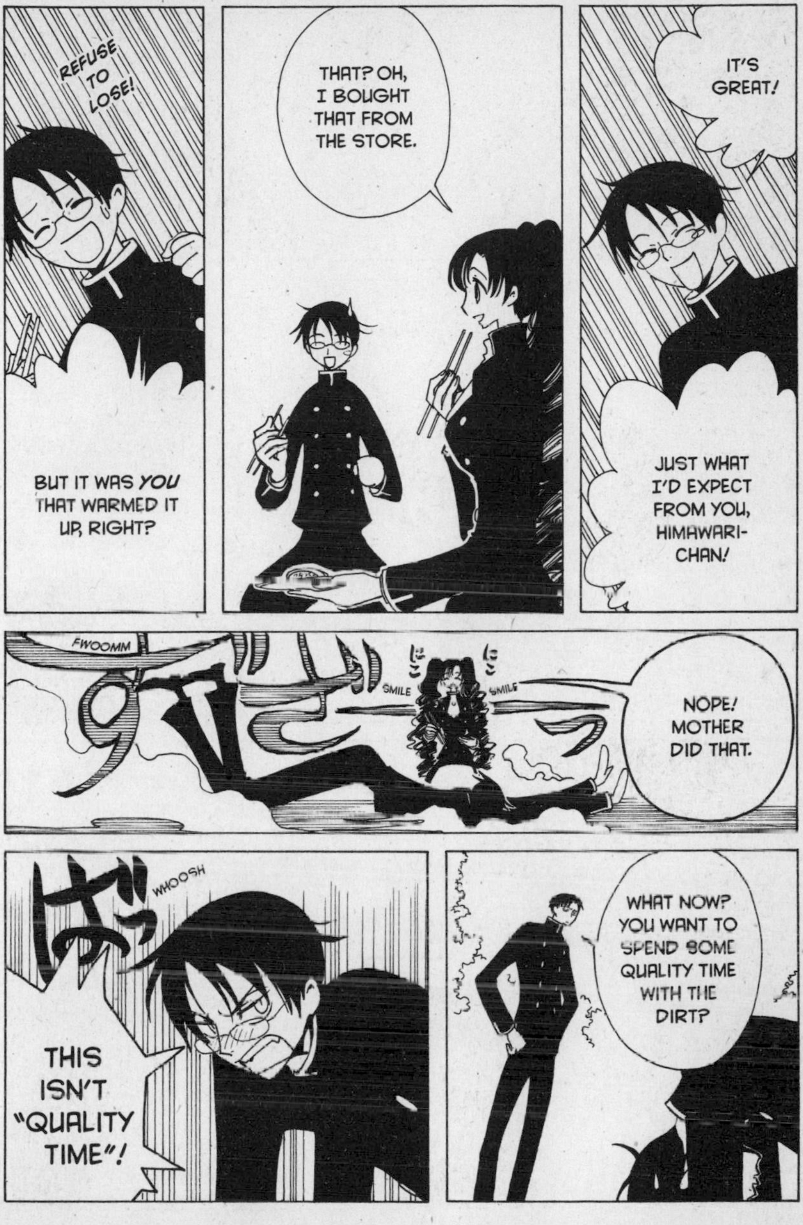
IT'S GREAT!
JUST WHAT I'D EXPECT FROM YOU, HIMAWARI-CHAN!
THAT? OH, I BOUGHT THAT FROM THE STORE.
REFUSE TO LOSE!
BUT IT WAS *YOU* THAT WARMED IT UP, RIGHT?
NOPE! MOTHER DID THAT.
SMILE
SMILE
FWOOMM
WHAT NOW? YOU WANT TO SPEND SOME QUALITY TIME WITH THE DIRT?
WHOOSH
THIS ISN'T "QUALITY TIME"!

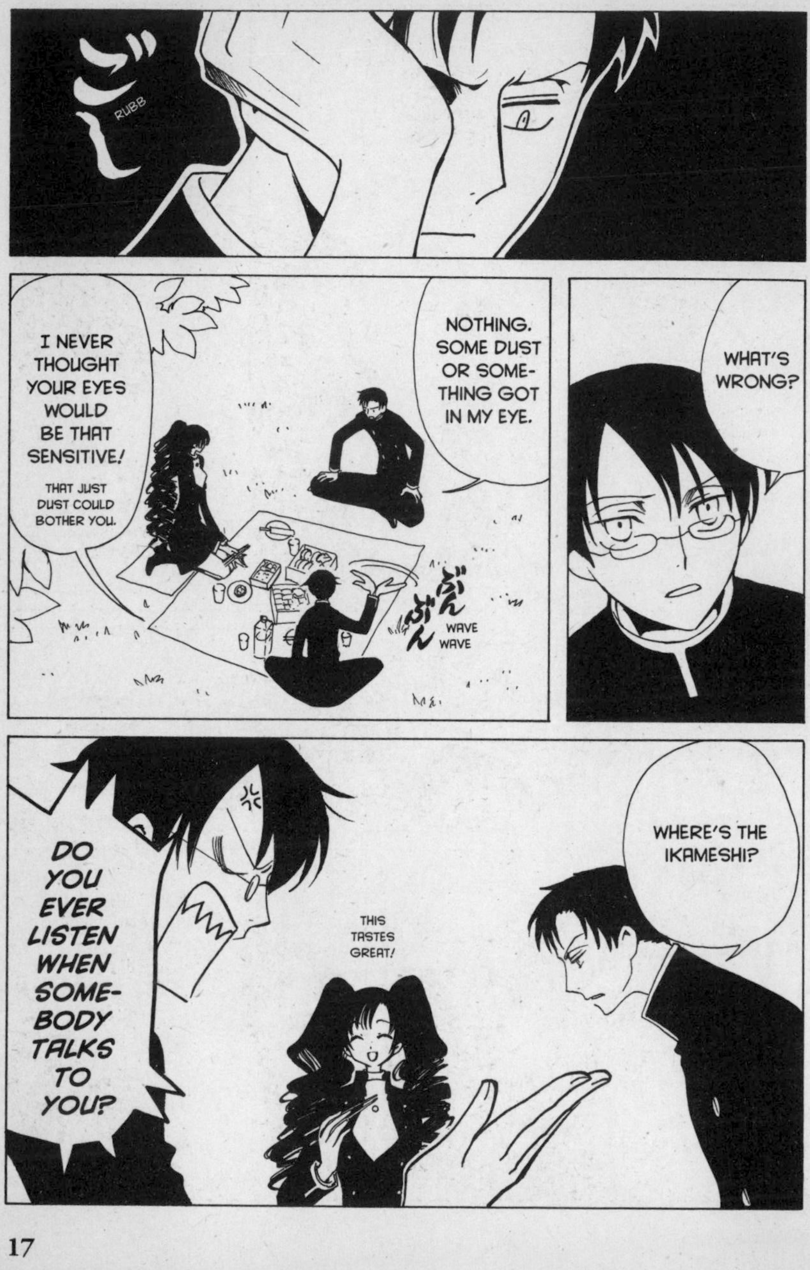
ごし
RUBB
WHAT'S WRONG?
NOTHING. SOME DUST OR SOME-THING GOT IN MY EYE.
I NEVER THOUGHT YOUR EYES WOULD BE THAT SENSITIVE!
THAT JUST DUST COULD BOTHER YOU.
ぶん ぶん
WAVE WAVE
WHERE'S THE IKAMESHI?
THIS TASTES GREAT!
DO YOU EVER LISTEN WHEN SOME-BODY TALKS TO YOU?

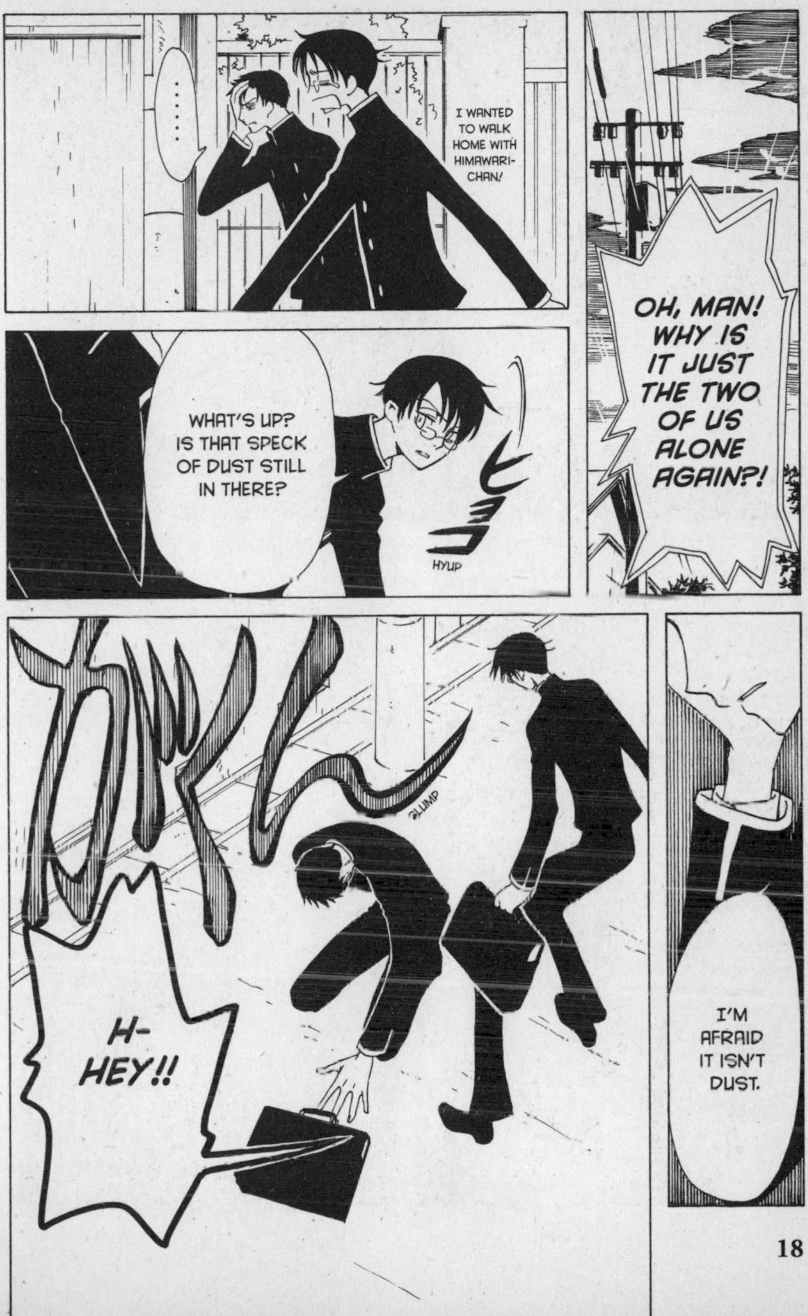
OH, MAN! WHY IS IT JUST THE TWO OF US ALONE AGAIN?!
I WANTED TO WALK HOME WITH HIMAWARI-CHAN!
......
WHAT'S UP? IS THAT SPECK OF DUST STILL IN THERE?
HYUP
I'M AFRAID IT ISN'T DUST.
CLUMP
H-HEY!!

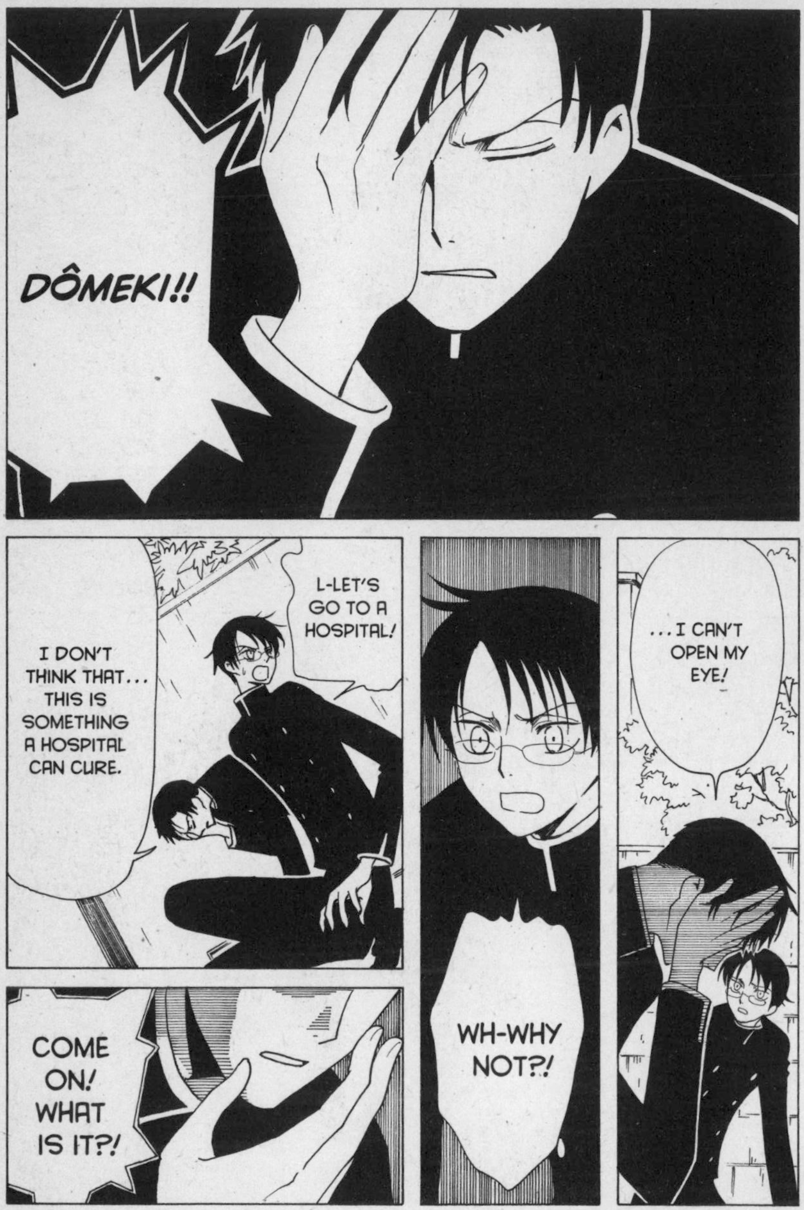
DÔMEKI!!
...I CAN'T OPEN MY EYE!
WH-WHY NOT?!
L-LET'S GO TO A HOSPITAL!
I DON'T THINK THAT... THIS IS SOMETHING A HOSPITAL CAN CURE.
COME ON! WHAT IS IT?!

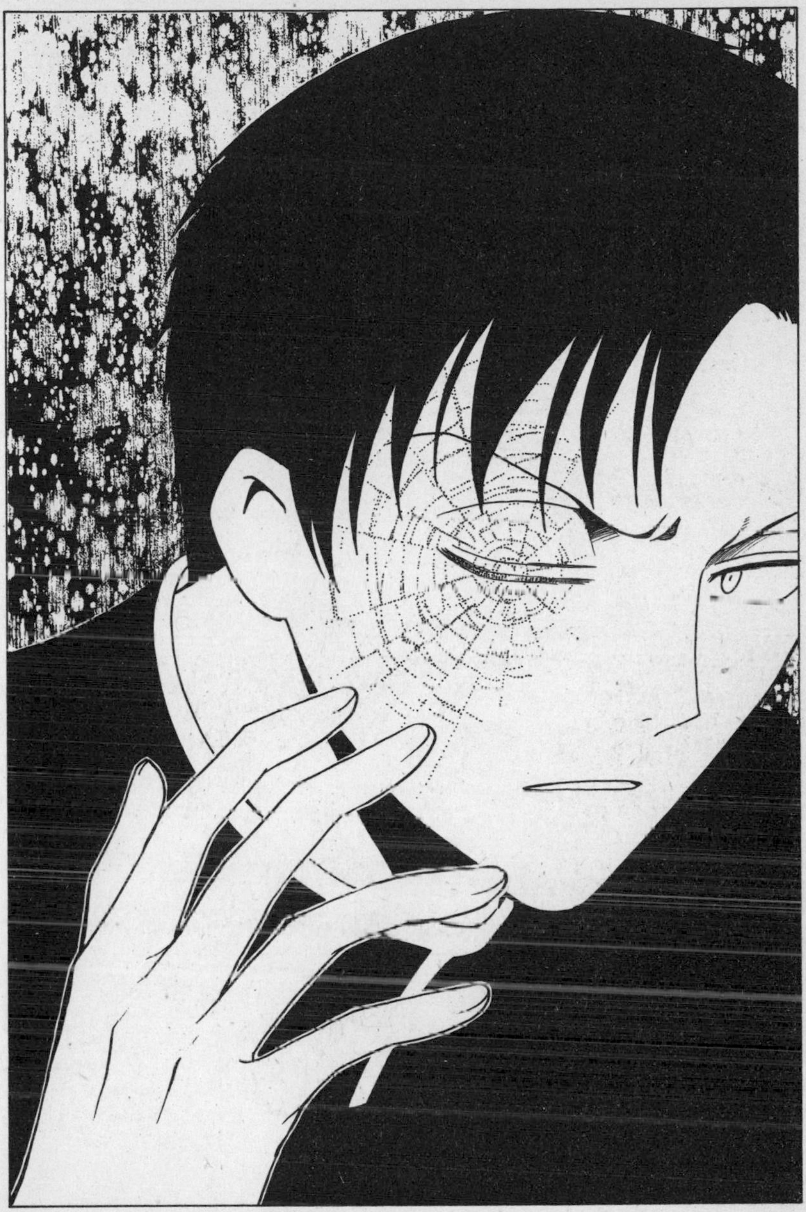

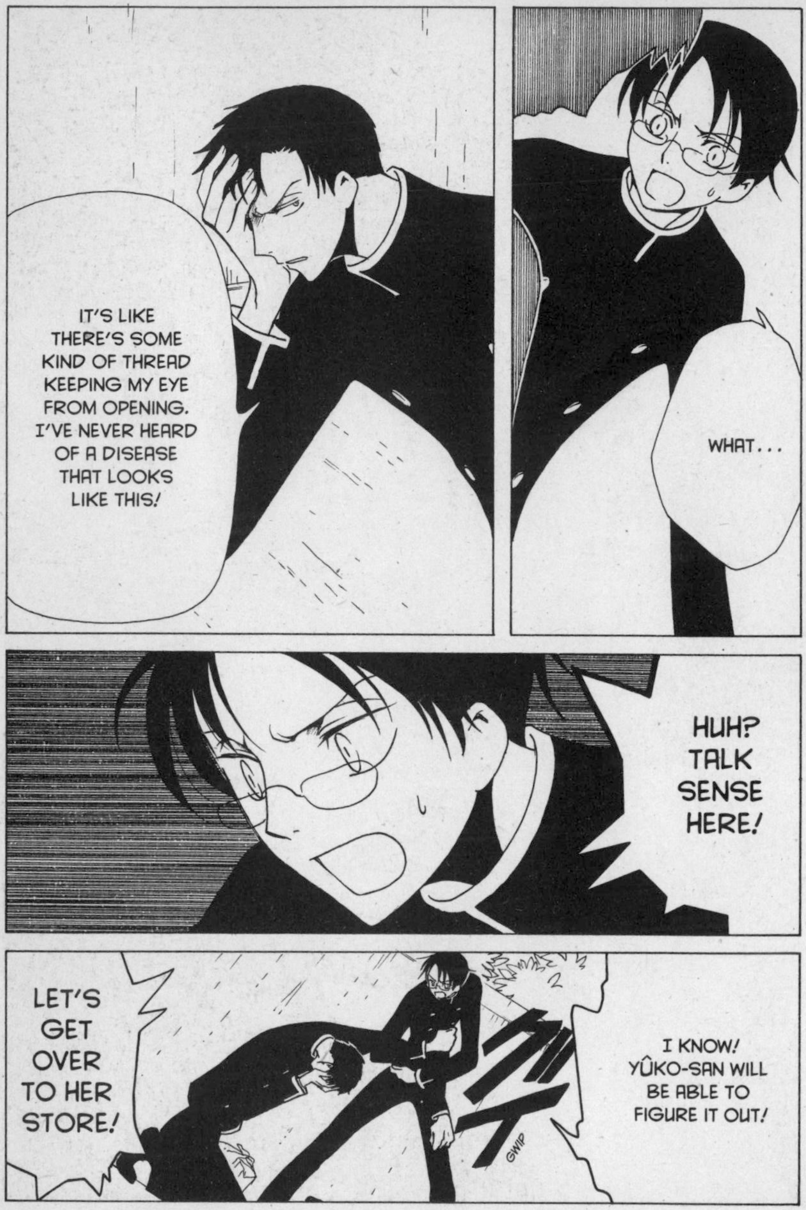
WHAT...
IT'S LIKE THERE'S SOME KIND OF THREAD KEEPING MY EYE FROM OPENING. I'VE NEVER HEARD OF A DISEASE THAT LOOKS LIKE THIS!
HUH? TALK SENSE HERE!
I KNOW! YÛKO-SAN WILL BE ABLE TO FIGURE IT OUT!
GWIP
LET'S GET OVER TO HER STORE!

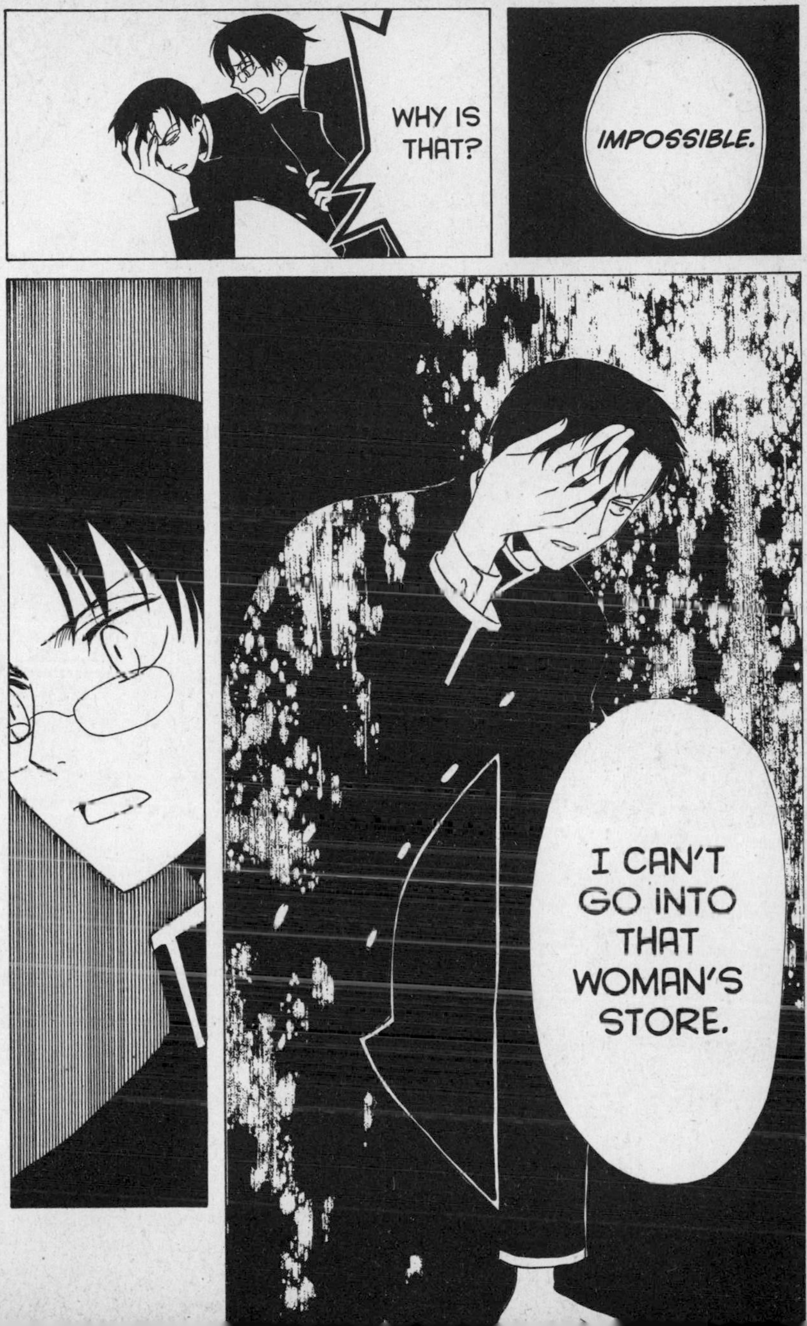
IMPOSSIBLE.
WHY IS THAT?
I CAN'T GO INTO THAT WOMAN'S STORE.

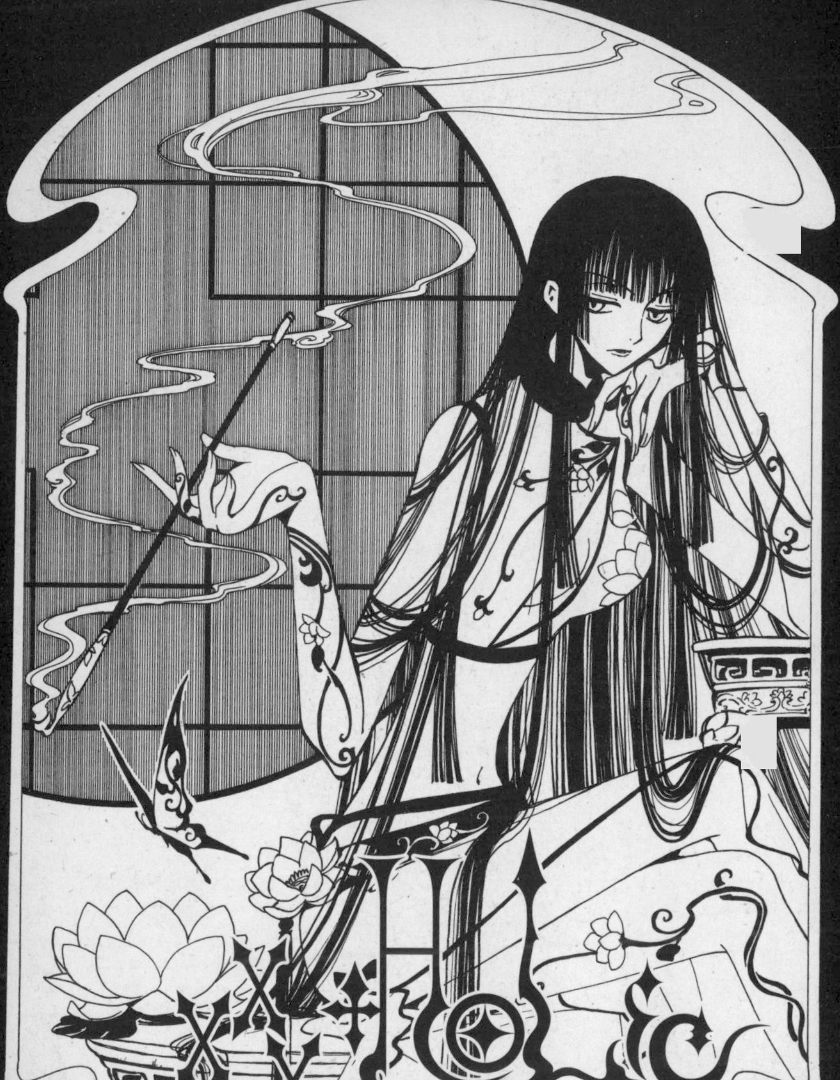
xxxHOLiC
~×××ホリック~

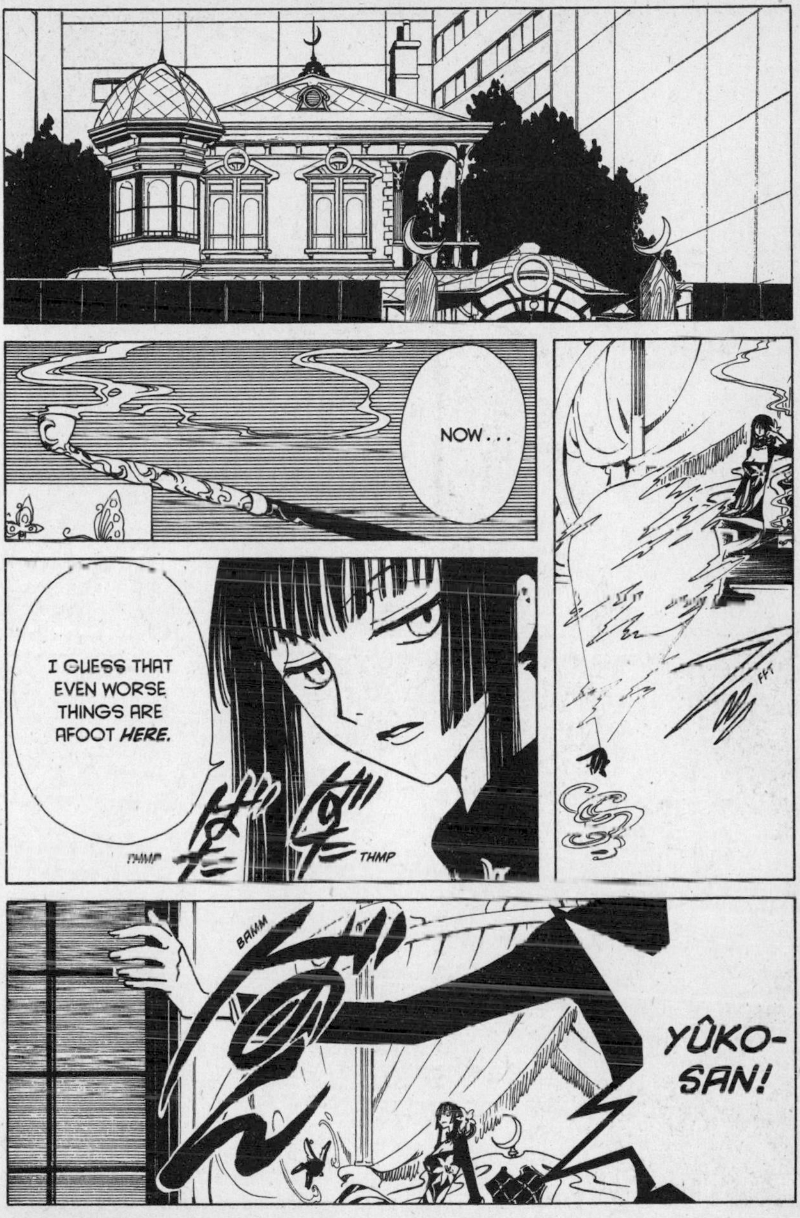
FFT
NOW...
I GUESS THAT EVEN WORSE THINGS ARE AFOOT *HERE.*
THMP
THMP
BAMM
YÛKO-SAN!

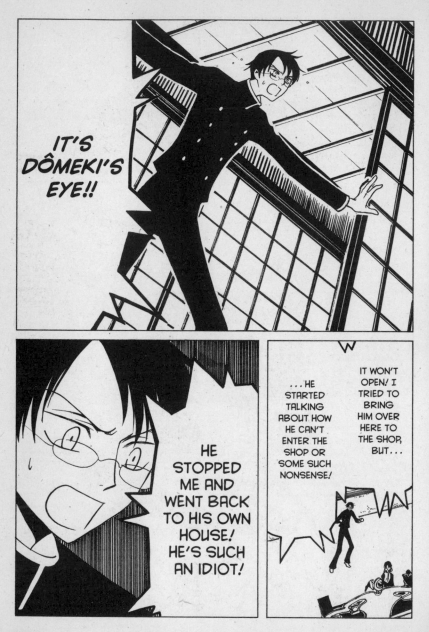

IT'S DÔMEKI'S EYE!!
IT WON'T OPEN! I TRIED TO BRING HIM OVER HERE TO THE SHOP, BUT...
...HE STARTED TALKING ABOUT HOW HE CAN'T ENTER THE SHOP OR SOME SUCH NONSENSE!
HE STOPPED ME AND WENT BACK TO HIS OWN HOUSE! HE'S SUCH AN IDIOT!

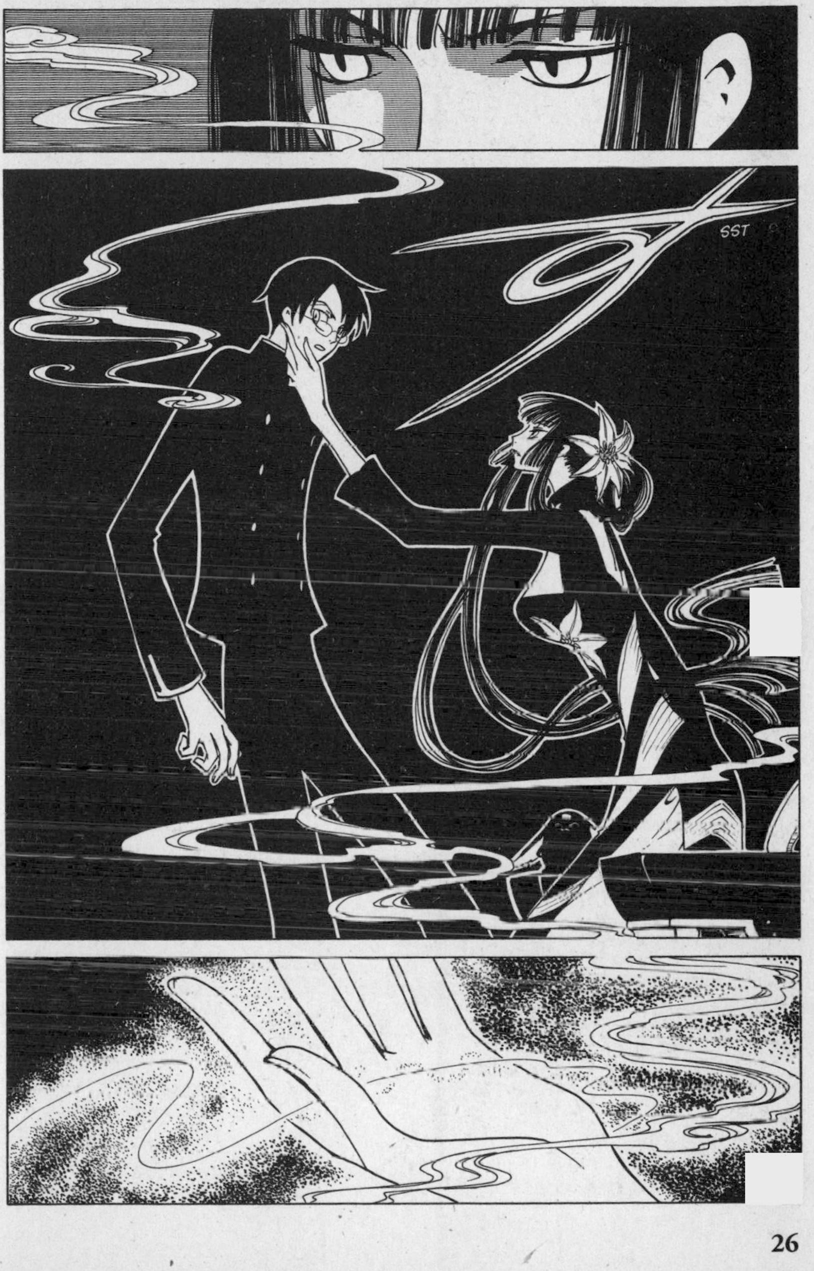
SST

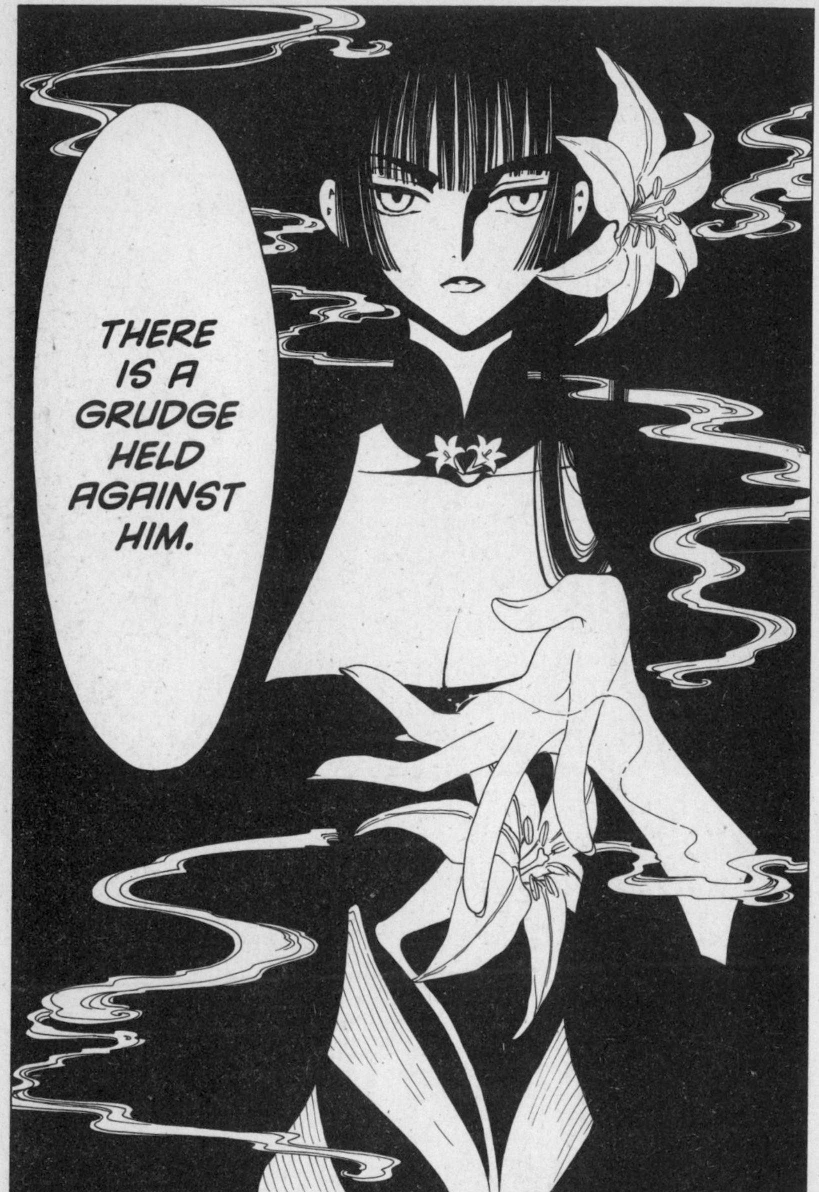
THERE IS A GRUDGE HELD AGAINST HIM.

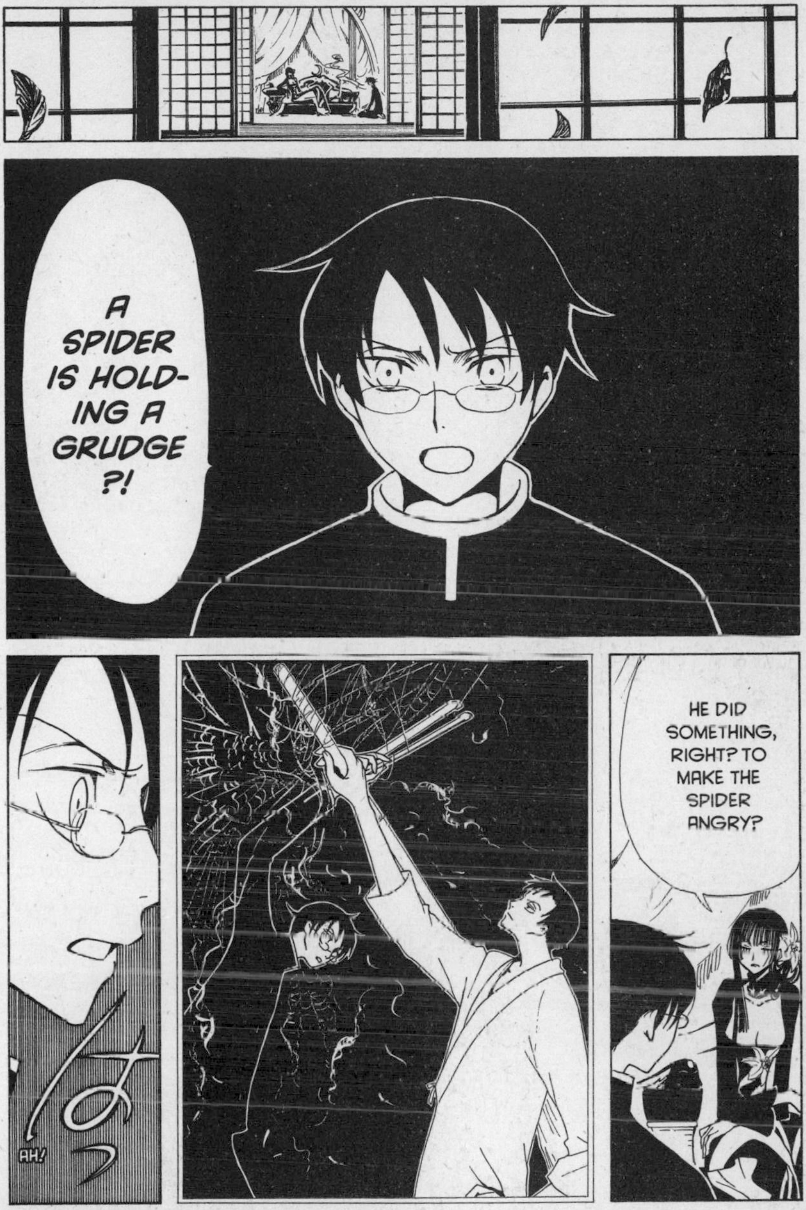
A SPIDER IS HOLDING A GRUDGE?!
HE DID SOMETHING, RIGHT? TO MAKE THE SPIDER ANGRY?
はっ
AH!

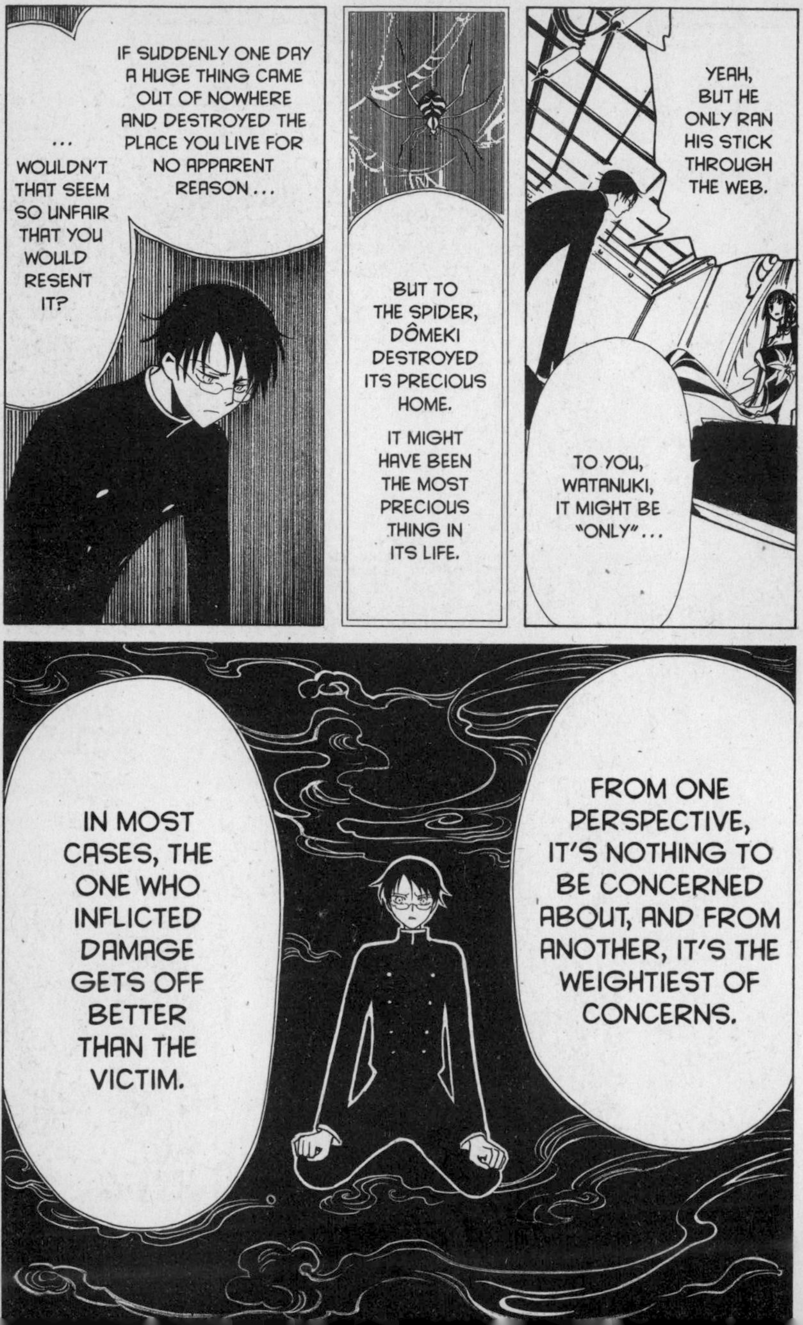
YEAH, BUT HE ONLY RAN HIS STICK THROUGH THE WEB.
TO YOU, WATANUKI, IT MIGHT BE "ONLY"...
BUT TO THE SPIDER, DÔMEKI DESTROYED ITS PRECIOUS HOME.
IT MIGHT HAVE BEEN THE MOST PRECIOUS THING IN ITS LIFE.
IF SUDDENLY ONE DAY A HUGE THING CAME OUT OF NOWHERE AND DESTROYED THE PLACE YOU LIVE FOR NO APPARENT REASON...
...WOULDN'T THAT SEEM SO UNFAIR THAT YOU WOULD RESENT IT?
FROM ONE PERSPECTIVE, IT'S NOTHING TO BE CONCERNED ABOUT, AND FROM ANOTHER, IT'S THE WEIGHTIEST OF CONCERNS.
IN MOST CASES, THE ONE WHO INFLICTED DAMAGE GETS OFF BETTER THAN THE VICTIM.

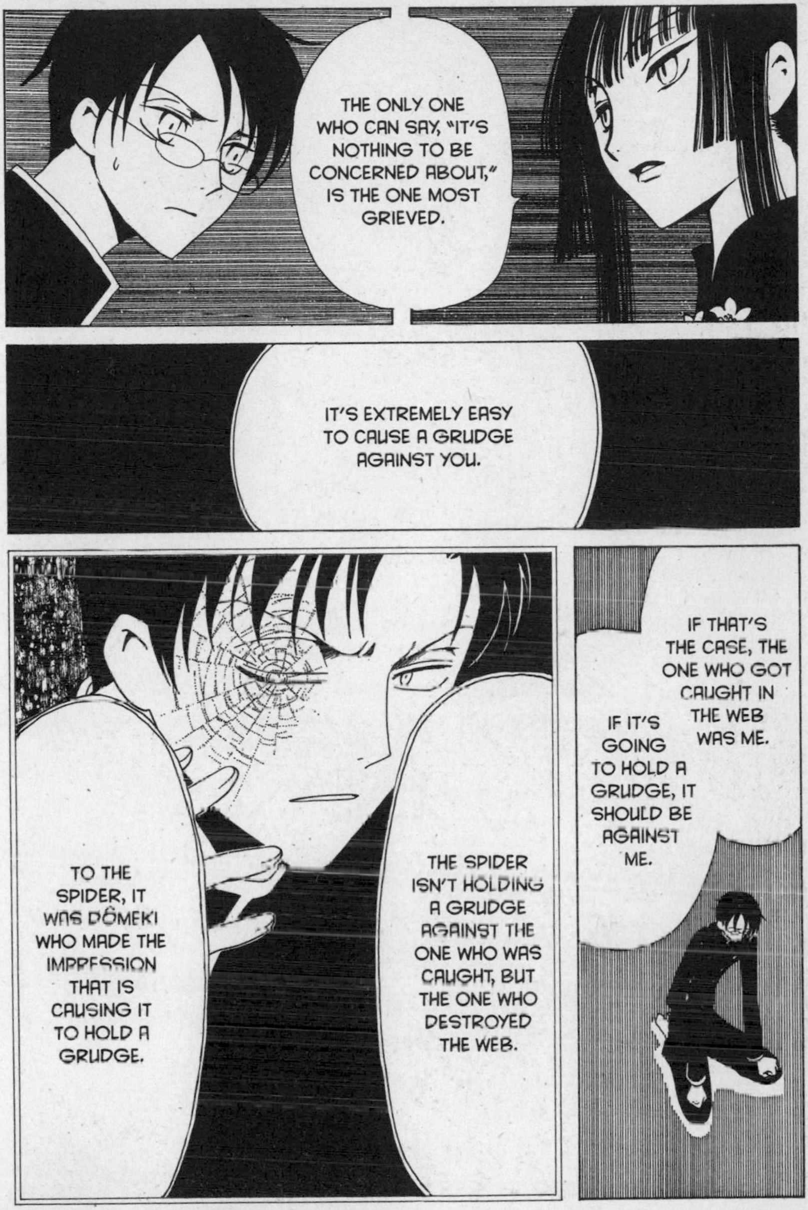

THE ONLY ONE WHO CAN SAY, "IT'S NOTHING TO BE CONCERNED ABOUT," IS THE ONE MOST GRIEVED.
IT'S EXTREMELY EASY TO CAUSE A GRUDGE AGAINST YOU.
IF THAT'S THE CASE, THE ONE WHO GOT CAUGHT IN THE WEB WAS ME.
IF IT'S GOING TO HOLD A GRUDGE, IT SHOULD BE AGAINST ME.
THE SPIDER ISN'T HOLDING A GRUDGE AGAINST THE ONE WHO WAS CAUGHT, BUT THE ONE WHO DESTROYED THE WEB.
TO THE SPIDER, IT WAS DŌMEKI WHO MADE THE IMPRESSION THAT IS CAUSING IT TO HOLD A GRUDGE.

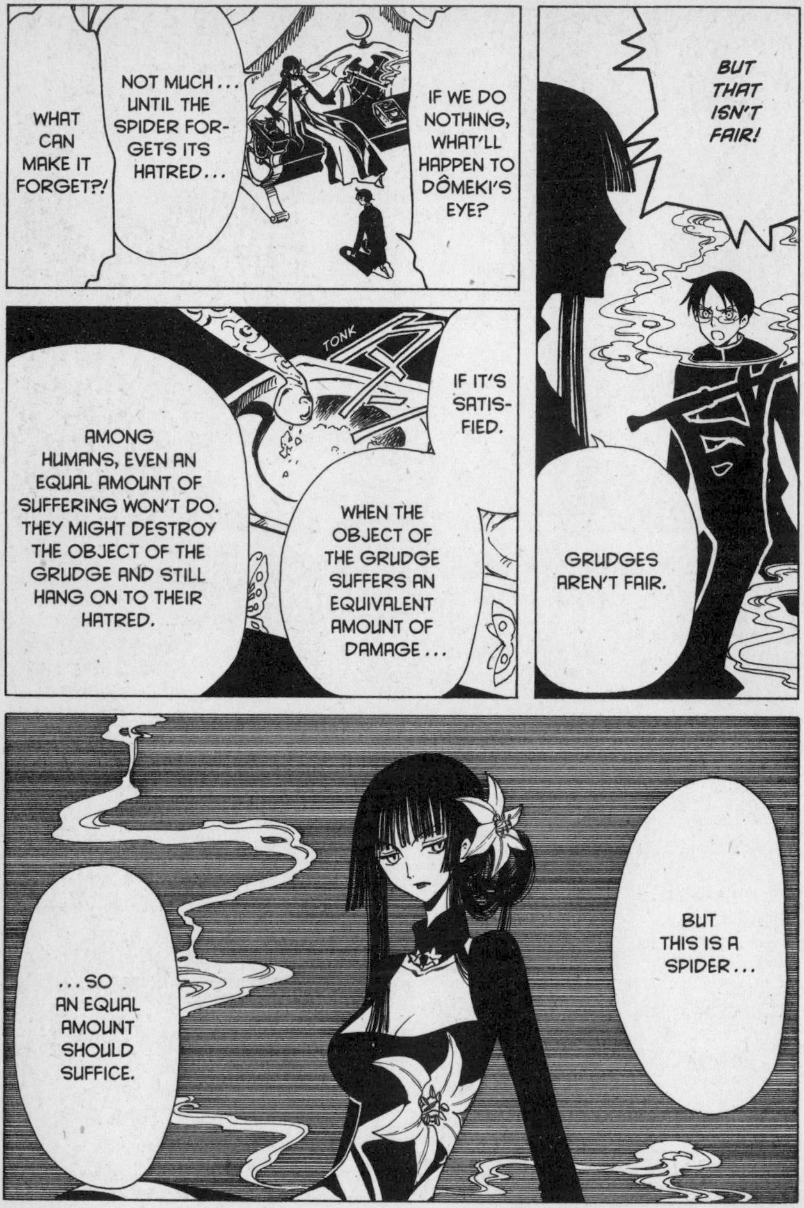
IF WE DO NOTHING, WHAT'LL HAPPEN TO DÔMEKI'S EYE?
NOT MUCH . . . UNTIL THE SPIDER FORGETS ITS HATRED . . .
WHAT CAN MAKE IT FORGET?!
TONK
IF IT'S SATISFIED.
WHEN THE OBJECT OF THE GRUDGE SUFFERS AN EQUIVALENT AMOUNT OF DAMAGE . . .
AMONG HUMANS, EVEN AN EQUAL AMOUNT OF SUFFERING WON'T DO. THEY MIGHT DESTROY THE OBJECT OF THE GRUDGE AND STILL HANG ON TO THEIR HATRED.
BUT THAT ISN'T FAIR!
GRUDGES AREN'T FAIR.
BUT THIS IS A SPIDER . . .
. . . SO AN EQUAL AMOUNT SHOULD SUFFICE.

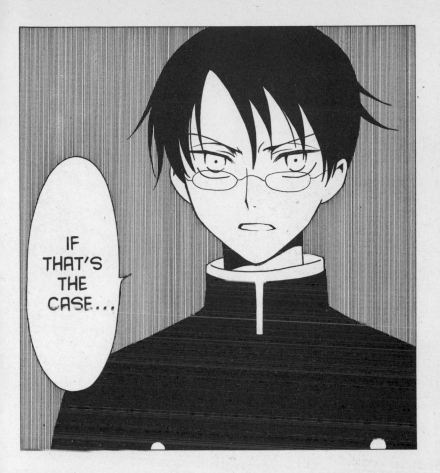

IF THAT'S THE CASE...

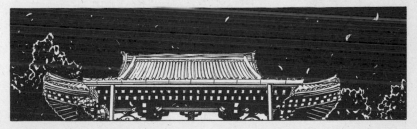

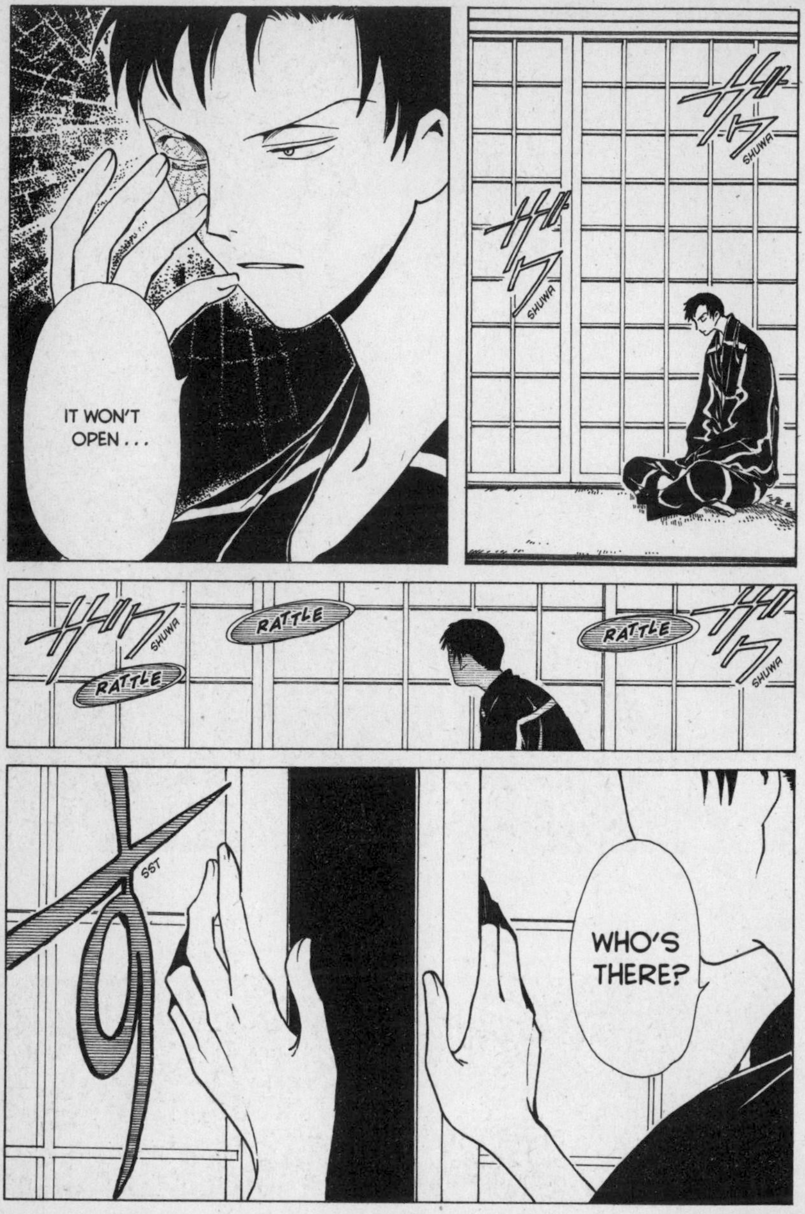
SHUWA
SHUWA
IT WON'T OPEN . . .
SHUWA
RATTLE
RATTLE
SHUWA
RATTLE
WHO'S THERE?
SST

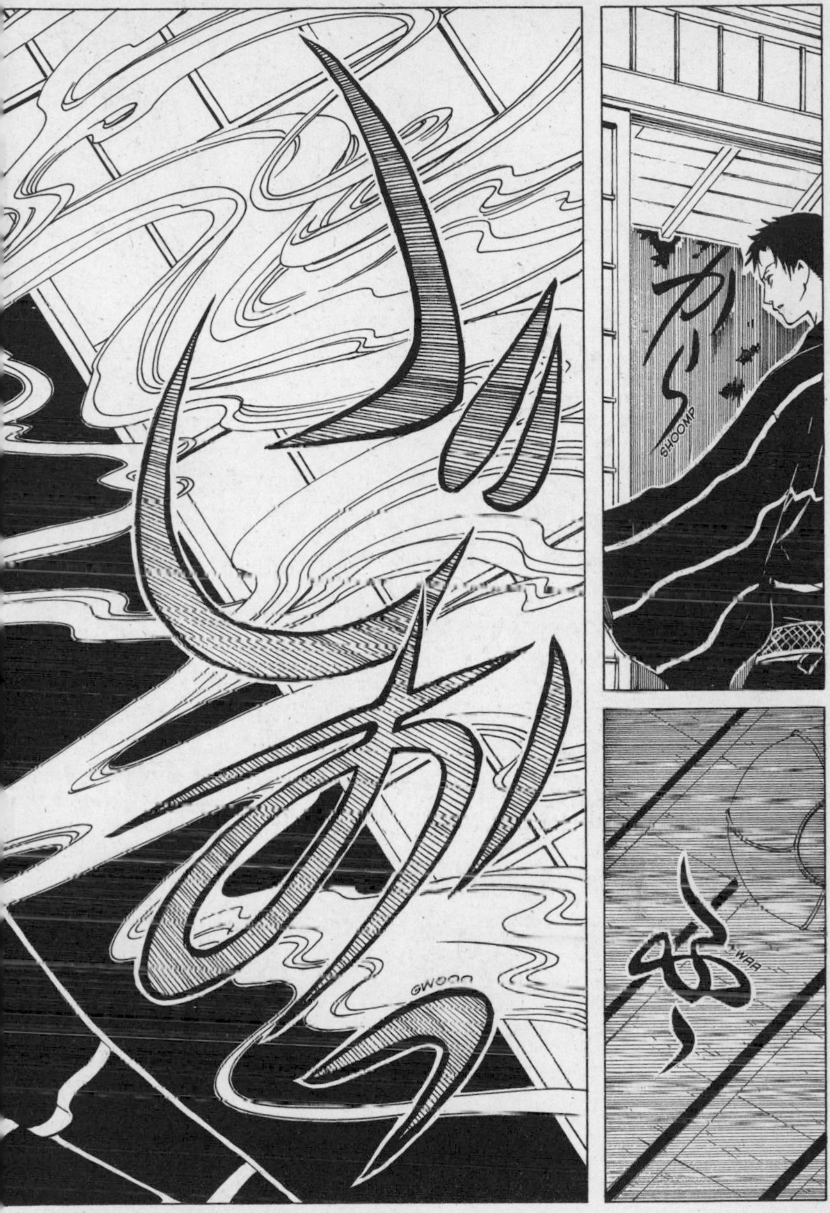
SHOOMP
WAA
GWOOO

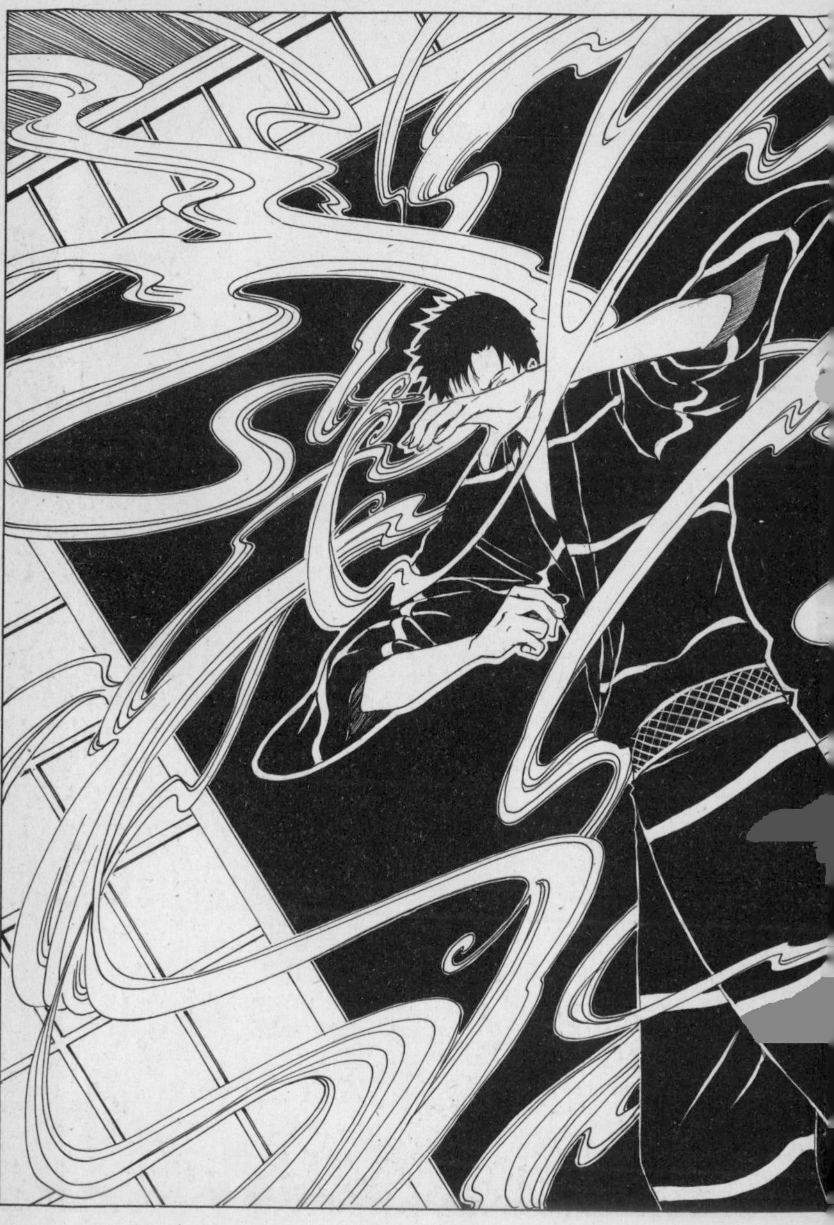

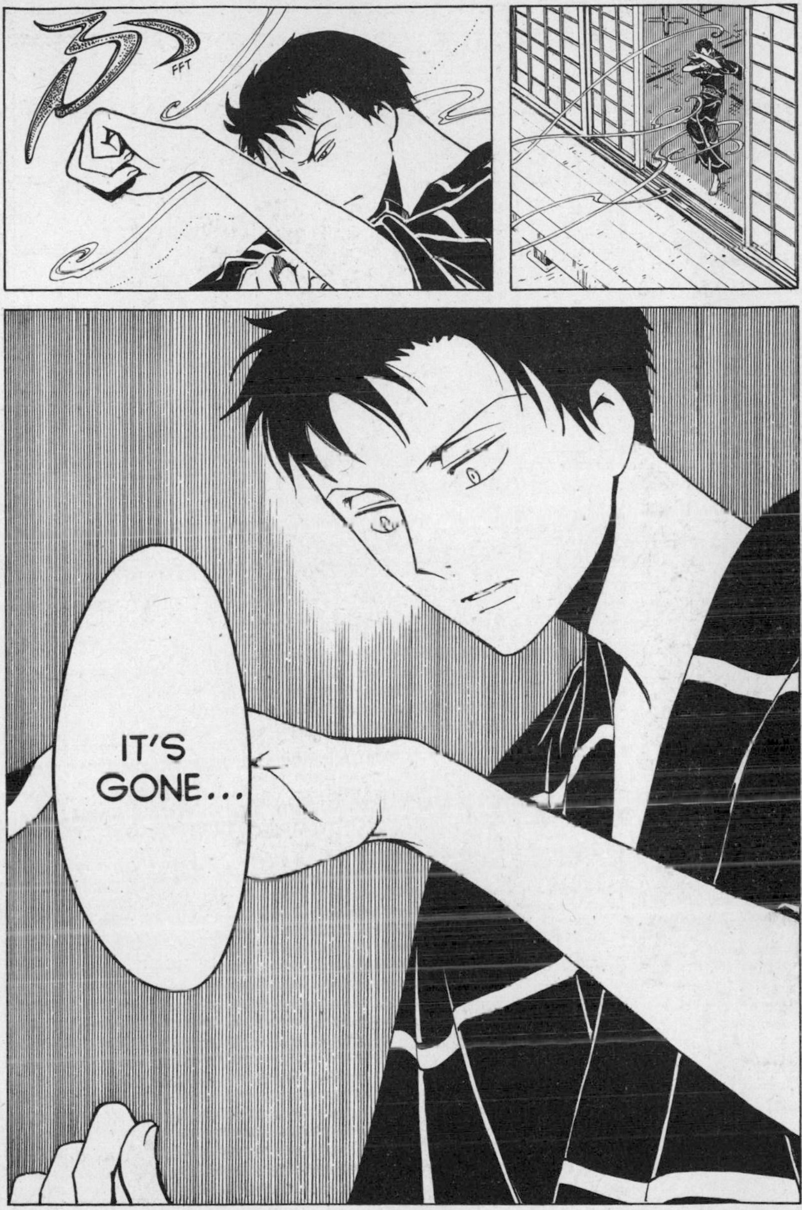
FFT
IT'S GONE...

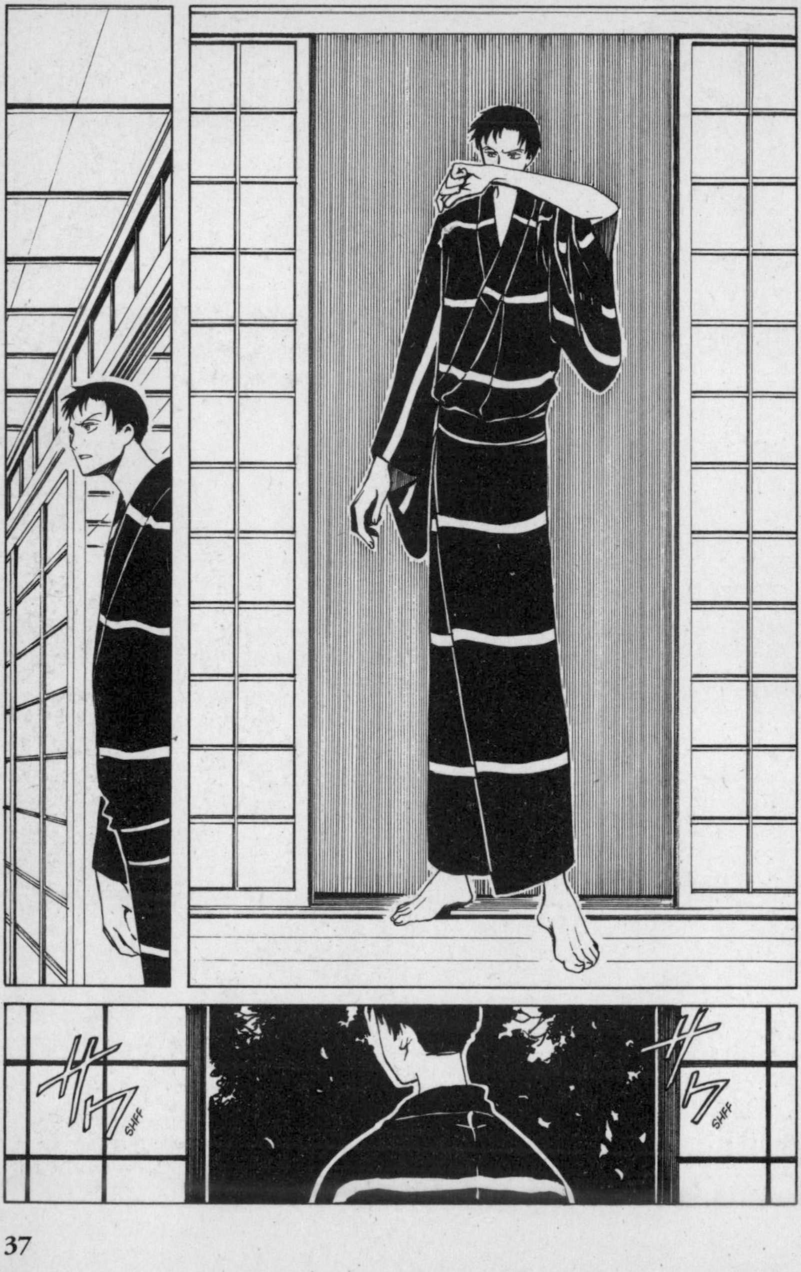
ザッ
SHFF
ザッ
SHFF

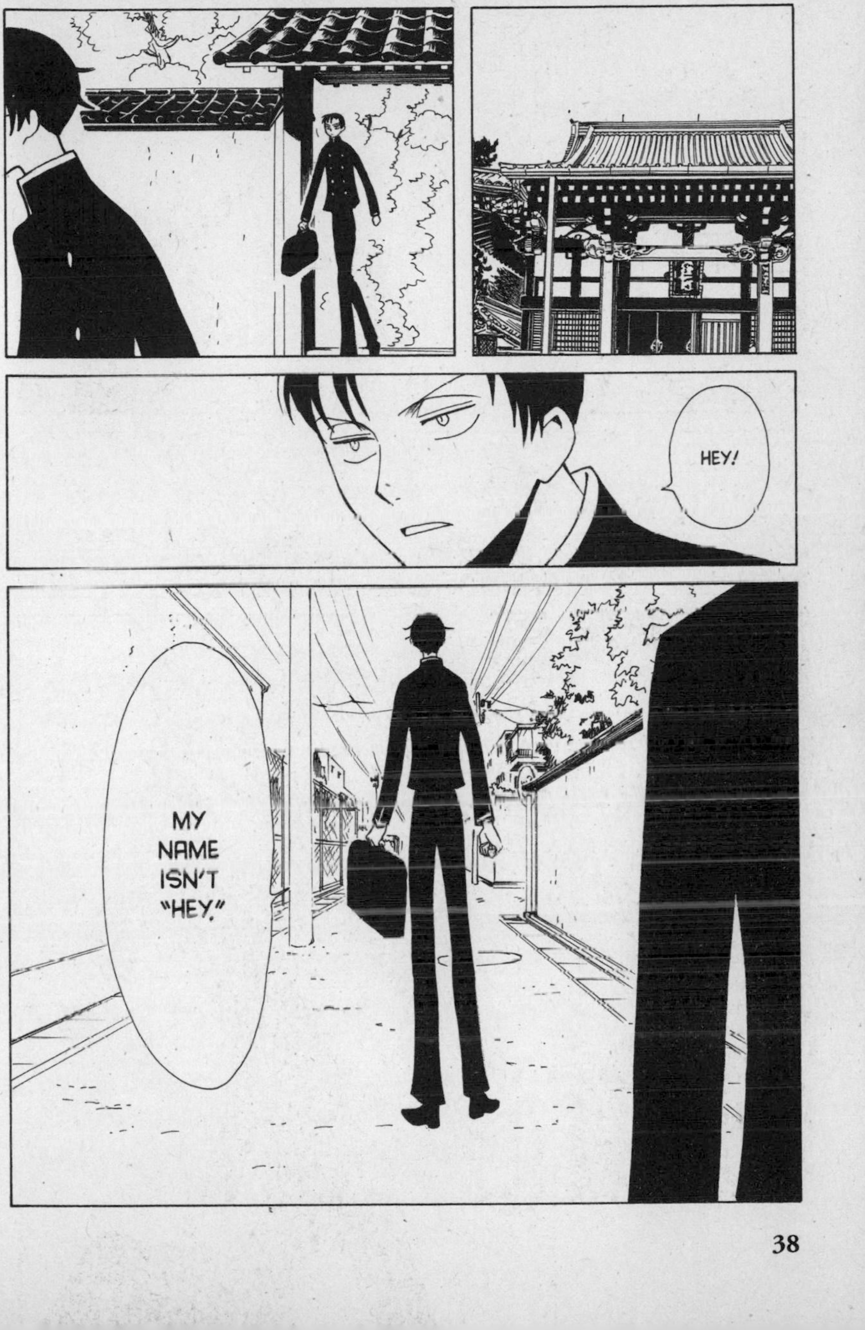
HEY!
MY NAME ISN'T "HEY."

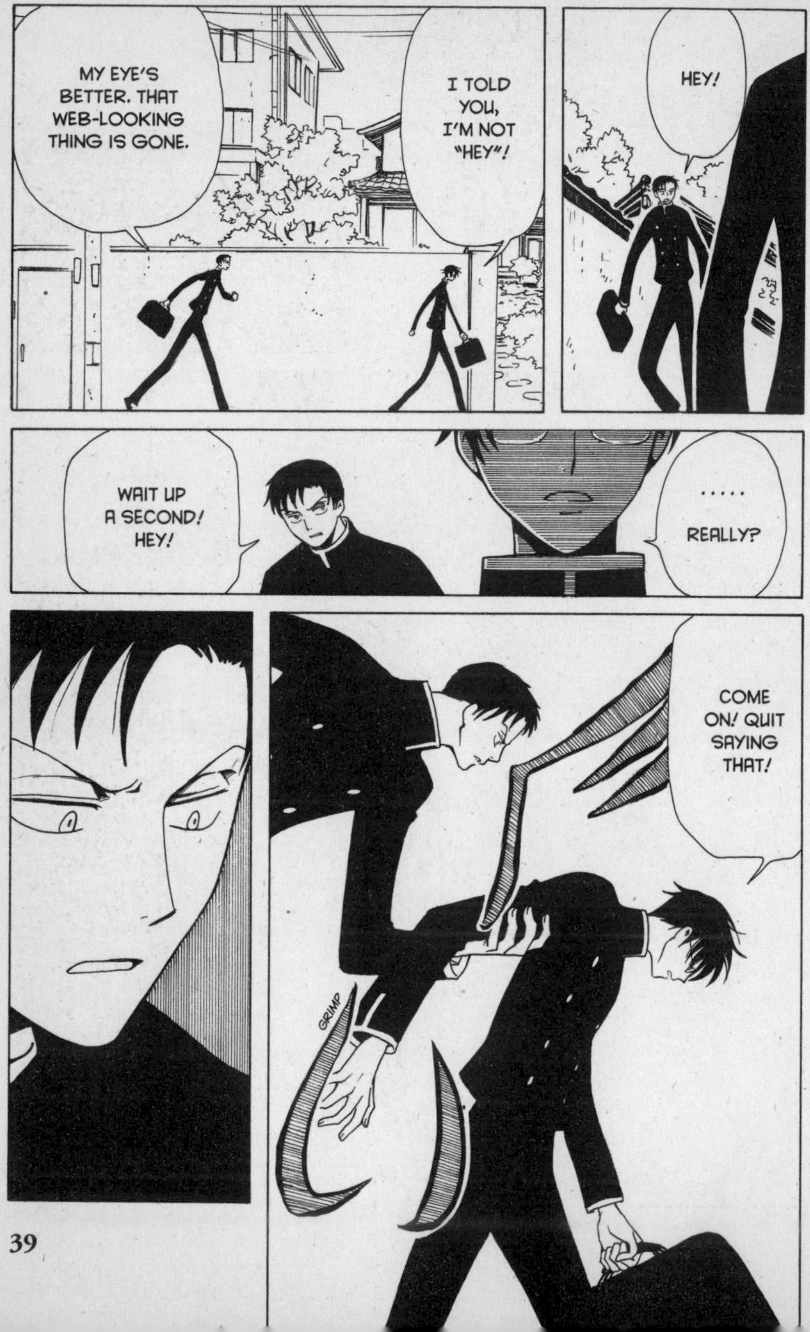
HEY!
I TOLD YOU, I'M NOT "HEY"!
MY EYE'S BETTER. THAT WEB-LOOKING THING IS GONE.
..... REALLY?
WAIT UP A SECOND! HEY!
COME ON! QUIT SAYING THAT!
GRIMP

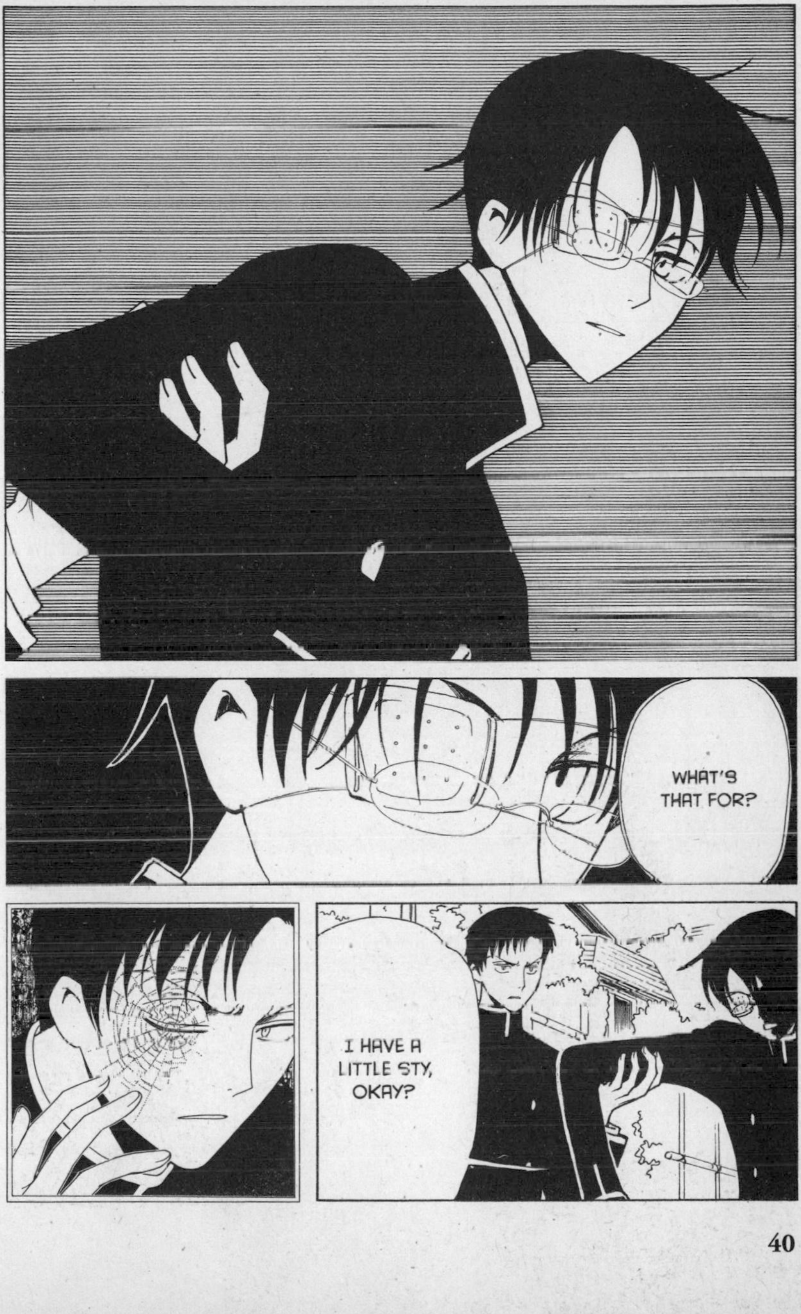
WHAT'S THAT FOR?
I HAVE A LITTLE STY, OKAY?

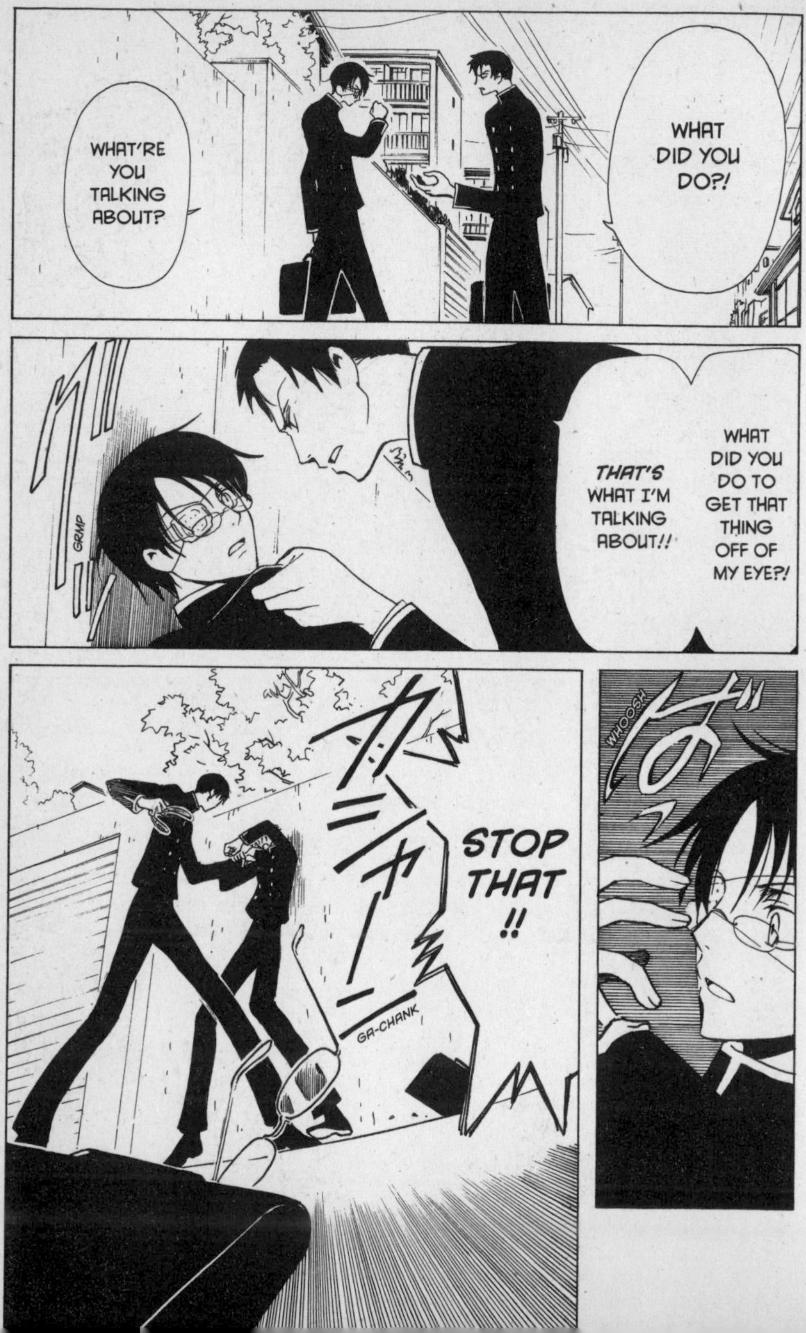
WHAT DID YOU DO?!
WHAT'RE YOU TALKING ABOUT?
WHAT DID YOU DO TO GET THAT THING OFF OF MY EYE?!
THAT'S WHAT I'M TALKING ABOUT!!
GRMP
WHOOSH
STOP THAT !!
GA-CHANK

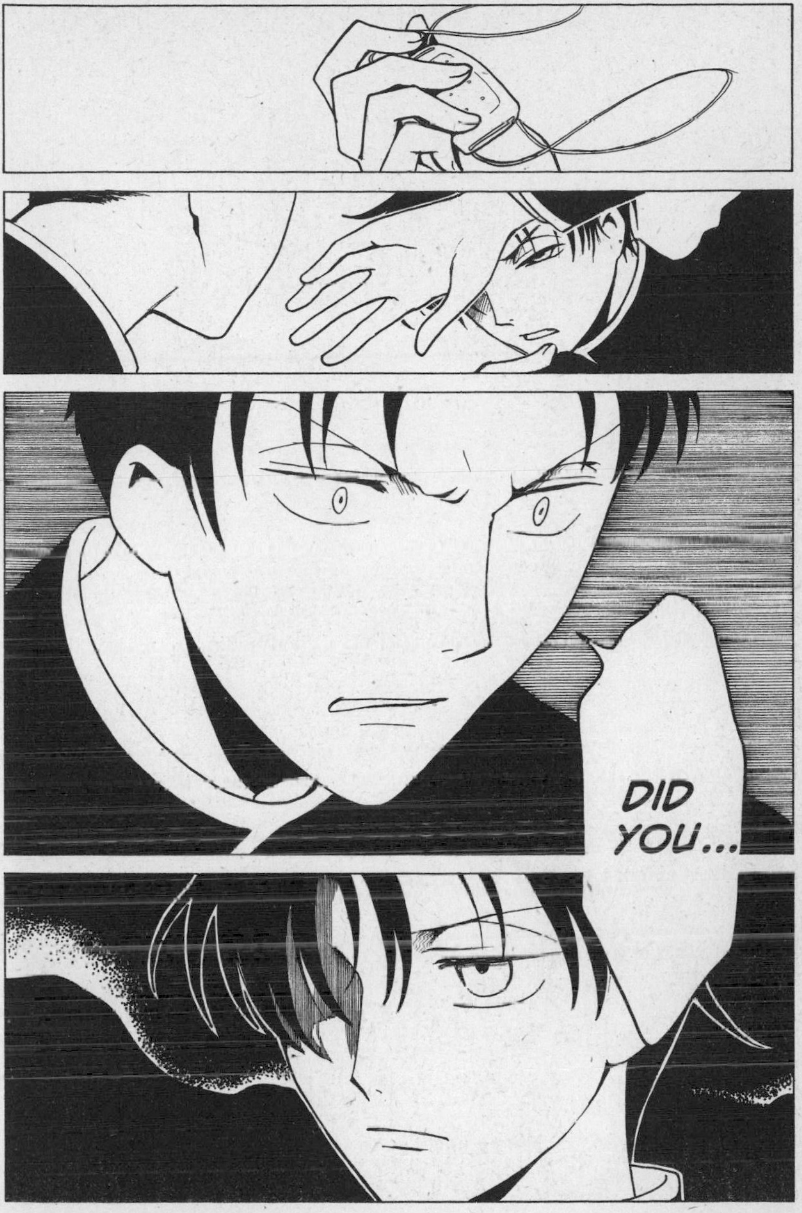
DID YOU...

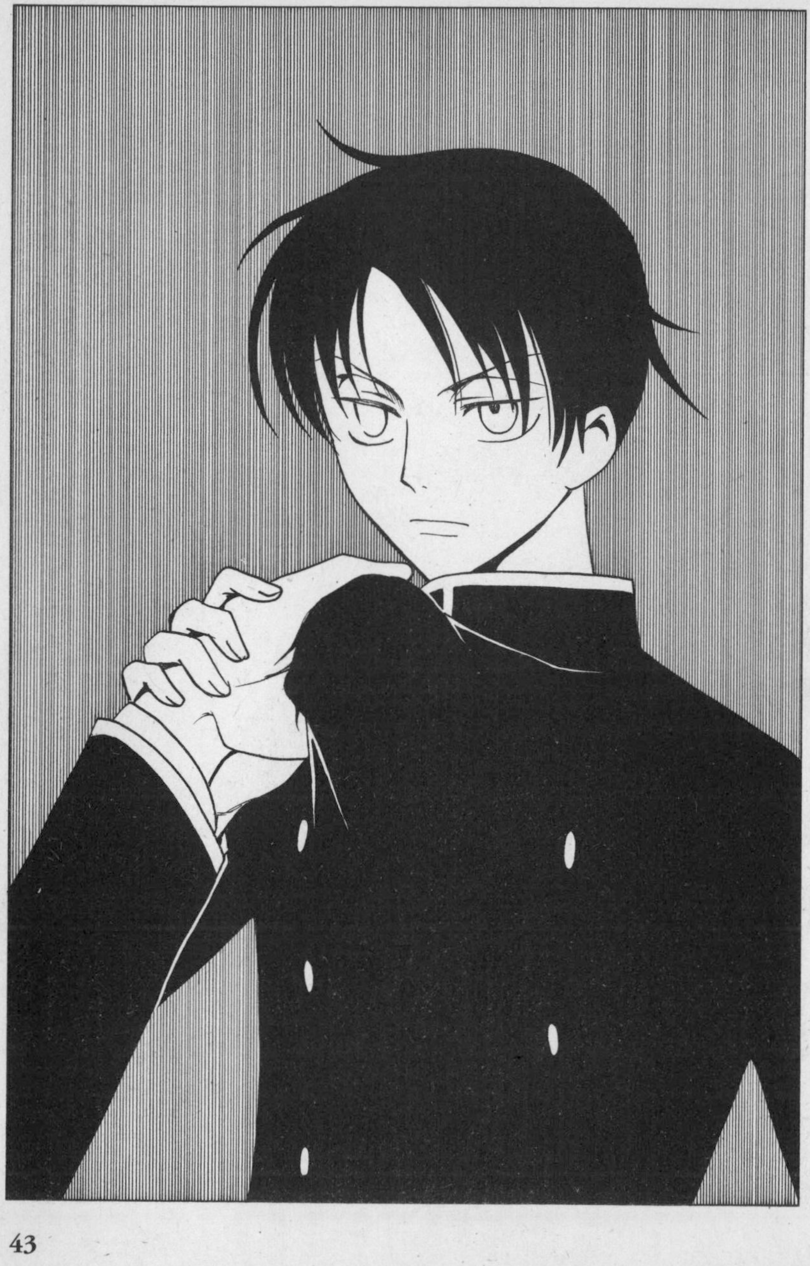

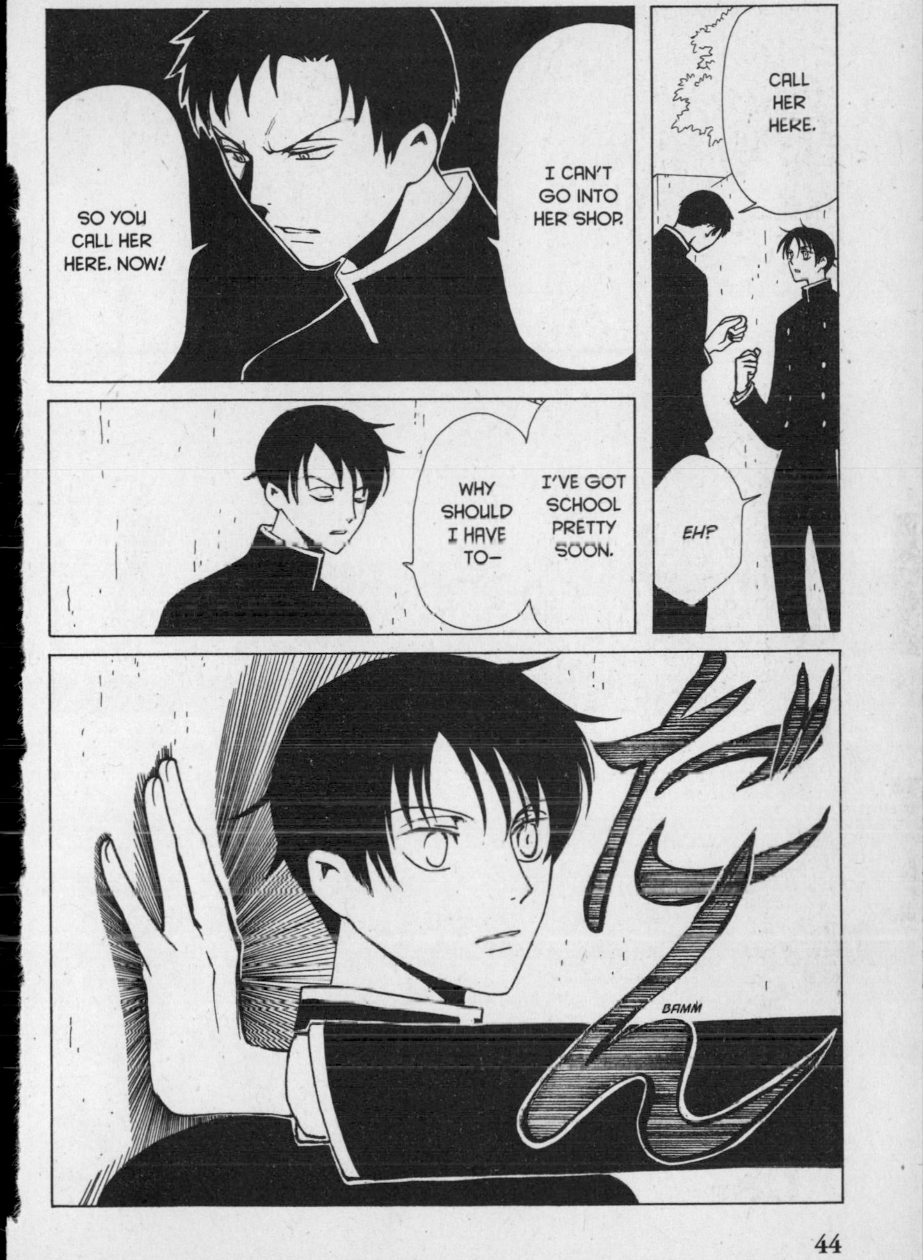
CALL HER HERE.
EH?
I CAN'T GO INTO HER SHOP.
SO YOU CALL HER HERE. NOW!
I'VE GOT SCHOOL PRETTY SOON.
WHY SHOULD I HAVE TO—
BAMM

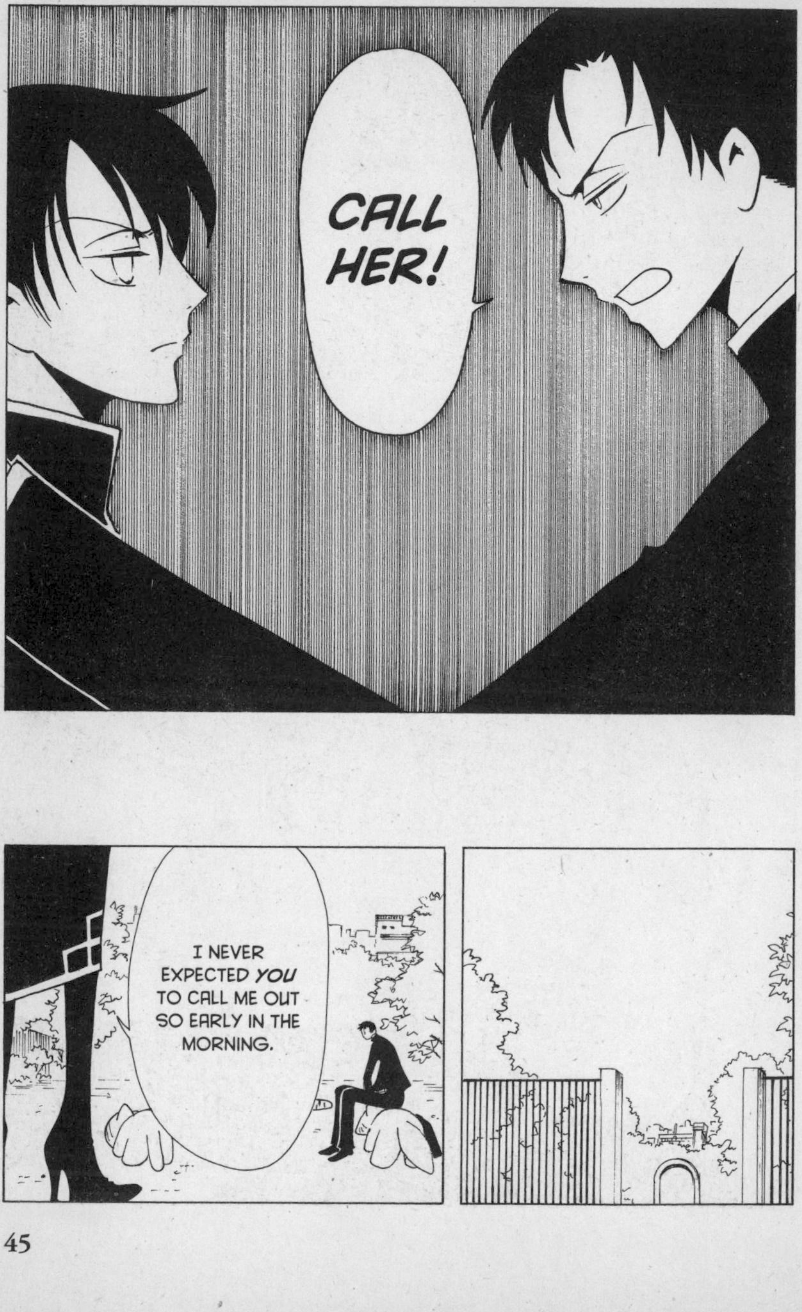
CALL HER!
I NEVER EXPECTED *YOU* TO CALL ME OUT SO EARLY IN THE MORNING.

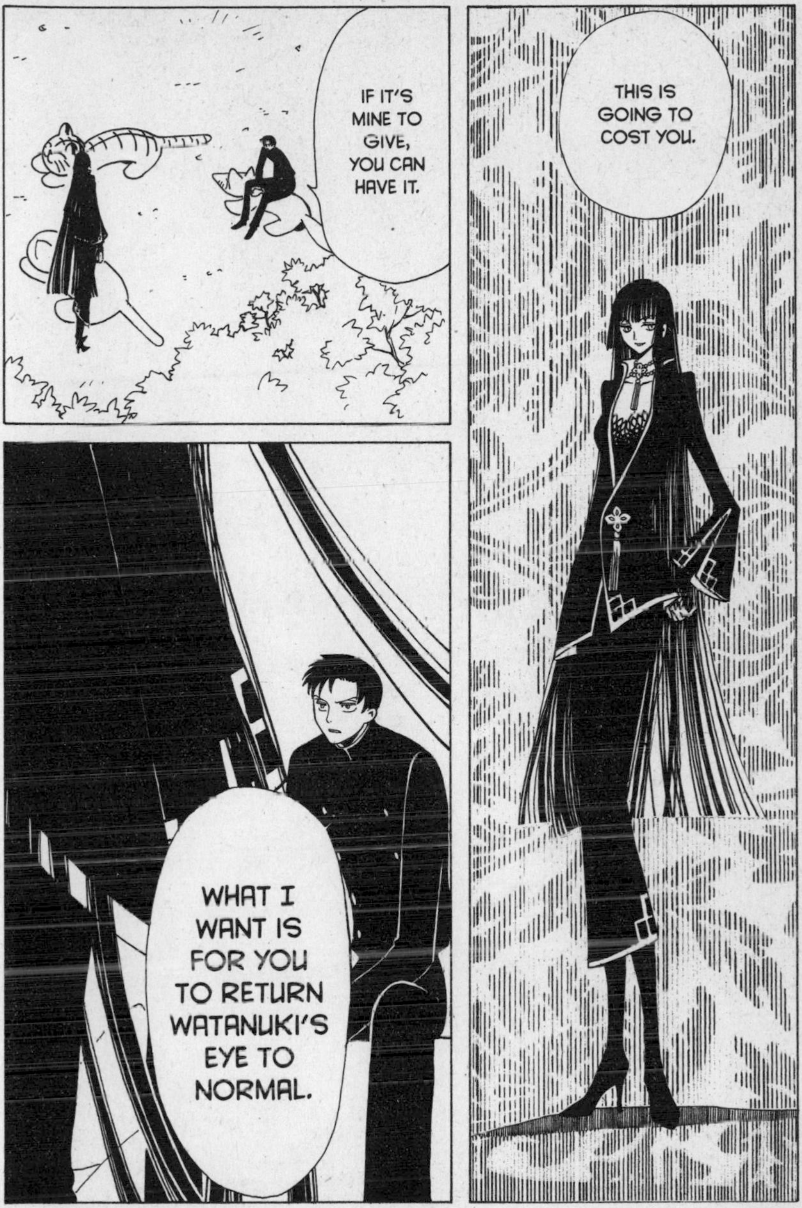
THIS IS GOING TO COST YOU.
IF IT'S MINE TO GIVE, YOU CAN HAVE IT.
WHAT I WANT IS FOR YOU TO RETURN WATANUKI'S EYE TO NORMAL.

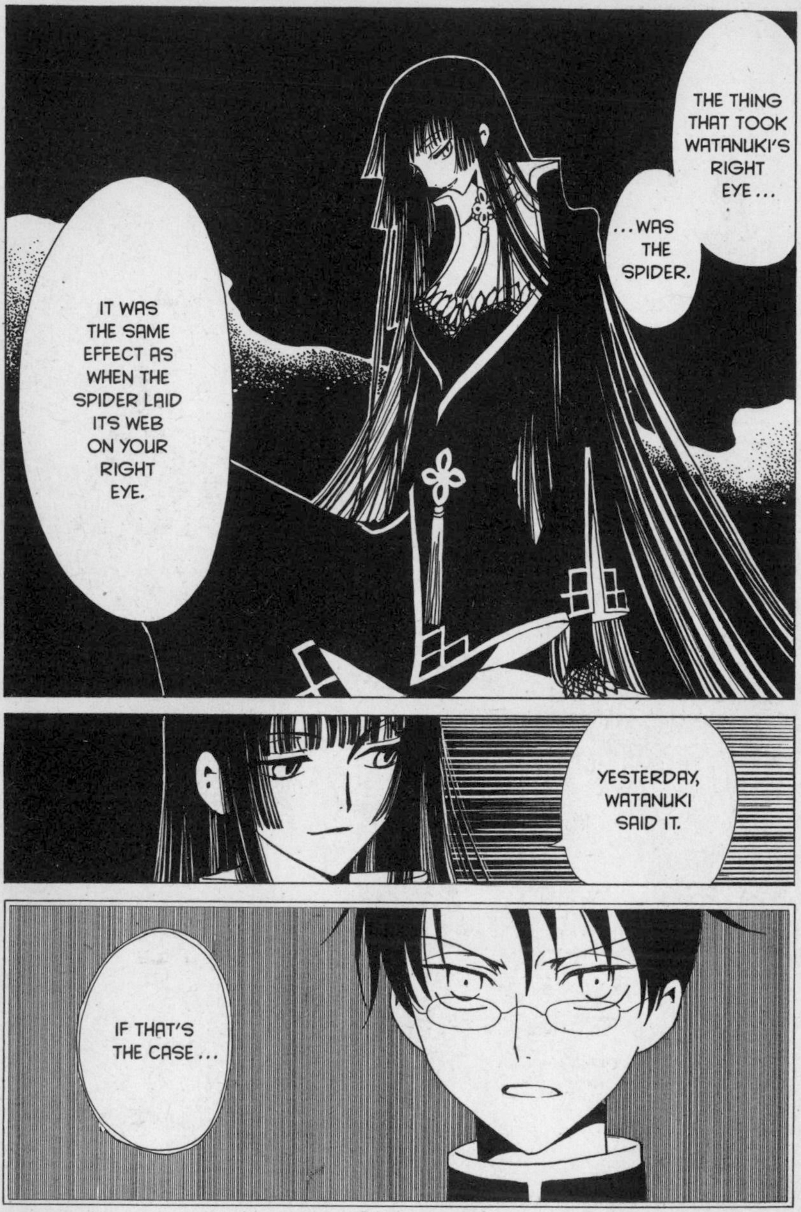
THE THING THAT TOOK WATANUKI'S RIGHT EYE...
...WAS THE SPIDER.
IT WAS THE SAME EFFECT AS WHEN THE SPIDER LAID ITS WEB ON YOUR RIGHT EYE.
YESTERDAY, WATANUKI SAID IT.
IF THAT'S THE CASE...

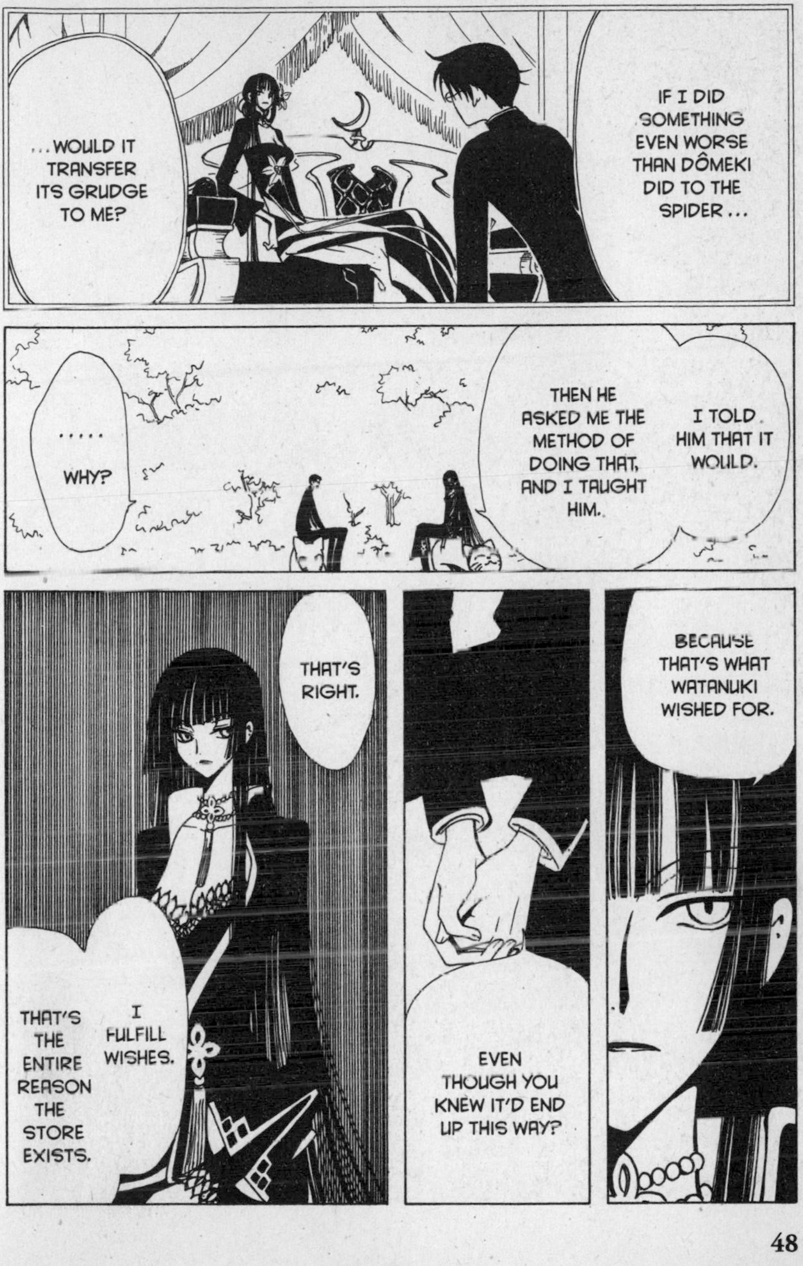
IF I DID SOMETHING EVEN WORSE THAN DÔMEKI DID TO THE SPIDER...
...WOULD IT TRANSFER ITS GRUDGE TO ME?
I TOLD HIM THAT IT WOULD.
THEN HE ASKED ME THE METHOD OF DOING THAT, AND I TAUGHT HIM.
.....
WHY?
BECAUSE THAT'S WHAT WATANUKI WISHED FOR.
EVEN THOUGH YOU KNEW IT'D END UP THIS WAY?
THAT'S RIGHT.
I FULFILL WISHES.
THAT'S THE ENTIRE REASON THE STORE EXISTS.

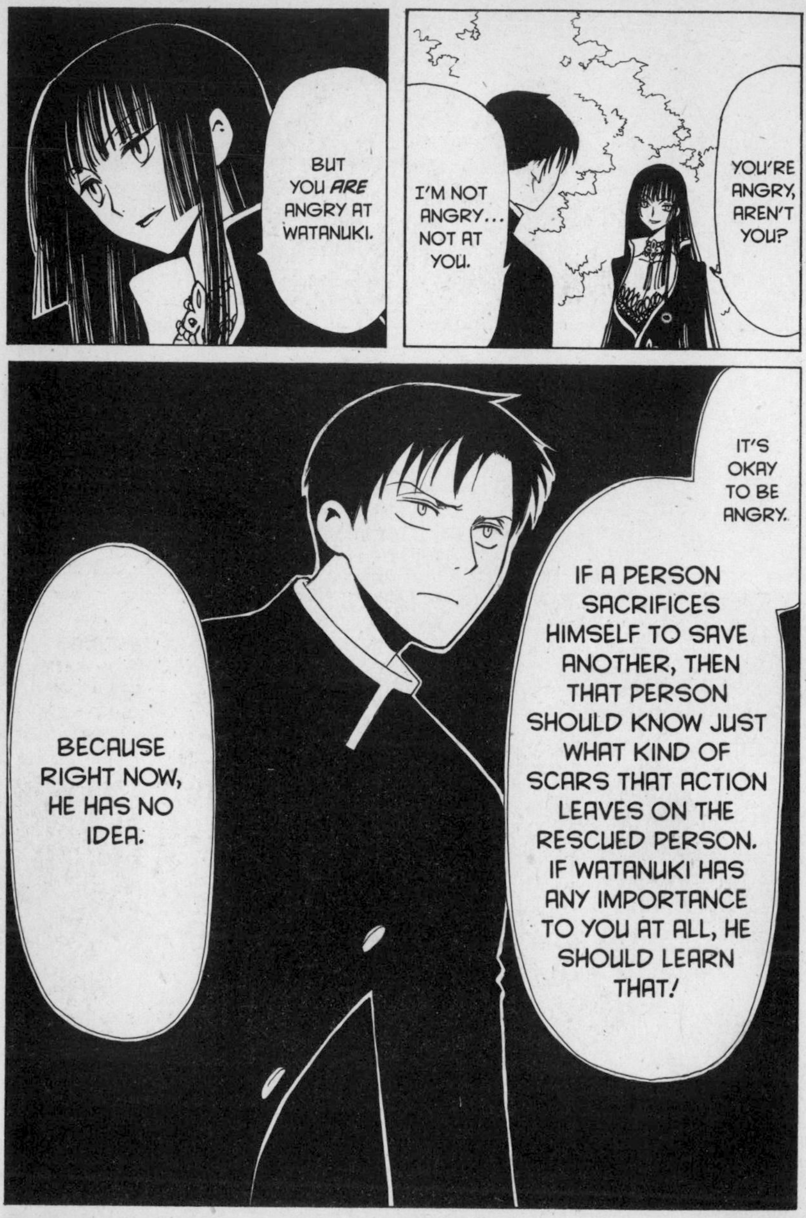
YOU'RE ANGRY, AREN'T YOU?
I'M NOT ANGRY... NOT AT YOU.
BUT YOU *ARE* ANGRY AT WATANUKI.
IT'S OKAY TO BE ANGRY.
IF A PERSON SACRIFICES HIMSELF TO SAVE ANOTHER, THEN THAT PERSON SHOULD KNOW JUST WHAT KIND OF SCARS THAT ACTION LEAVES ON THE RESCUED PERSON. IF WATANUKI HAS ANY IMPORTANCE TO YOU AT ALL, HE SHOULD LEARN THAT!
BECAUSE RIGHT NOW, HE HAS NO IDEA.

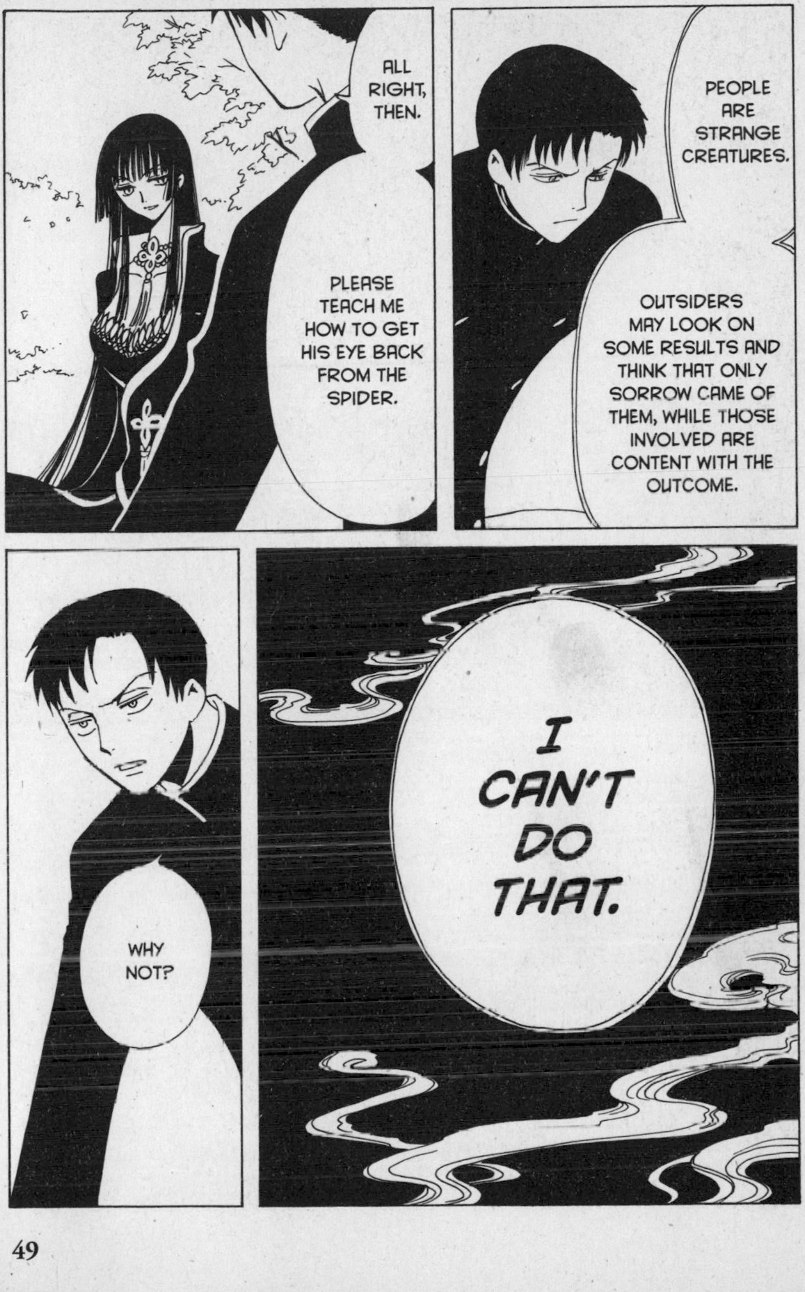
PEOPLE ARE STRANGE CREATURES.
OUTSIDERS MAY LOOK ON SOME RESULTS AND THINK THAT ONLY SORROW CAME OF THEM, WHILE THOSE INVOLVED ARE CONTENT WITH THE OUTCOME.
ALL RIGHT, THEN.
PLEASE TEACH ME HOW TO GET HIS EYE BACK FROM THE SPIDER.
I CAN'T DO THAT.
WHY NOT?

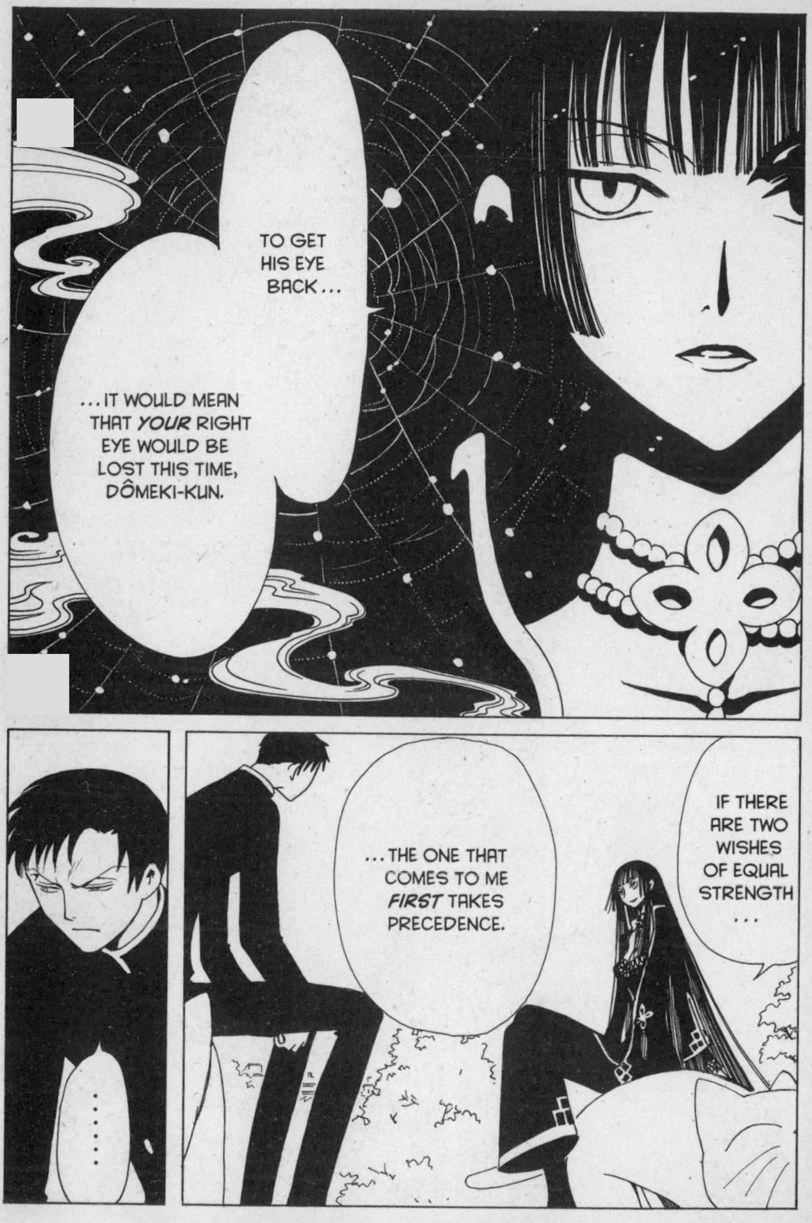
TO GET HIS EYE BACK...
...IT WOULD MEAN THAT *YOUR* RIGHT EYE WOULD BE LOST THIS TIME, DÔMEKI-KUN.
IF THERE ARE TWO WISHES OF EQUAL STRENGTH ...
...THE ONE THAT COMES TO ME *FIRST* TAKES PRECEDENCE.
......

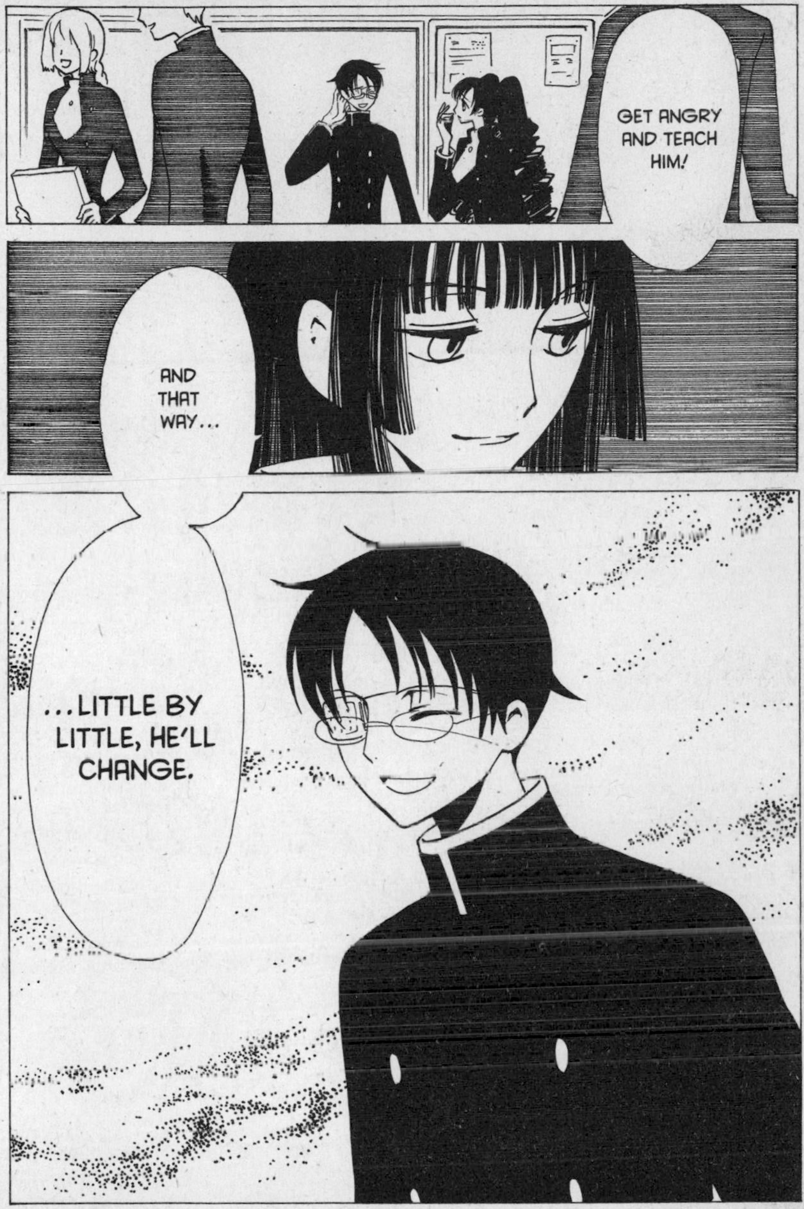
GET ANGRY AND TEACH HIM!
AND THAT WAY...
...LITTLE BY LITTLE, HE'LL CHANGE.

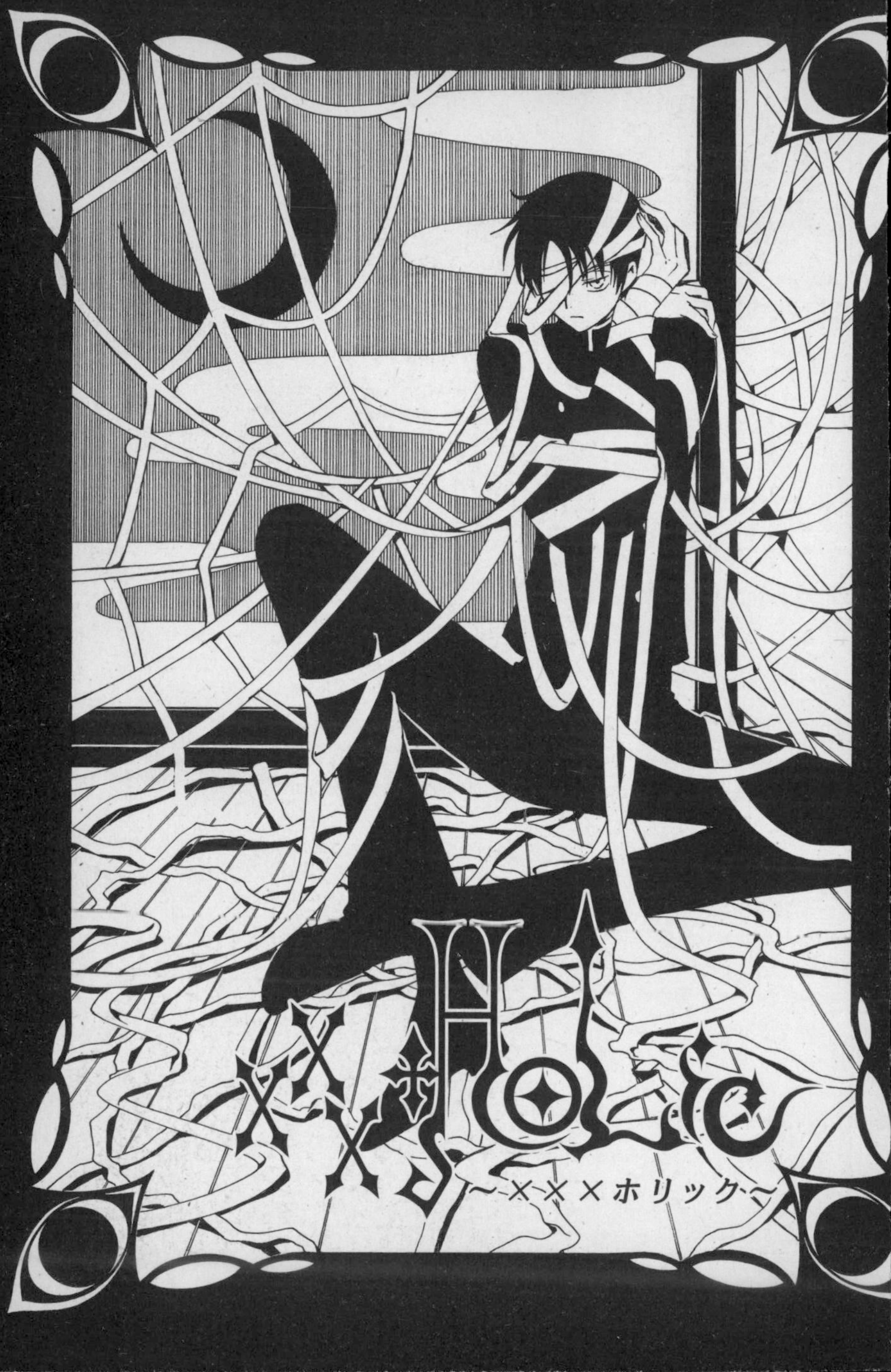
xxxHOLiC
~×××ホリック~

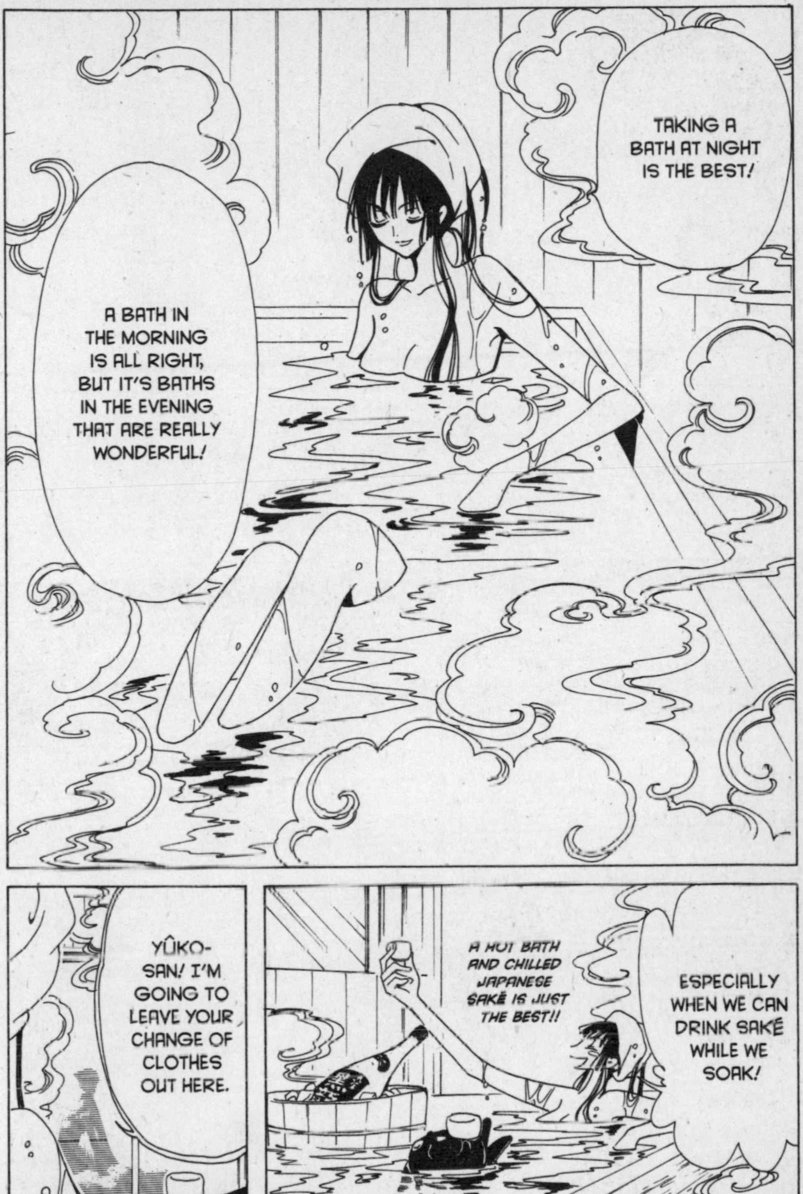
TAKING A BATH AT NIGHT IS THE BEST!
A BATH IN THE MORNING IS ALL RIGHT, BUT IT'S BATHS IN THE EVENING THAT ARE REALLY WONDERFUL!
ESPECIALLY WHEN WE CAN DRINK SAKÉ WHILE WE SOAK!
A HOT BATH AND CHILLED JAPANESE SAKÉ IS JUST THE BEST!!
YÛKO-SAN! I'M GOING TO LEAVE YOUR CHANGE OF CLOTHES OUT HERE.

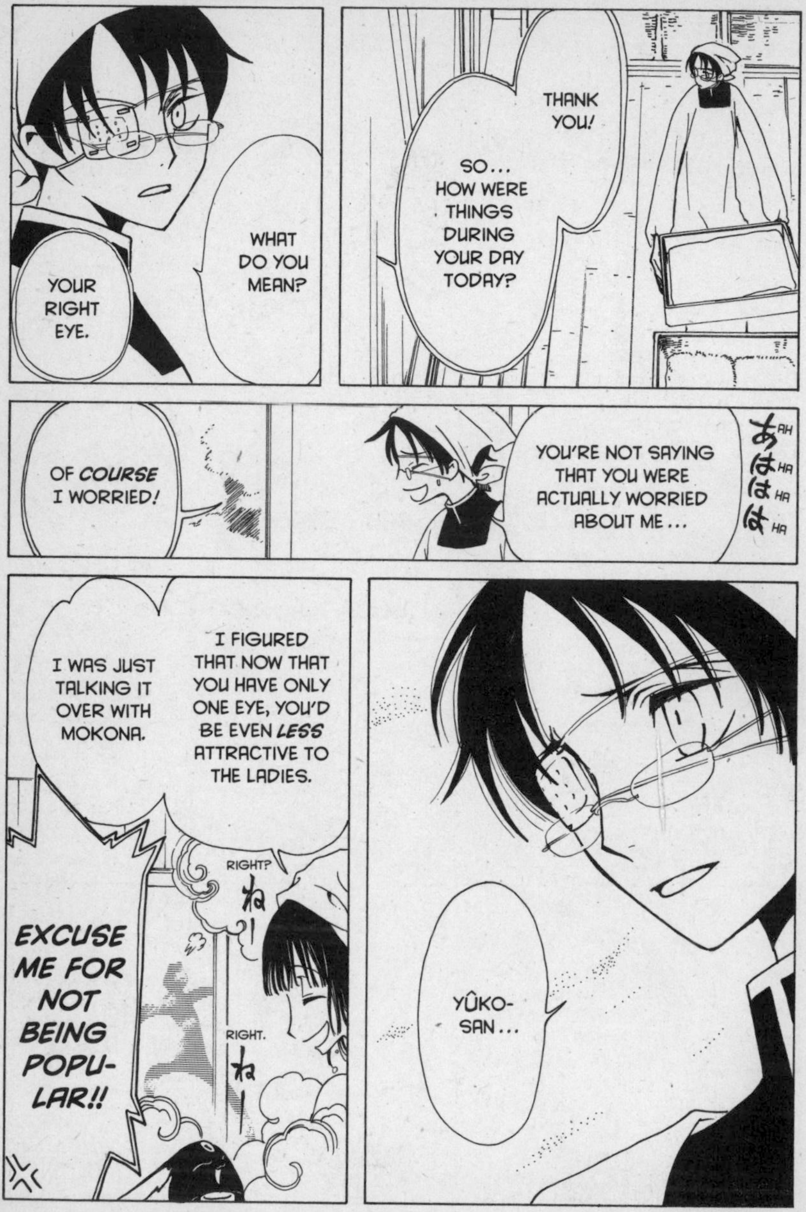
THANK YOU!
SO... HOW WERE THINGS DURING YOUR DAY TODAY?
WHAT DO YOU MEAN?
YOUR RIGHT EYE.
あ AH は HA は HA は HA
YOU'RE NOT SAYING THAT YOU WERE ACTUALLY WORRIED ABOUT ME...
OF COURSE I WORRIED!
YÛKO-SAN...
I FIGURED THAT NOW THAT YOU HAVE ONLY ONE EYE, YOU'D BE EVEN LESS ATTRACTIVE TO THE LADIES.
I WAS JUST TALKING IT OVER WITH MOKONA.
RIGHT? ね
RIGHT. ね
EXCUSE ME FOR NOT BEING POPU-LAR!!

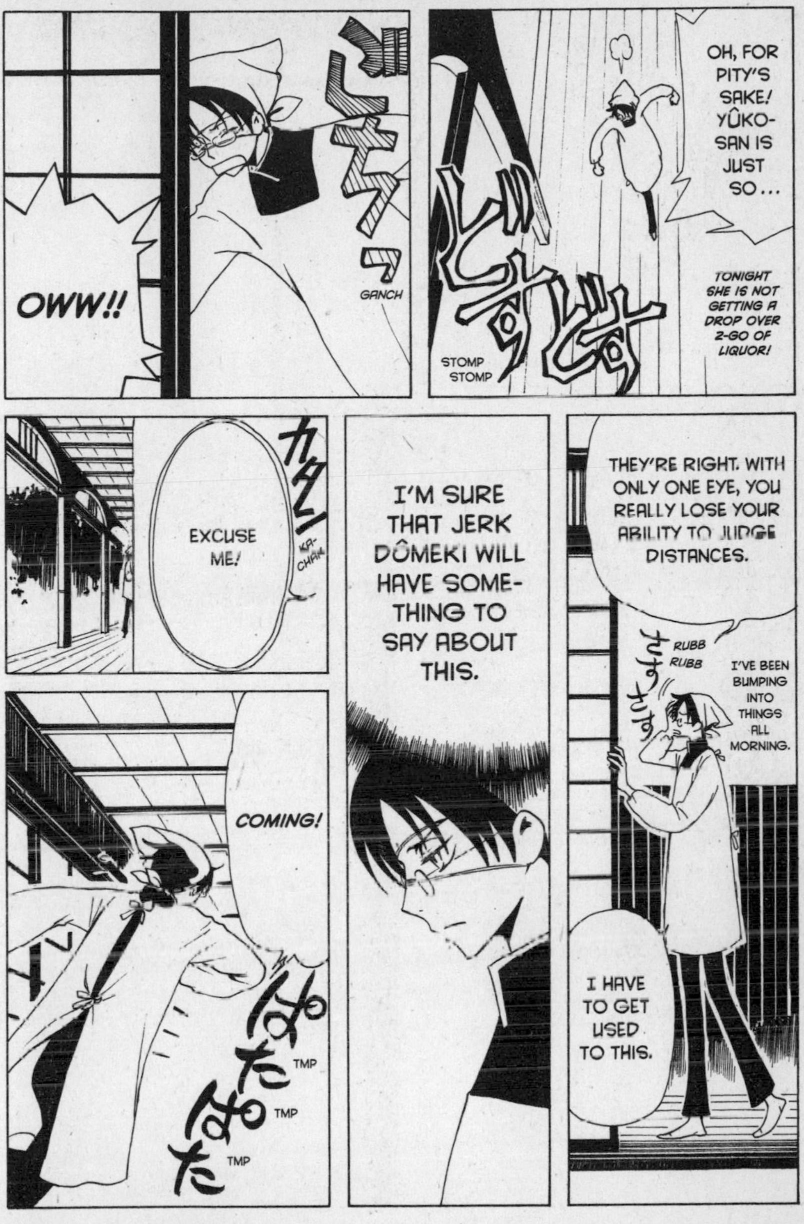

OH, FOR PITY'S SAKE! YÛKO-SAN IS JUST SO...
TONIGHT SHE IS NOT GETTING A DROP OVER 2-GO OF LIQUOR!
STOMP STOMP
GANCH
OWW!!
THEY'RE RIGHT. WITH ONLY ONE EYE, YOU REALLY LOSE YOUR ABILITY TO JUDGE DISTANCES.
RUBB RUBB
I'VE BEEN BUMPING INTO THINGS ALL MORNING.
I HAVE TO GET USED TO THIS.
I'M SURE THAT JERK DÔMEKI WILL HAVE SOME-THING TO SAY ABOUT THIS.
EXCUSE ME!
KA-CHAK
COMING!
TMP
TMP
TMP

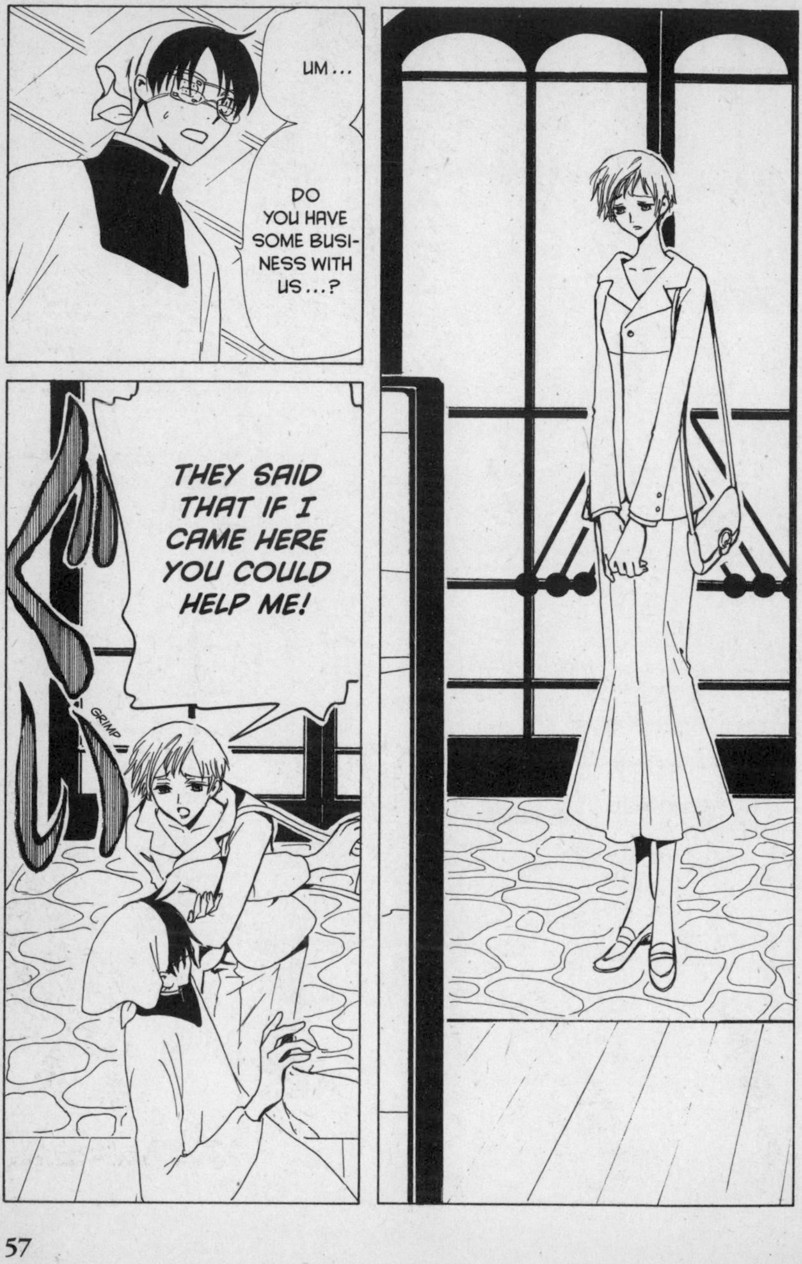
UM...
DO YOU HAVE SOME BUSINESS WITH US...?
THEY SAID THAT IF I CAME HERE YOU COULD HELP ME!
GRIMP

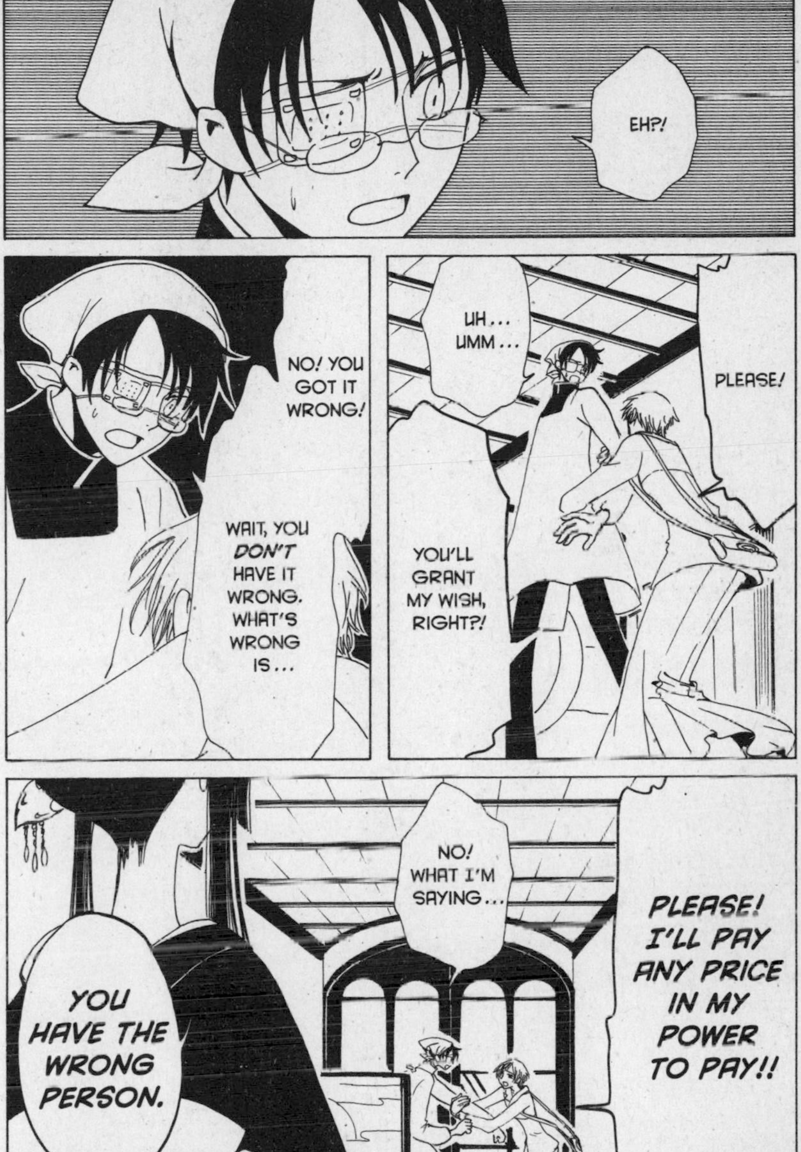
EH?!
PLEASE!
UH... UMM...
YOU'LL GRANT MY WISH, RIGHT?!
NO! YOU GOT IT WRONG!
WAIT, YOU *DON'T* HAVE IT WRONG. WHAT'S WRONG IS...
PLEASE! I'LL PAY ANY PRICE IN MY POWER TO PAY!!
NO! WHAT I'M SAYING...
YOU HAVE THE WRONG PERSON.

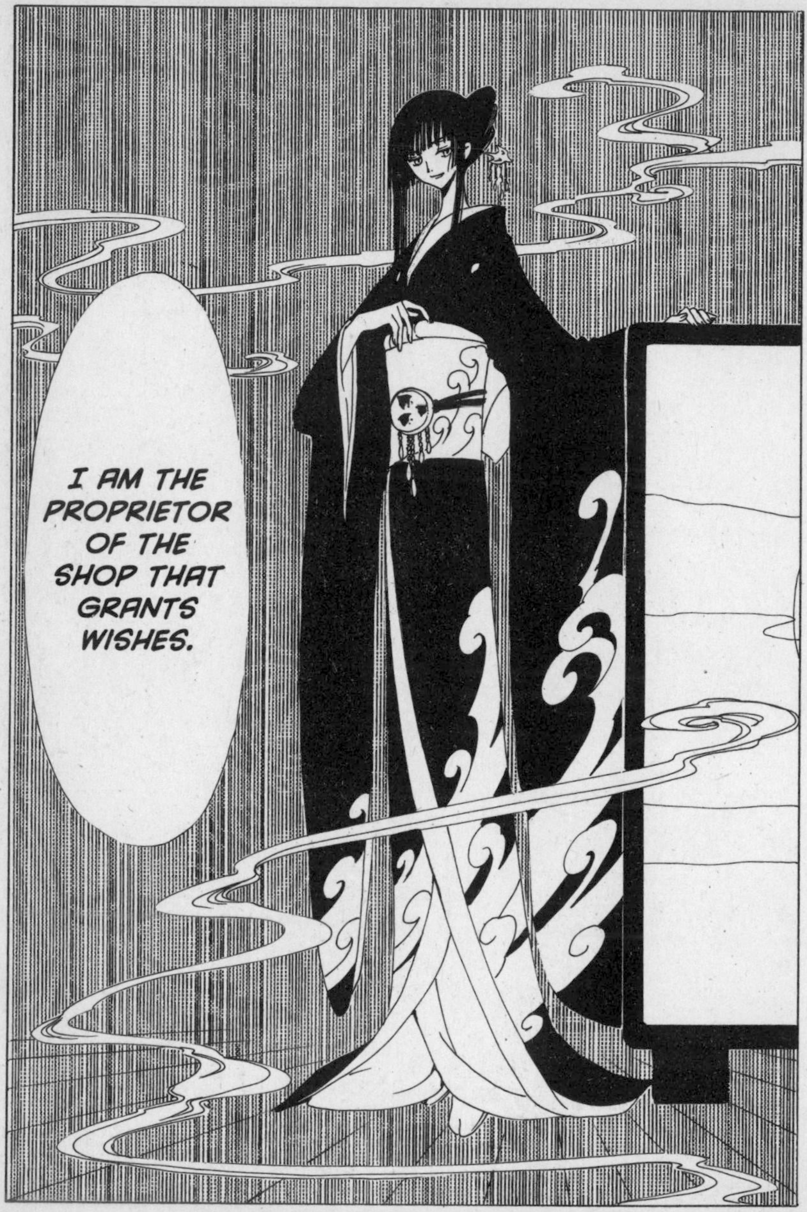
I AM THE PROPRIETOR OF THE SHOP THAT GRANTS WISHES.

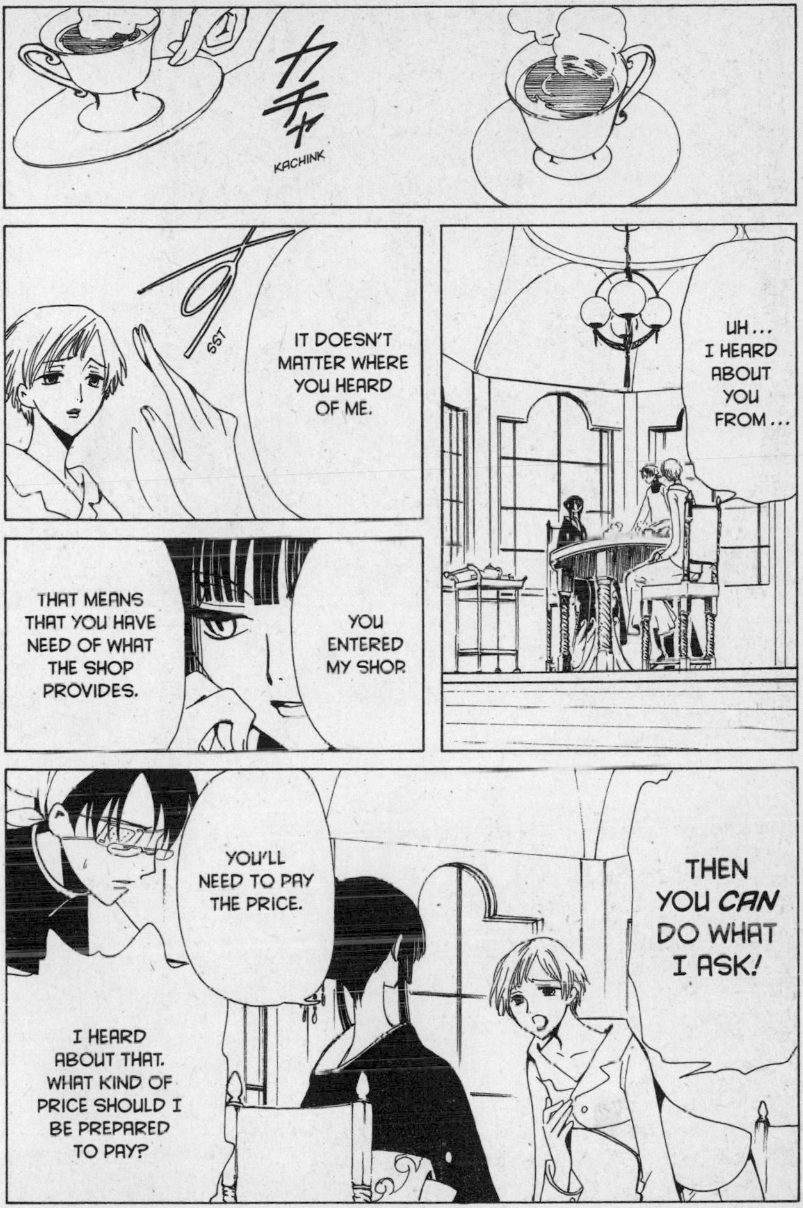
カチャ
KACHINK
UH... I HEARD ABOUT YOU FROM...
IT DOESN'T MATTER WHERE YOU HEARD OF ME.
SST
YOU ENTERED MY SHOP.
THAT MEANS THAT YOU HAVE NEED OF WHAT THE SHOP PROVIDES.
THEN YOU *CAN* DO WHAT I ASK!
YOU'LL NEED TO PAY THE PRICE.
I HEARD ABOUT THAT. WHAT KIND OF PRICE SHOULD I BE PREPARED TO PAY?

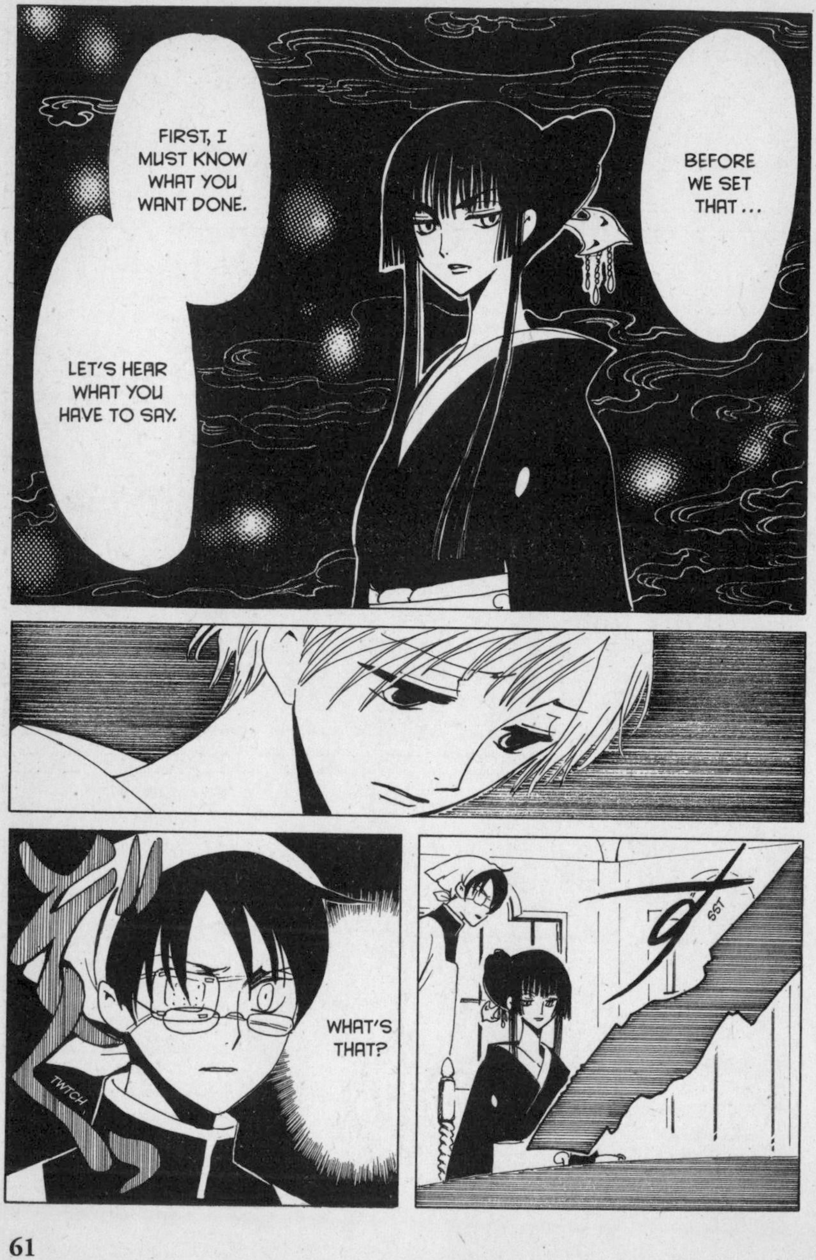
BEFORE WE SET THAT...
FIRST, I MUST KNOW WHAT YOU WANT DONE.
LET'S HEAR WHAT YOU HAVE TO SAY.
SST
WHAT'S THAT?
TWTCH

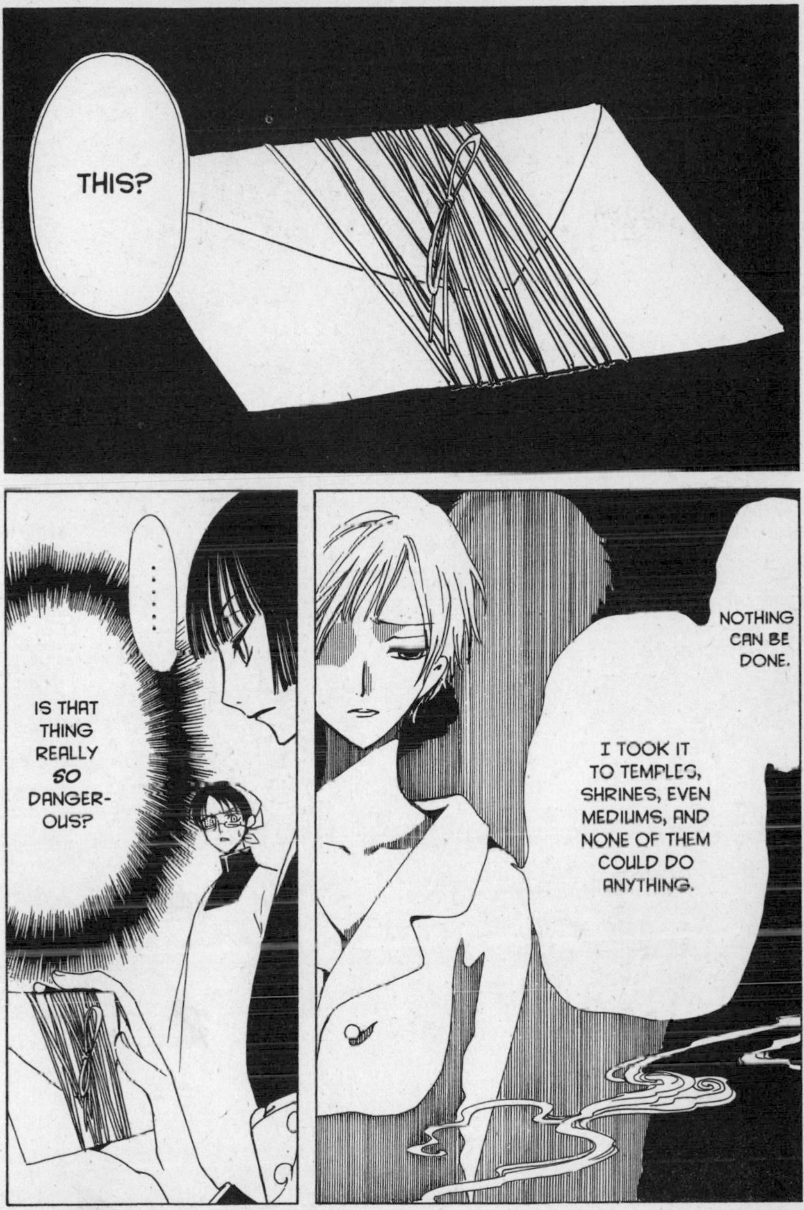
THIS?
NOTHING CAN BE DONE.
I TOOK IT TO TEMPLES, SHRINES, EVEN MEDIUMS, AND NONE OF THEM COULD DO ANYTHING.
......
IS THAT THING REALLY SO DANGEROUS?

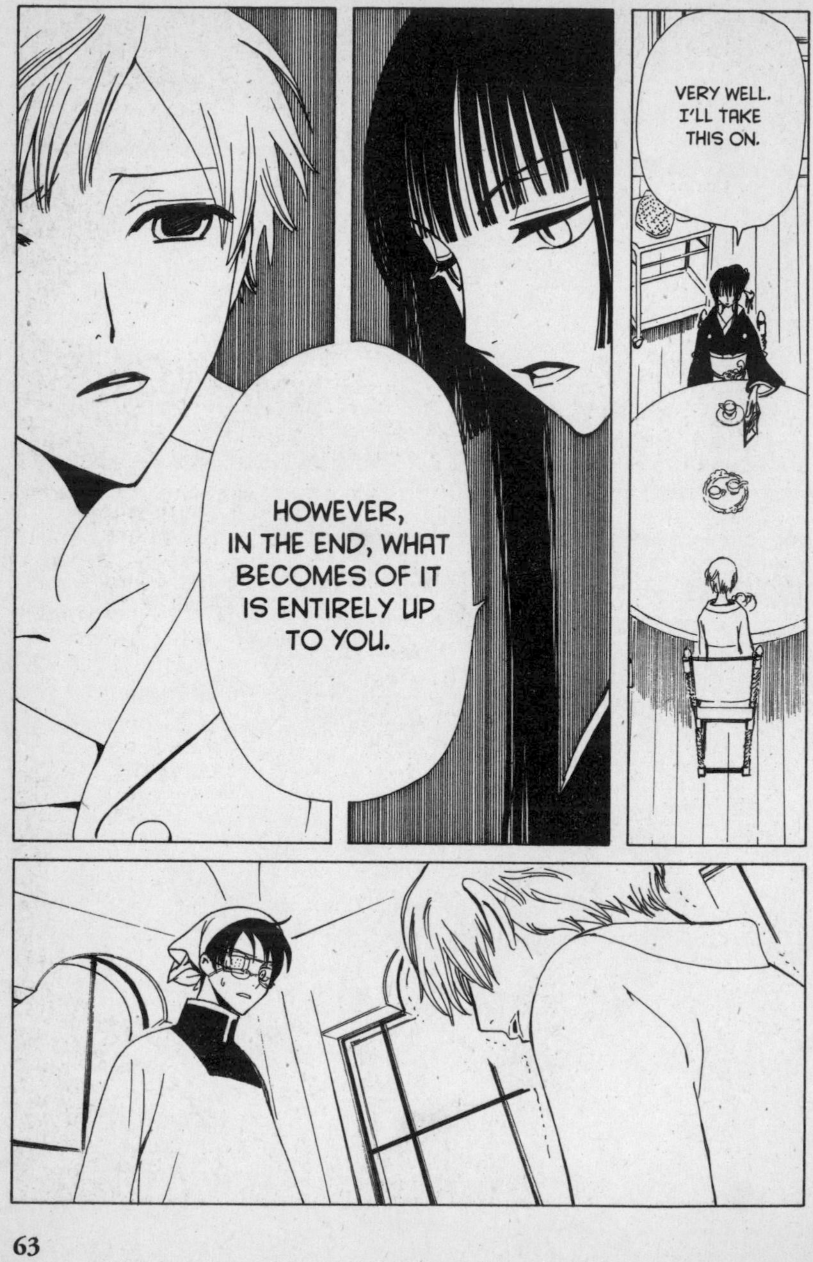
VERY WELL. I'LL TAKE THIS ON.
HOWEVER, IN THE END, WHAT BECOMES OF IT IS ENTIRELY UP TO YOU.

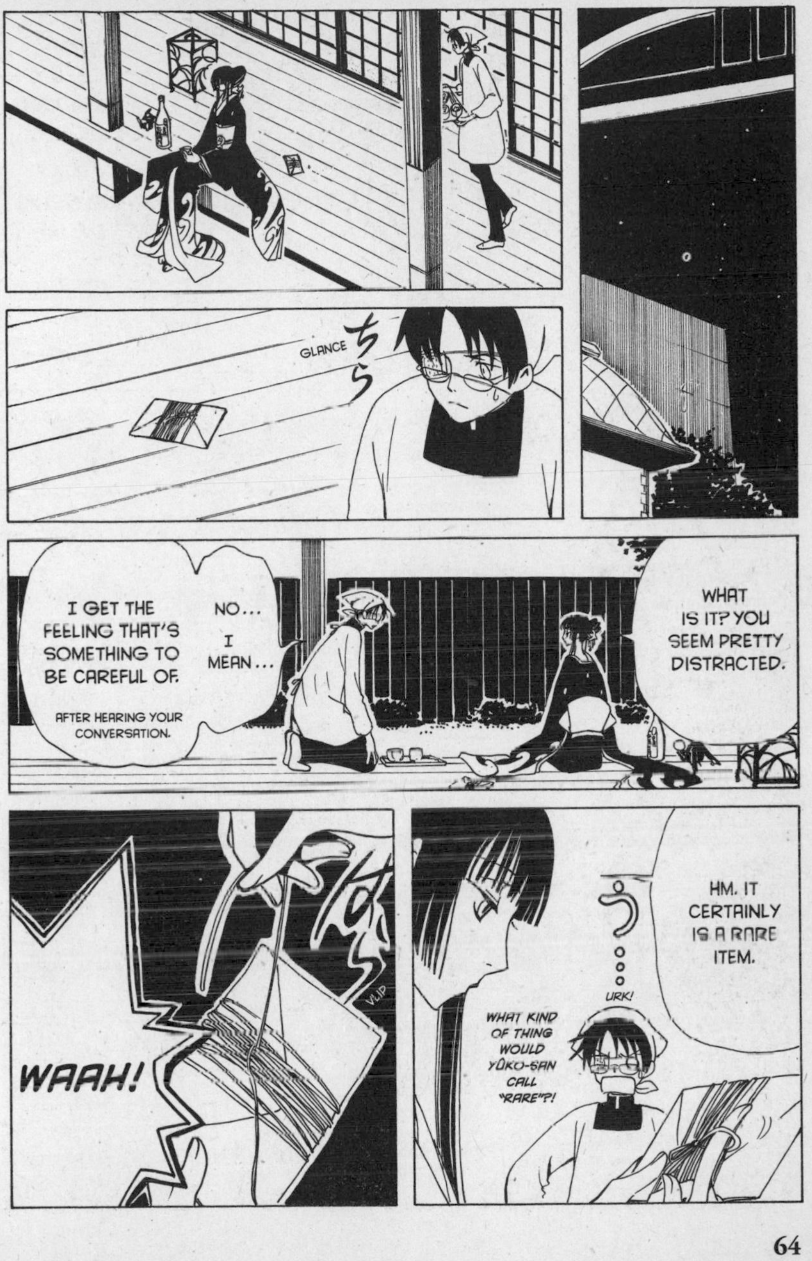

GLANCE
ちら
WHAT IS IT? YOU SEEM PRETTY DISTRACTED.
NO... I MEAN...
I GET THE FEELING THAT'S SOMETHING TO BE CAREFUL OF.
AFTER HEARING YOUR CONVERSATION.
HM. IT CERTAINLY IS A RARE ITEM.
う
URK!
WHAT KIND OF THING WOULD YŪKO-SAN CALL "RARE"?!
VLIP
WAAH!

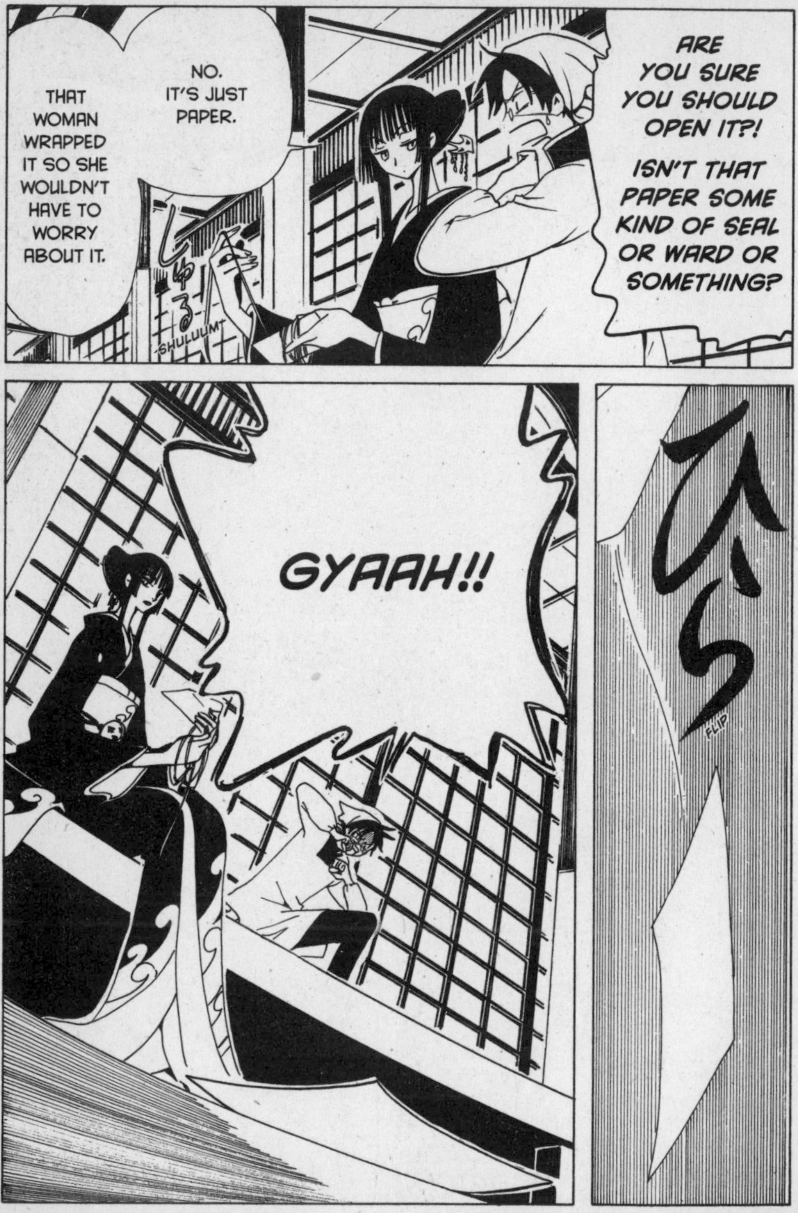
ARE YOU SURE YOU SHOULD OPEN IT?!
ISN'T THAT PAPER SOME KIND OF SEAL OR WARD OR SOMETHING?
NO. IT'S JUST PAPER.
THAT WOMAN WRAPPED IT SO SHE WOULDN'T HAVE TO WORRY ABOUT IT.
SHULUUM
FLIP
GYAAH!!

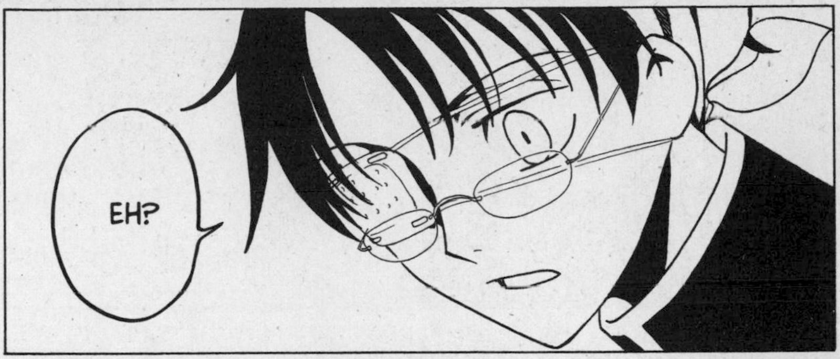
EH?
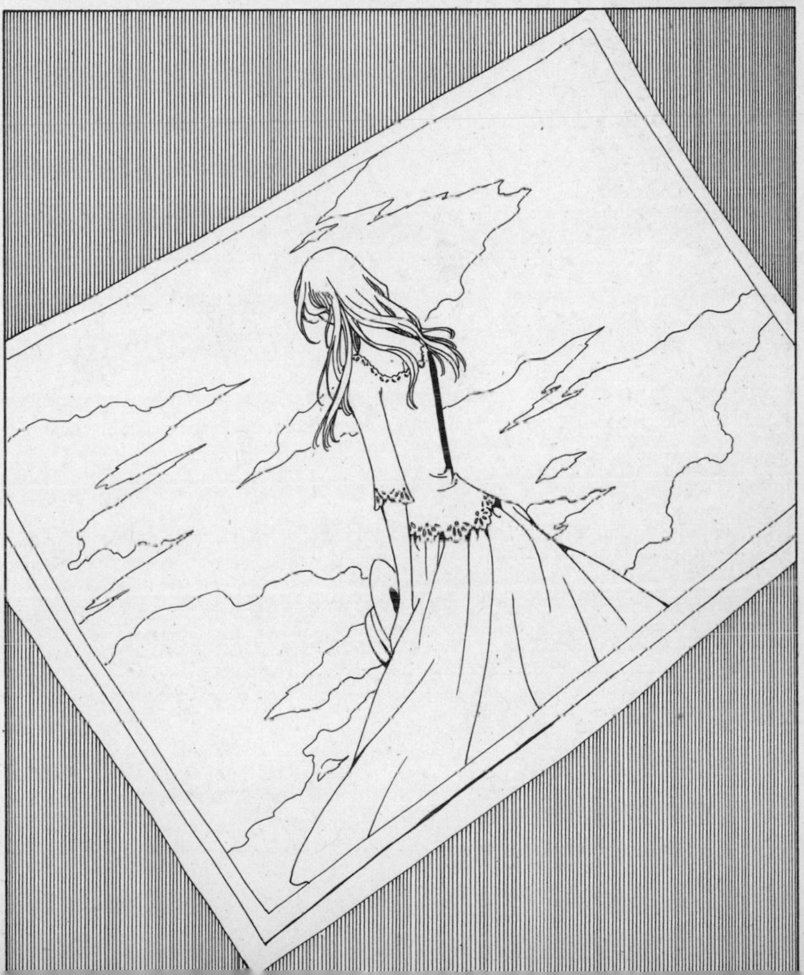

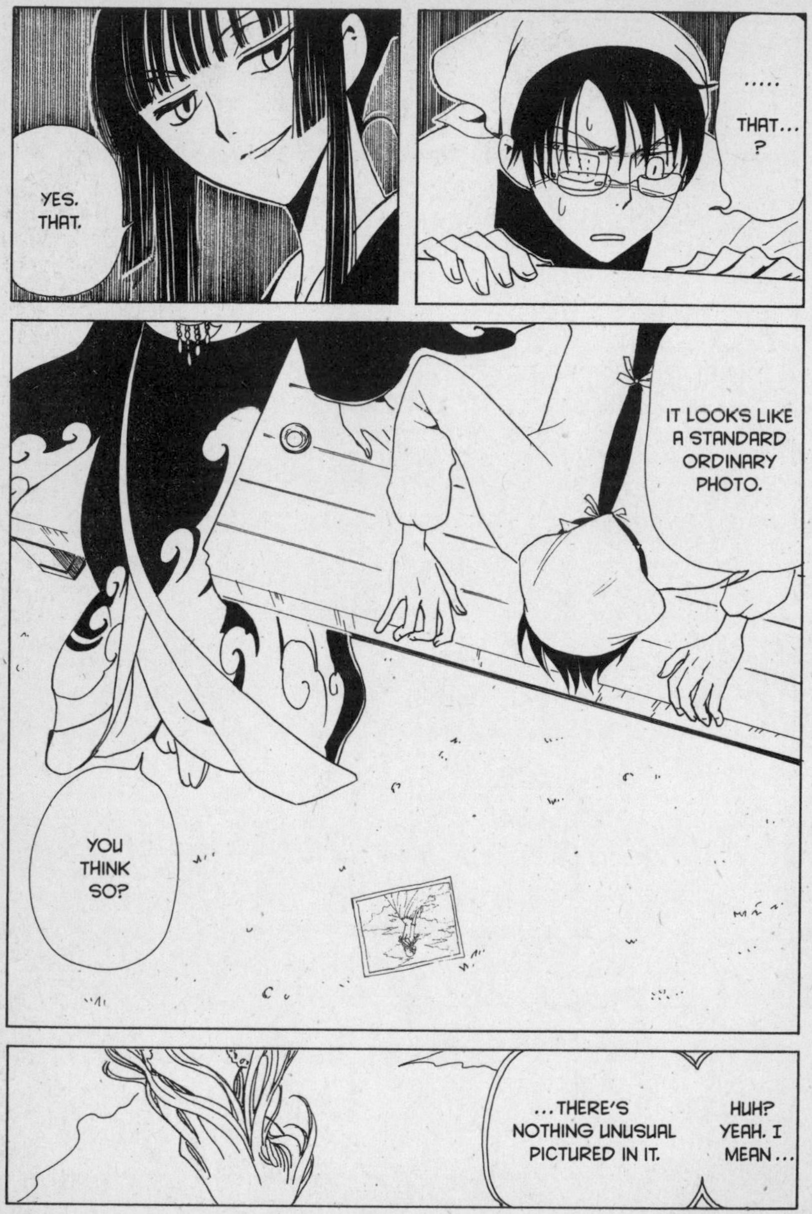
.....
THAT...?
YES. THAT.
IT LOOKS LIKE A STANDARD ORDINARY PHOTO.
YOU THINK SO?
HUH? YEAH. I MEAN...
...THERE'S NOTHING UNUSUAL PICTURED IN IT.

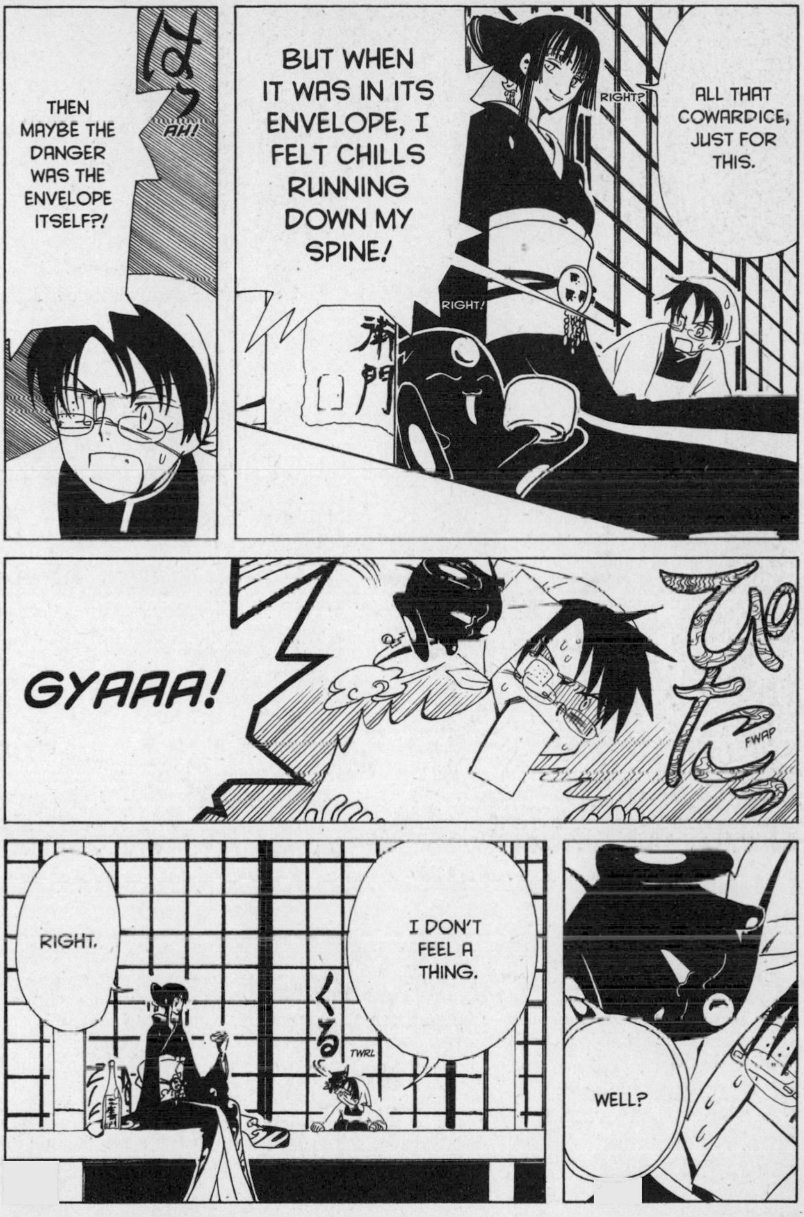
ALL THAT COWARDICE, JUST FOR THIS.
RIGHT?
BUT WHEN IT WAS IN ITS ENVELOPE, I FELT CHILLS RUNNING DOWN MY SPINE!
RIGHT!
はっ
AH!
THEN MAYBE THE DANGER WAS THE ENVELOPE ITSELF?!
ぴたっ
FWAP
GYAAA!
WELL?
I DON'T FEEL A THING.
くる
TWRL
RIGHT.

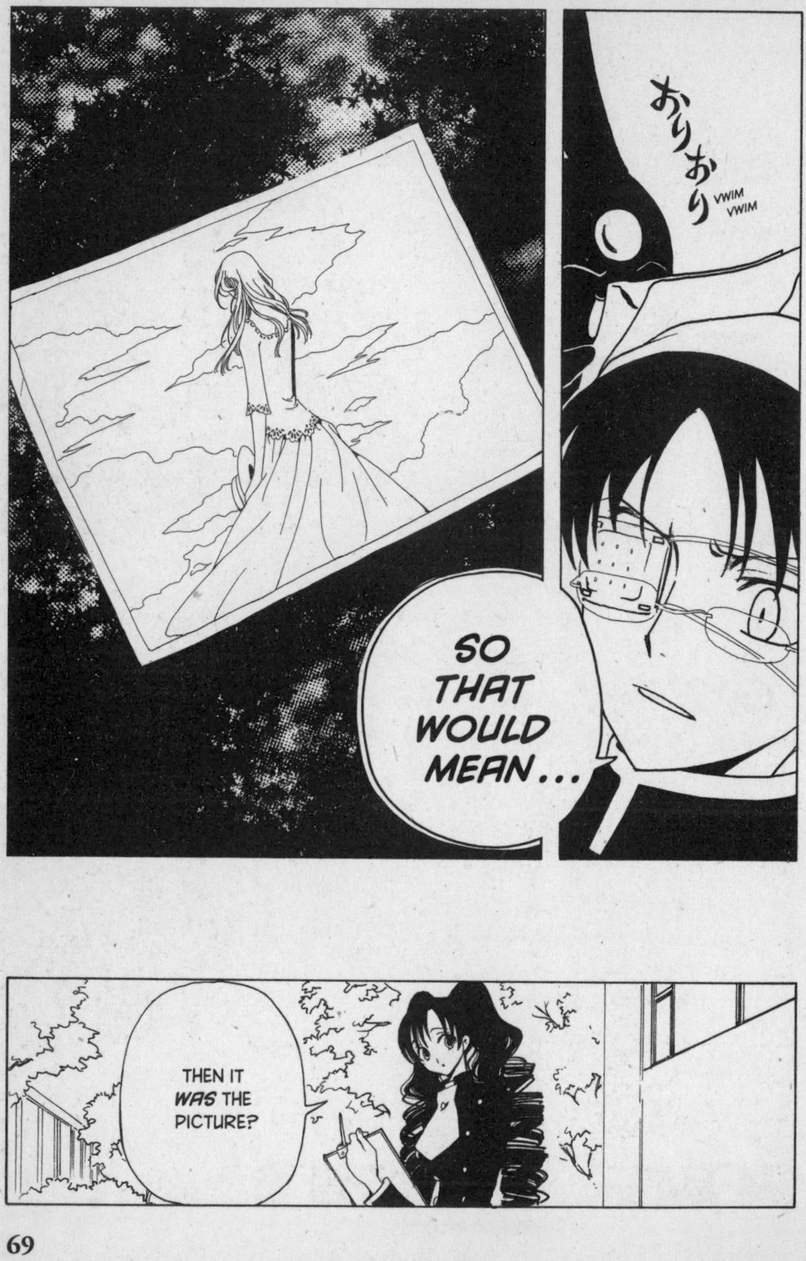
おりおり
VWIM VWIM
SO THAT WOULD MEAN...
THEN IT *WAS* THE PICTURE?

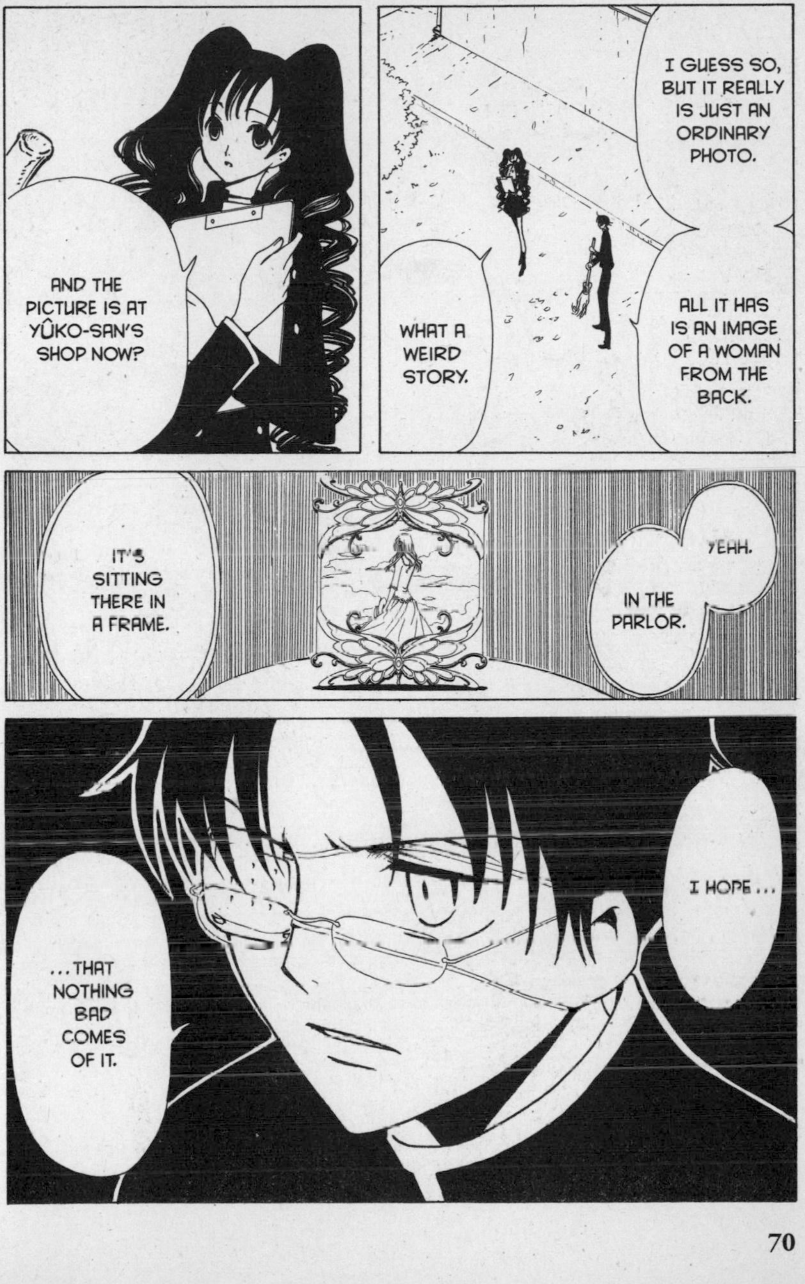
I GUESS SO, BUT IT REALLY IS JUST AN ORDINARY PHOTO.
ALL IT HAS IS AN IMAGE OF A WOMAN FROM THE BACK.
WHAT A WEIRD STORY.
AND THE PICTURE IS AT YÛKO-SAN'S SHOP NOW?
YEAH.
IN THE PARLOR.
IT'S SITTING THERE IN A FRAME.
I HOPE . . .
. . . THAT NOTHING BAD COMES OF IT.

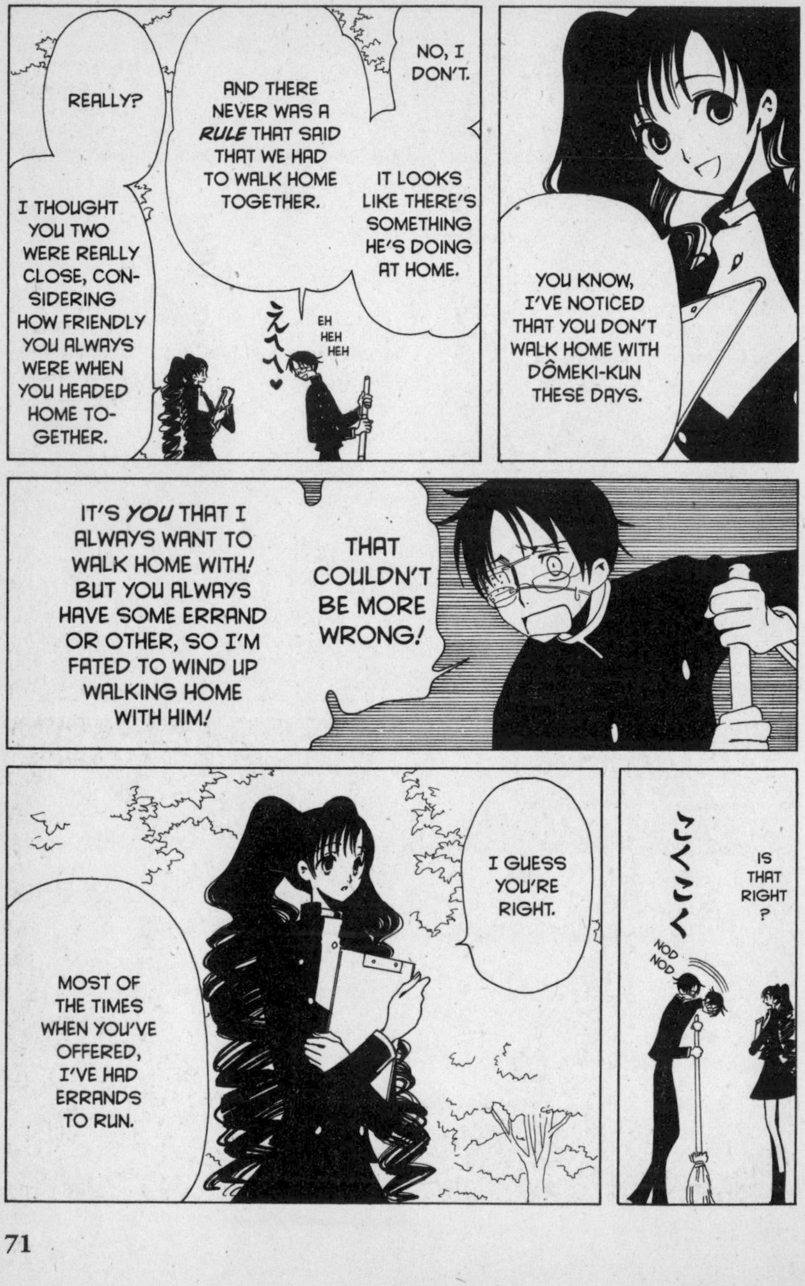
YOU KNOW, I'VE NOTICED THAT YOU DON'T WALK HOME WITH DÔMEKI-KUN THESE DAYS.
NO, I DON'T.
IT LOOKS LIKE THERE'S SOMETHING HE'S DOING AT HOME.
AND THERE NEVER WAS A RULE THAT SAID THAT WE HAD TO WALK HOME TOGETHER.
えへへ♥
EH HEH HEH
REALLY?
I THOUGHT YOU TWO WERE REALLY CLOSE, CONSIDERING HOW FRIENDLY YOU ALWAYS WERE WHEN YOU HEADED HOME TOGETHER.
THAT COULDN'T BE MORE WRONG!
IT'S YOU THAT I ALWAYS WANT TO WALK HOME WITH! BUT YOU ALWAYS HAVE SOME ERRAND OR OTHER, SO I'M FATED TO WIND UP WALKING HOME WITH HIM!
IS THAT RIGHT?
こくこく
NOD NOD
I GUESS YOU'RE RIGHT.
MOST OF THE TIMES WHEN YOU'VE OFFERED, I'VE HAD ERRANDS TO RUN.

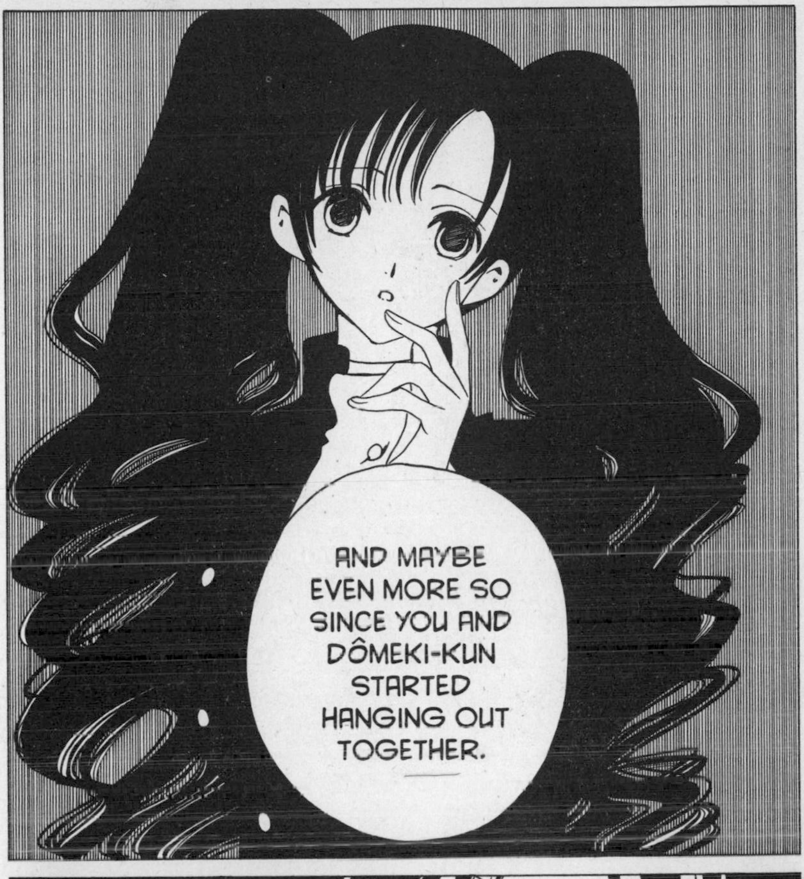
AND MAYBE EVEN MORE SO SINCE YOU AND DÔMEKI-KUN STARTED HANGING OUT TOGETHER.
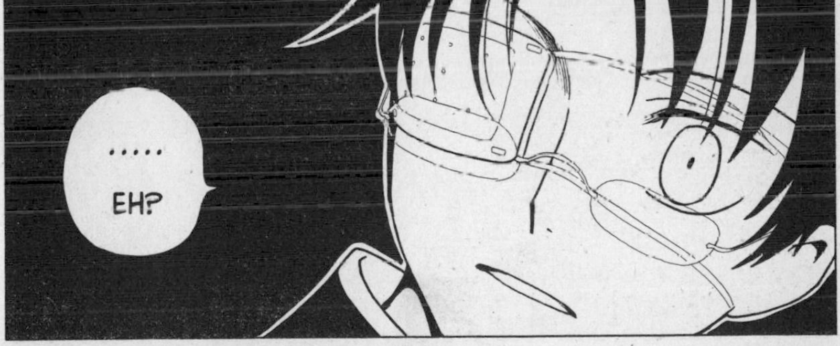
..... EH?

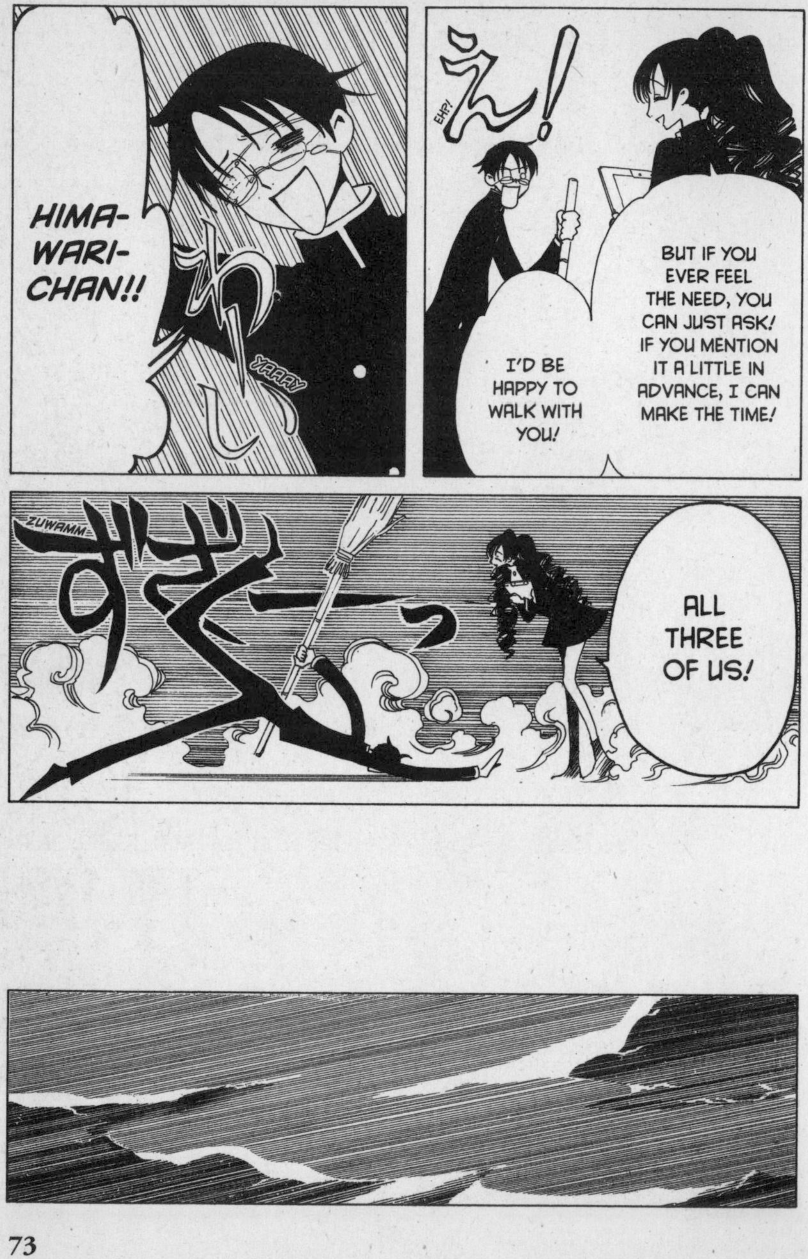
BUT IF YOU EVER FEEL THE NEED, YOU CAN JUST ASK! IF YOU MENTION IT A LITTLE IN ADVANCE, I CAN MAKE THE TIME!
I'D BE HAPPY TO WALK WITH YOU!
EH?!
HIMA-WARI-CHAN!!
YAAAY
ALL THREE OF US!
ZUWAMM

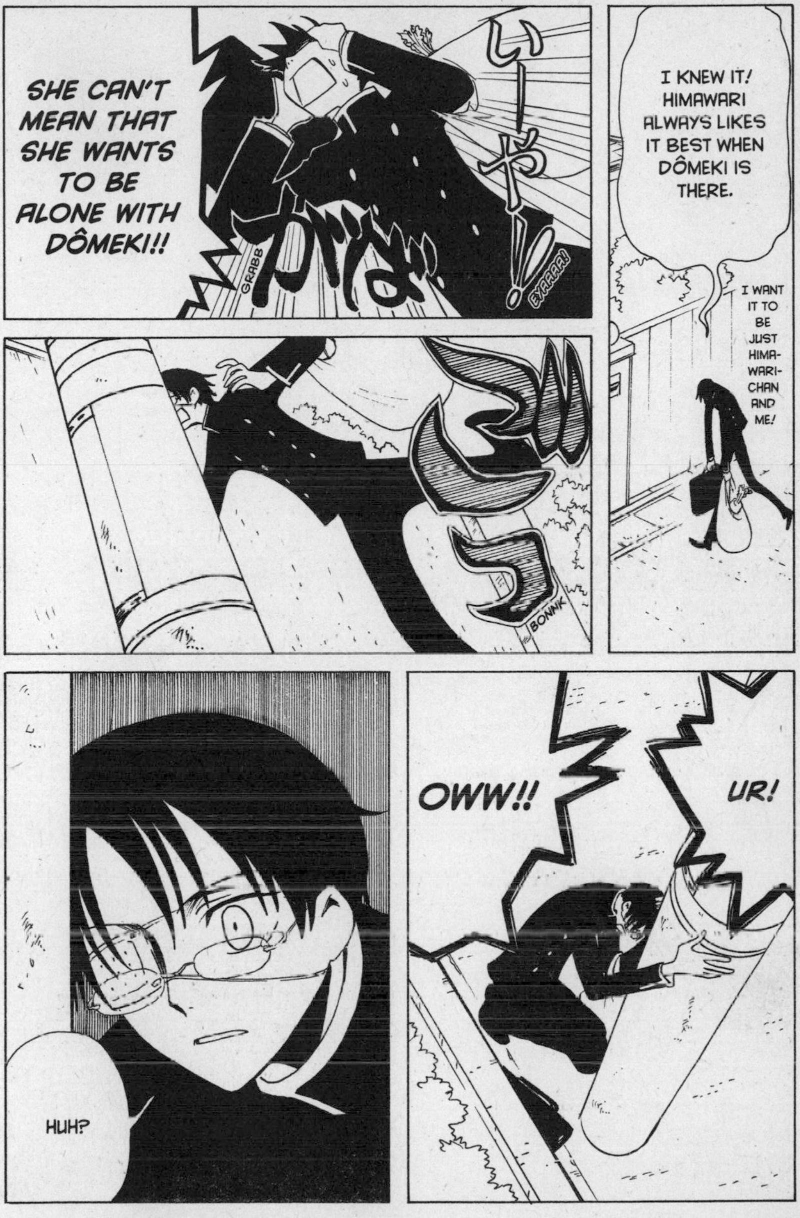
I KNEW IT! HIMAWARI ALWAYS LIKES IT BEST WHEN DÔMEKI IS THERE.
I WANT IT TO BE JUST HIMA-WARI-CHAN AND ME!
EYAAAA!
SHE CAN'T MEAN THAT SHE WANTS TO BE ALONE WITH DÔMEKI!!
GRABB
BONNK
UR!
OWW!!
HUH?

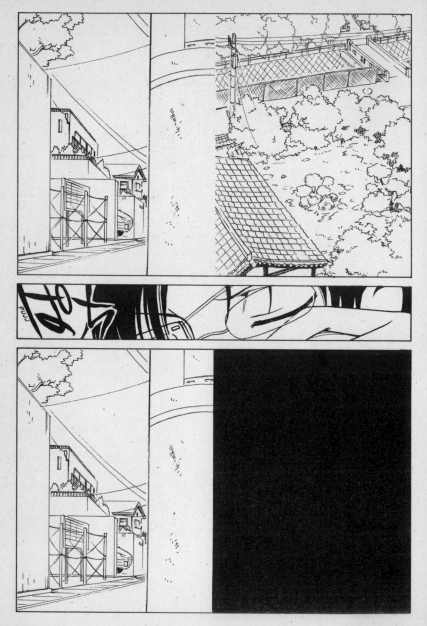

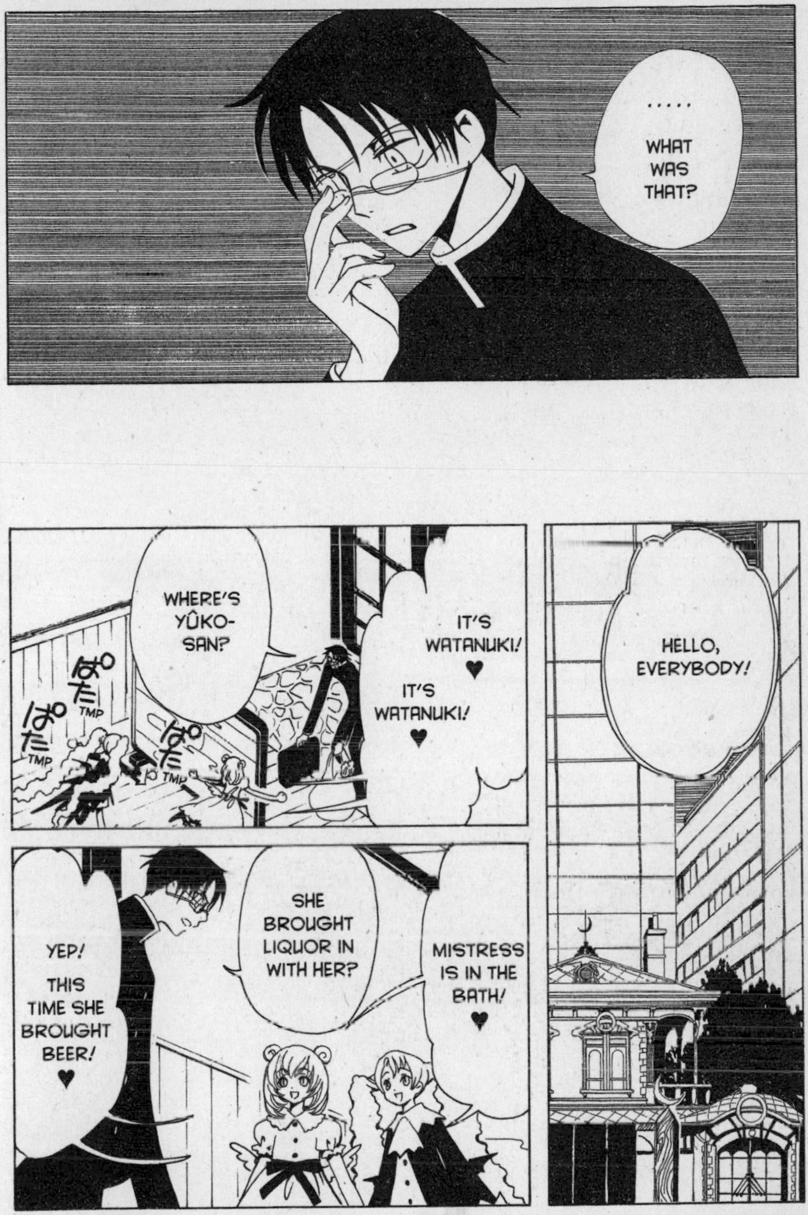
.....
WHAT WAS THAT?
HELLO, EVERYBODY!
IT'S WATANUKI! ♥
IT'S WATANUKI! ♥
WHERE'S YÛKO-SAN?
ぱた TMP
ぱた TMP
ぱた TMP
MISTRESS IS IN THE BATH! ♥
SHE BROUGHT LIQUOR IN WITH HER?
YEP! THIS TIME SHE BROUGHT BEER! ♥

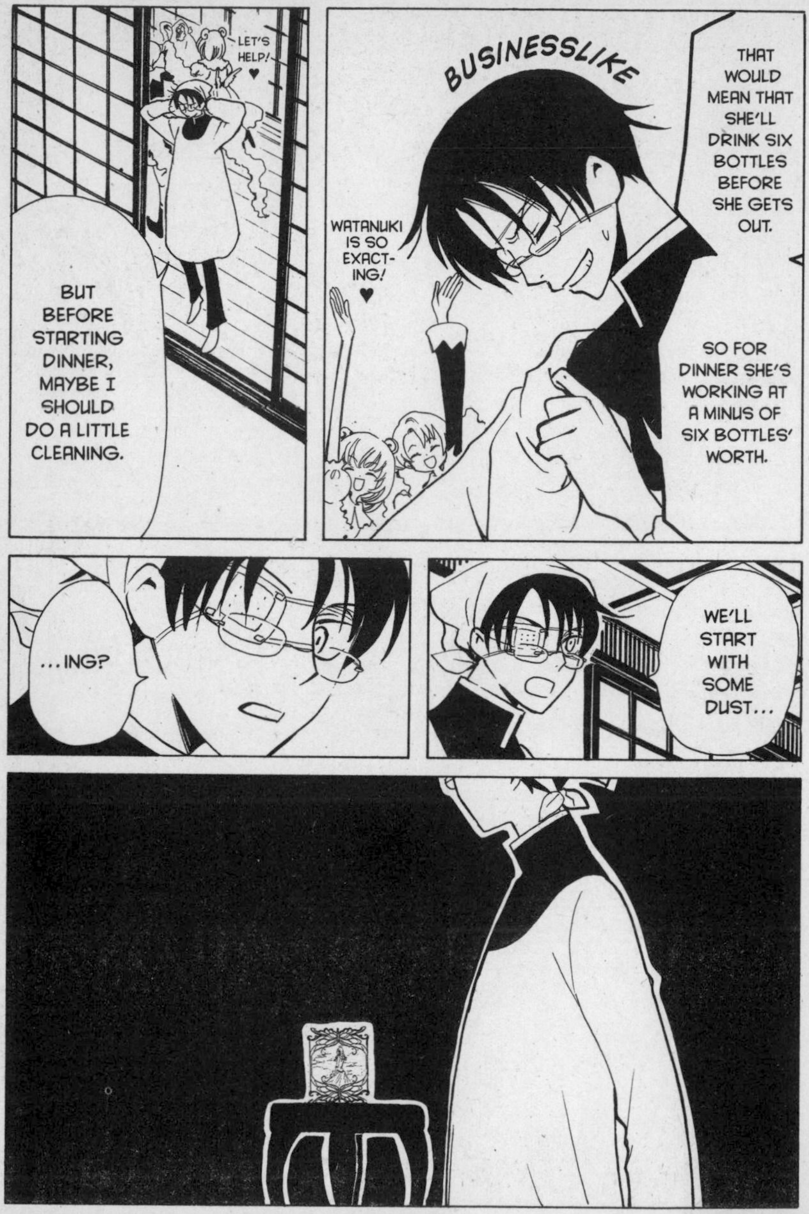
BUSINESSLIKE
THAT WOULD MEAN THAT SHE'LL DRINK SIX BOTTLES BEFORE SHE GETS OUT.
SO FOR DINNER SHE'S WORKING AT A MINUS OF SIX BOTTLES' WORTH.
WATANUKI IS SO EXACTING! ♥
BUT BEFORE STARTING DINNER, MAYBE I SHOULD DO A LITTLE CLEANING.
LET'S HELP! ♥
WE'LL START WITH SOME DUST...
...ING?

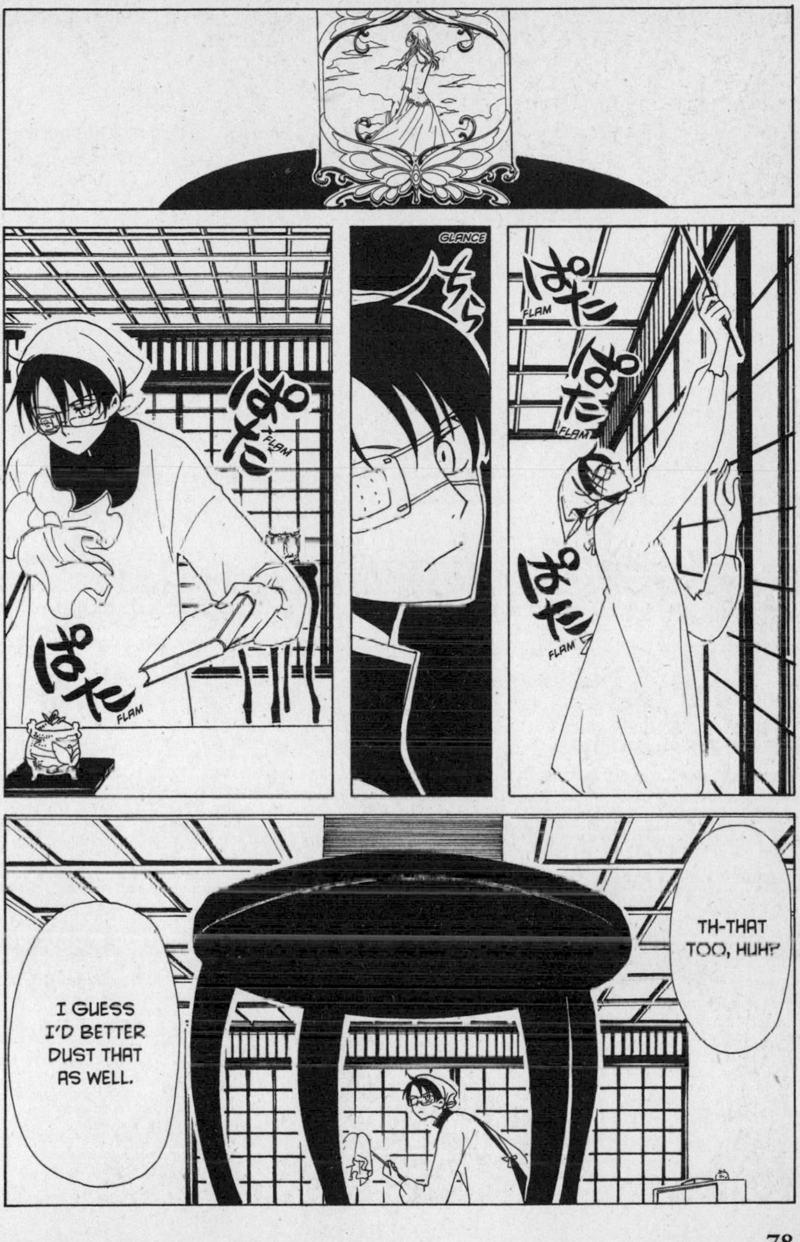
ぱた
FLAM
ぱた
FLAM
ぱた
FLAM
GLANCE
ちら
ぱた
FLAM
ぱた
FLAM
TH-THAT TOO, HUH?
I GUESS I'D BETTER DUST THAT AS WELL.

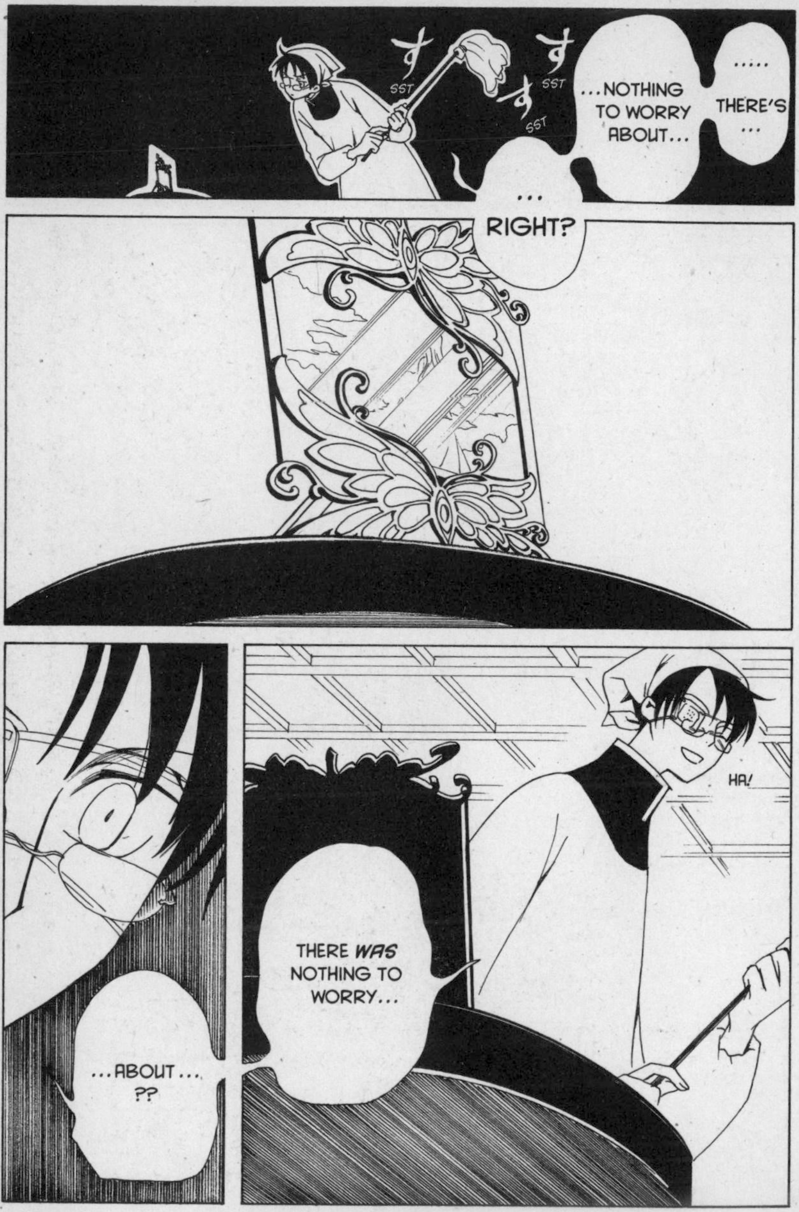
.....
THERE'S
...
...NOTHING
TO WORRY
ABOUT...
す
SST
す
SST
す
SST
...
RIGHT?
HA!
THERE *WAS*
NOTHING TO
WORRY...
...ABOUT....
??

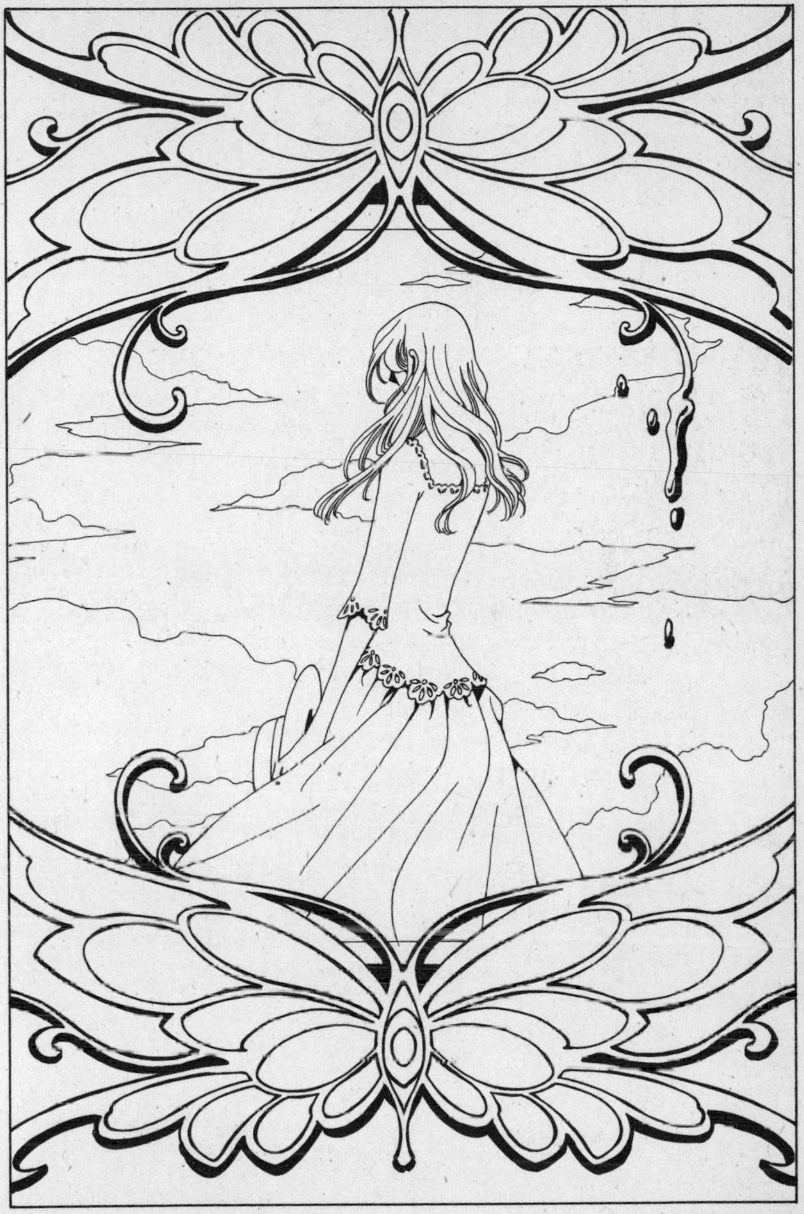

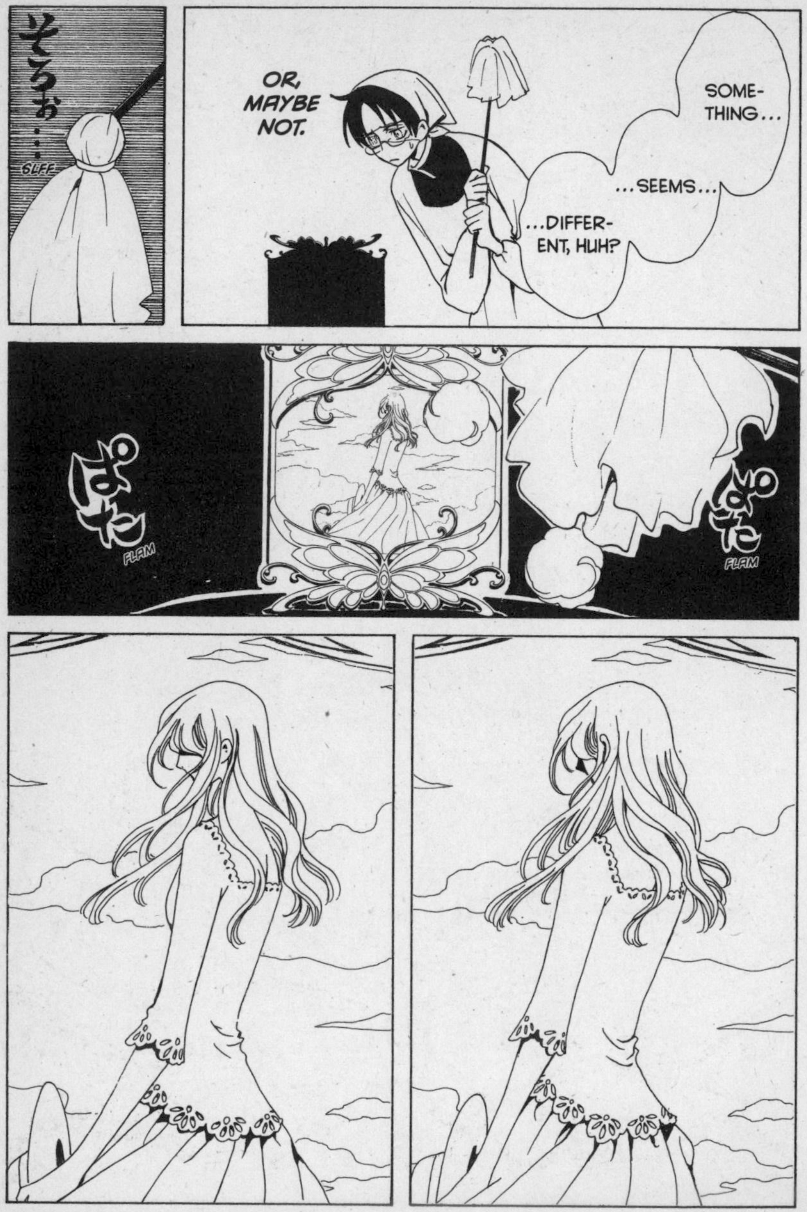
SOME-
THING...
...SEEMS...
...DIFFER-
ENT, HUH?
OR, MAYBE NOT.
そろぉ…
SLFF
ぱた
FLAM
ぱた
FLAM

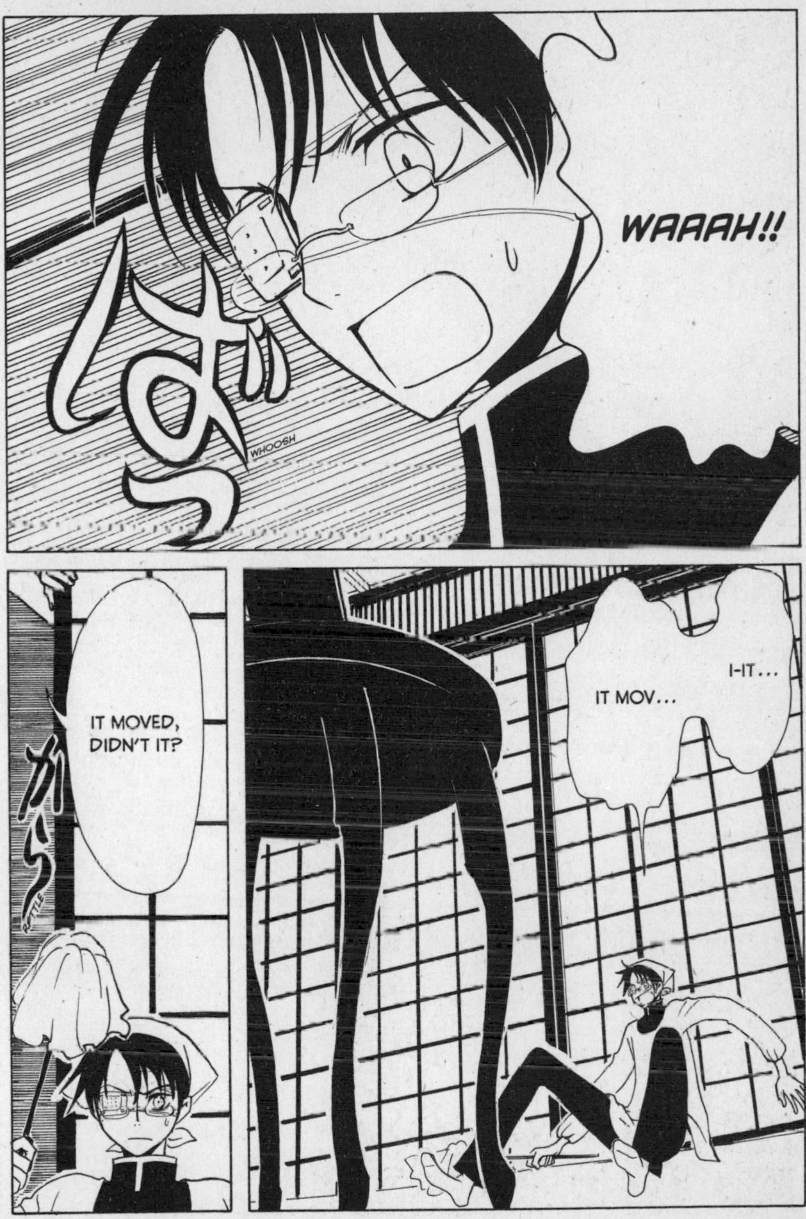
WAAAH!!
WHOOSH
I-IT...
IT MOV...
IT MOVED, DIDN'T IT?
RATTLE

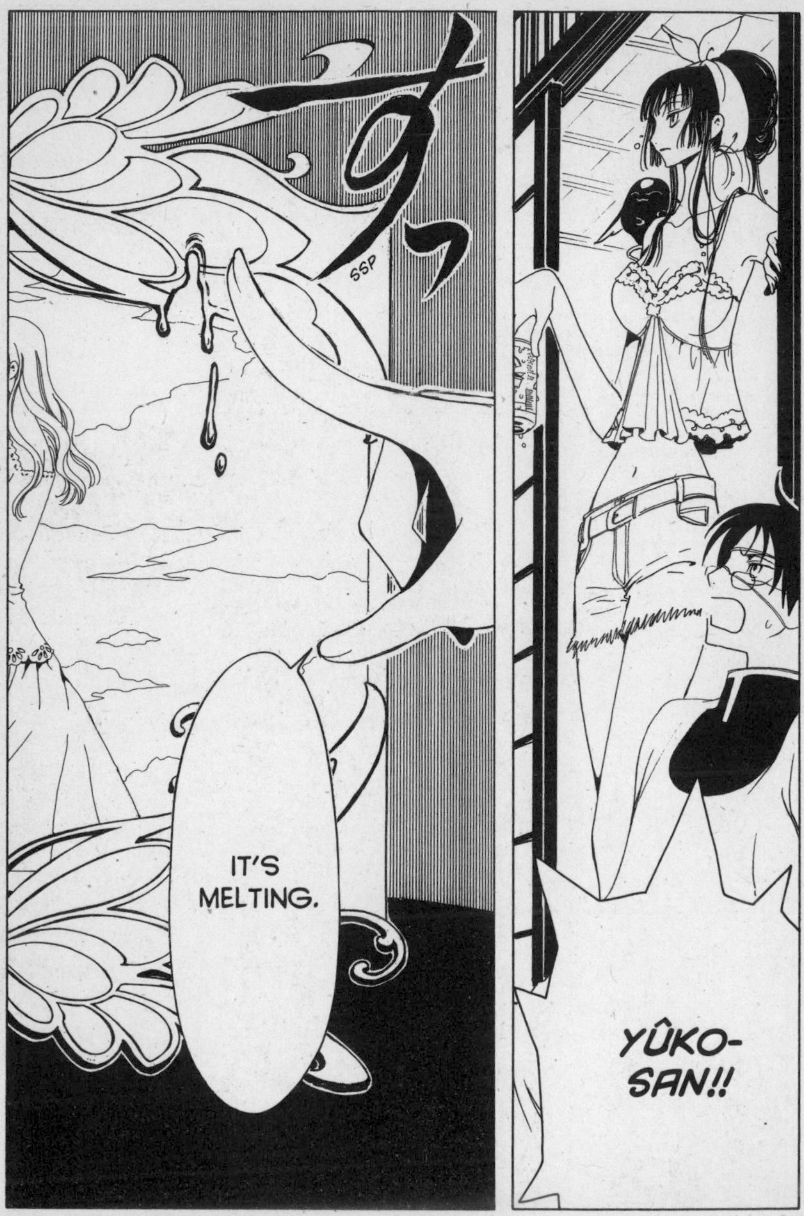
YÛKO-SAN!!
すっ
SSP
IT'S MELTING.

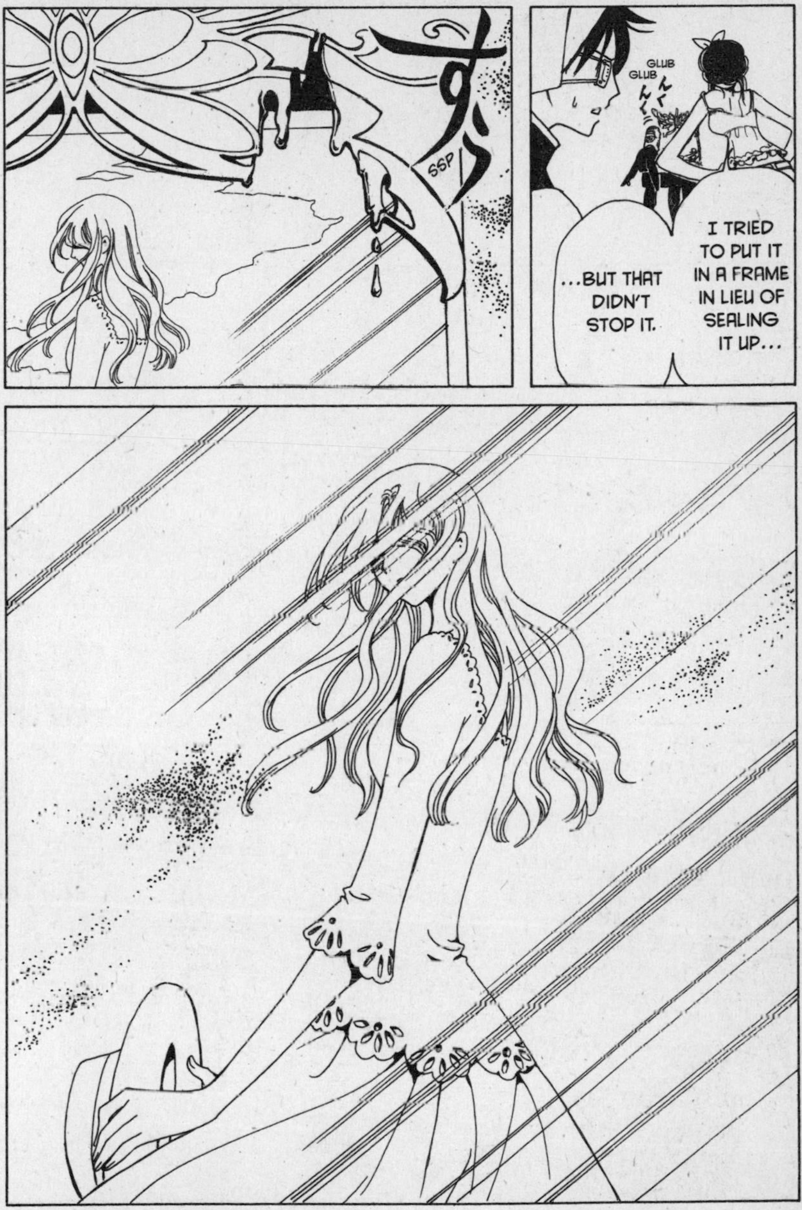
GLUB GLUB
んく んく
I TRIED TO PUT IT IN A FRAME IN LIEU OF SEALING IT UP...
...BUT THAT DIDN'T STOP IT.
すぅ
SSP

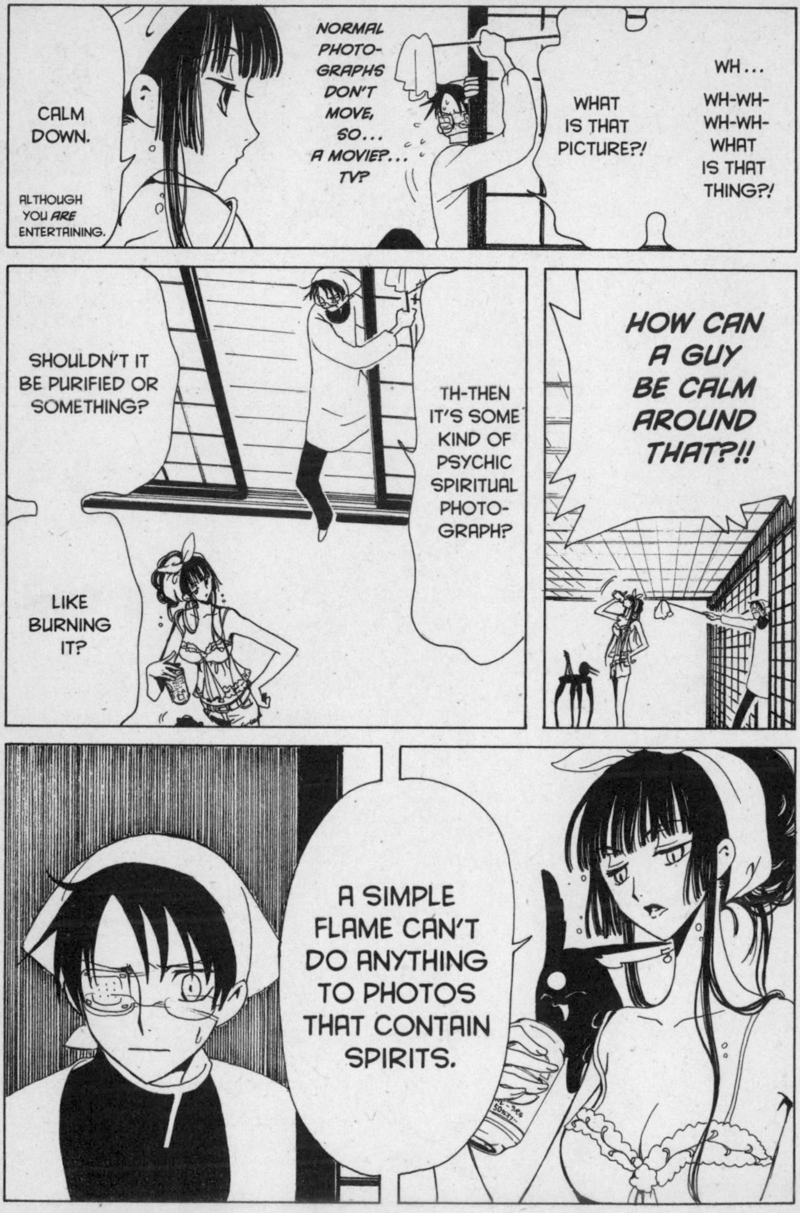
WH...
WH-WH-WH-WH-WHAT IS THAT THING?!
WHAT IS THAT PICTURE?!
NORMAL PHOTOGRAPHS DON'T MOVE, SO... A MOVIE?... TV?
CALM DOWN.
ALTHOUGH YOU *ARE* ENTERTAINING.
HOW CAN A GUY BE CALM AROUND THAT?!!
TH-THEN IT'S SOME KIND OF PSYCHIC SPIRITUAL PHOTOGRAPH?
SHOULDN'T IT BE PURIFIED OR SOMETHING?
LIKE BURNING IT?
A SIMPLE FLAME CAN'T DO ANYTHING TO PHOTOS THAT CONTAIN SPIRITS.

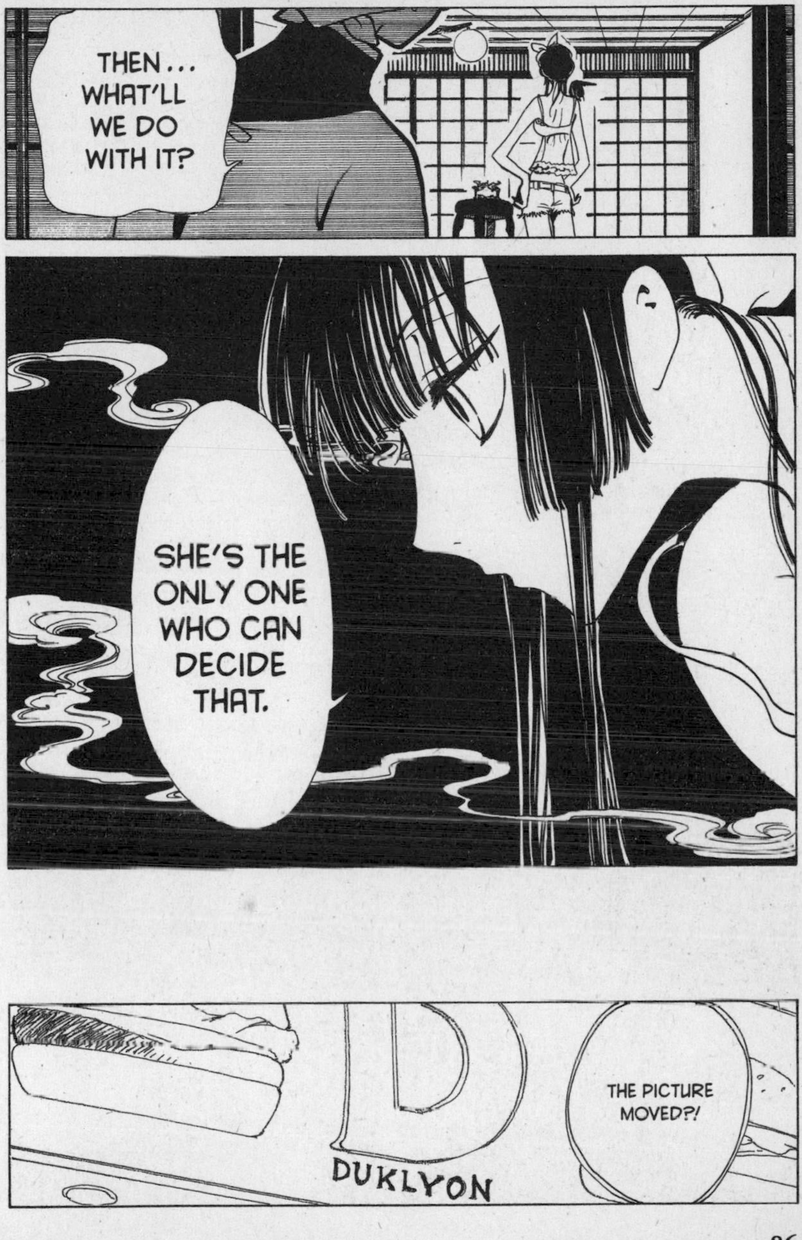
THEN... WHAT'LL WE DO WITH IT?
SHE'S THE ONLY ONE WHO CAN DECIDE THAT.
THE PICTURE MOVED?!
DUKLYON

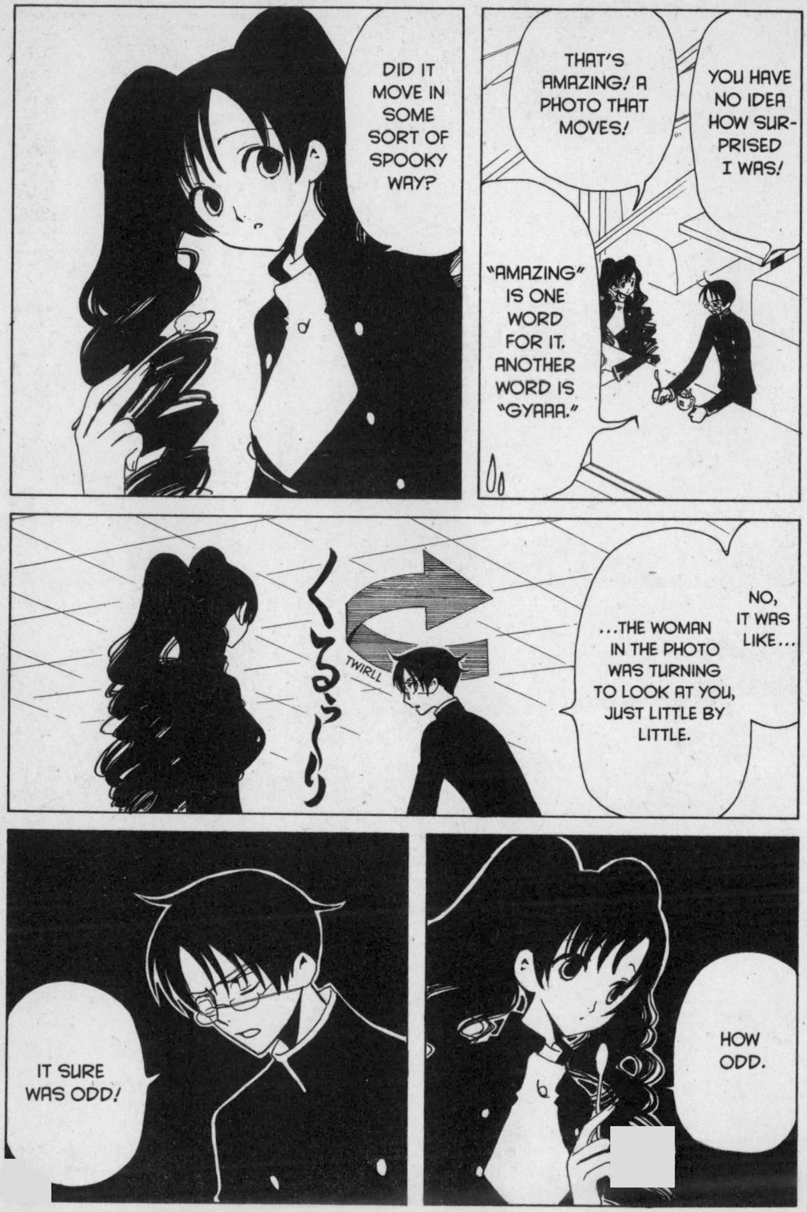
YOU HAVE NO IDEA HOW SUR-PRISED I WAS!
THAT'S AMAZING! A PHOTO THAT MOVES!
"AMAZING" IS ONE WORD FOR IT. ANOTHER WORD IS "GYAAA."
DID IT MOVE IN SOME SORT OF SPOOKY WAY?
NO, IT WAS LIKE...
...THE WOMAN IN THE PHOTO WAS TURNING TO LOOK AT YOU, JUST LITTLE BY LITTLE.
くるぅ～り
TWIRLL
HOW ODD.
IT SURE WAS ODD!

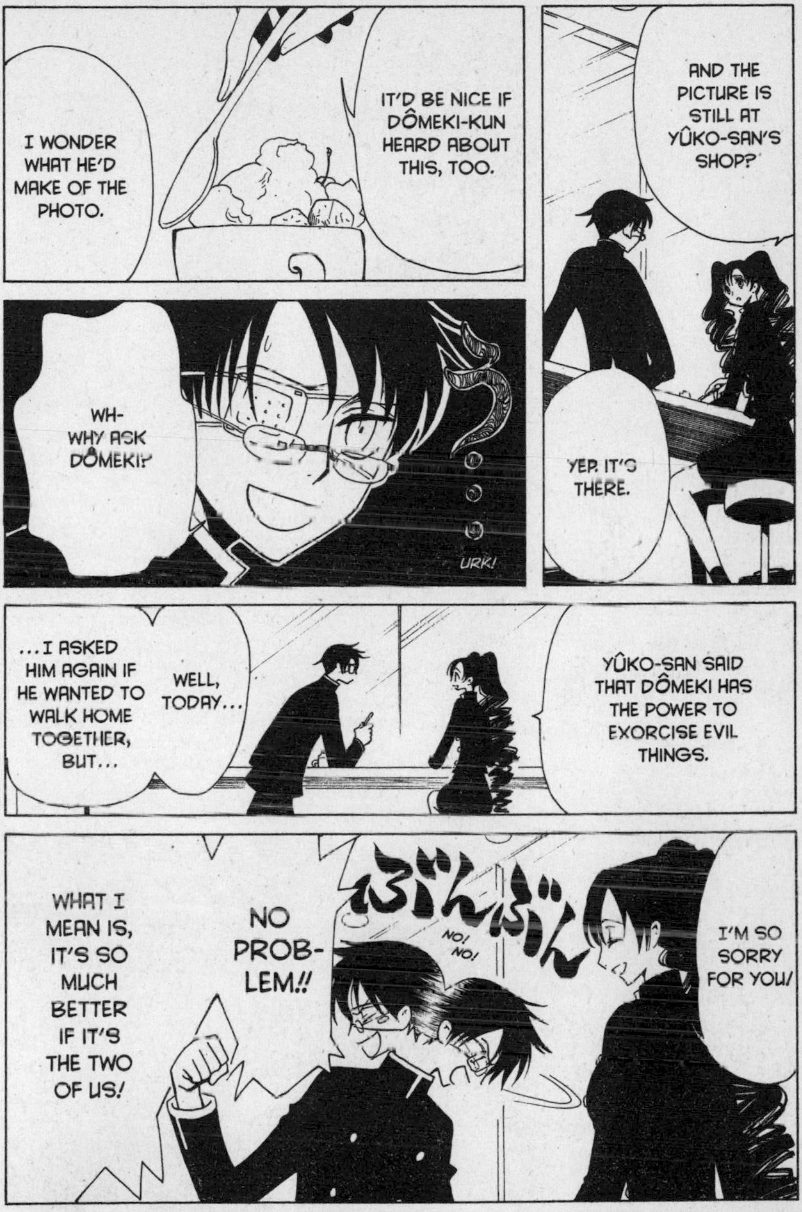
AND THE PICTURE IS STILL AT YÛKO-SAN'S SHOP?
YEP. IT'S THERE.
IT'D BE NICE IF DÔMEKI-KUN HEARD ABOUT THIS, TOO.
I WONDER WHAT HE'D MAKE OF THE PHOTO.
URK!
WH- WHY ASK DÔMEKI!?
YÛKO-SAN SAID THAT DÔMEKI HAS THE POWER TO EXORCISE EVIL THINGS.
WELL, TODAY...
...I ASKED HIM AGAIN IF HE WANTED TO WALK HOME TOGETHER, BUT...
I'M SO SORRY FOR YOU!
ぶんぶん
NO! NO!
NO PROBLEM!!
WHAT I MEAN IS, IT'S SO MUCH BETTER IF IT'S THE TWO OF US!

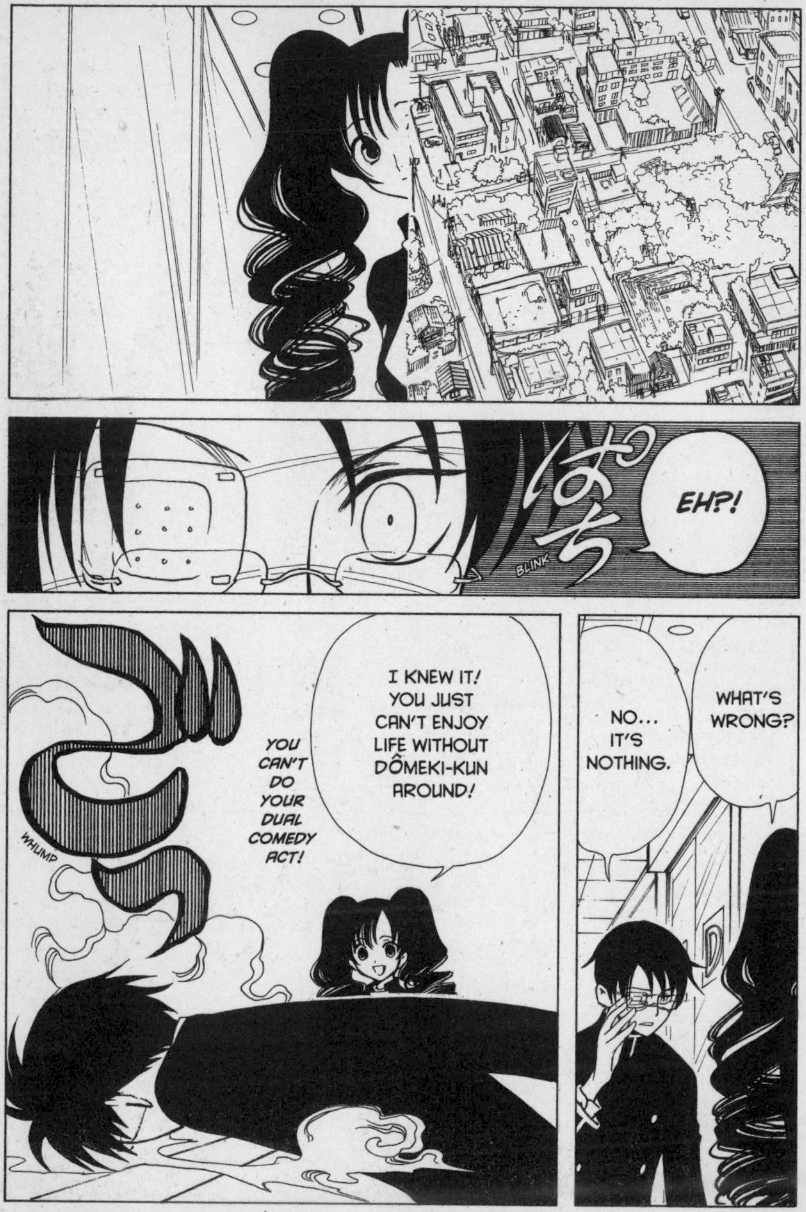
EH?!
ぱち
BLINK
WHAT'S WRONG?
NO... IT'S NOTHING.
I KNEW IT! YOU JUST CAN'T ENJOY LIFE WITHOUT DÔMEKI-KUN AROUND!
YOU CAN'T DO YOUR DUAL COMEDY ACT!
WHUMP

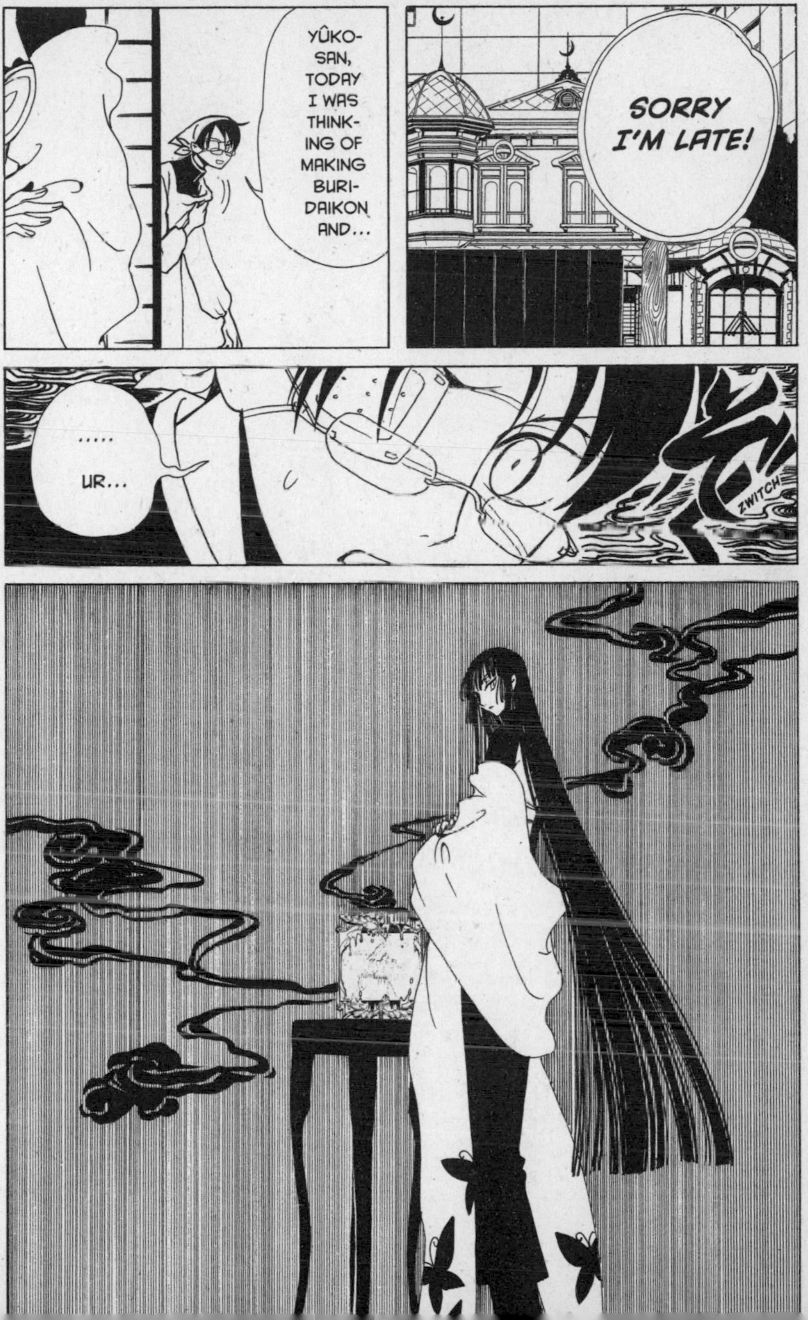
SORRY I'M LATE!
YÛKO-SAN, TODAY I WAS THINKING OF MAKING BURI-DAIKON AND...
ZWITCH
......
UR...

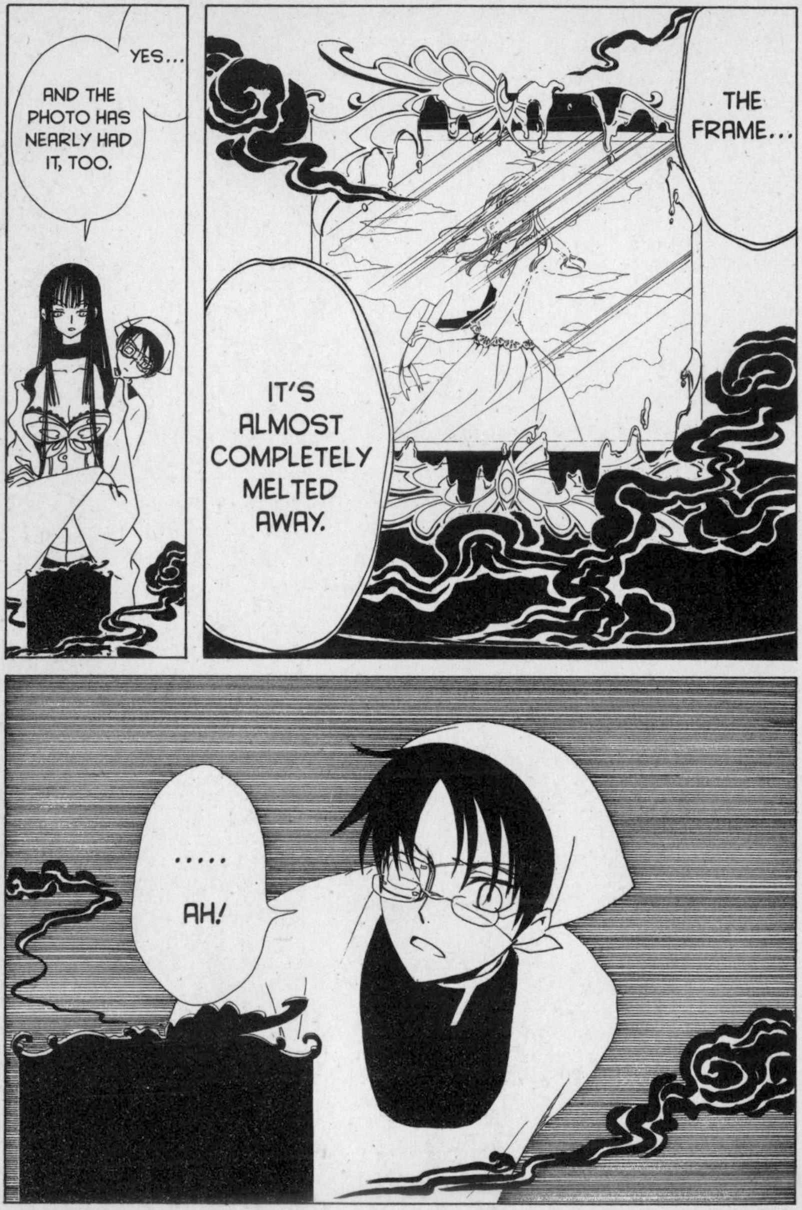
THE FRAME...
IT'S ALMOST COMPLETELY MELTED AWAY.
YES...
AND THE PHOTO HAS NEARLY HAD IT, TOO.
.....
AH!

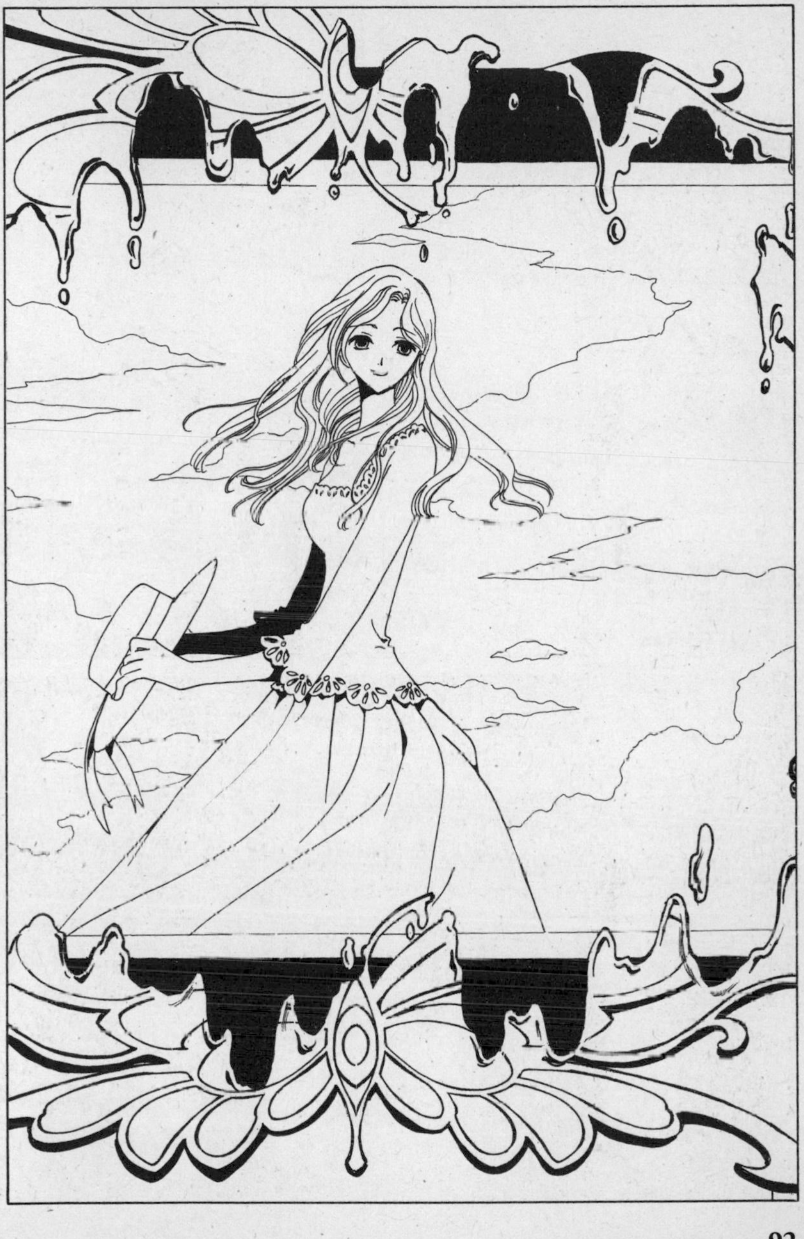

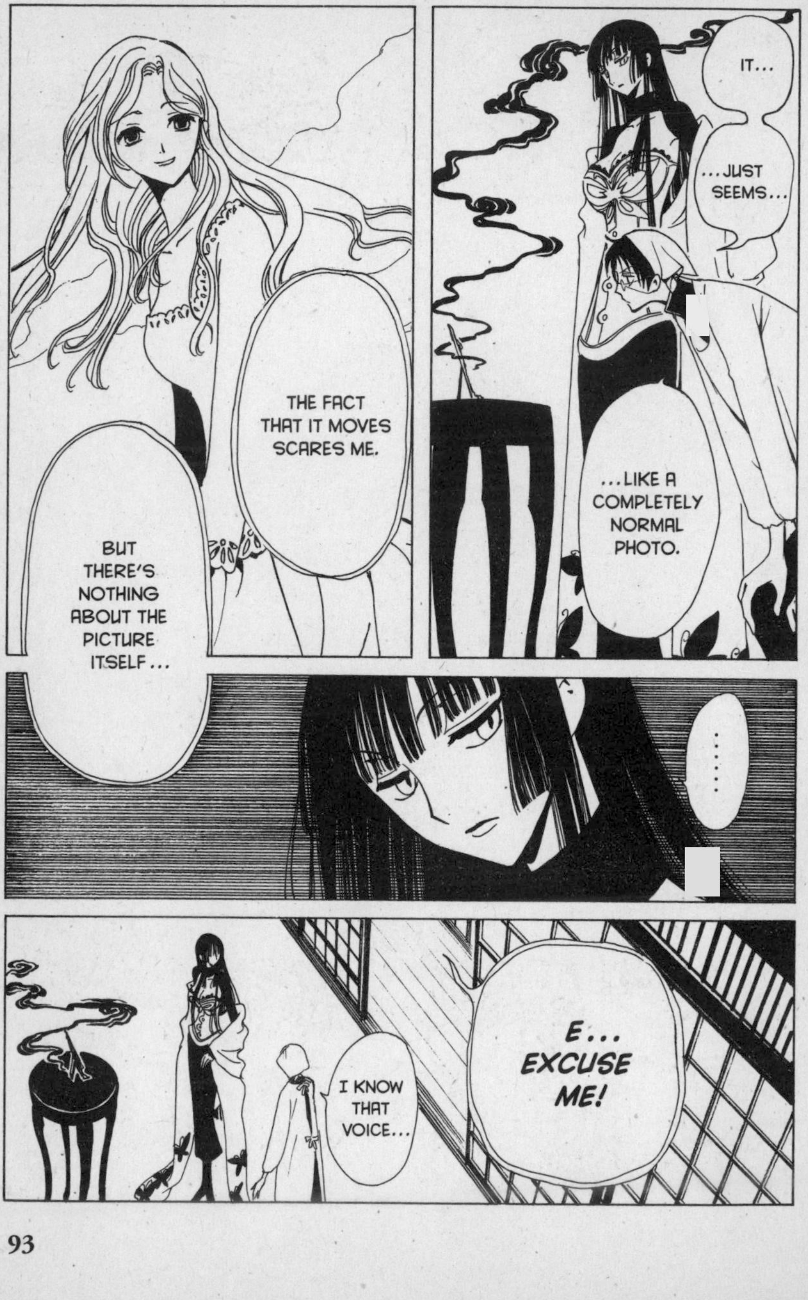
IT...
...JUST SEEMS...
...LIKE A COMPLETELY NORMAL PHOTO.
THE FACT THAT IT MOVES SCARES ME.
BUT THERE'S NOTHING ABOUT THE PICTURE ITSELF...
......
E... EXCUSE ME!
I KNOW THAT VOICE...

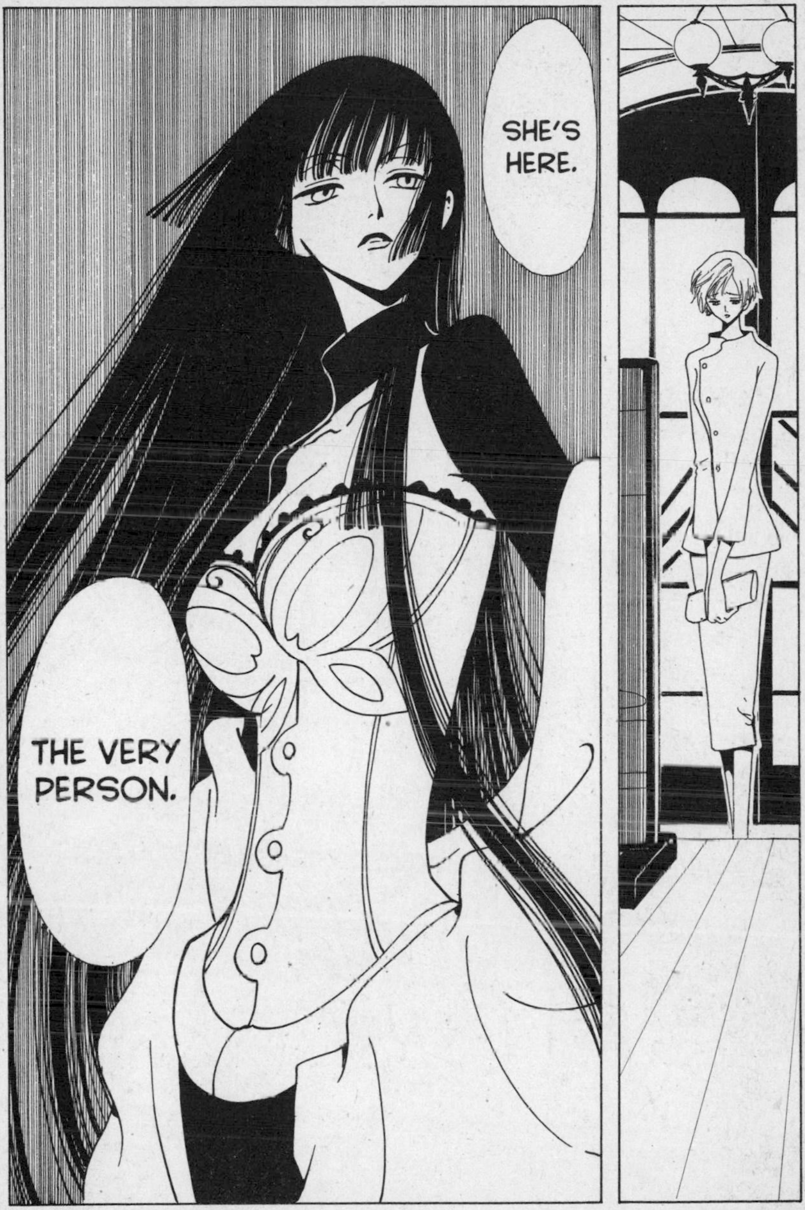
SHE'S HERE.
THE VERY PERSON.

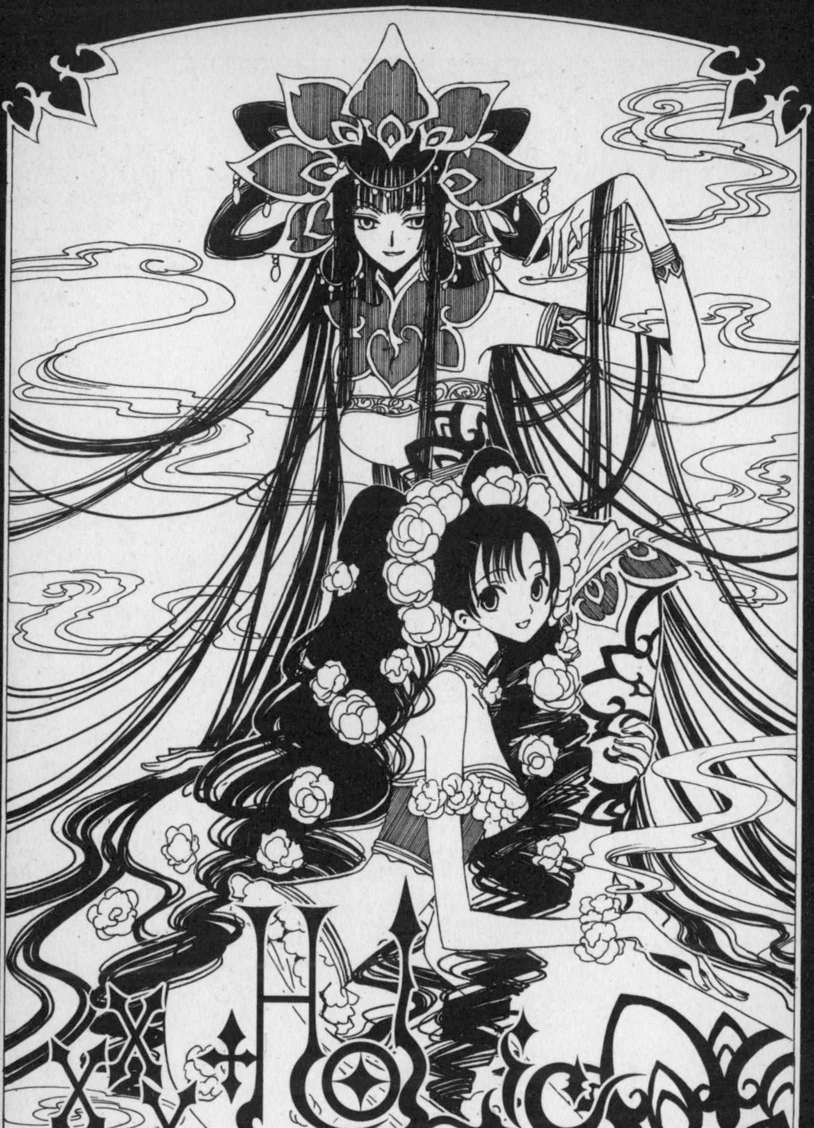
xxxHOLiC
〜×××ホリック〜

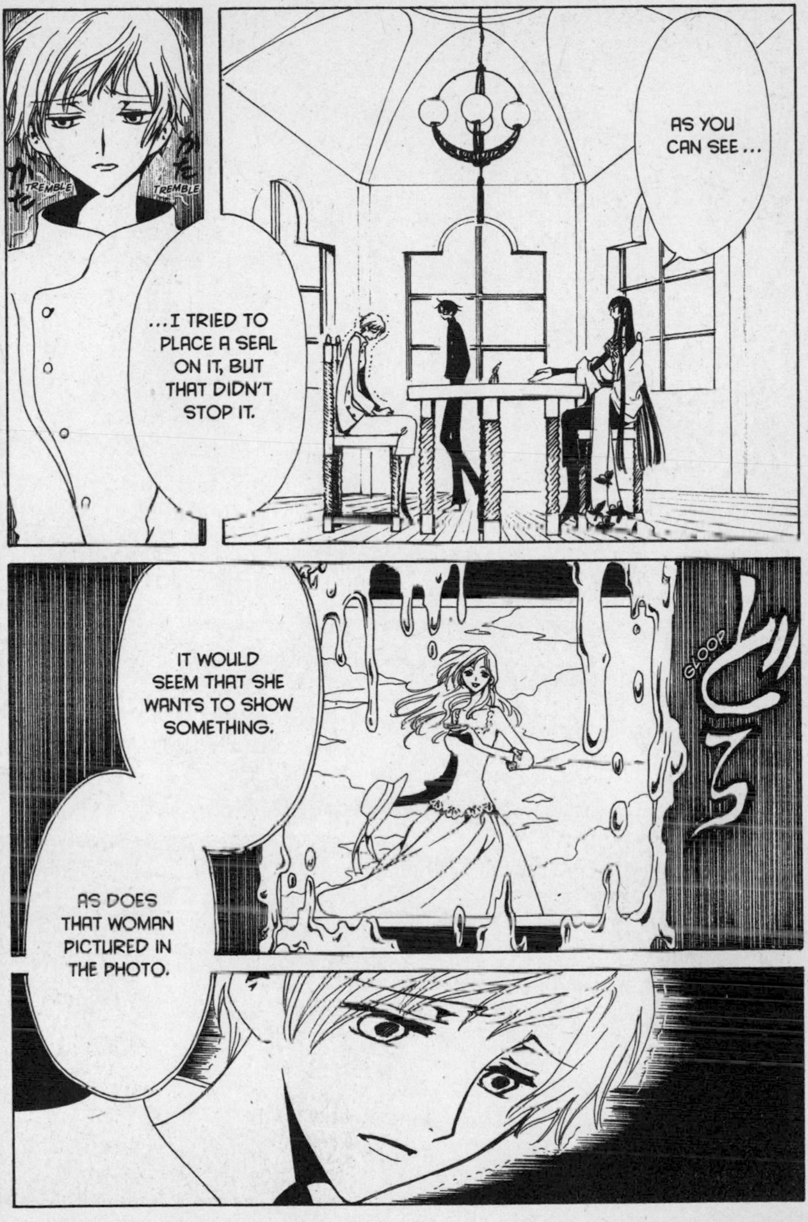
AS YOU CAN SEE ...
TREMBLE
TREMBLE
...I TRIED TO PLACE A SEAL ON IT, BUT THAT DIDN'T STOP IT.
GLOOP
IT WOULD SEEM THAT SHE WANTS TO SHOW SOMETHING.
AS DOES THAT WOMAN PICTURED IN THE PHOTO.

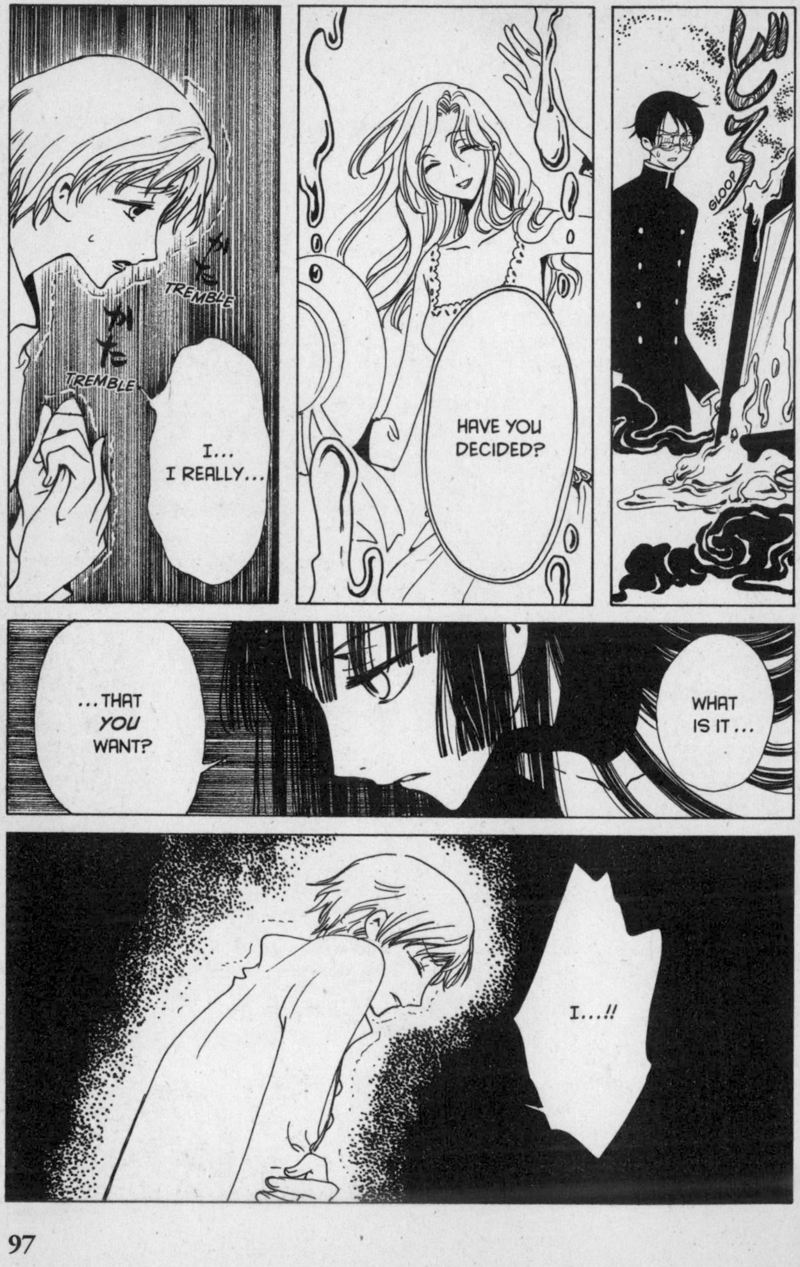
GLOOP
HAVE YOU DECIDED?
かた
TREMBLE
かた
TREMBLE
I... I REALLY...
WHAT IS IT...
...THAT *YOU* WANT?
I...!!

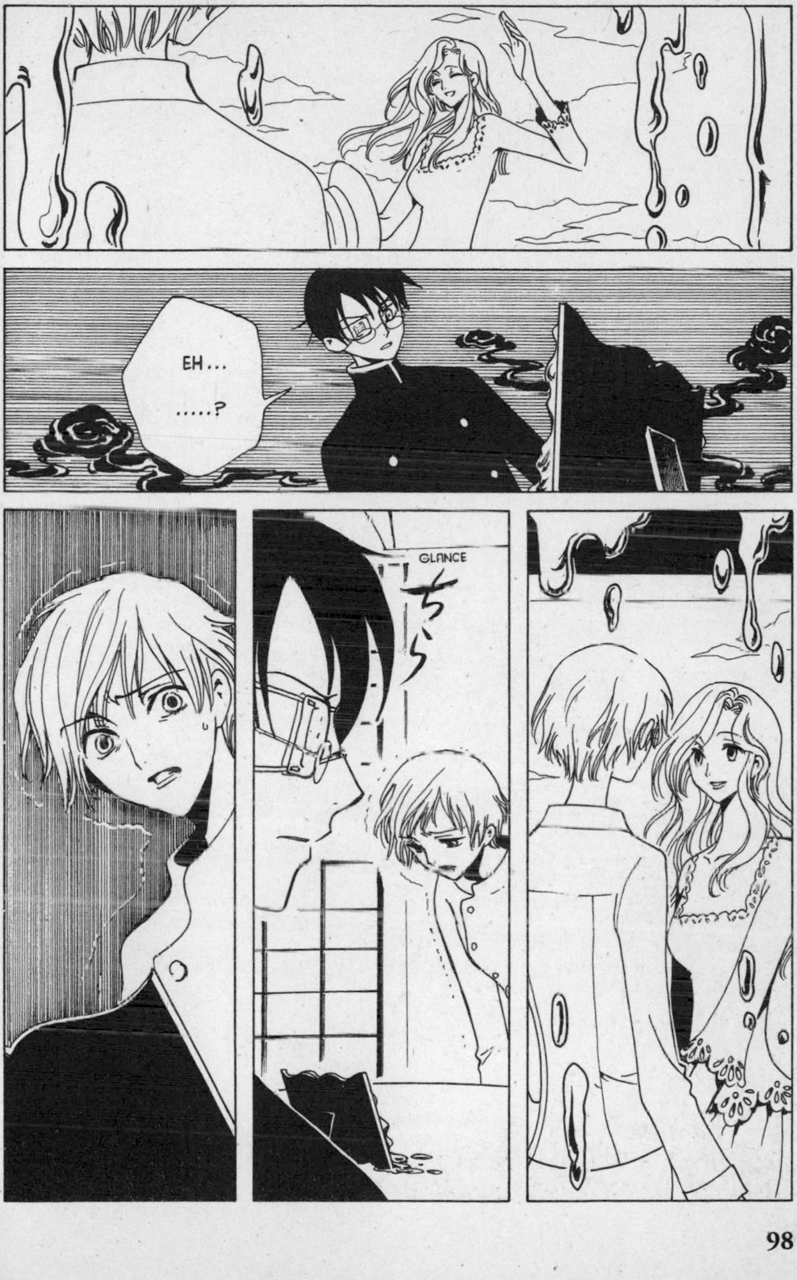
EH...
.....?
GLANCE
ちら

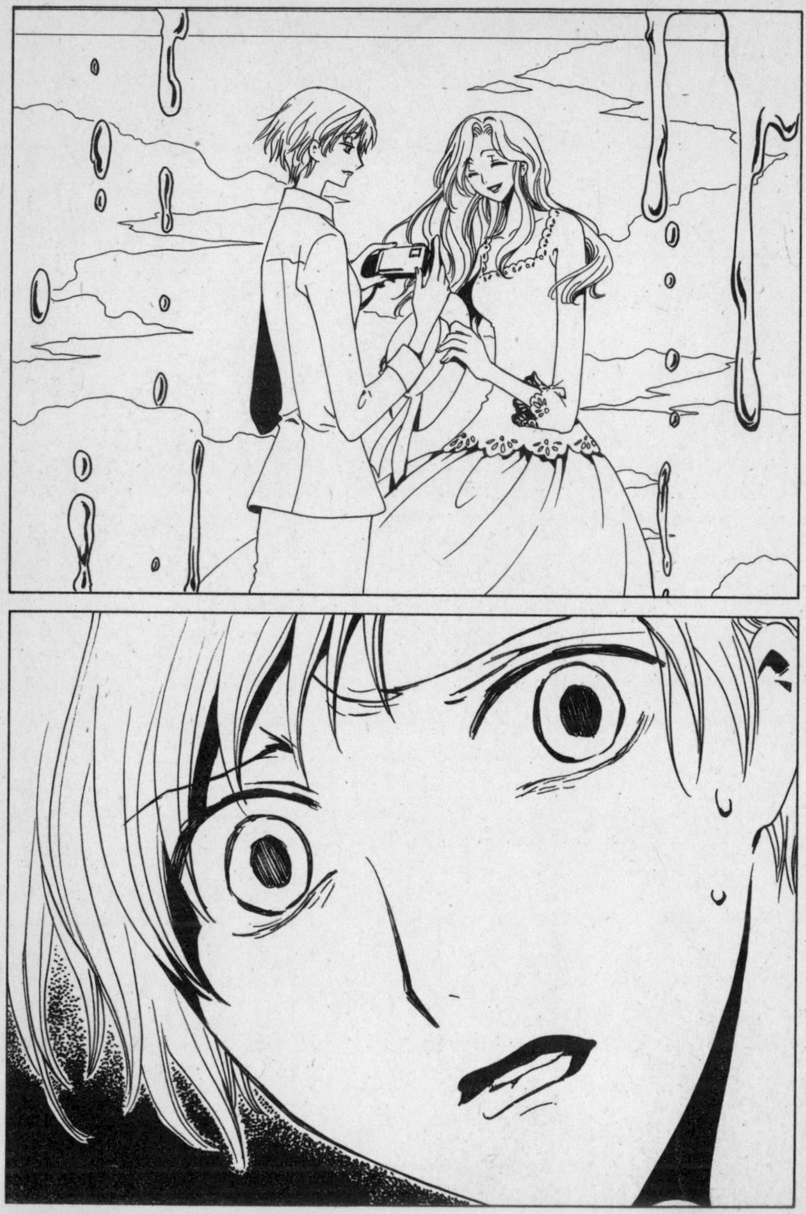

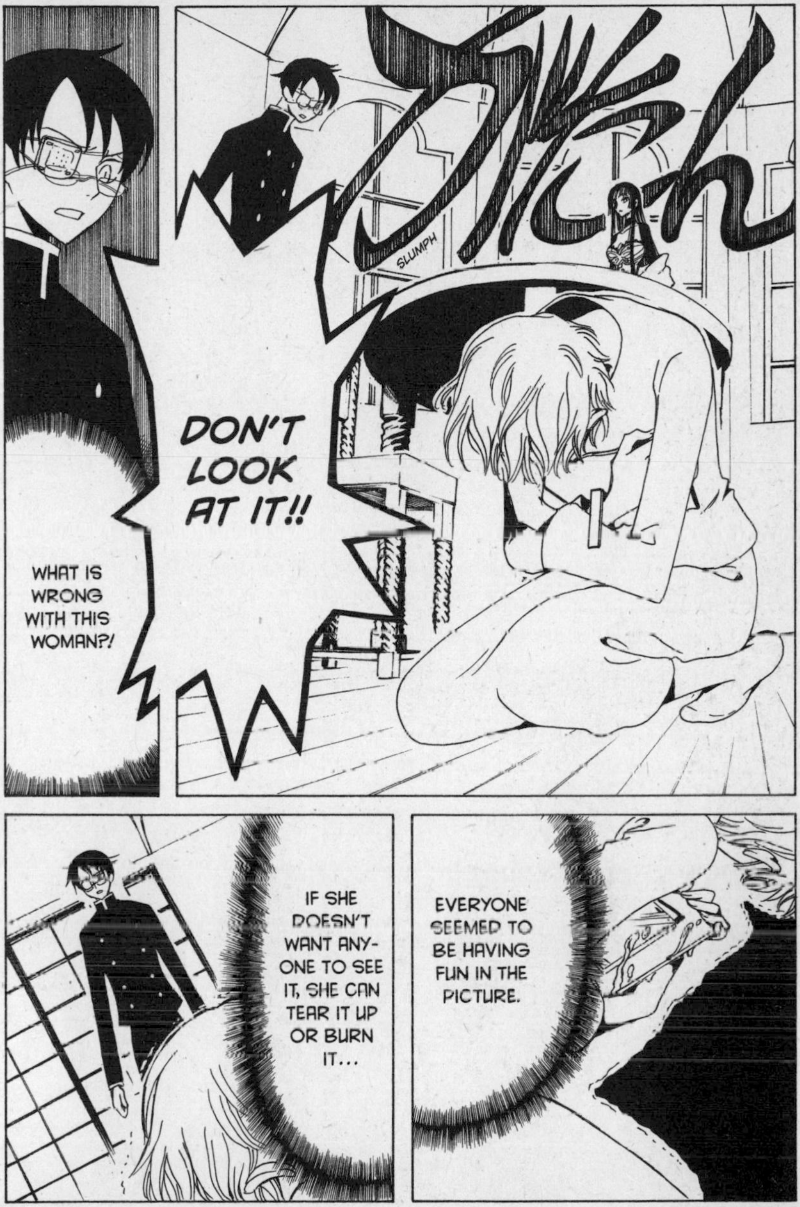
SLUMPH
DON'T LOOK AT IT!!
WHAT IS WRONG WITH THIS WOMAN?!
EVERYONE SEEMED TO BE HAVING FUN IN THE PICTURE.
IF SHE DOESN'T WANT ANY-ONE TO SEE IT, SHE CAN TEAR IT UP OR BURN IT...

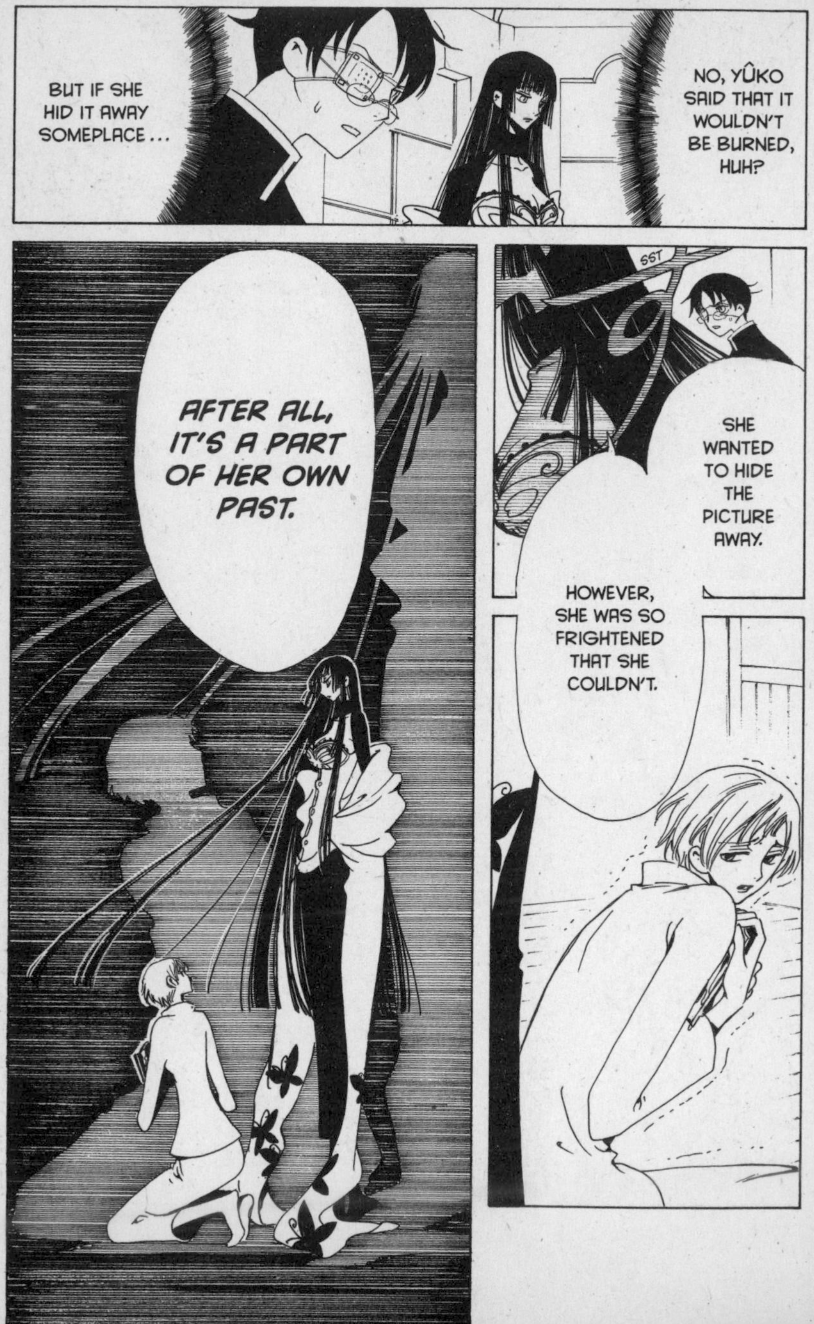
NO, YÛKO SAID THAT IT WOULDN'T BE BURNED, HUH?
BUT IF SHE HID IT AWAY SOMEPLACE...
SST
SHE WANTED TO HIDE THE PICTURE AWAY.
HOWEVER, SHE WAS SO FRIGHTENED THAT SHE COULDN'T.
AFTER ALL, IT'S A PART OF HER OWN PAST.

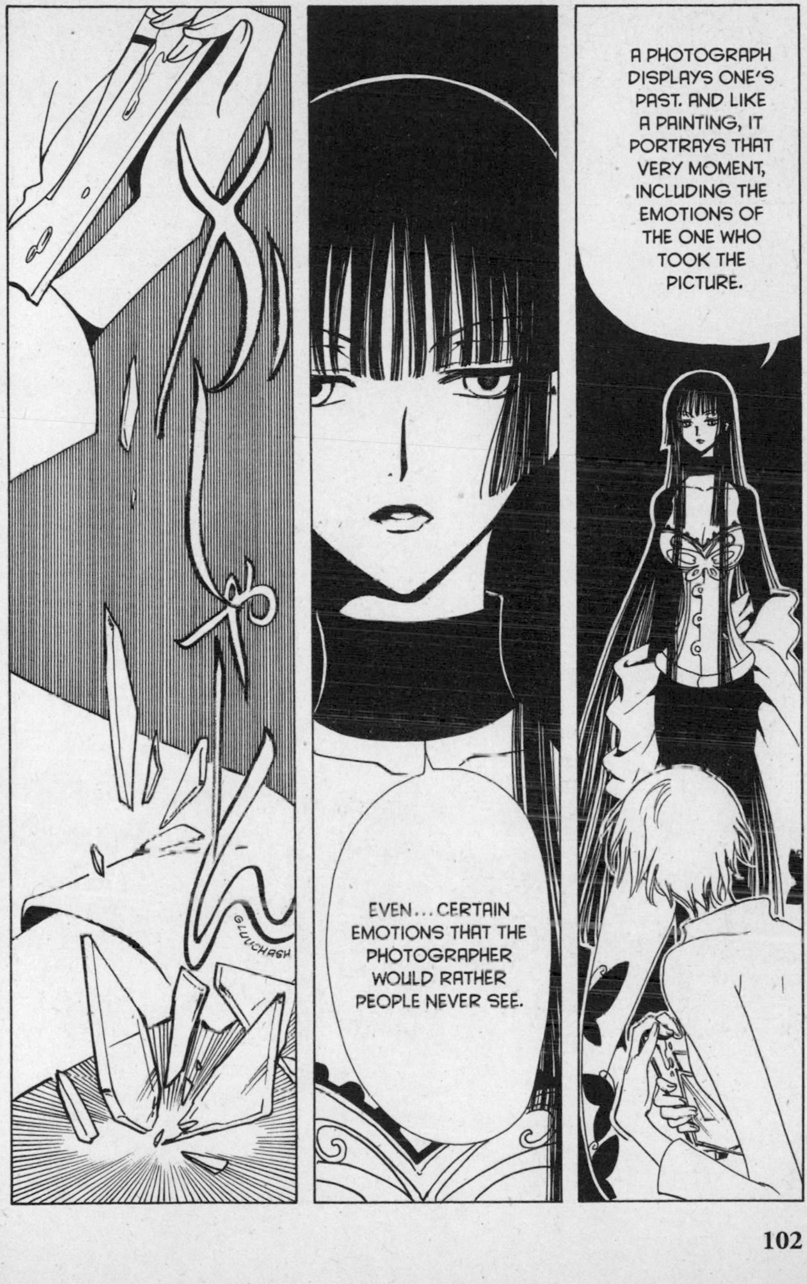
A PHOTOGRAPH DISPLAYS ONE'S PAST. AND LIKE A PAINTING, IT PORTRAYS THAT VERY MOMENT, INCLUDING THE EMOTIONS OF THE ONE WHO TOOK THE PICTURE.
EVEN... CERTAIN EMOTIONS THAT THE PHOTOGRAPHER WOULD RATHER PEOPLE NEVER SEE.
GLUUCHASH

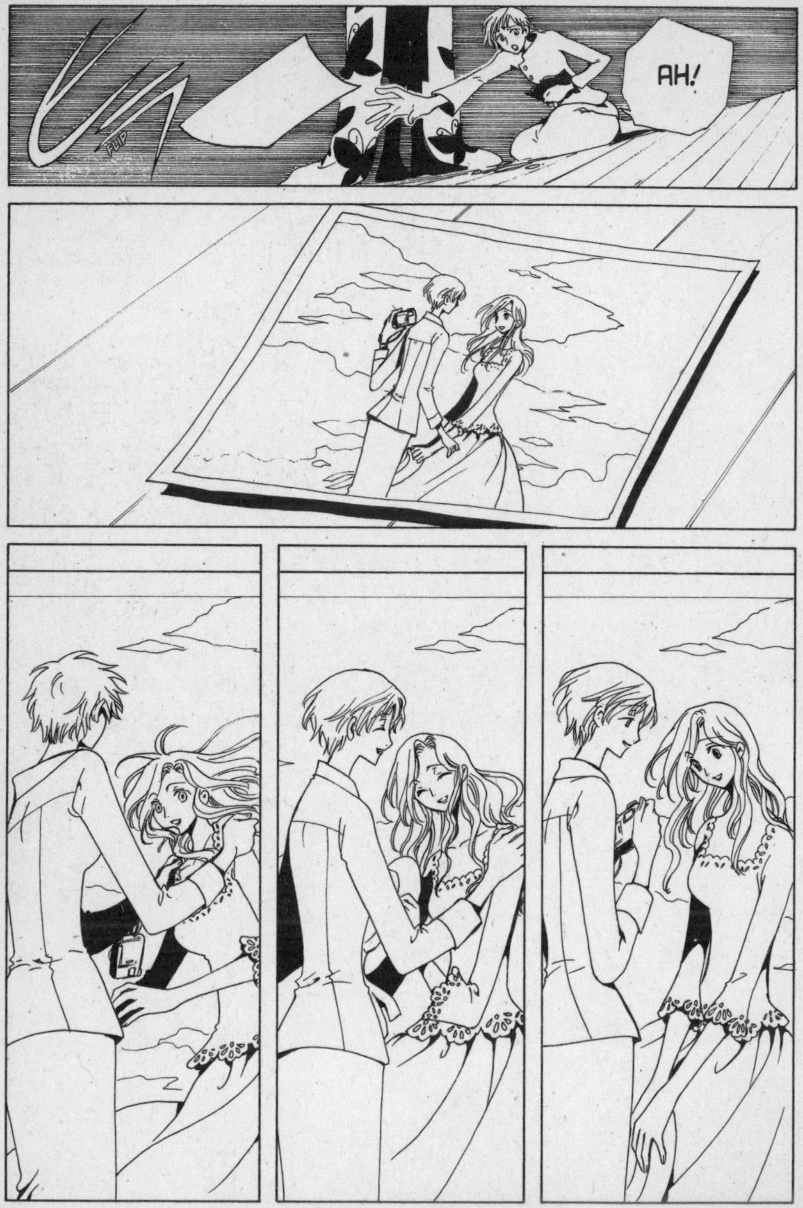
AH!
FLIP

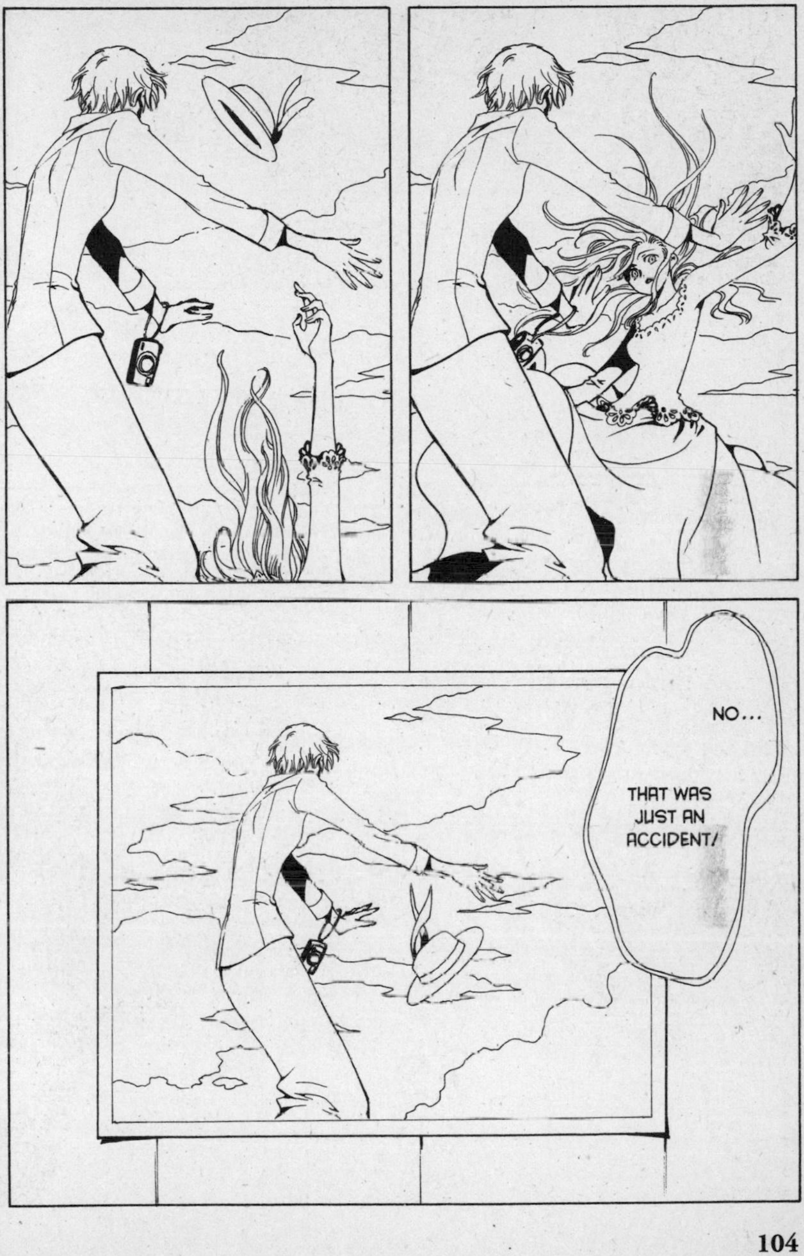
NO...
THAT WAS JUST AN ACCIDENT!

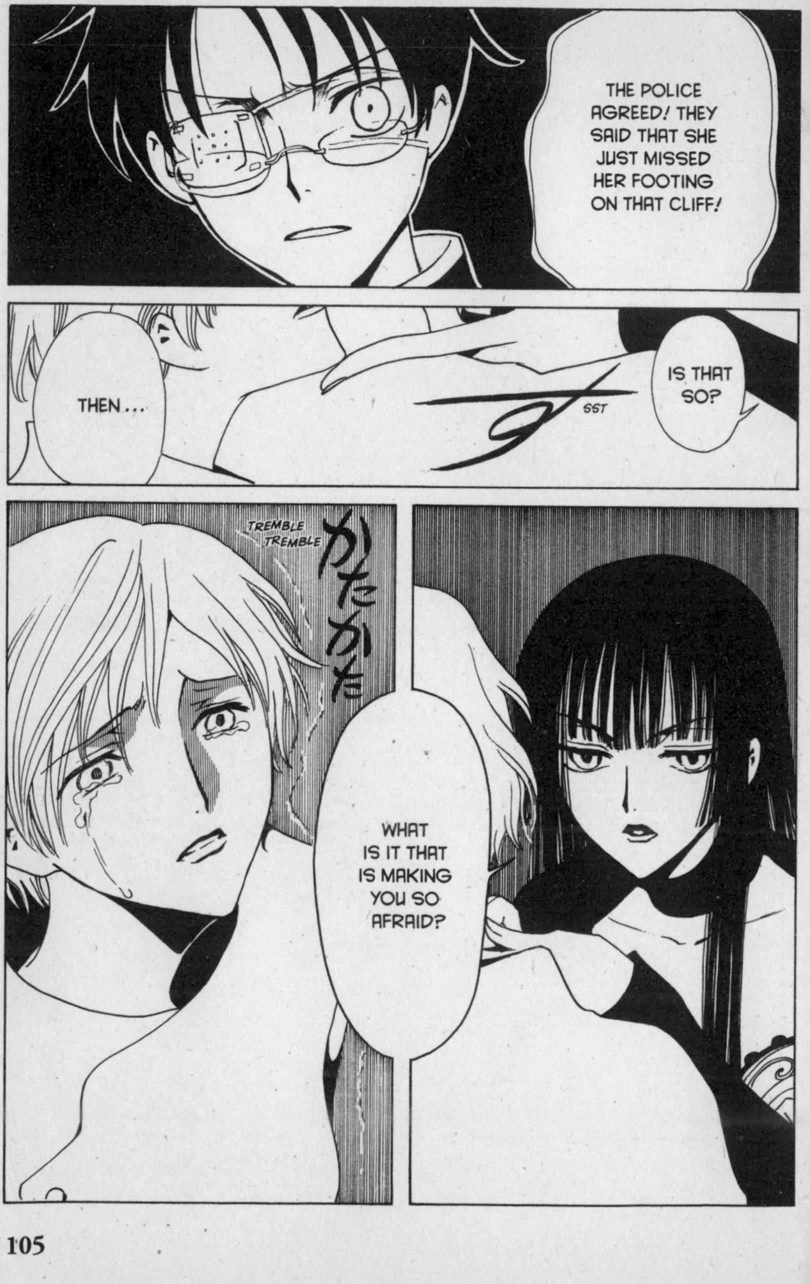
THE POLICE AGREED! THEY SAID THAT SHE JUST MISSED HER FOOTING ON THAT CLIFF!
IS THAT SO?
SST
THEN...
WHAT IS IT THAT IS MAKING YOU SO AFRAID?
かたかた
TREMBLE TREMBLE

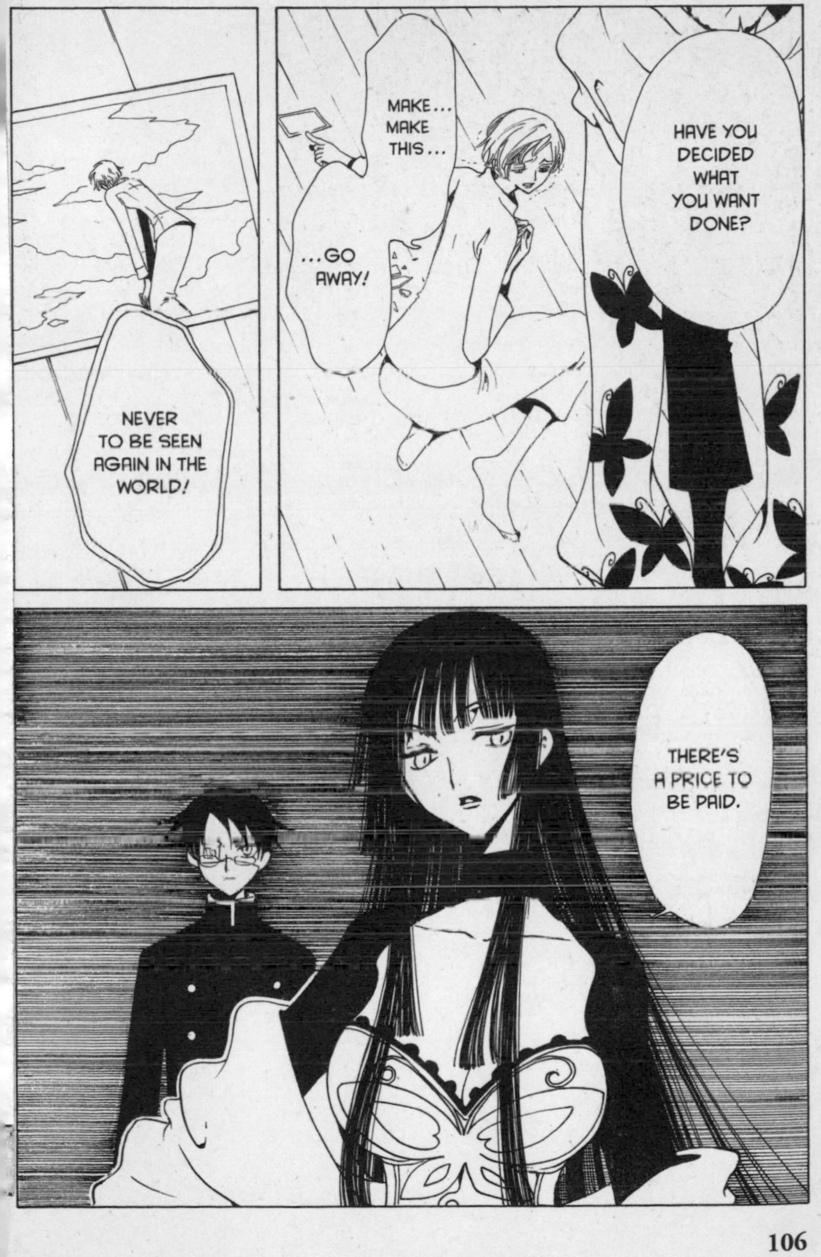
HAVE YOU DECIDED WHAT YOU WANT DONE?
MAKE... MAKE THIS...
...GO AWAY!
NEVER TO BE SEEN AGAIN IN THE WORLD!
THERE'S A PRICE TO BE PAID.

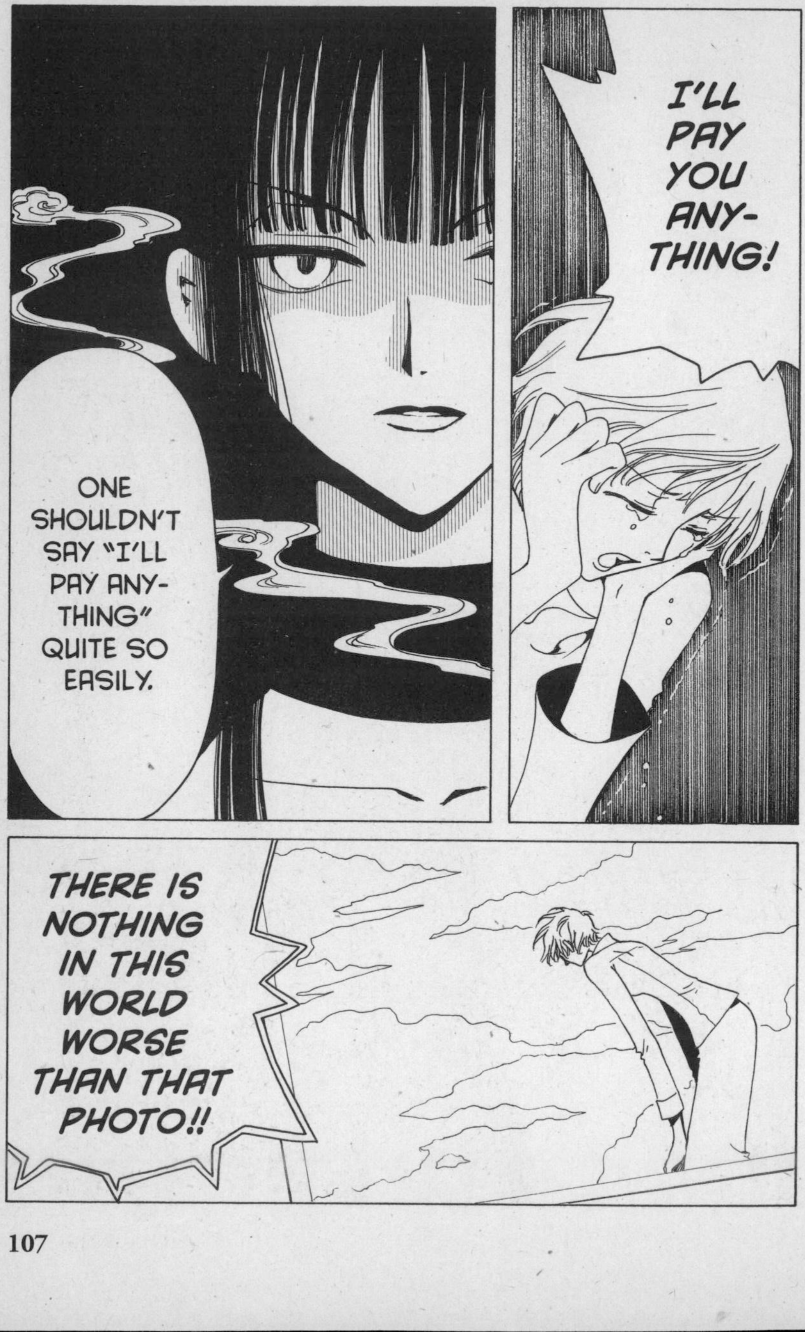
I'LL PAY YOU ANY-THING!
ONE SHOULDN'T SAY "I'LL PAY ANY-THING" QUITE SO EASILY.
THERE IS NOTHING IN THIS WORLD WORSE THAN THAT PHOTO!!

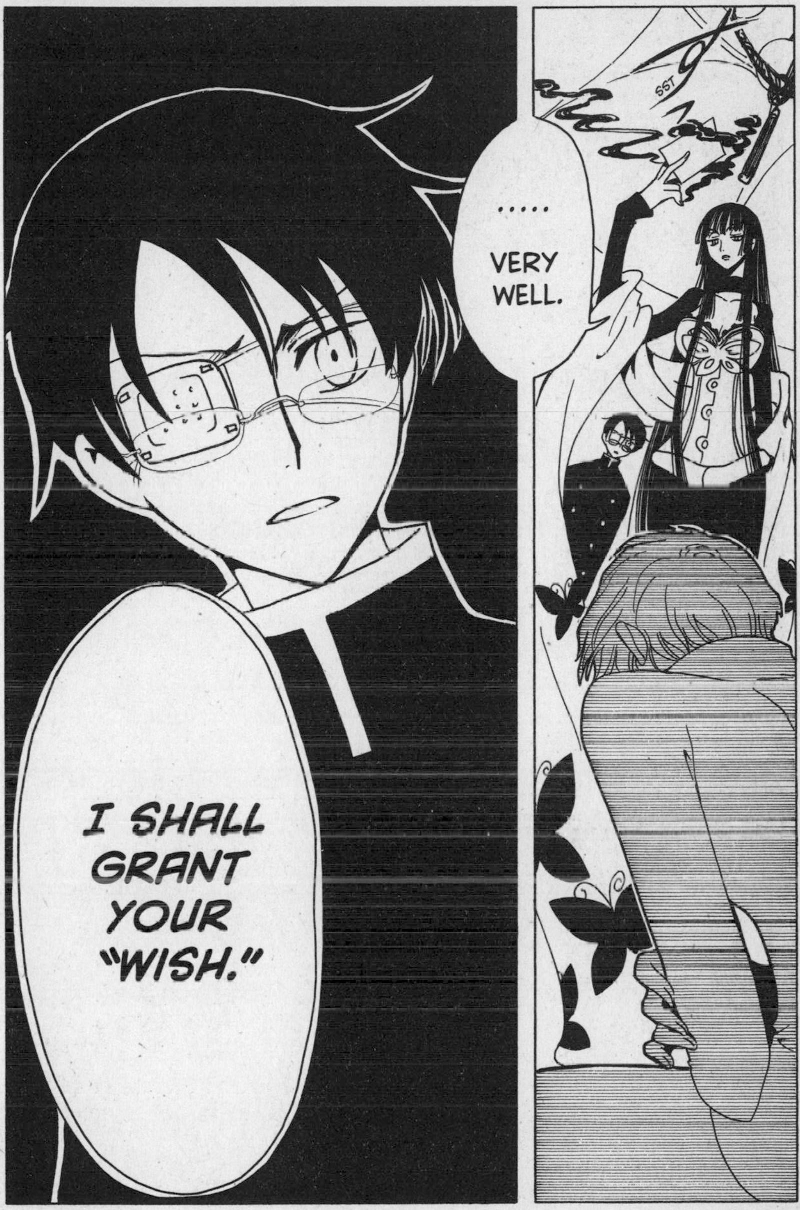
SST
.....
VERY WELL.
I SHALL GRANT YOUR "WISH."

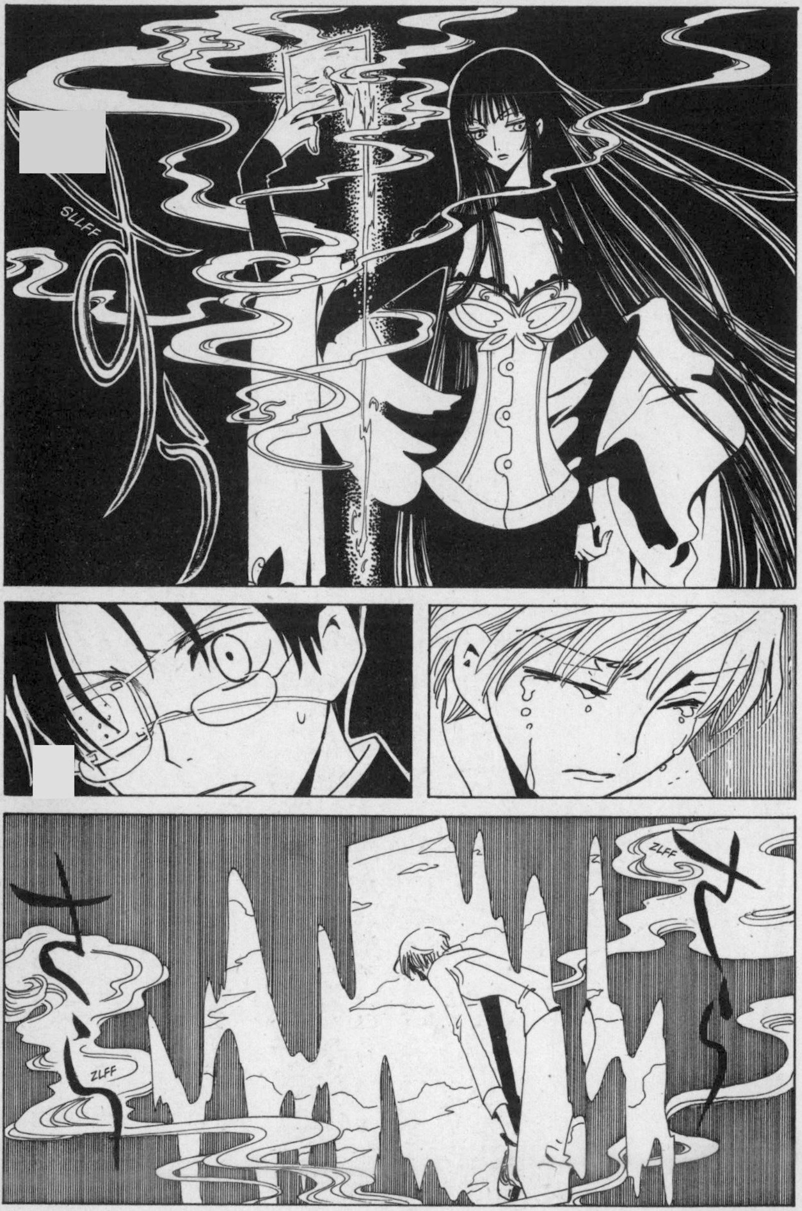
SLLFF
ZLFF
ZLFF

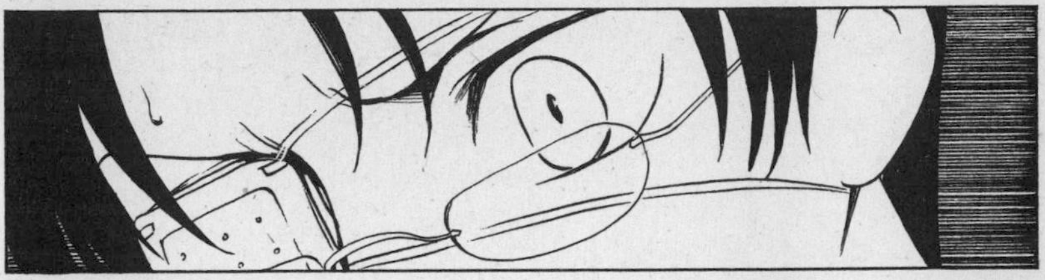
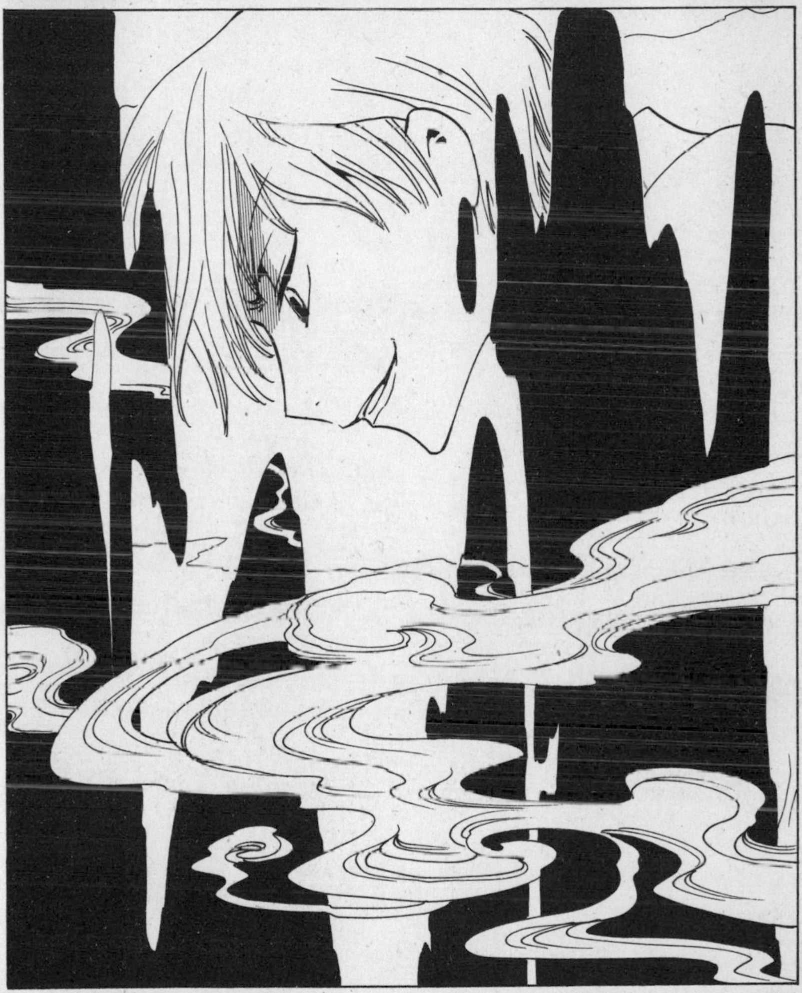

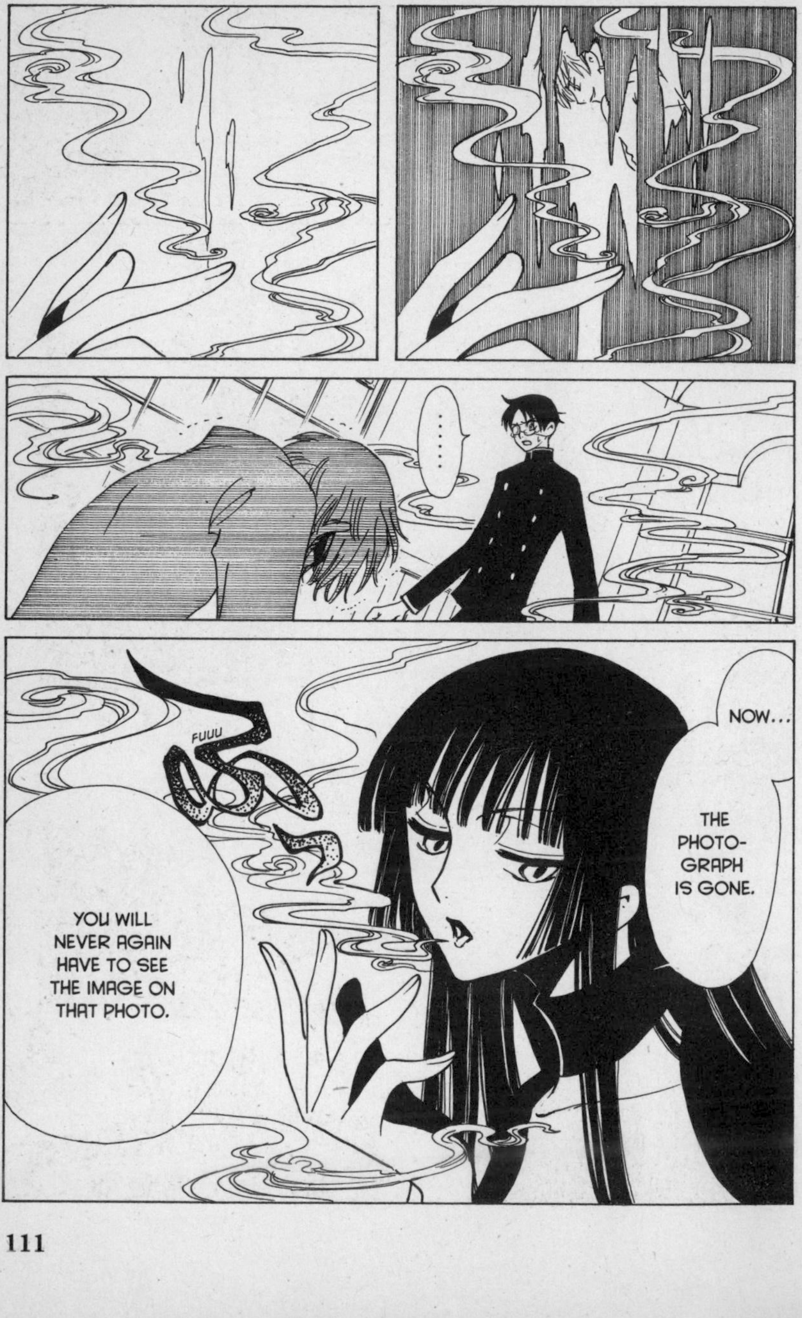
......
NOW...
THE PHOTO-GRAPH IS GONE.
FUUU
YOU WILL NEVER AGAIN HAVE TO SEE THE IMAGE ON THAT PHOTO.

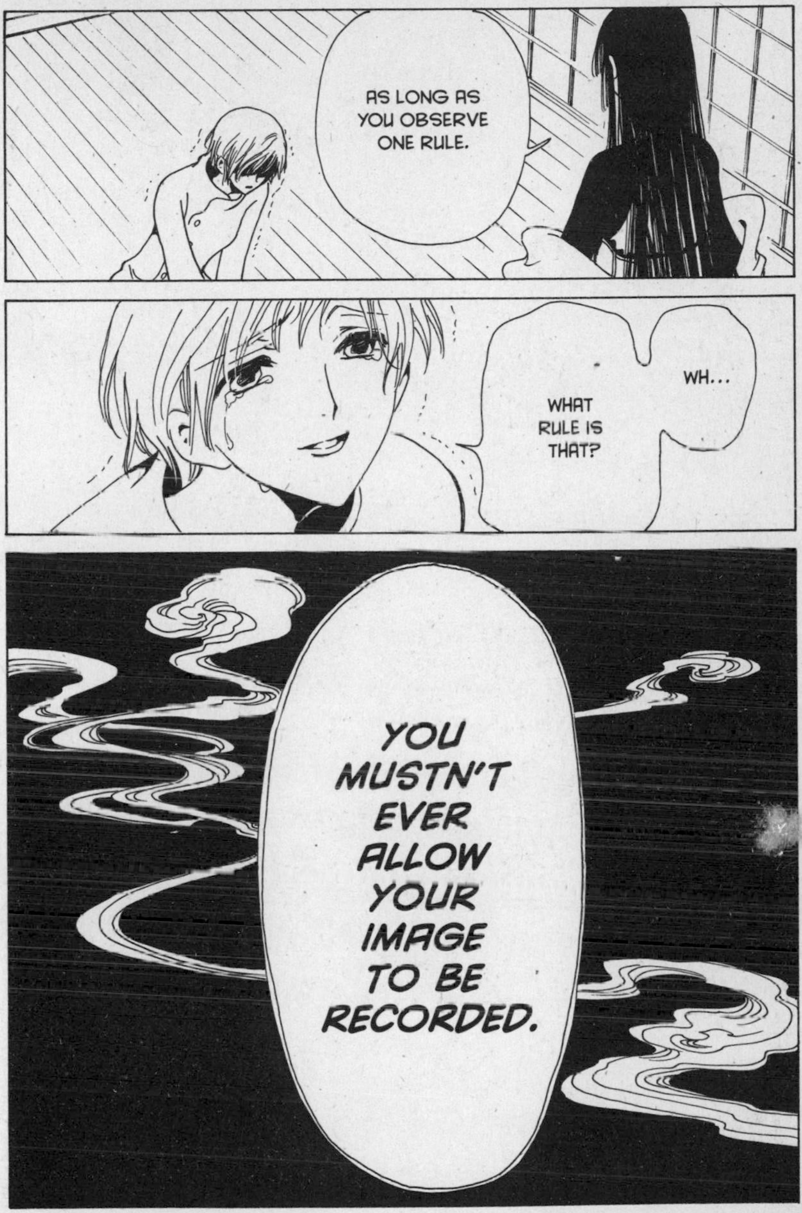
AS LONG AS YOU OBSERVE ONE RULE.
WH...
WHAT RULE IS THAT?
YOU MUSTN'T EVER ALLOW YOUR IMAGE TO BE RECORDED.

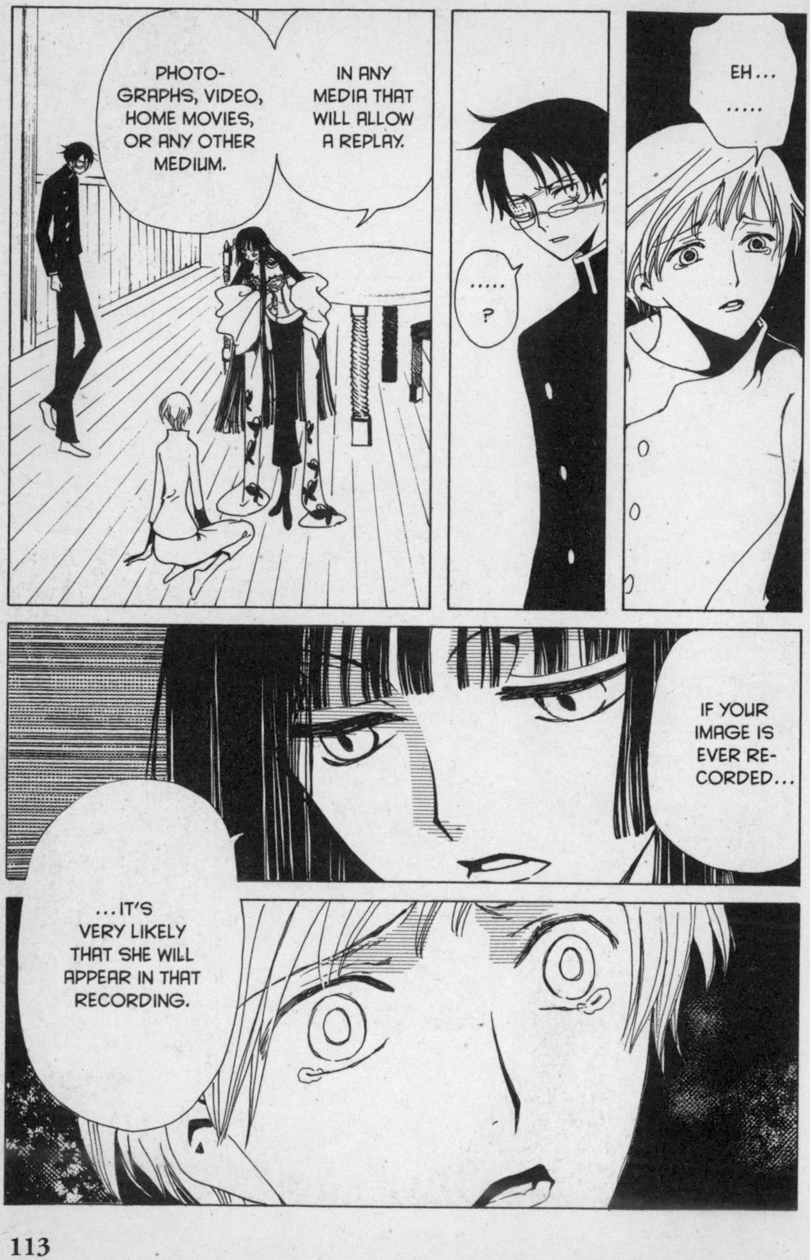
EH... .....
..... ?
IN ANY MEDIA THAT WILL ALLOW A REPLAY.
PHOTO-GRAPHS, VIDEO, HOME MOVIES, OR ANY OTHER MEDIUM.
IF YOUR IMAGE IS EVER RE-CORDED...
...IT'S VERY LIKELY THAT SHE WILL APPEAR IN THAT RECORDING.

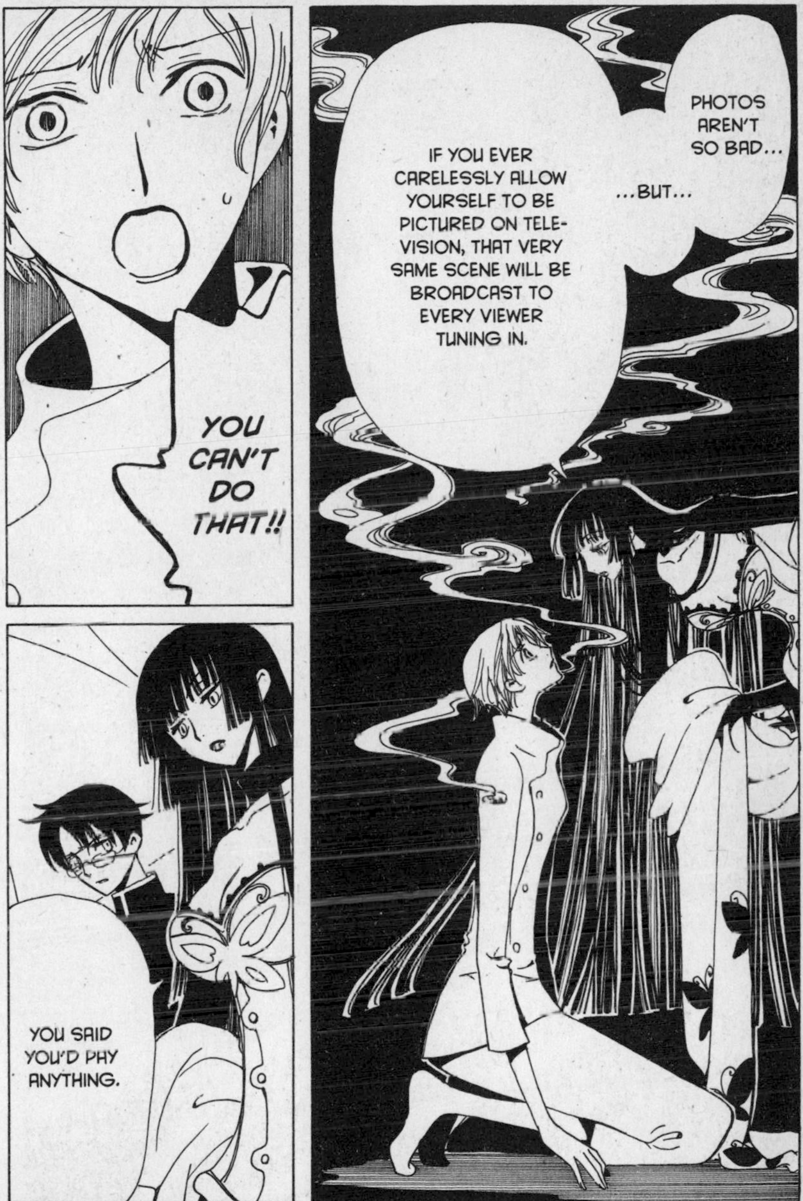
PHOTOS AREN'T SO BAD...
...BUT...
IF YOU EVER CARELESSLY ALLOW YOURSELF TO BE PICTURED ON TELE-VISION, THAT VERY SAME SCENE WILL BE BROADCAST TO EVERY VIEWER TUNING IN.
YOU CAN'T DO THAT!!
YOU SAID YOU'D PAY ANYTHING.

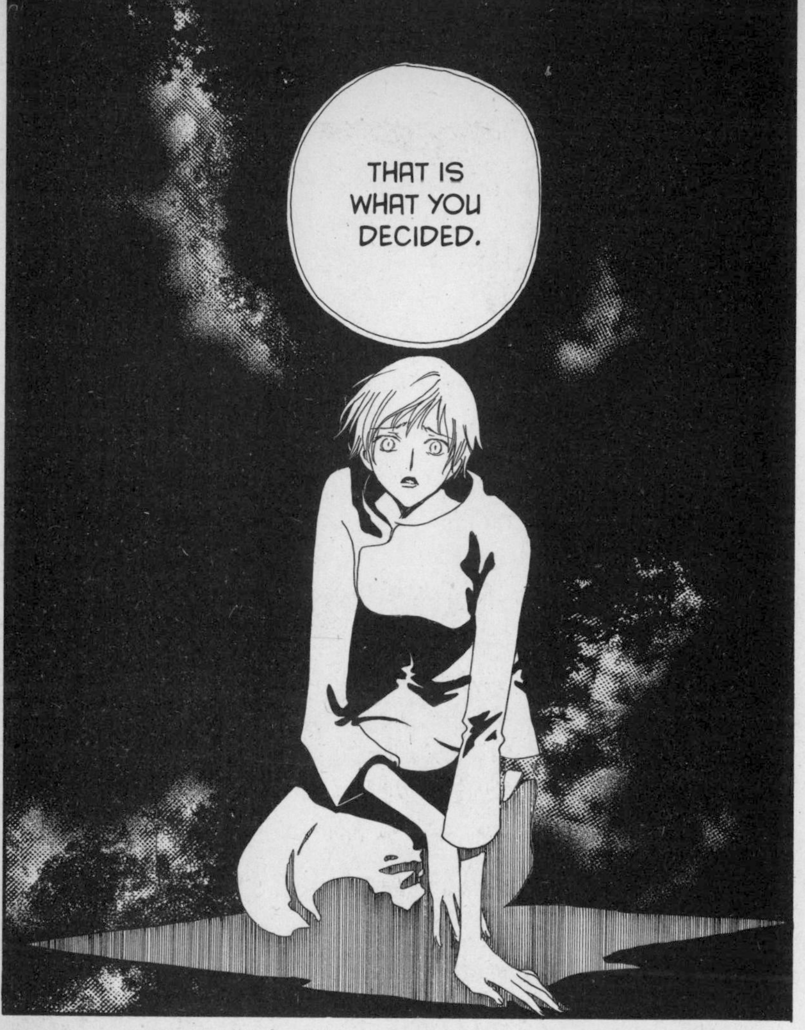
THAT IS WHAT YOU DECIDED.
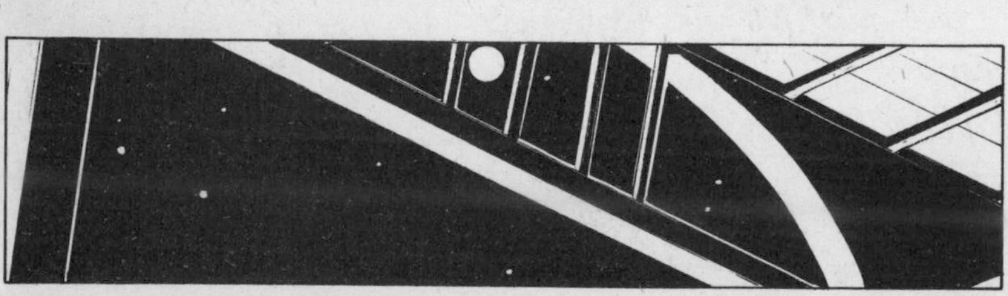

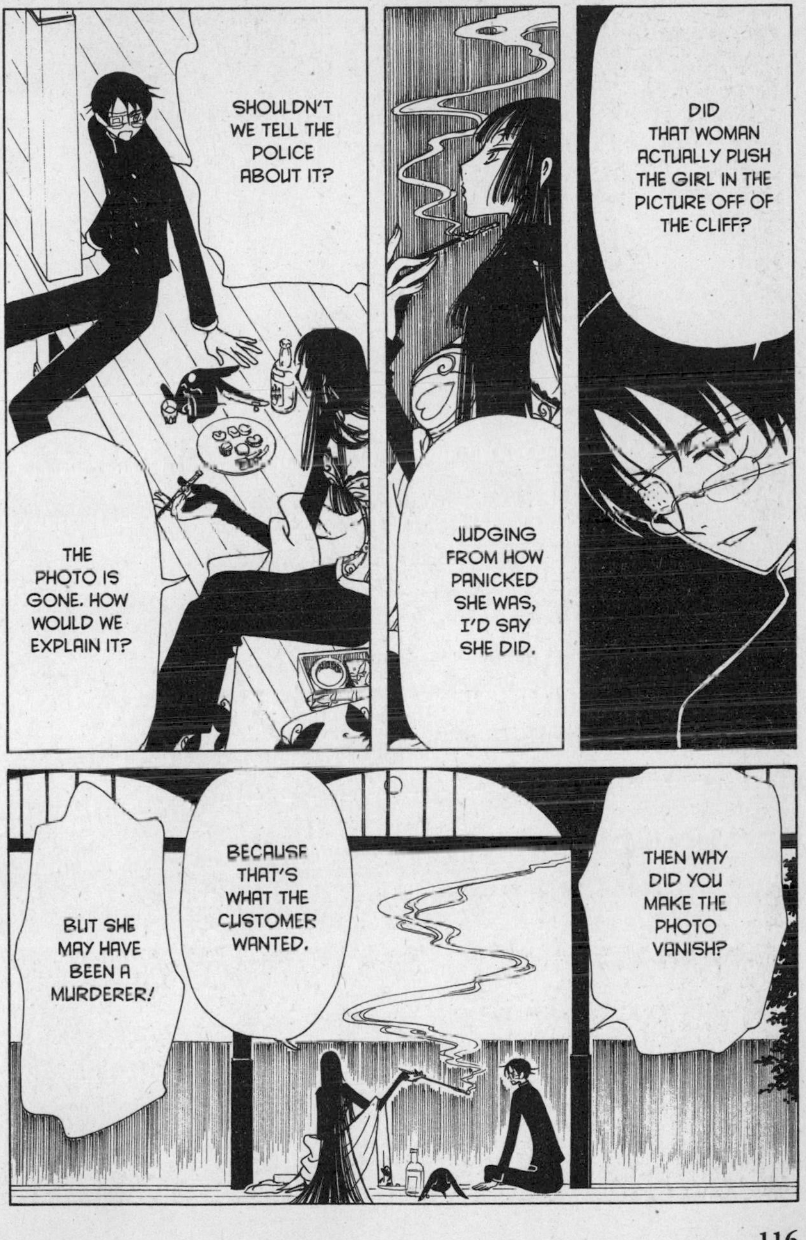
DID THAT WOMAN ACTUALLY PUSH THE GIRL IN THE PICTURE OFF OF THE CLIFF?
JUDGING FROM HOW PANICKED SHE WAS, I'D SAY SHE DID.
SHOULDN'T WE TELL THE POLICE ABOUT IT?
THE PHOTO IS GONE. HOW WOULD WE EXPLAIN IT?
THEN WHY DID YOU MAKE THE PHOTO VANISH?
BECAUSE THAT'S WHAT THE CUSTOMER WANTED.
BUT SHE MAY HAVE BEEN A MURDERER!

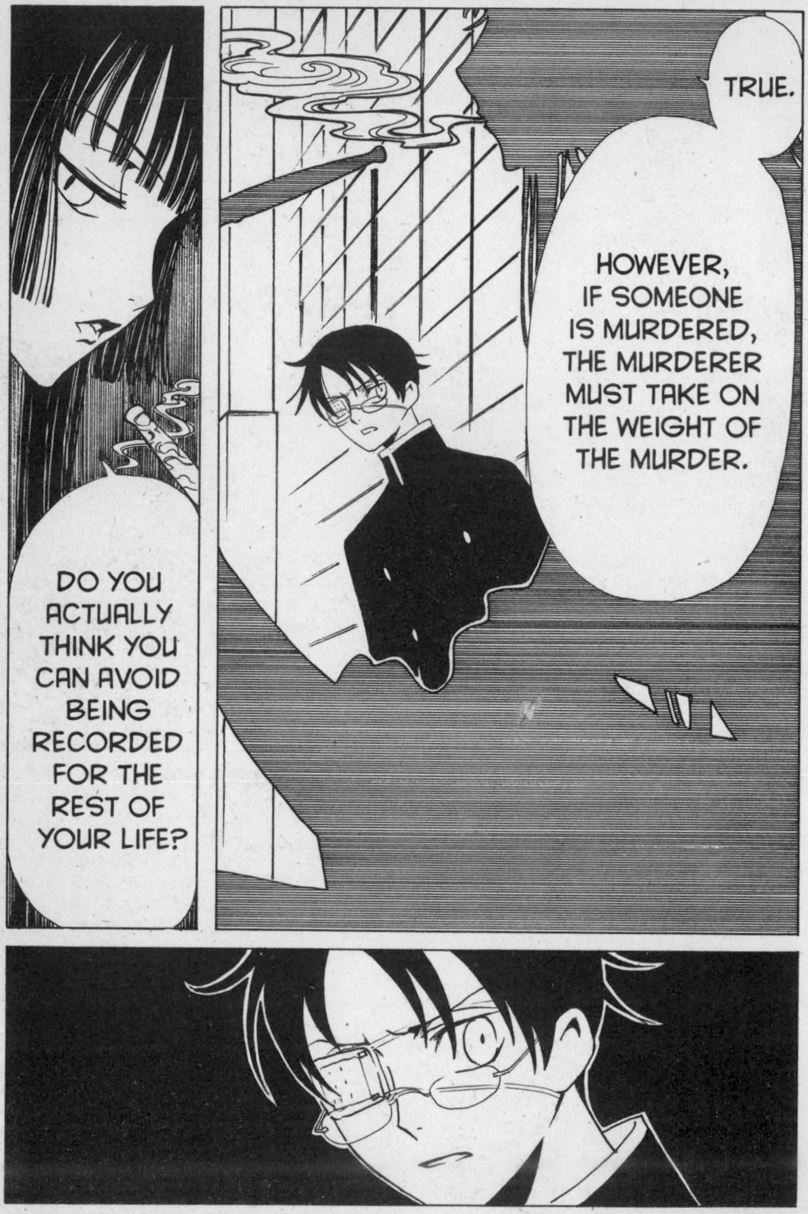
TRUE.
HOWEVER, IF SOMEONE IS MURDERED, THE MURDERER MUST TAKE ON THE WEIGHT OF THE MURDER.
DO YOU ACTUALLY THINK YOU CAN AVOID BEING RECORDED FOR THE REST OF YOUR LIFE?

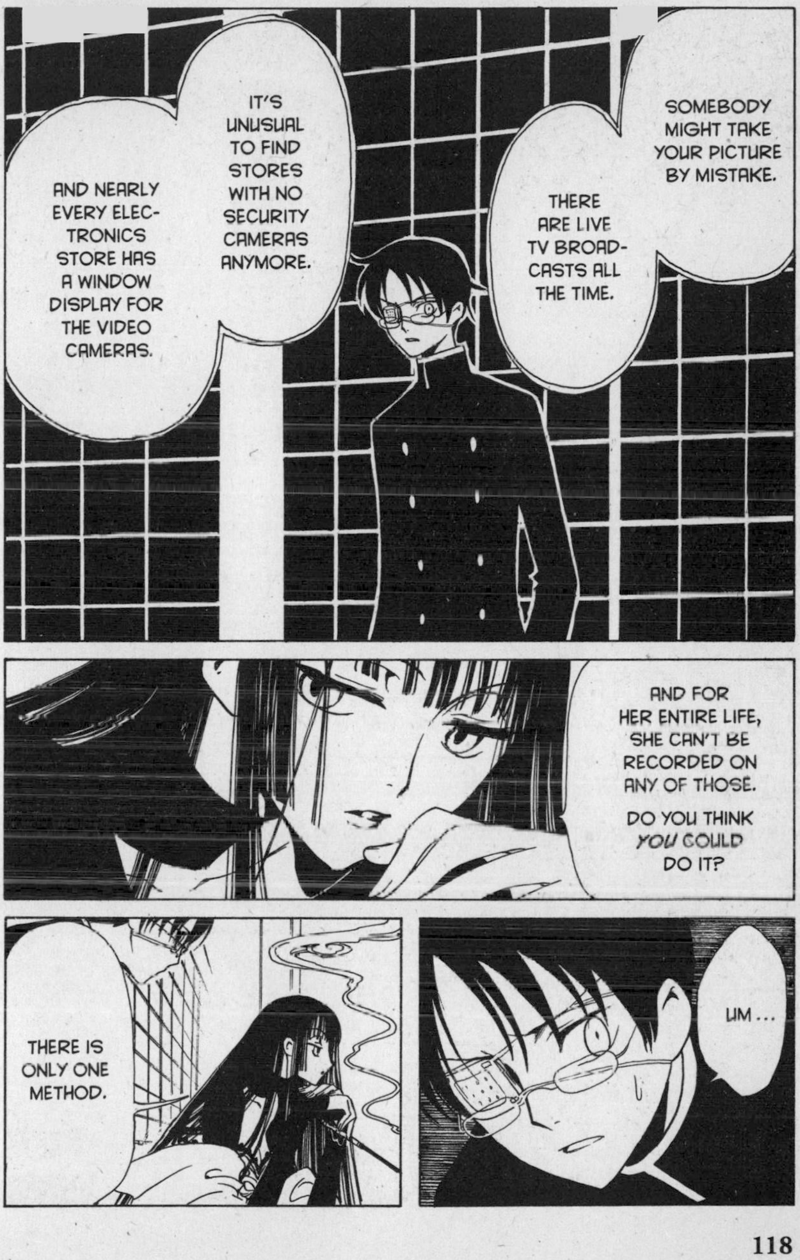
SOMEBODY MIGHT TAKE YOUR PICTURE BY MISTAKE.
THERE ARE LIVE TV BROAD-CASTS ALL THE TIME.
IT'S UNUSUAL TO FIND STORES WITH NO SECURITY CAMERAS ANYMORE.
AND NEARLY EVERY ELEC-TRONICS STORE HAS A WINDOW DISPLAY FOR THE VIDEO CAMERAS.
AND FOR HER ENTIRE LIFE, SHE CAN'T BE RECORDED ON ANY OF THOSE.
DO YOU THINK *YOU* COULD DO IT?
UM ...
THERE IS ONLY ONE METHOD.

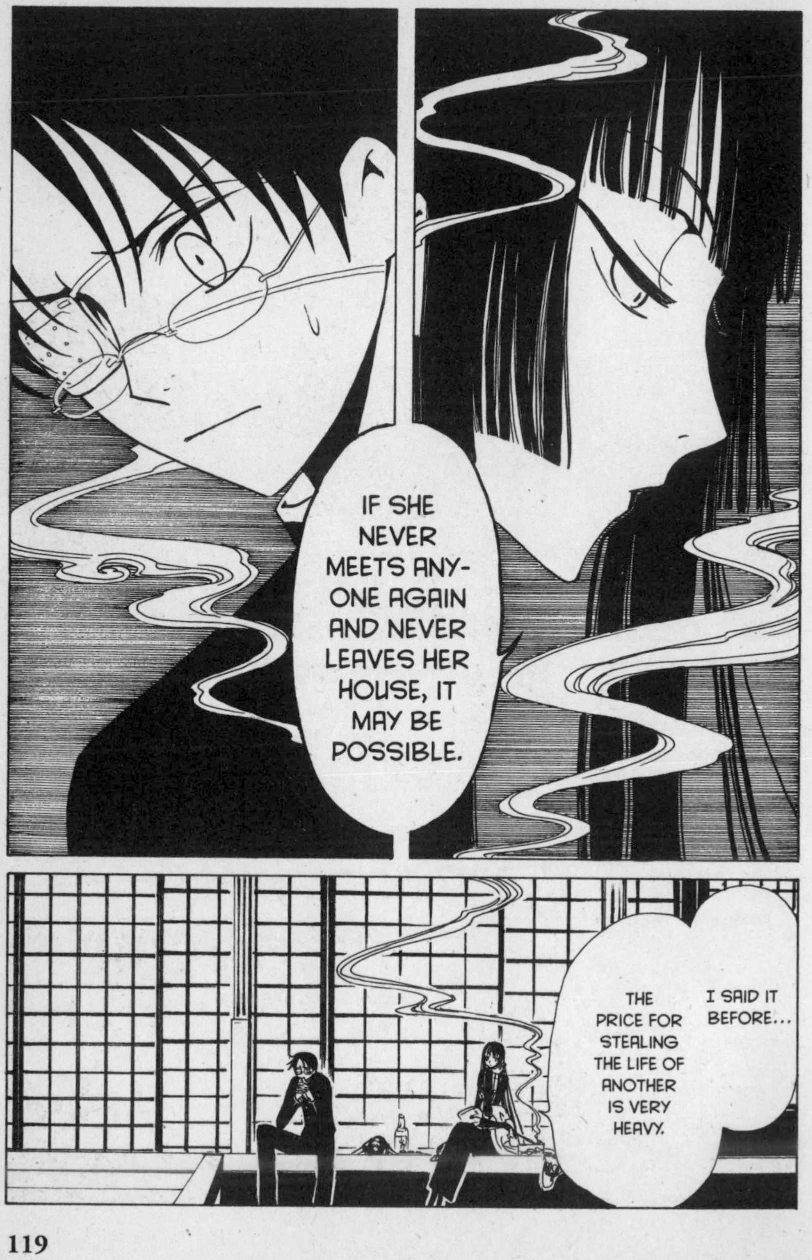
IF SHE NEVER MEETS ANY-ONE AGAIN AND NEVER LEAVES HER HOUSE, IT MAY BE POSSIBLE.
I SAID IT BEFORE...
THE PRICE FOR STEALING THE LIFE OF ANOTHER IS VERY HEAVY.

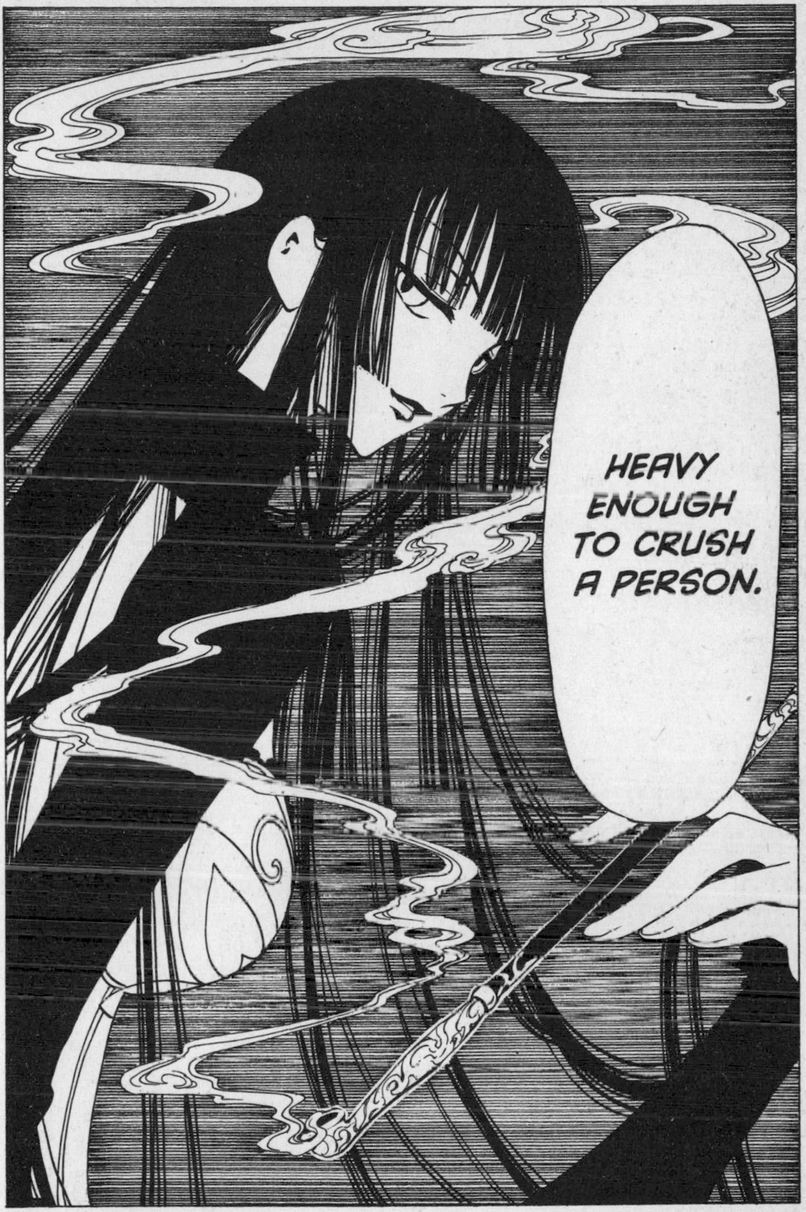
HEAVY ENOUGH TO CRUSH A PERSON.

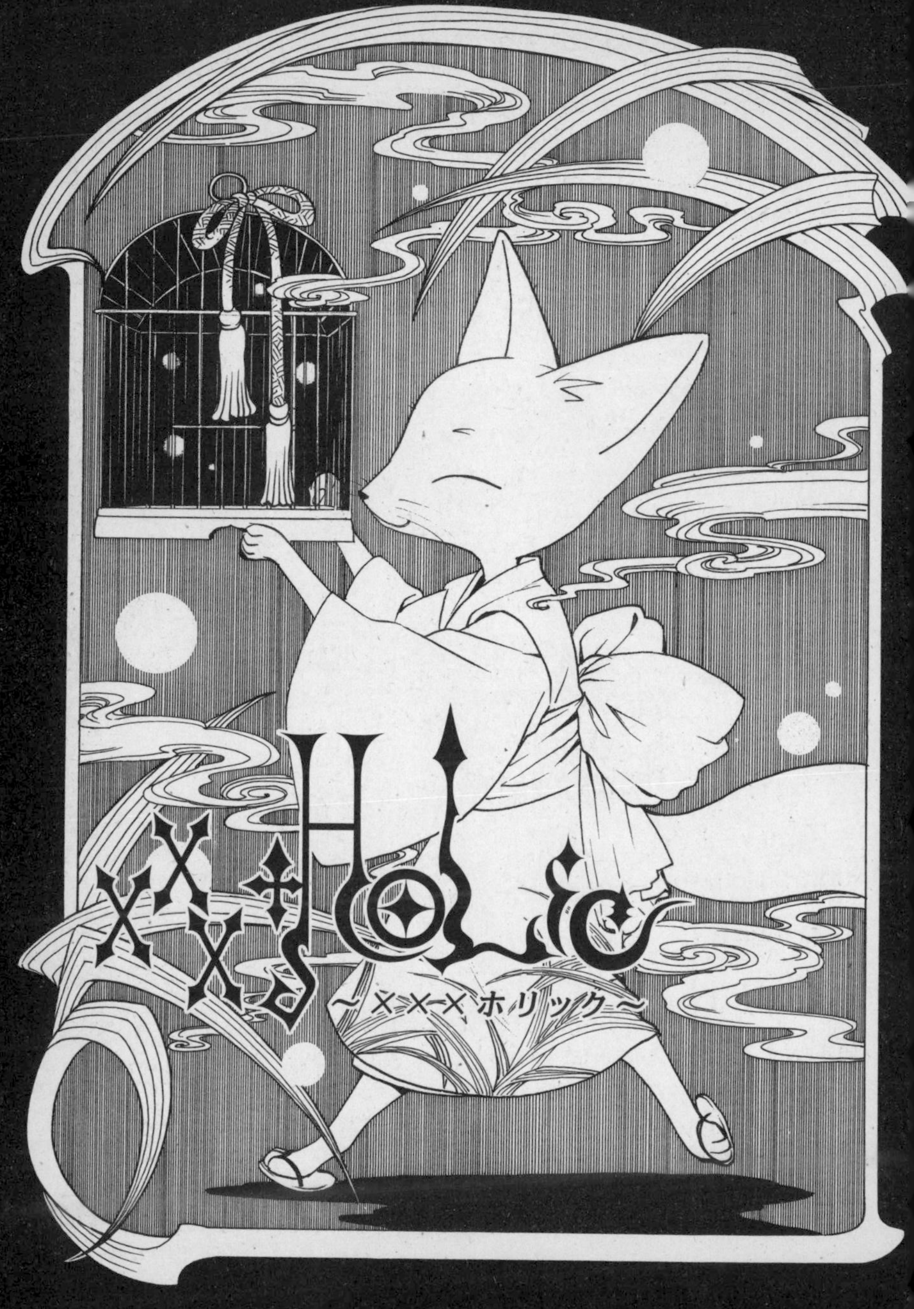
xxxHolic
~×××ホリック~

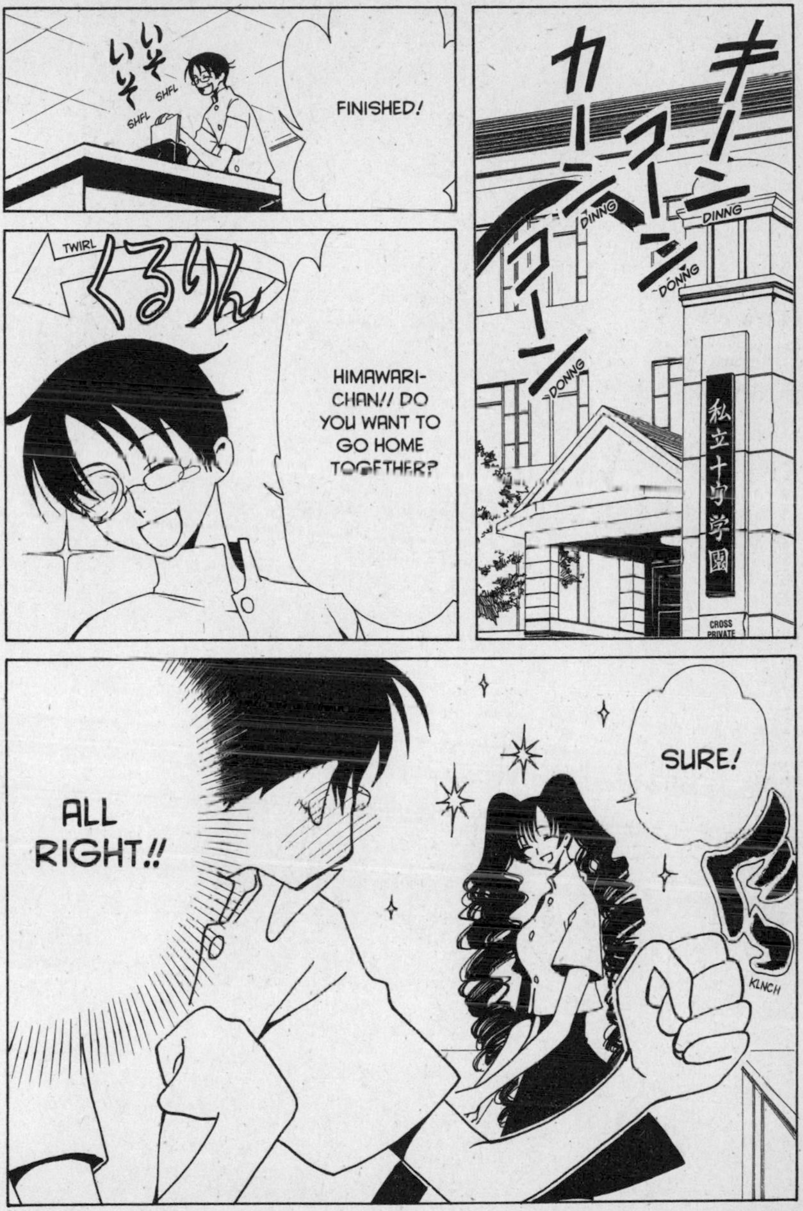
DINNG
DINNG
DONNG
DONNG
私立十字学園
CROSS PRIVATE
いそいそ
SHFL
SHFL
FINISHED!
くるりん
TWIRL
HIMAWARI-CHAN!! DO YOU WANT TO GO HOME TOGETHER?
SURE!
KLNCH
ALL RIGHT!!

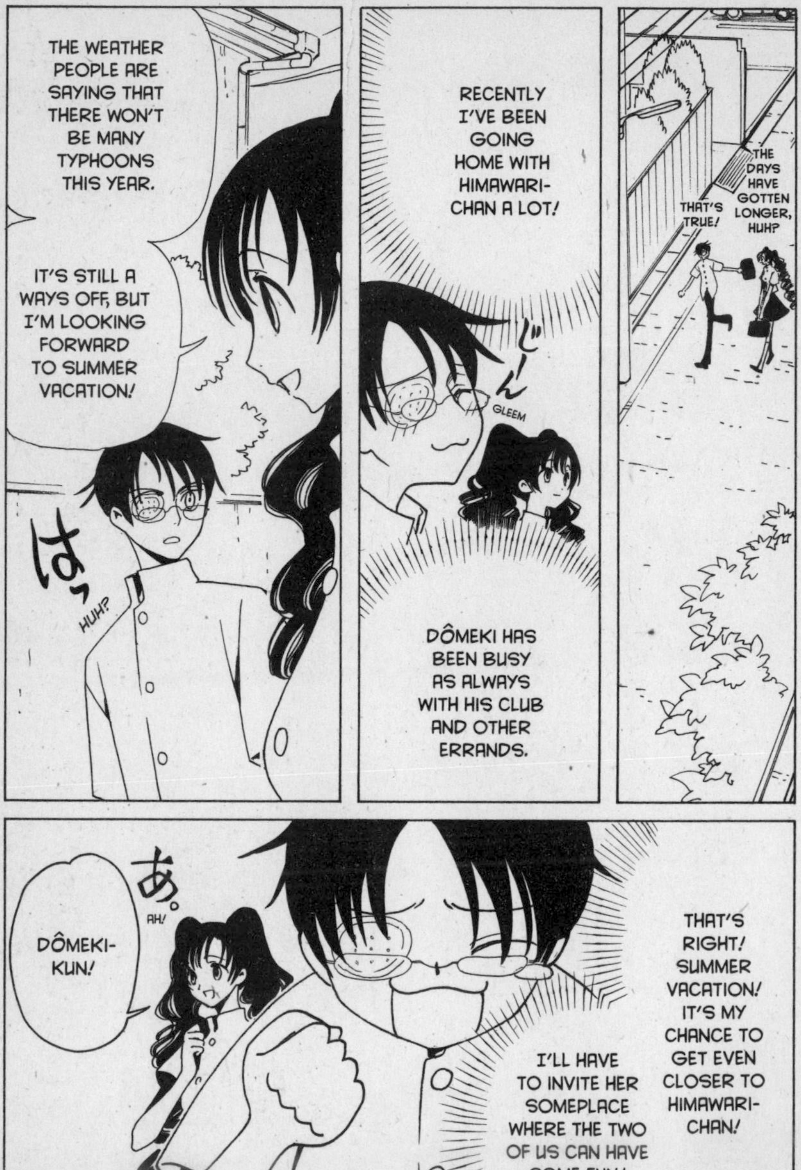
THE DAYS HAVE GOTTEN LONGER, HUH?
THAT'S TRUE!
RECENTLY I'VE BEEN GOING HOME WITH HIMAWARI-CHAN A LOT!
じーん
GLEEM
DÔMEKI HAS BEEN BUSY AS ALWAYS WITH HIS CLUB AND OTHER ERRANDS.
THE WEATHER PEOPLE ARE SAYING THAT THERE WON'T BE MANY TYPHOONS THIS YEAR.
IT'S STILL A WAYS OFF, BUT I'M LOOKING FORWARD TO SUMMER VACATION!
は、
HUH?
THAT'S RIGHT! SUMMER VACATION! IT'S MY CHANCE TO GET EVEN CLOSER TO HIMAWARI-CHAN!
I'LL HAVE TO INVITE HER SOMEPLACE WHERE THE TWO OF US CAN HAVE SOME FUN!
あ。
AH!
DÔMEKI-KUN!

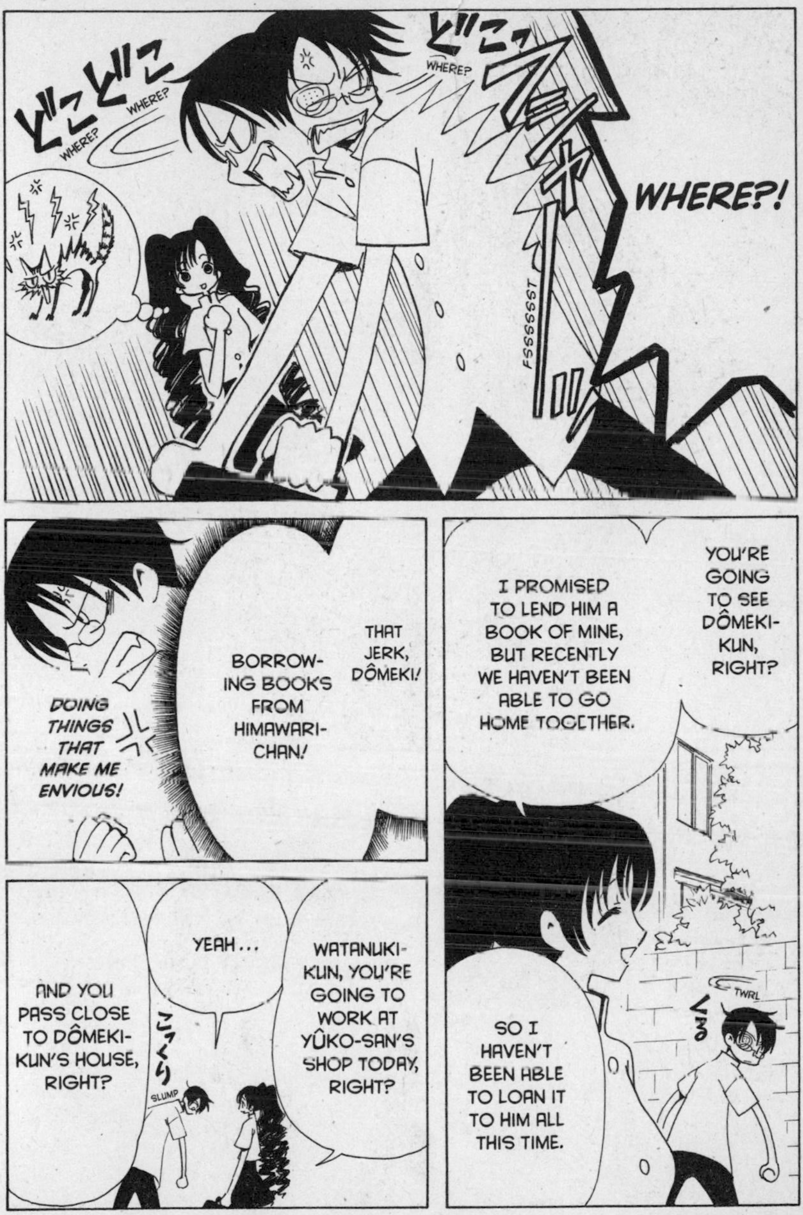

どこっ
WHERE?
WHERE?!
FSSSSSST
どこどこ
WHERE?
WHERE?
YOU'RE GOING TO SEE DÔMEKI-KUN, RIGHT?
I PROMISED TO LEND HIM A BOOK OF MINE, BUT RECENTLY WE HAVEN'T BEEN ABLE TO GO HOME TOGETHER.
SO I HAVEN'T BEEN ABLE TO LOAN IT TO HIM ALL THIS TIME.
TWRL
THAT JERK, DÔMEKI!
BORROWING BOOKS FROM HIMAWARI-CHAN!
DOING THINGS THAT MAKE ME ENVIOUS!
WATANUKI-KUN, YOU'RE GOING TO WORK AT YÛKO-SAN'S SHOP TODAY, RIGHT?
YEAH...
こっくり
SLUMP
AND YOU PASS CLOSE TO DÔMEKI-KUN'S HOUSE, RIGHT?

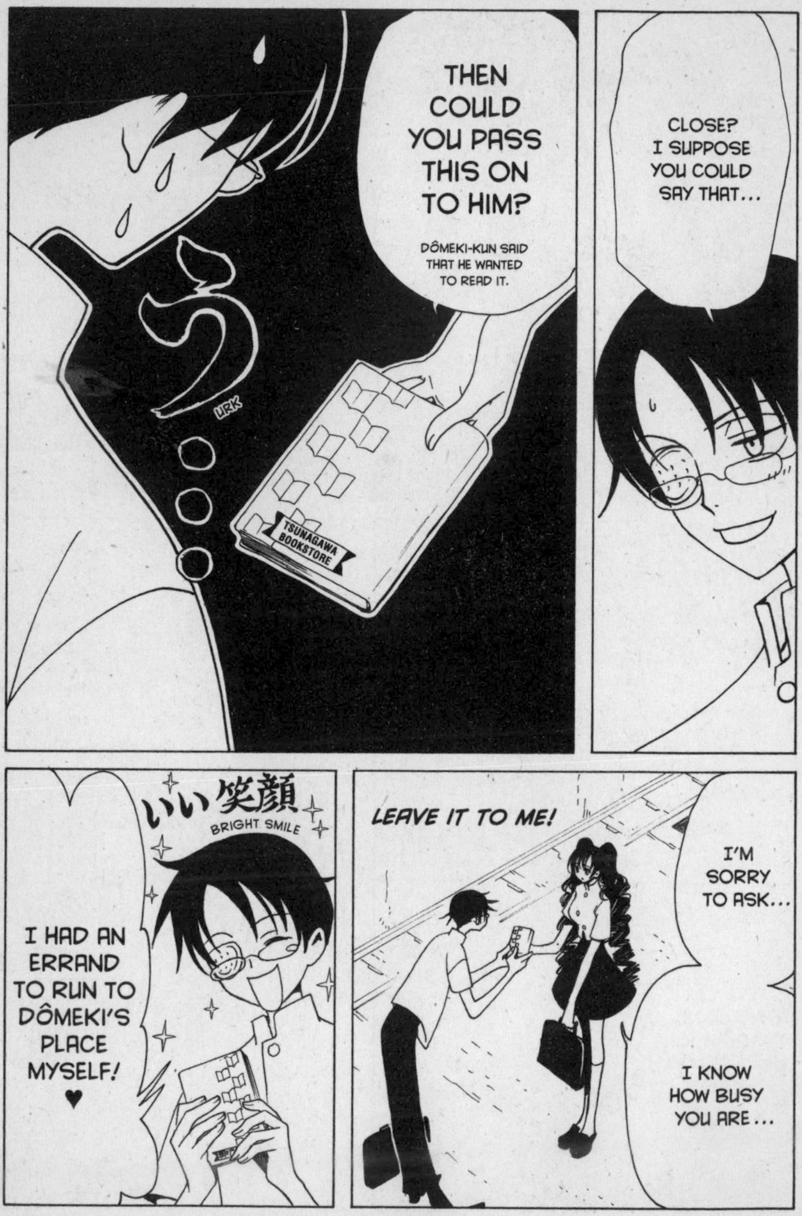
CLOSE? I SUPPOSE YOU COULD SAY THAT...
THEN COULD YOU PASS THIS ON TO HIM?
DÔMEKI-KUN SAID THAT HE WANTED TO READ IT.
う
URK
TSUNAGAWA BOOKSTORE
I'M SORRY TO ASK...
I KNOW HOW BUSY YOU ARE...
LEAVE IT TO ME!
いい笑顔
BRIGHT SMILE
I HAD AN ERRAND TO RUN TO DÔMEKI'S PLACE MYSELF! ♥

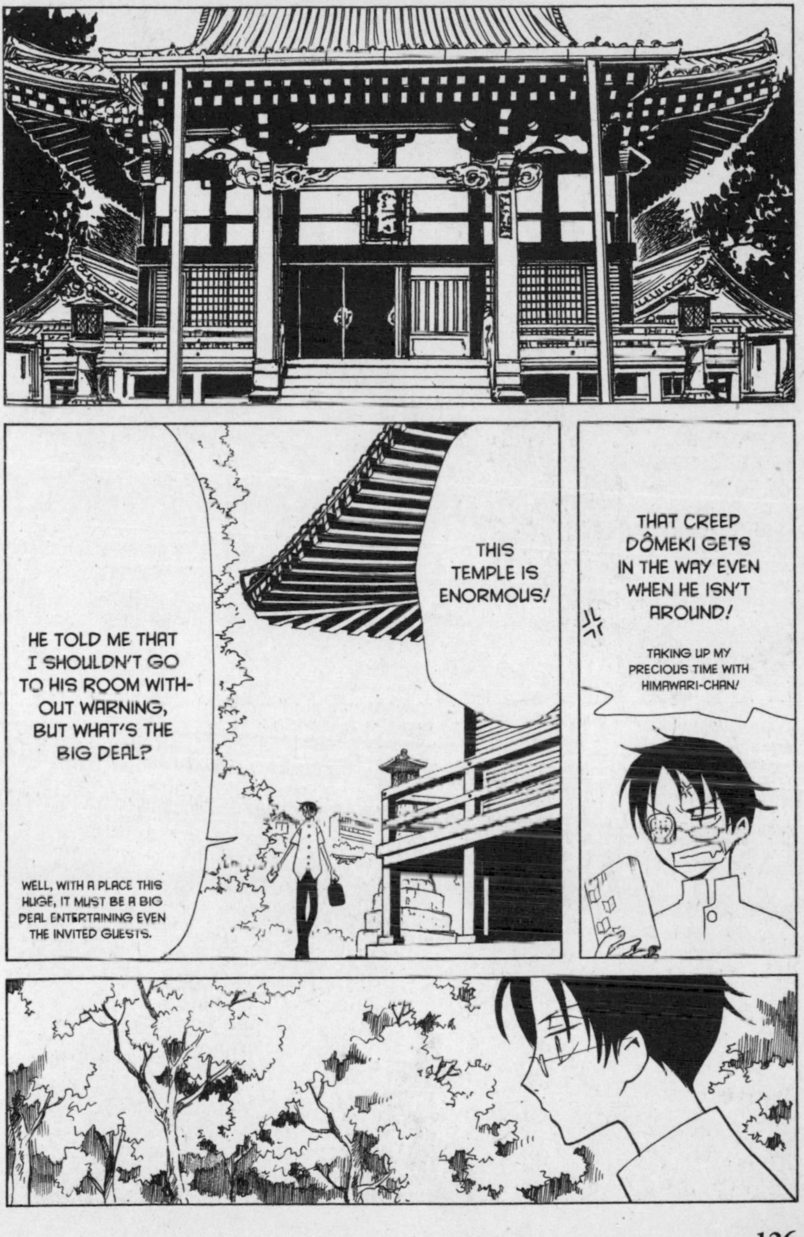
THAT CREEP DÔMEKI GETS IN THE WAY EVEN WHEN HE ISN'T AROUND!
TAKING UP MY PRECIOUS TIME WITH HIMAWARI-CHAN!
THIS TEMPLE IS ENORMOUS!
HE TOLD ME THAT I SHOULDN'T GO TO HIS ROOM WITH-OUT WARNING, BUT WHAT'S THE BIG DEAL?
WELL, WITH A PLACE THIS HUGE, IT MUST BE A BIG DEAL ENTERTAINING EVEN THE INVITED GUESTS.

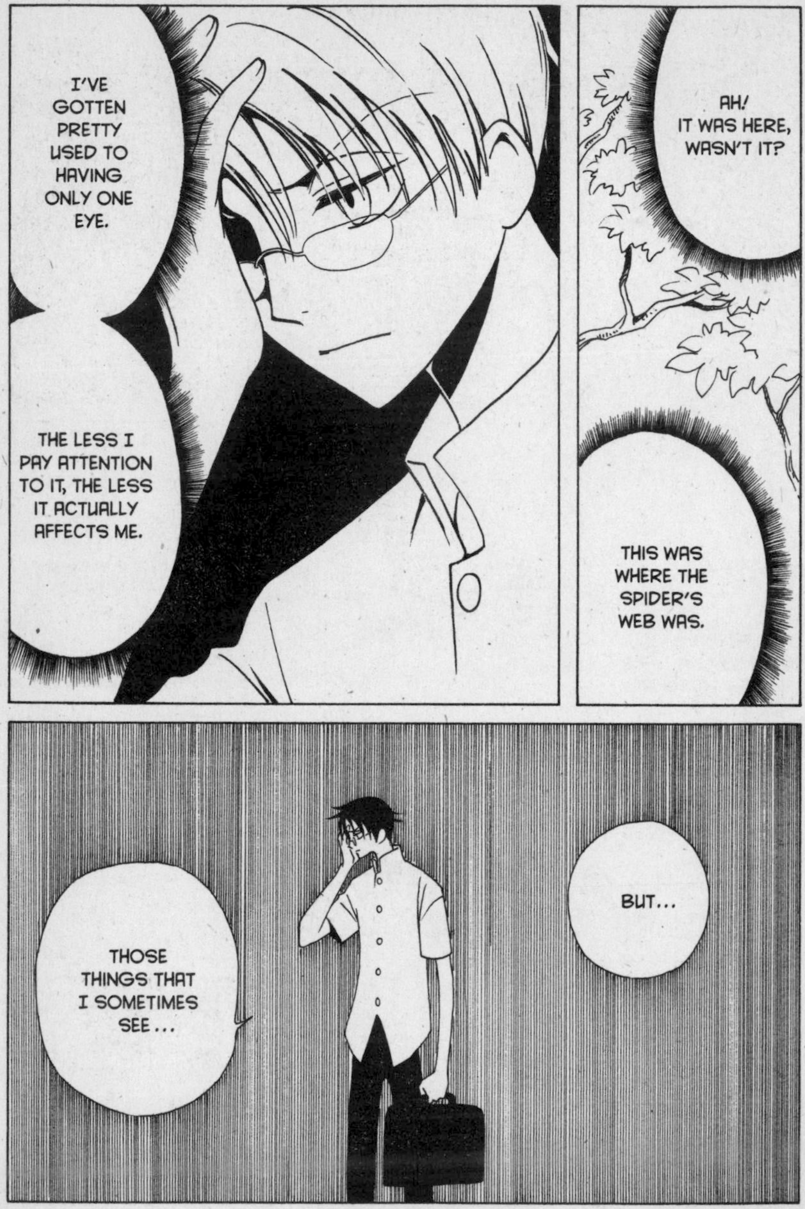
AH! IT WAS HERE, WASN'T IT?
THIS WAS WHERE THE SPIDER'S WEB WAS.
I'VE GOTTEN PRETTY USED TO HAVING ONLY ONE EYE.
THE LESS I PAY ATTENTION TO IT, THE LESS IT ACTUALLY AFFECTS ME.
BUT...
THOSE THINGS THAT I SOMETIMES SEE...

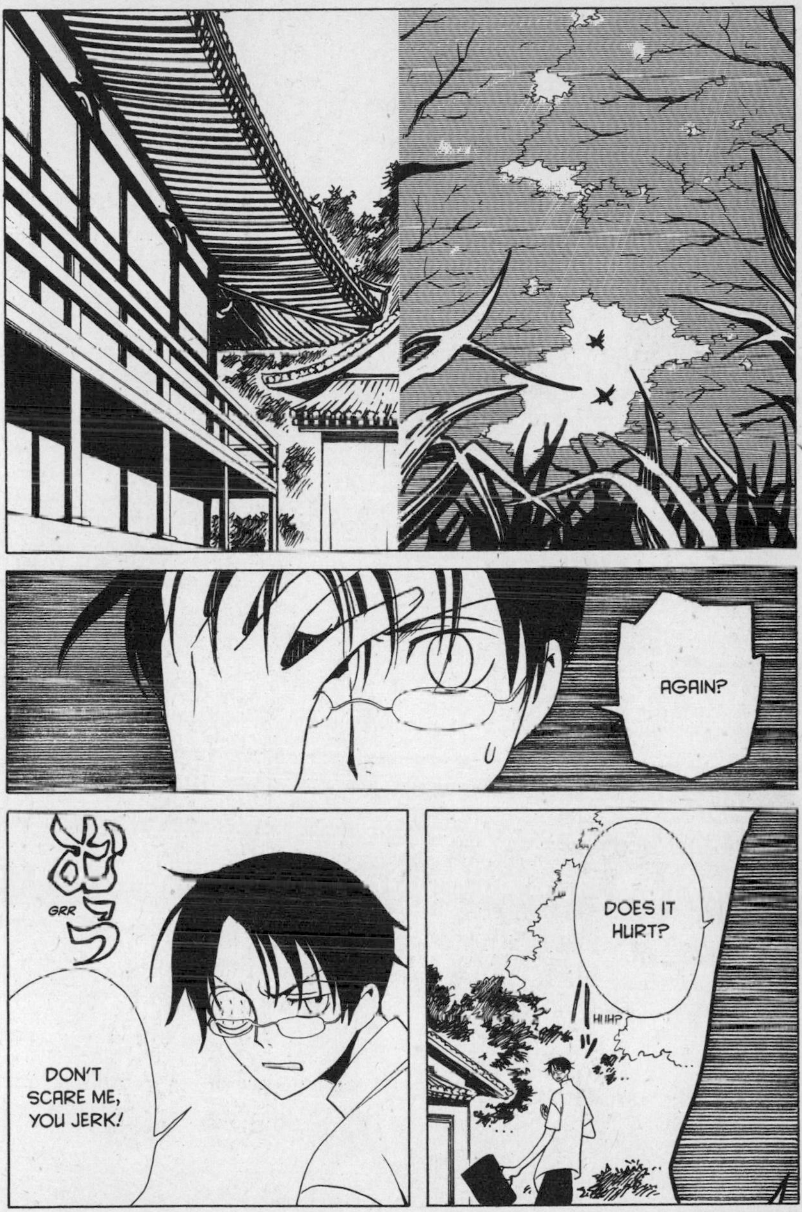
AGAIN?
DOES IT HURT?
HUH?
...
...
GRR
DON'T SCARE ME, YOU JERK!

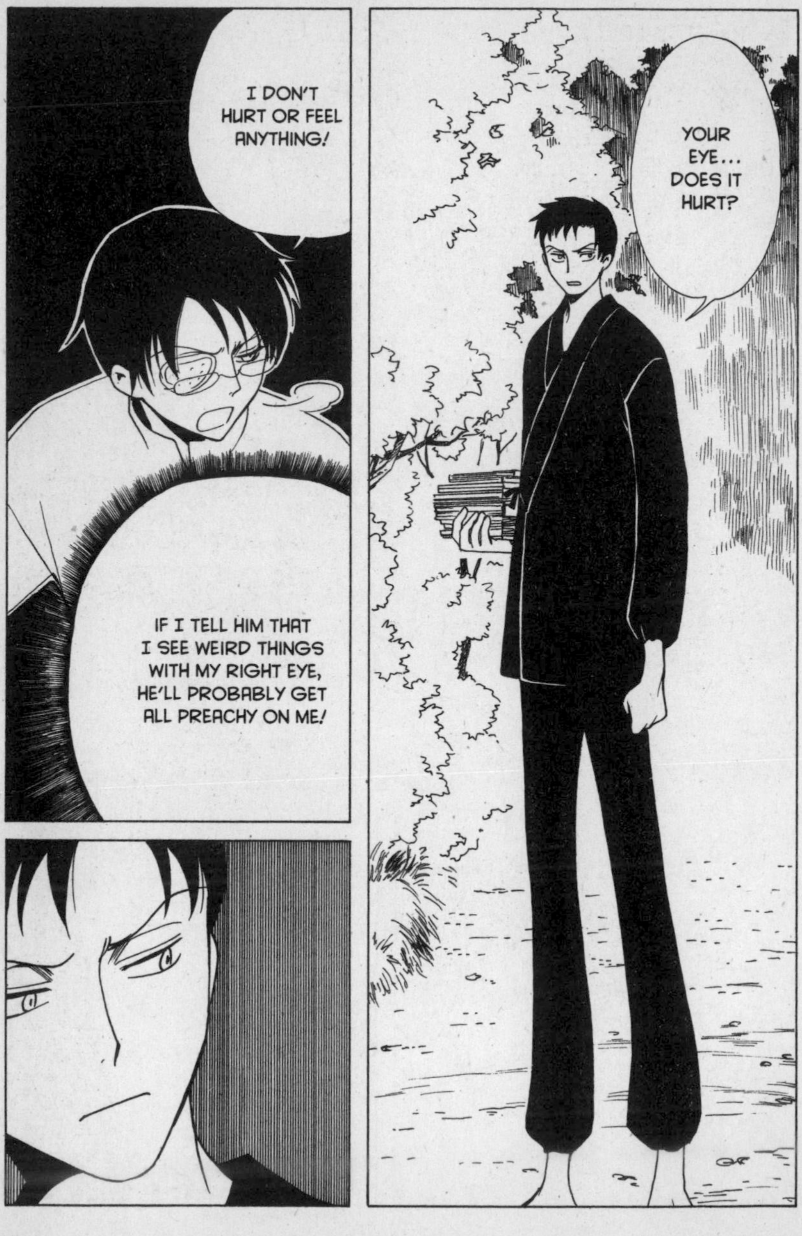
YOUR EYE... DOES IT HURT?
I DON'T HURT OR FEEL ANYTHING!
IF I TELL HIM THAT I SEE WEIRD THINGS WITH MY RIGHT EYE, HE'LL PROBABLY GET ALL PREACHY ON ME!

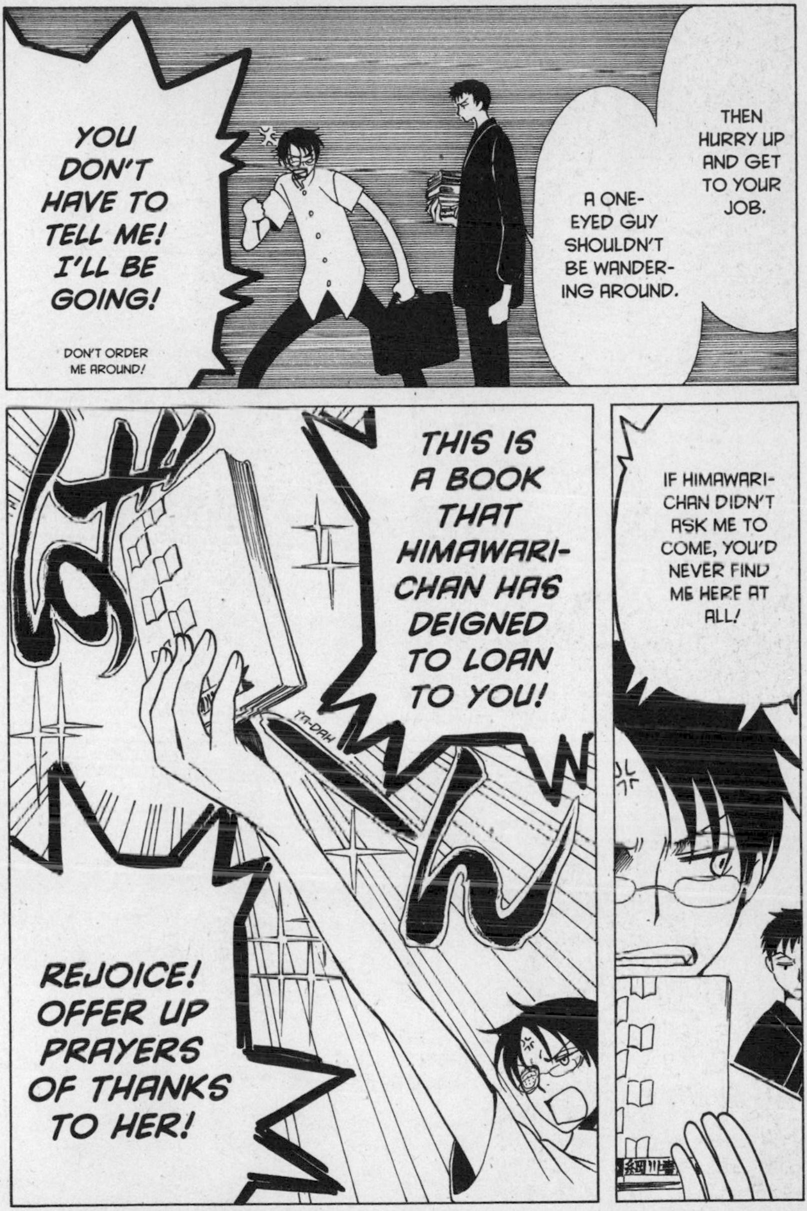
THEN HURRY UP AND GET TO YOUR JOB.
A ONE-EYED GUY SHOULDN'T BE WANDERING AROUND.
YOU DON'T HAVE TO TELL ME! I'LL BE GOING!
DON'T ORDER ME AROUND!
IF HIMAWARI-CHAN DIDN'T ASK ME TO COME, YOU'D NEVER FIND ME HERE AT ALL!
THIS IS A BOOK THAT HIMAWARI-CHAN HAS DEIGNED TO LOAN TO YOU!
YA-DAH
REJOICE! OFFER UP PRAYERS OF THANKS TO HER!

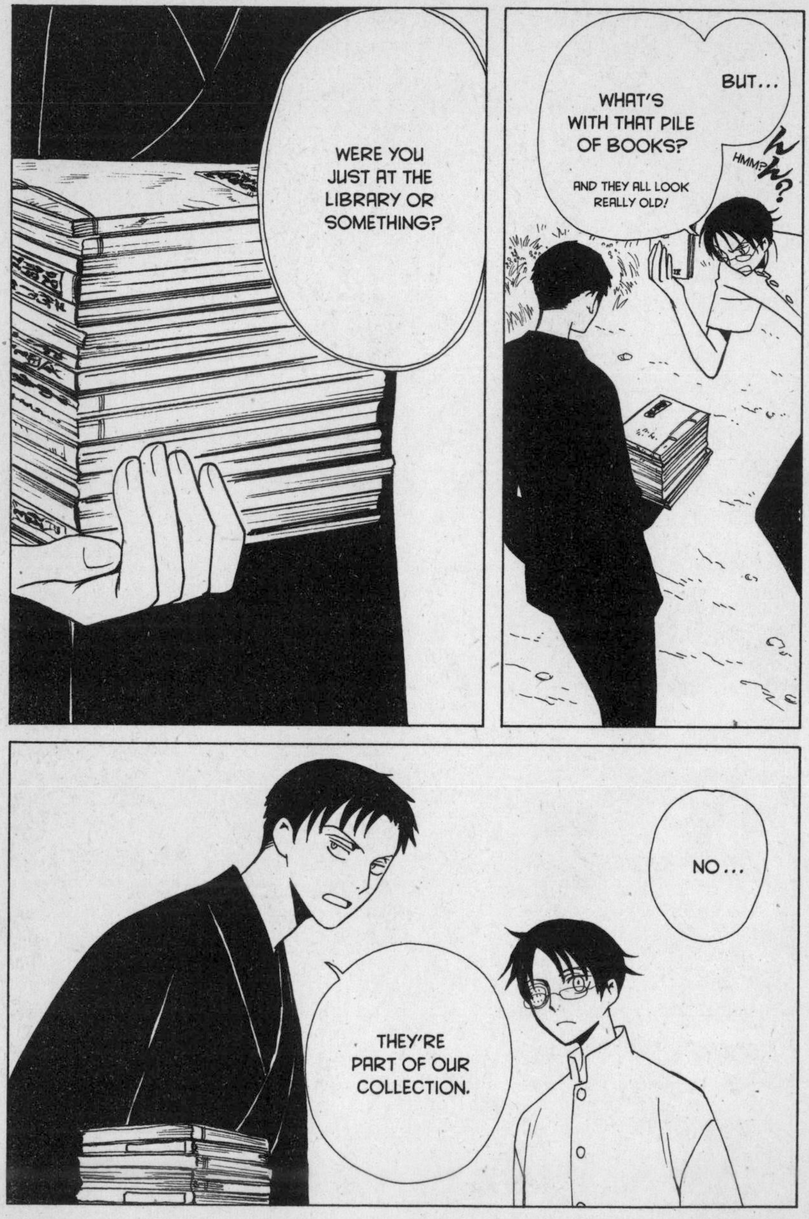
BUT...
WHAT'S WITH THAT PILE OF BOOKS?
AND THEY ALL LOOK REALLY OLD!
HMM?
WERE YOU JUST AT THE LIBRARY OR SOMETHING?
NO...
THEY'RE PART OF OUR COLLECTION.

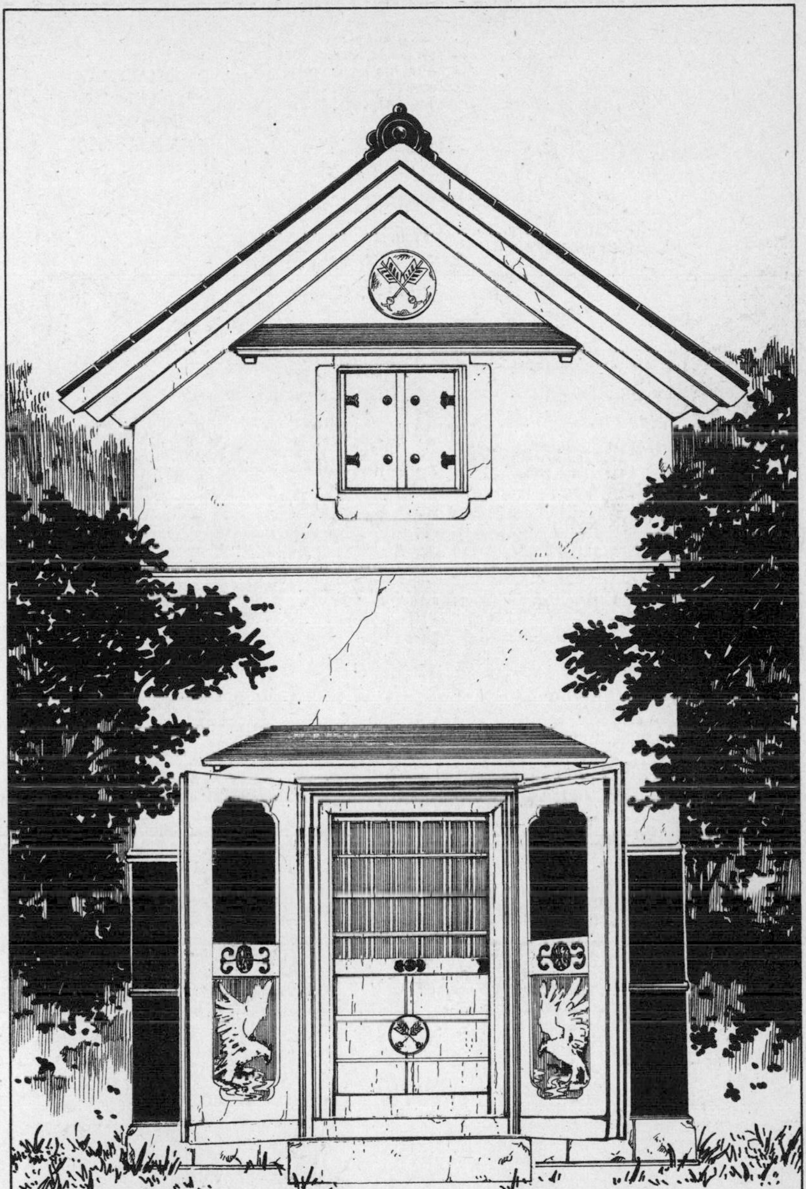

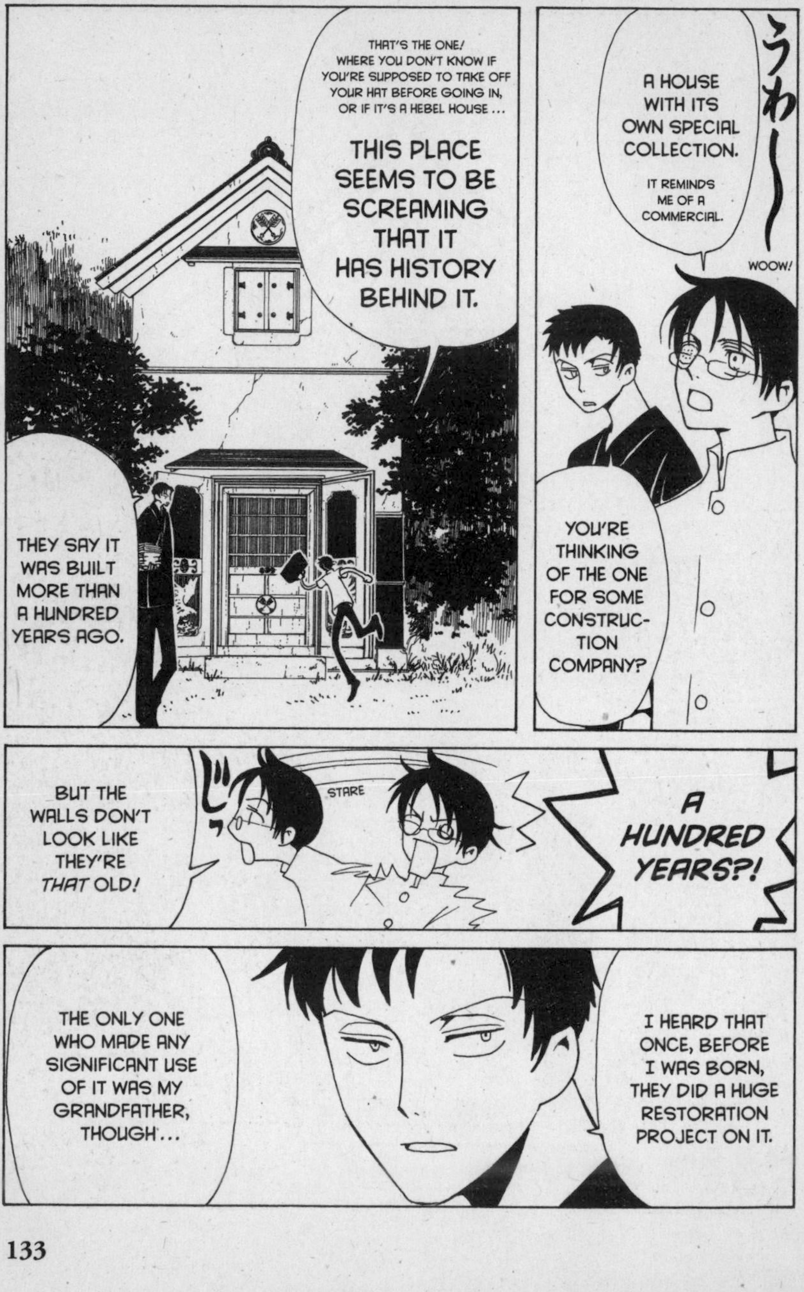
うわ〜
WOOW!
A HOUSE WITH ITS OWN SPECIAL COLLECTION.
IT REMINDS ME OF A COMMERCIAL.
YOU'RE THINKING OF THE ONE FOR SOME CONSTRUC-TION COMPANY?
THAT'S THE ONE! WHERE YOU DON'T KNOW IF YOU'RE SUPPOSED TO TAKE OFF YOUR HAT BEFORE GOING IN, OR IF IT'S A HEBEL HOUSE...
THIS PLACE SEEMS TO BE SCREAMING THAT IT HAS HISTORY BEHIND IT.
THEY SAY IT WAS BUILT MORE THAN A HUNDRED YEARS AGO.
A HUNDRED YEARS?!
STARE
BUT THE WALLS DON'T LOOK LIKE THEY'RE *THAT* OLD!
I HEARD THAT ONCE, BEFORE I WAS BORN, THEY DID A HUGE RESTORATION PROJECT ON IT.
THE ONLY ONE WHO MADE ANY SIGNIFICANT USE OF IT WAS MY GRANDFATHER, THOUGH...

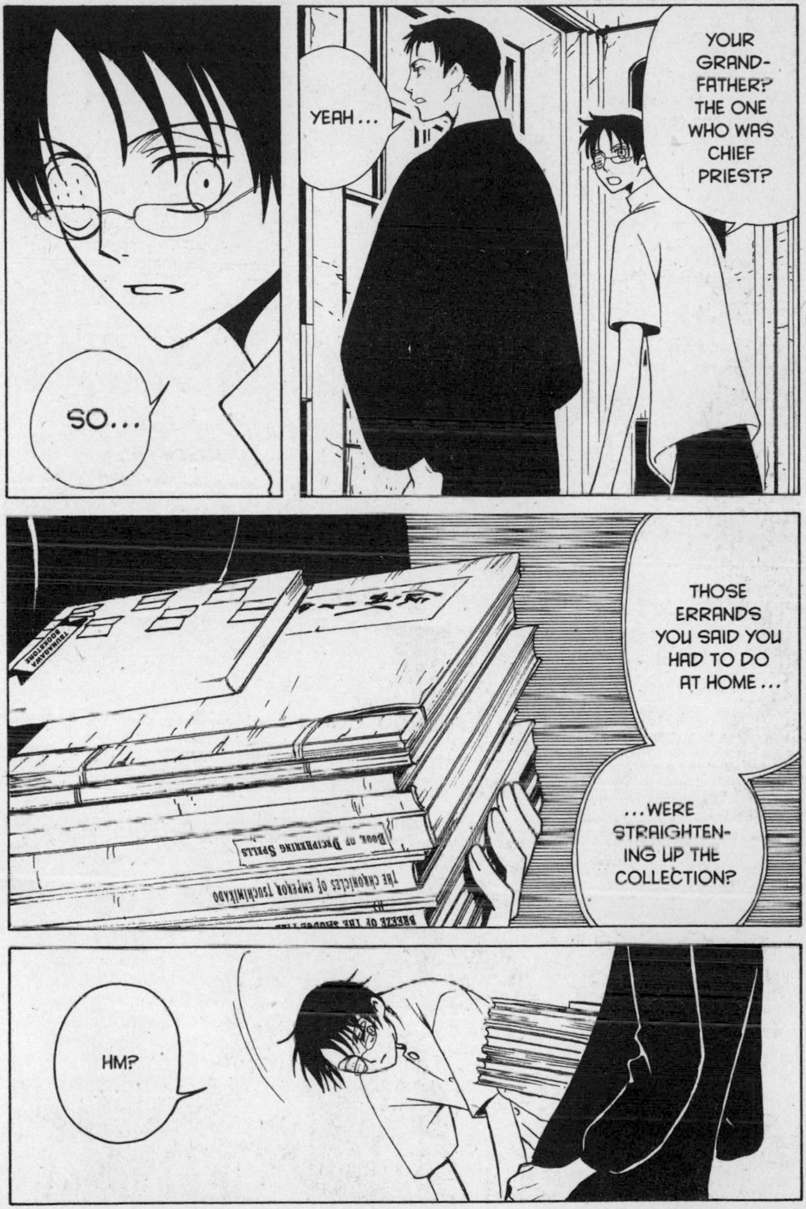
YOUR GRAND-FATHER? THE ONE WHO WAS CHIEF PRIEST?
YEAH...
SO...
THOSE ERRANDS YOU SAID YOU HAD TO DO AT HOME...
...WERE STRAIGHTEN-ING UP THE COLLECTION?
TSUNAGAWA BOOKSTORE
Book of Deciphering Spells
The Chronicles of Emperor Tsuchimikado
HM?

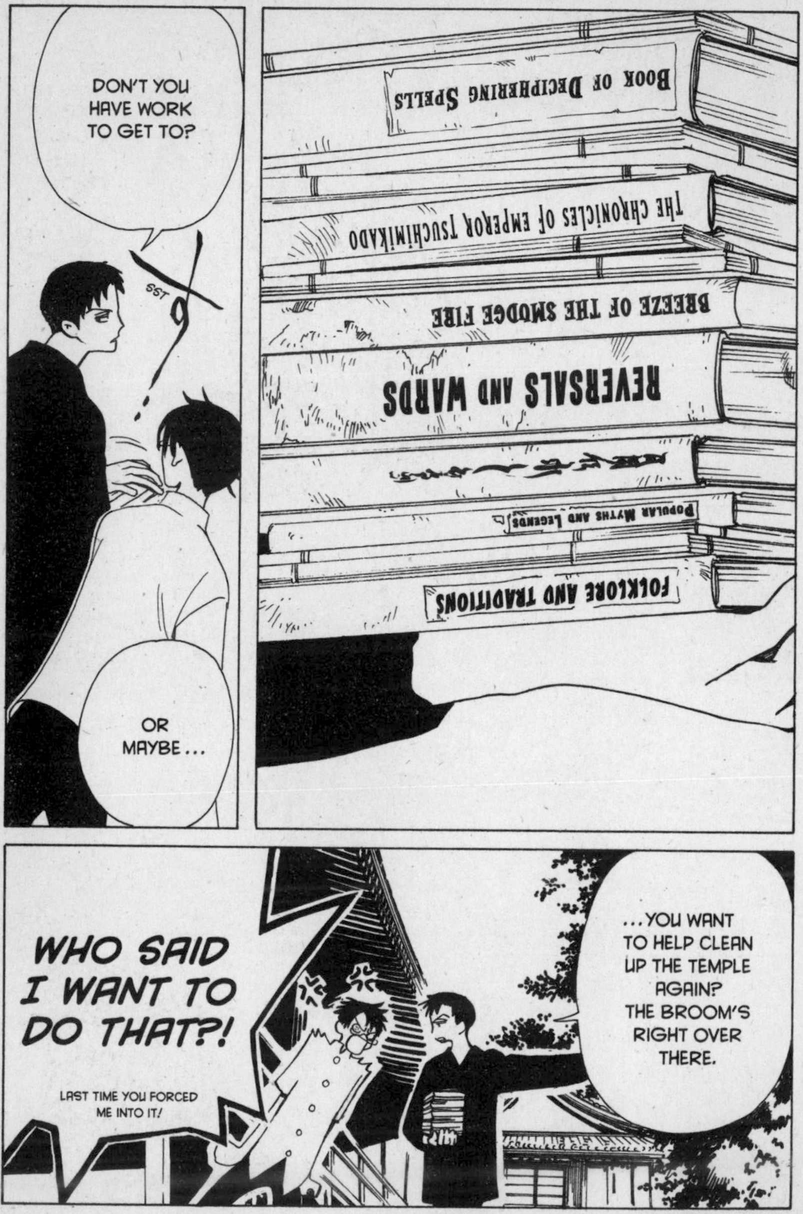
BOOK OF DECIPHERING SPELLS
THE CHRONICLES OF EMPEROR TSUCHIMIKADO
BREEZE OF THE SMUDGE FIRE
REVERSALS AND WARDS
POPULAR MYTHS AND LEGENDS
FOLKLORE AND TRADITIONS
DON'T YOU HAVE WORK TO GET TO?
SST
OR MAYBE...
...YOU WANT TO HELP CLEAN UP THE TEMPLE AGAIN? THE BROOM'S RIGHT OVER THERE.
WHO SAID I WANT TO DO THAT?!
LAST TIME YOU FORCED ME INTO IT!

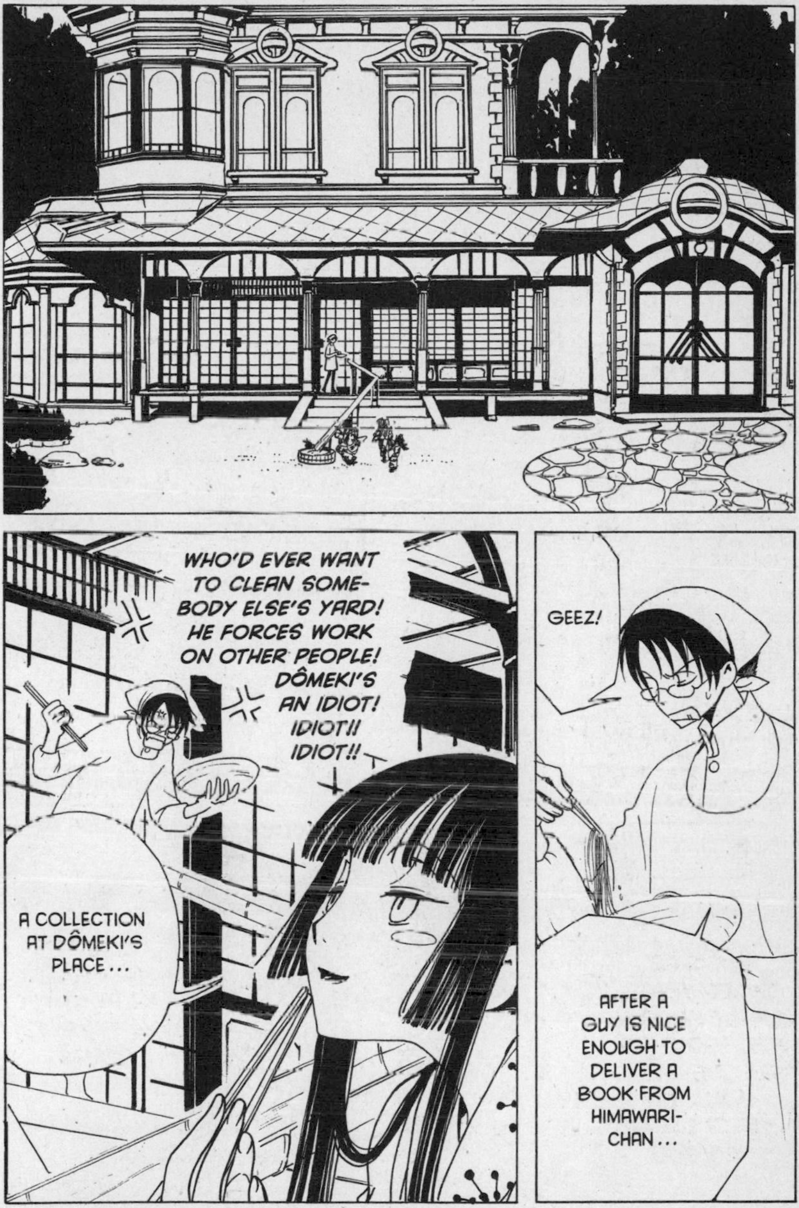
GEEZ!
AFTER A GUY IS NICE ENOUGH TO DELIVER A BOOK FROM HIMAWARI-CHAN...
WHO'D EVER WANT TO CLEAN SOMEBODY ELSE'S YARD! HE FORCES WORK ON OTHER PEOPLE! DÔMEKI'S AN IDIOT! IDIOT!! IDIOT!!
A COLLECTION AT DÔMEKI'S PLACE...

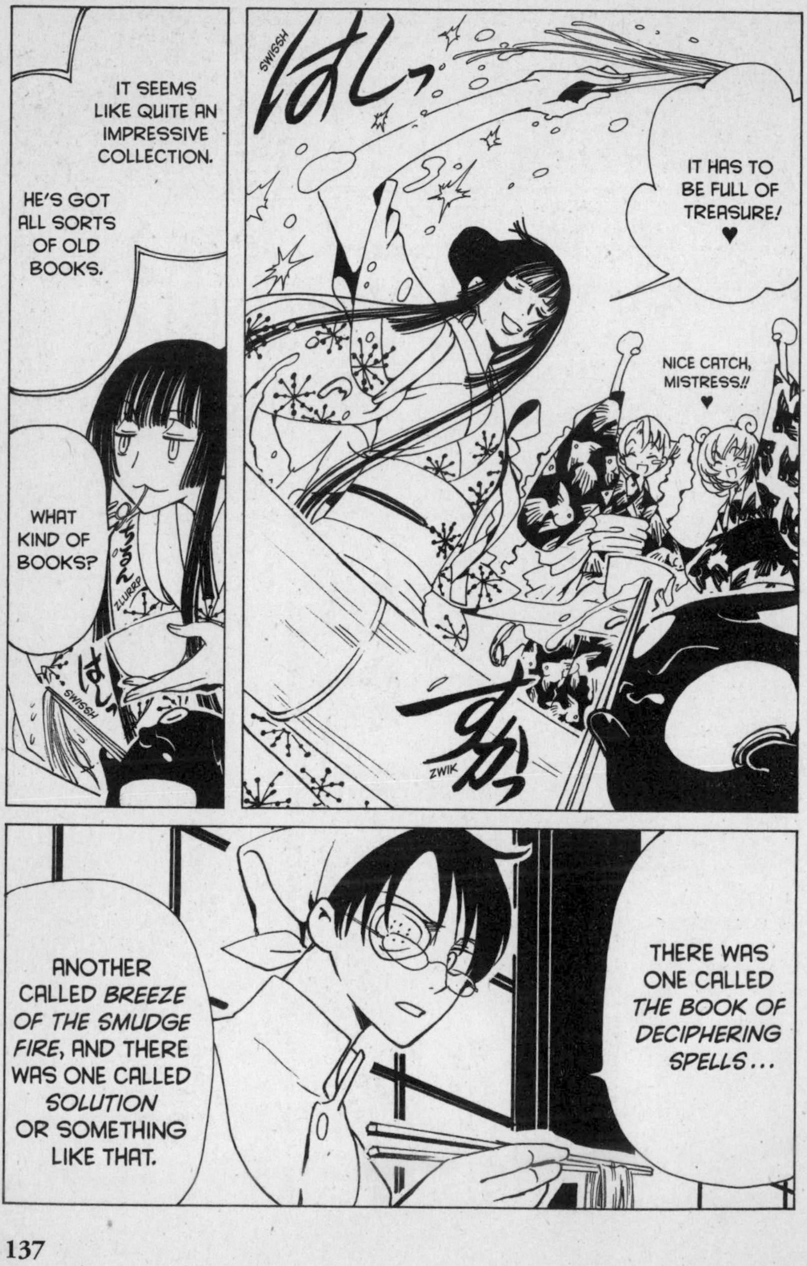
はしっ
SWISSH
IT HAS TO BE FULL OF TREASURE! ♥
NICE CATCH, MISTRESS!! ♥
すかっ
ZWIK
IT SEEMS LIKE QUITE AN IMPRESSIVE COLLECTION.
HE'S GOT ALL SORTS OF OLD BOOKS.
WHAT KIND OF BOOKS?
ZLURRP
はしっ
SWISSH
THERE WAS ONE CALLED *THE BOOK OF DECIPHERING SPELLS*...
ANOTHER CALLED *BREEZE OF THE SMUDGE FIRE*, AND THERE WAS ONE CALLED *SOLUTION* OR SOMETHING LIKE THAT.

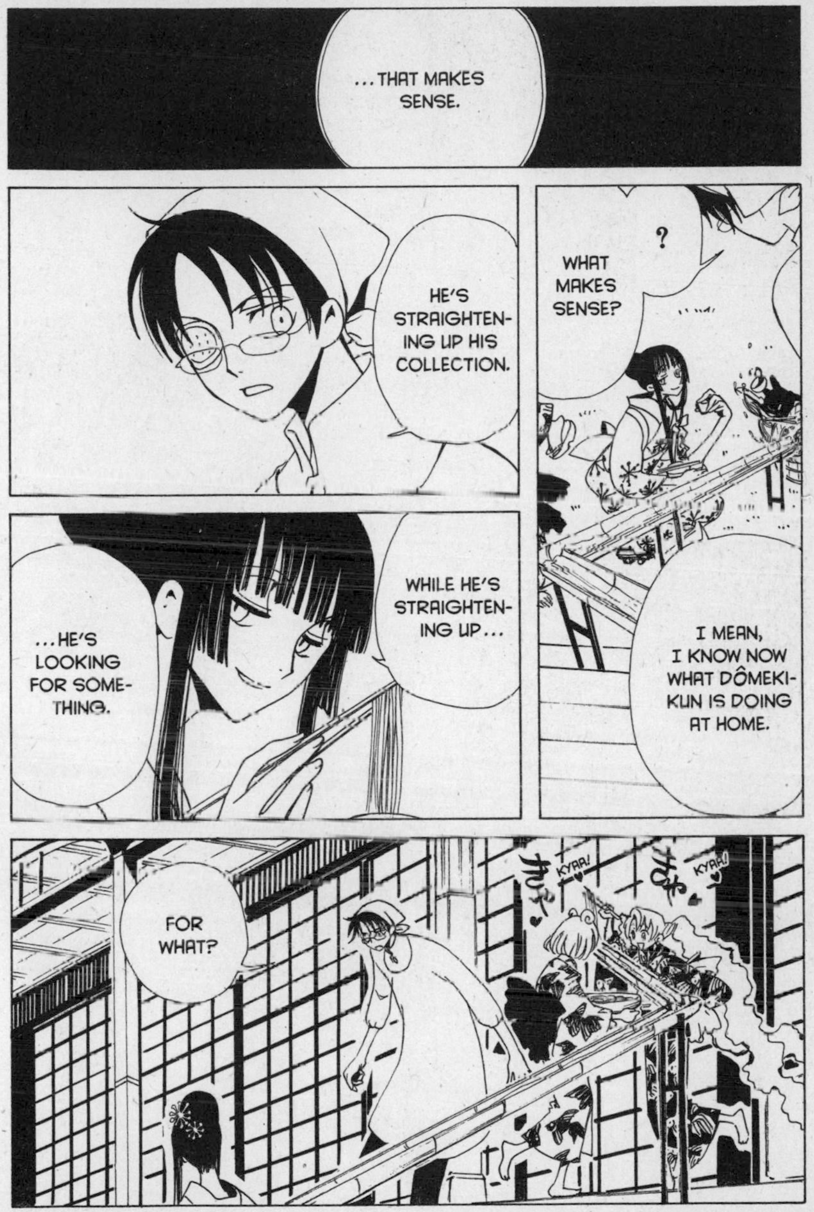
...THAT MAKES SENSE.
?
WHAT MAKES SENSE?
I MEAN, I KNOW NOW WHAT DÔMEKI-KUN IS DOING AT HOME.
HE'S STRAIGHTEN-ING UP HIS COLLECTION.
WHILE HE'S STRAIGHTEN-ING UP...
...HE'S LOOKING FOR SOME-THING.
KYAA!
KYAA!
FOR WHAT?

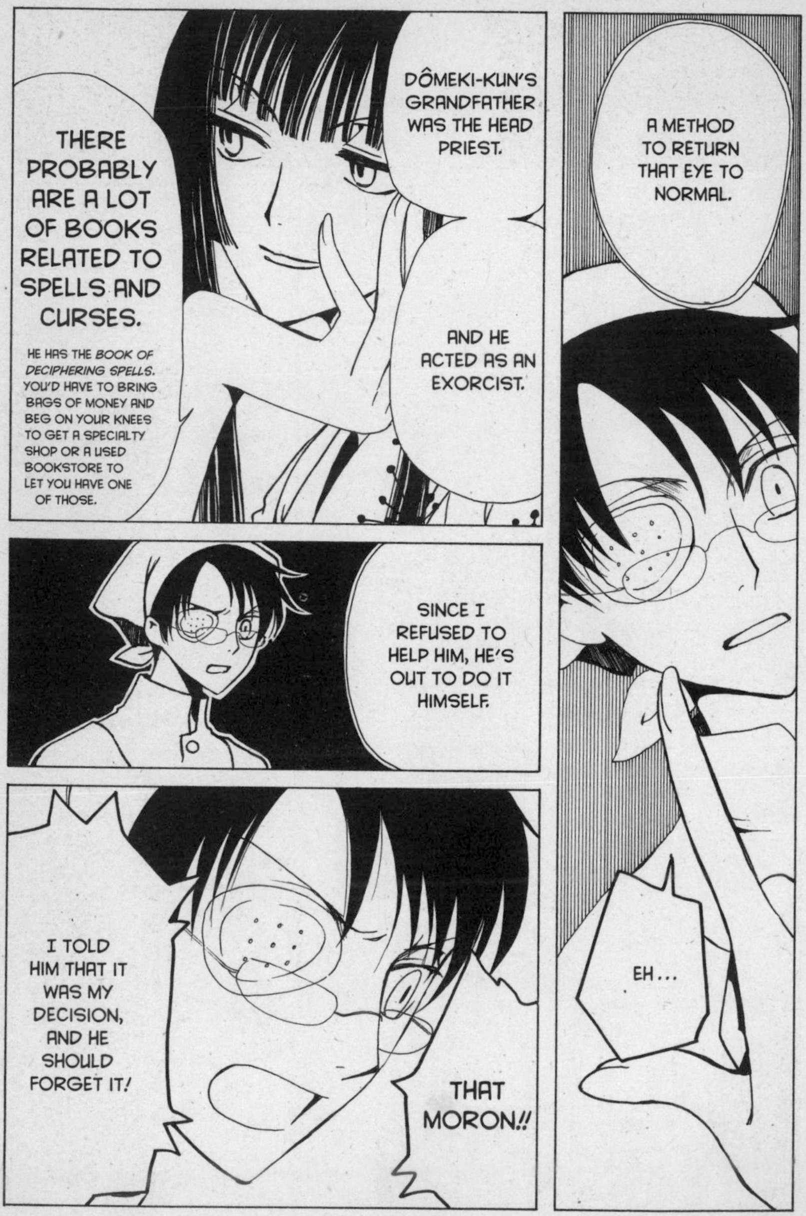
A METHOD TO RETURN THAT EYE TO NORMAL.
EH...
DÔMEKI-KUN'S GRANDFATHER WAS THE HEAD PRIEST.
AND HE ACTED AS AN EXORCIST.
THERE PROBABLY ARE A LOT OF BOOKS RELATED TO SPELLS AND CURSES.
HE HAS THE *BOOK OF DECIPHERING SPELLS*. YOU'D HAVE TO BRING BAGS OF MONEY AND BEG ON YOUR KNEES TO GET A SPECIALTY SHOP OR A USED BOOKSTORE TO LET YOU HAVE ONE OF THOSE.
SINCE I REFUSED TO HELP HIM, HE'S OUT TO DO IT HIMSELF.
I TOLD HIM THAT IT WAS MY DECISION, AND HE SHOULD FORGET IT!
THAT MORON!!

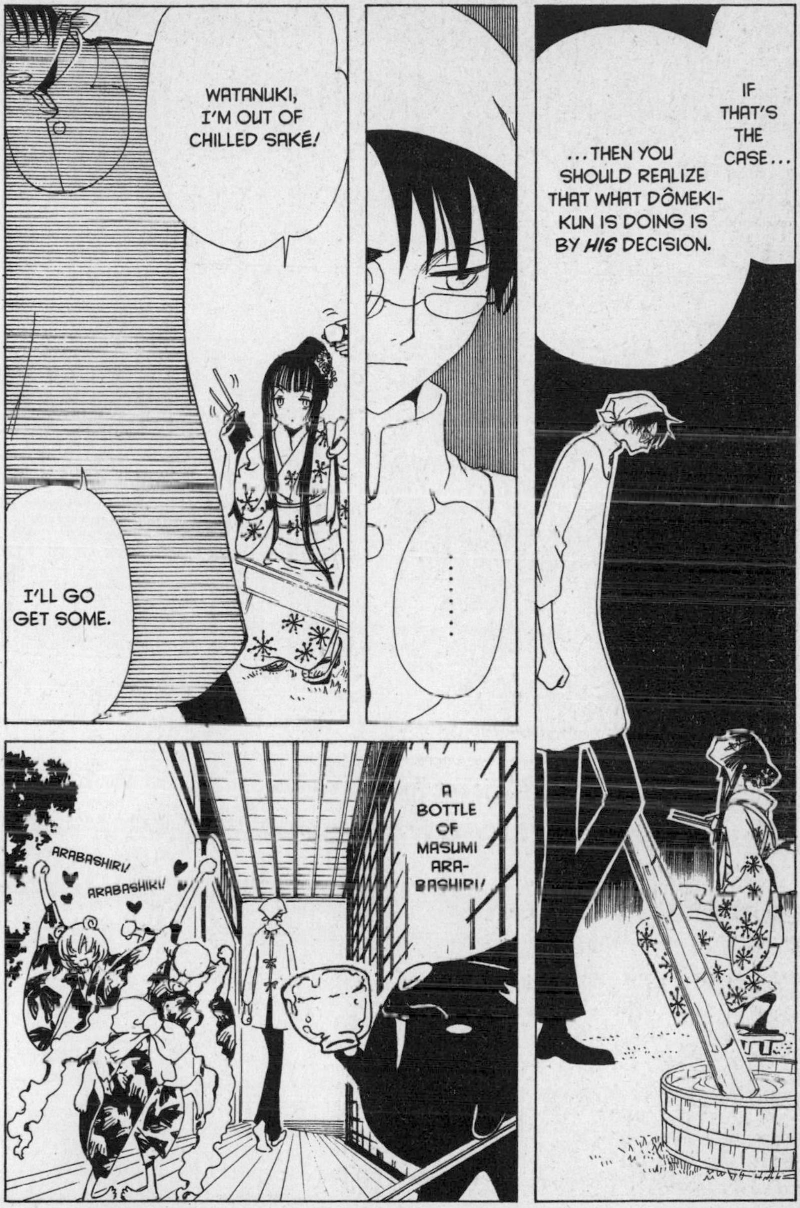
IF THAT'S THE CASE...
...THEN YOU SHOULD REALIZE THAT WHAT DÔMEKI-KUN IS DOING IS BY *HIS* DECISION.
......
WATANUKI, I'M OUT OF CHILLED SAKÉ!
I'LL GO GET SOME.
A BOTTLE OF MASUMI ARA-BASHIRI!
ARABASHIRI!
ARABASHIRI!

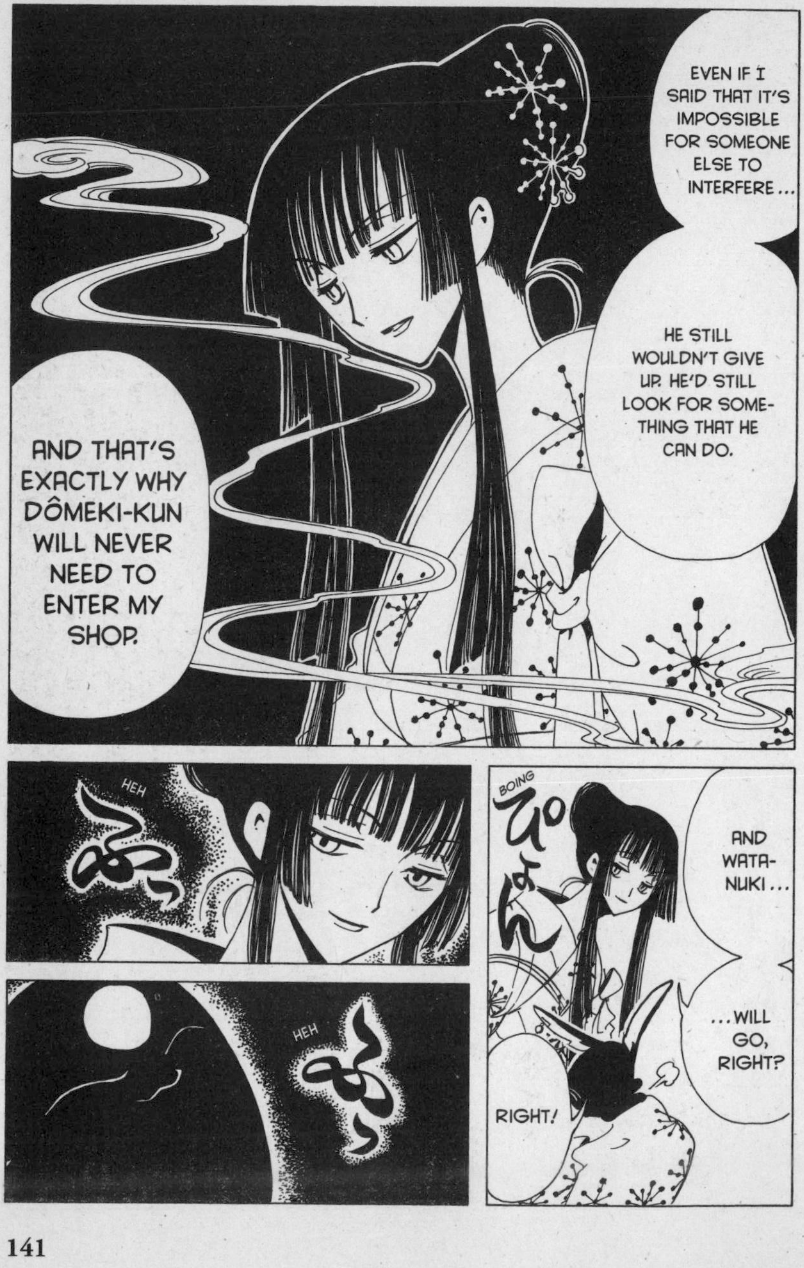
EVEN IF I SAID THAT IT'S IMPOSSIBLE FOR SOMEONE ELSE TO INTERFERE...
HE STILL WOULDN'T GIVE UP. HE'D STILL LOOK FOR SOMETHING THAT HE CAN DO.
AND THAT'S EXACTLY WHY DÔMEKI-KUN WILL NEVER NEED TO ENTER MY SHOP.
BOING
ぴょん
AND WATANUKI...
...WILL GO, RIGHT?
RIGHT!
HEH
ふっ
HEH
ふっ

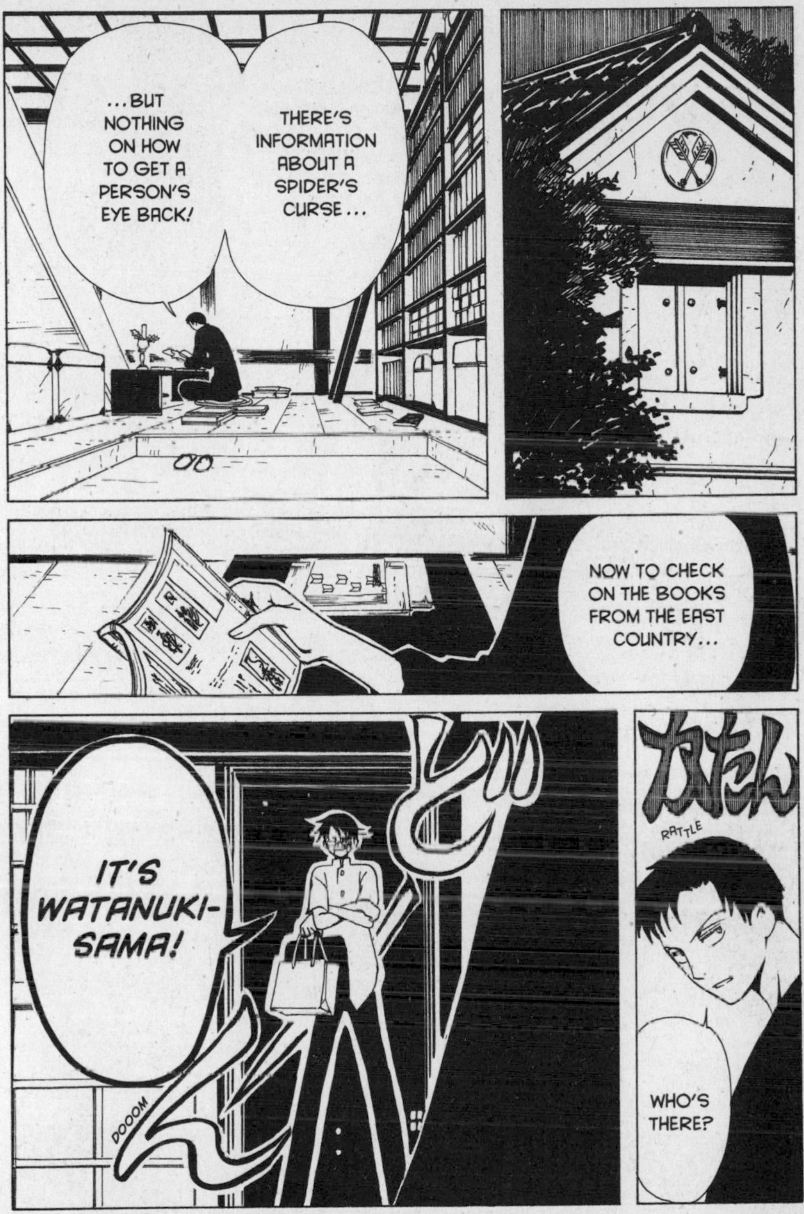
THERE'S INFORMATION ABOUT A SPIDER'S CURSE...
...BUT NOTHING ON HOW TO GET A PERSON'S EYE BACK!
NOW TO CHECK ON THE BOOKS FROM THE EAST COUNTRY...
かたん
RATTLE
WHO'S THERE?
IT'S WATANUKI-SAMA!
DOOOM

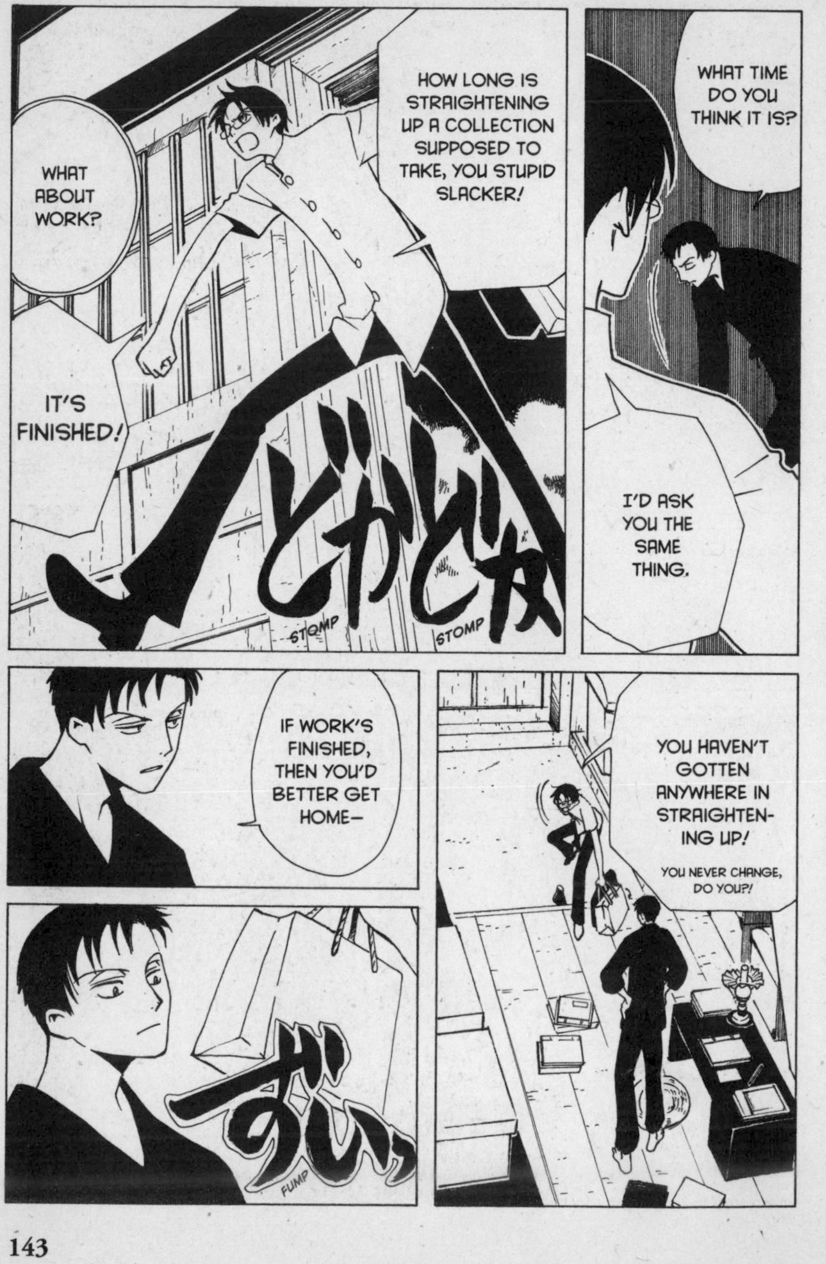
WHAT TIME DO YOU THINK IT IS?
I'D ASK YOU THE SAME THING.
HOW LONG IS STRAIGHTENING UP A COLLECTION SUPPOSED TO TAKE, YOU STUPID SLACKER!
WHAT ABOUT WORK?
IT'S FINISHED!
STOMP
STOMP
YOU HAVEN'T GOTTEN ANYWHERE IN STRAIGHTEN-ING UP!
YOU NEVER CHANGE, DO YOU?!
IF WORK'S FINISHED, THEN YOU'D BETTER GET HOME—
FUMP

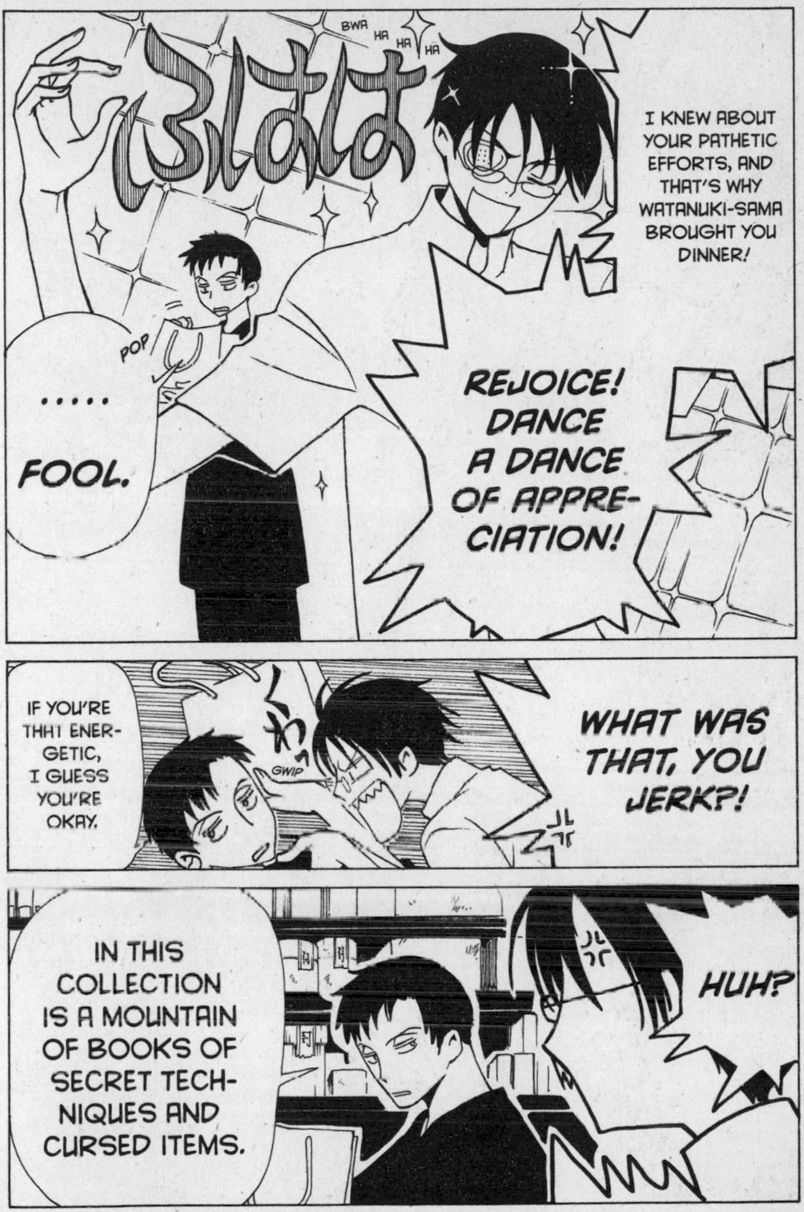
ふはは
BWA HA HA HA
I KNEW ABOUT YOUR PATHETIC EFFORTS, AND THAT'S WHY WATANUKI-SAMA BROUGHT YOU DINNER!
REJOICE! DANCE A DANCE OF APPRE-CIATION!
POP
.....
FOOL.
WHAT WAS THAT, YOU JERK?!
GWIP
IF YOU'RE THAT ENER-GETIC, I GUESS YOU'RE OKAY.
HUH?
IN THIS COLLECTION IS A MOUNTAIN OF BOOKS OF SECRET TECH-NIQUES AND CURSED ITEMS.

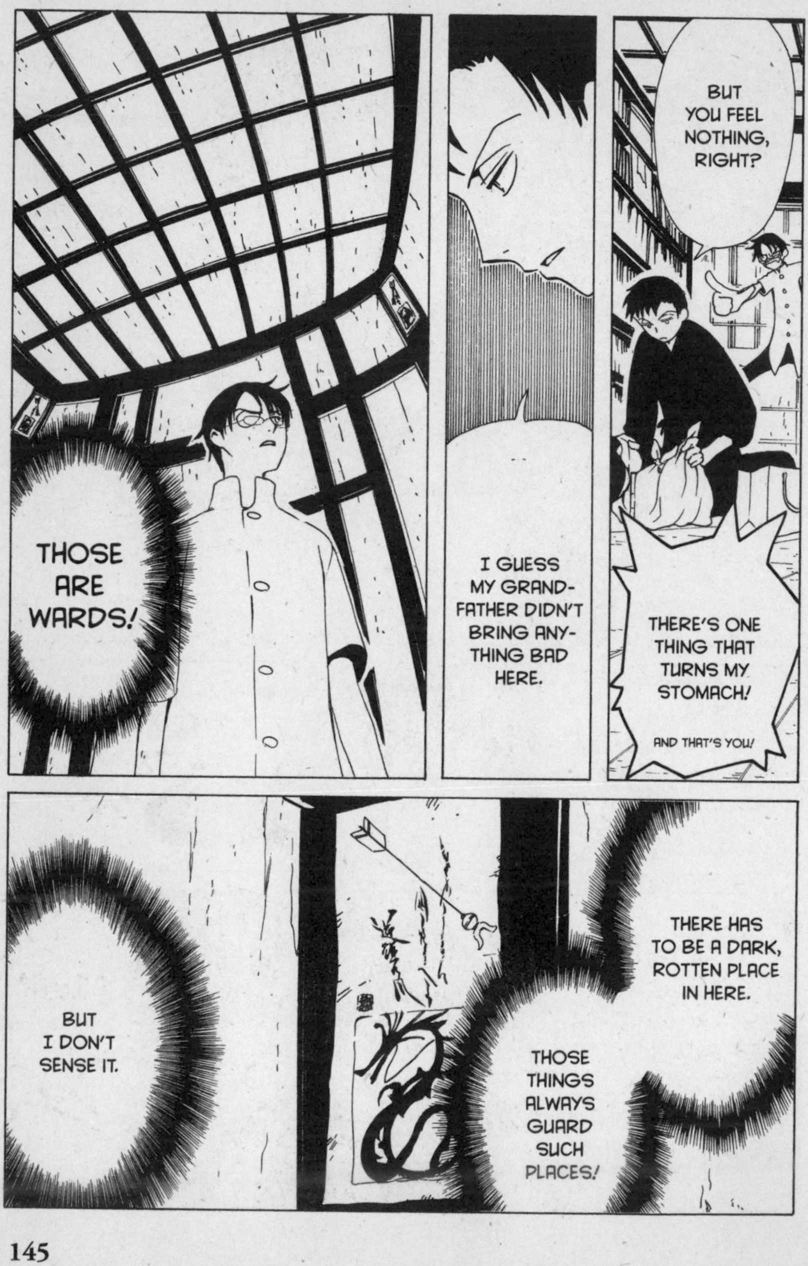
BUT YOU FEEL NOTHING, RIGHT?
THERE'S ONE THING THAT TURNS MY STOMACH!
AND THAT'S YOU!
I GUESS MY GRAND-FATHER DIDN'T BRING ANY-THING BAD HERE.
THOSE ARE WARDS!
THERE HAS TO BE A DARK, ROTTEN PLACE IN HERE.
THOSE THINGS ALWAYS GUARD SUCH PLACES!
BUT I DON'T SENSE IT.

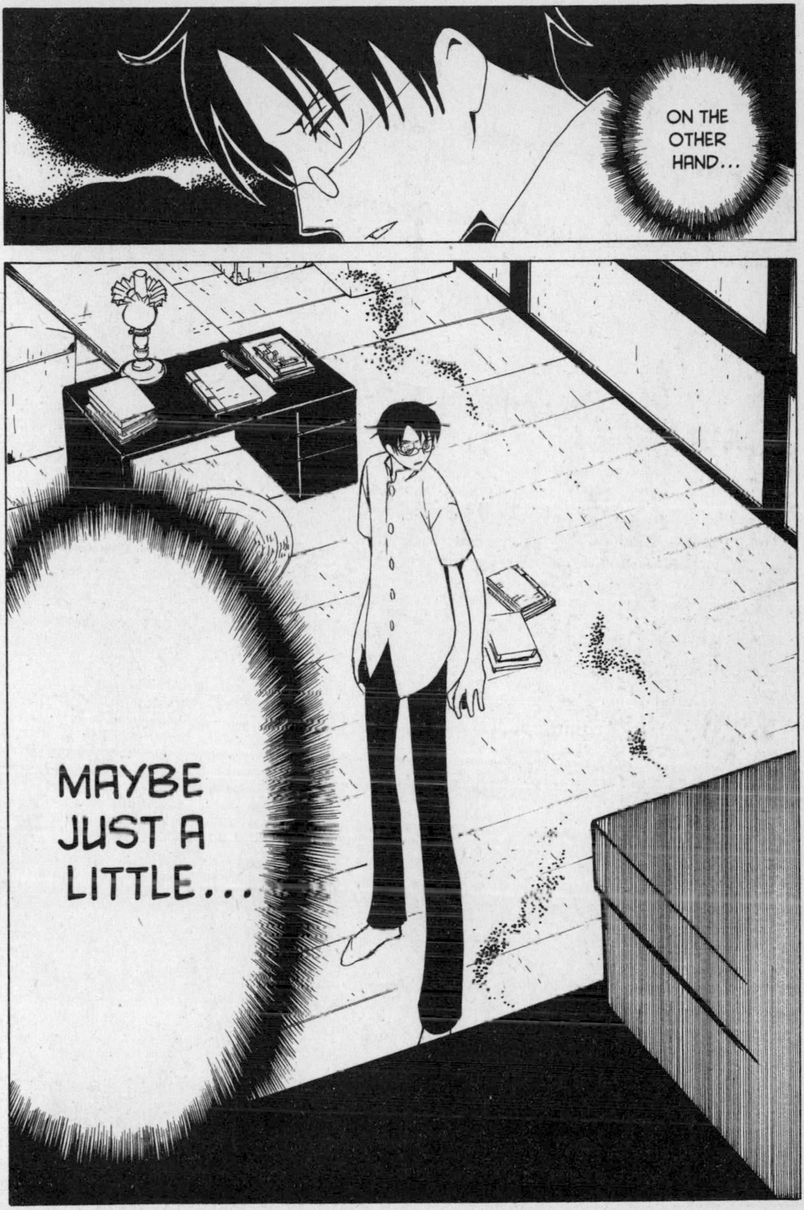
ON THE OTHER HAND...
MAYBE JUST A LITTLE...

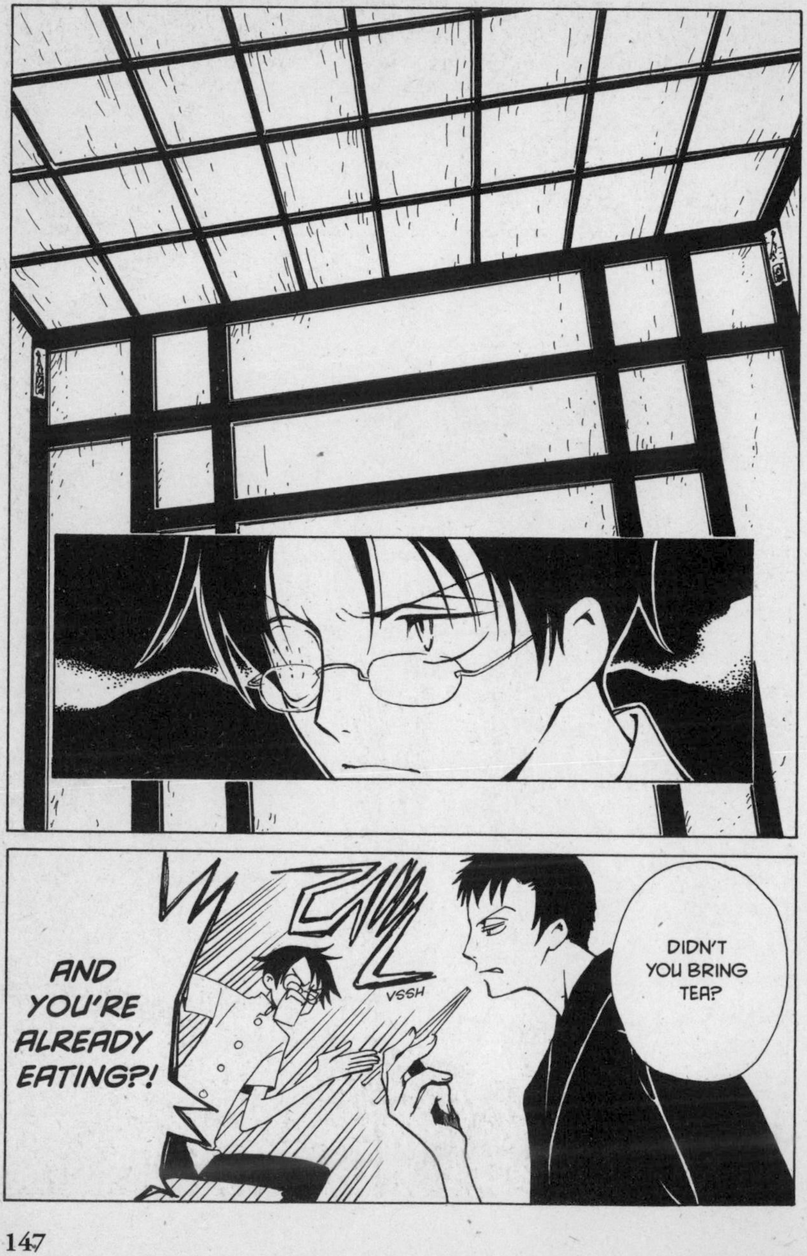
DIDN'T YOU BRING TEA?
VSSH
AND YOU'RE ALREADY EATING?!

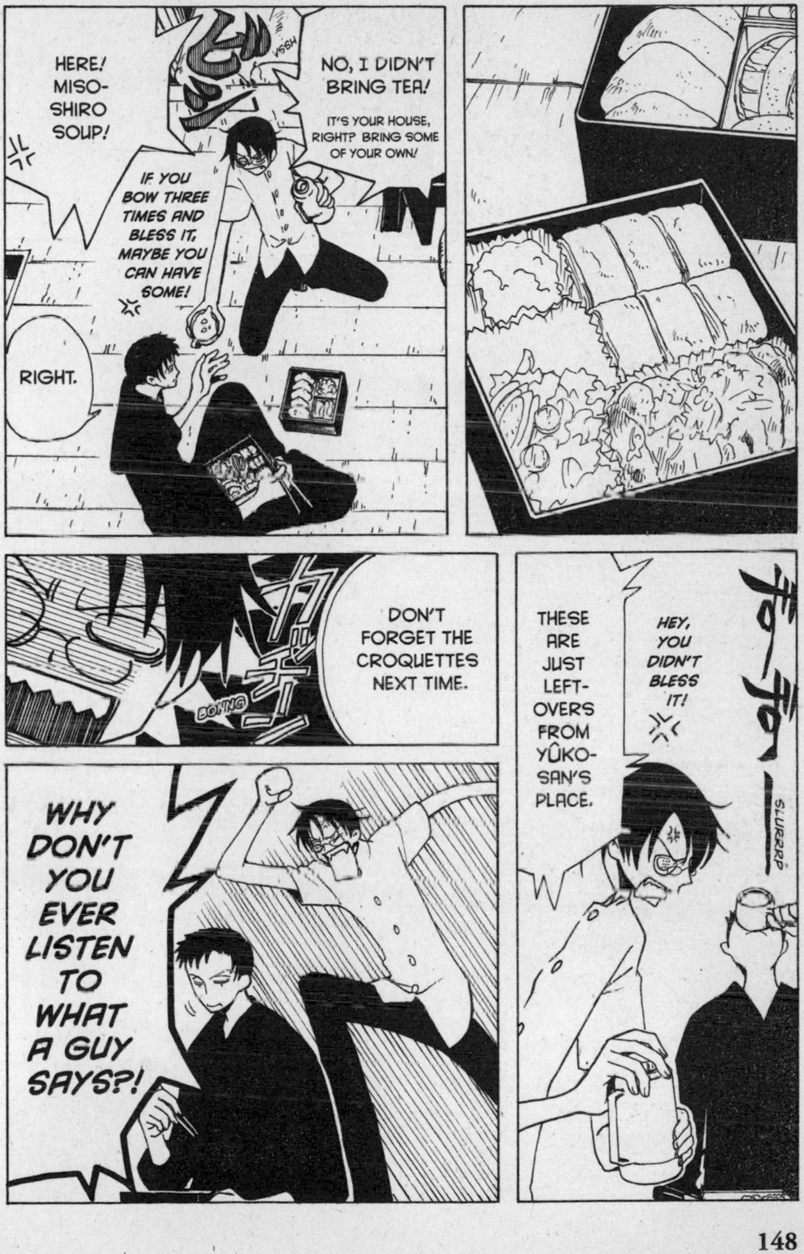
VSSH
NO, I DIDN'T BRING TEA!
IT'S YOUR HOUSE, RIGHT? BRING SOME OF YOUR OWN!
HERE! MISO-SHIRO SOUP!
IF YOU BOW THREE TIMES AND BLESS IT, MAYBE YOU CAN HAVE SOME!
RIGHT.
SLURRRP
HEY, YOU DIDN'T BLESS IT!
THESE ARE JUST LEFT-OVERS FROM YÛKO-SAN'S PLACE.
DON'T FORGET THE CROQUETTES NEXT TIME.
BONNG
WHY DON'T YOU EVER LISTEN TO WHAT A GUY SAYS?!

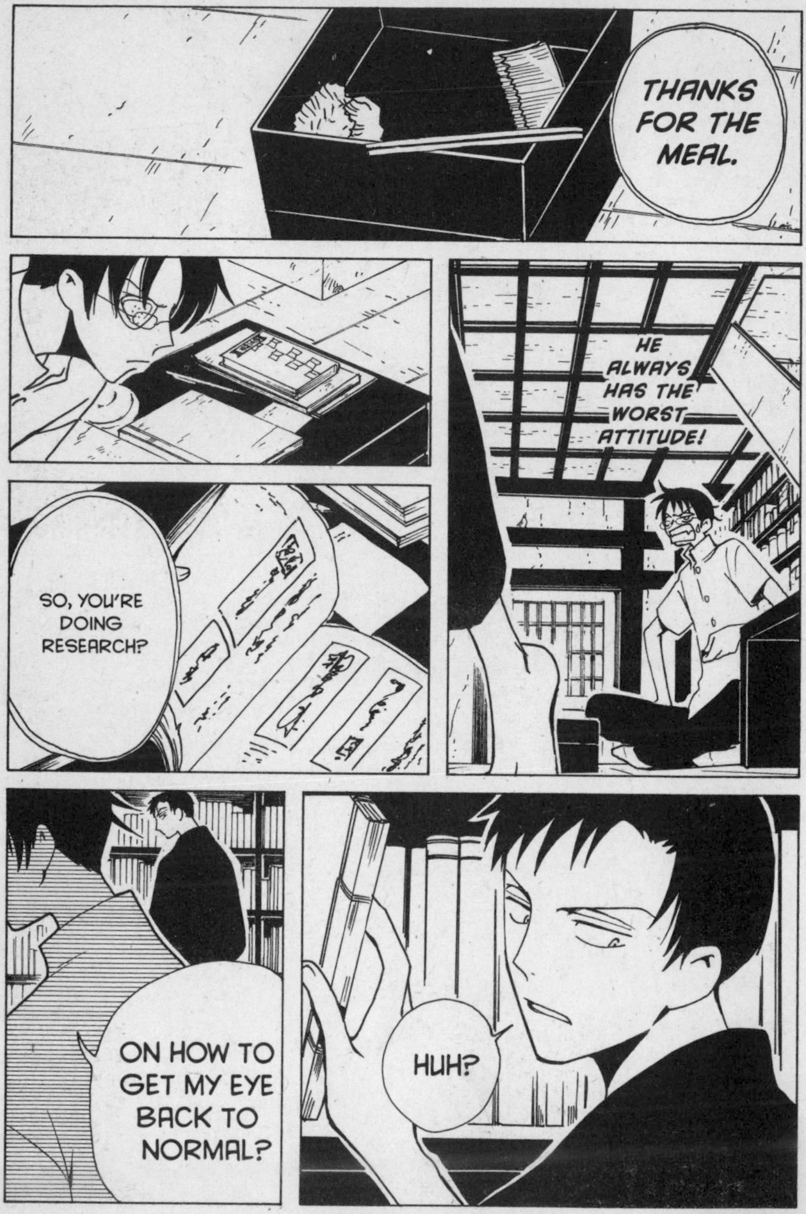
THANKS FOR THE MEAL.
HE ALWAYS HAS THE WORST ATTITUDE!
SO, YOU'RE DOING RESEARCH?
HUH?
ON HOW TO GET MY EYE BACK TO NORMAL?

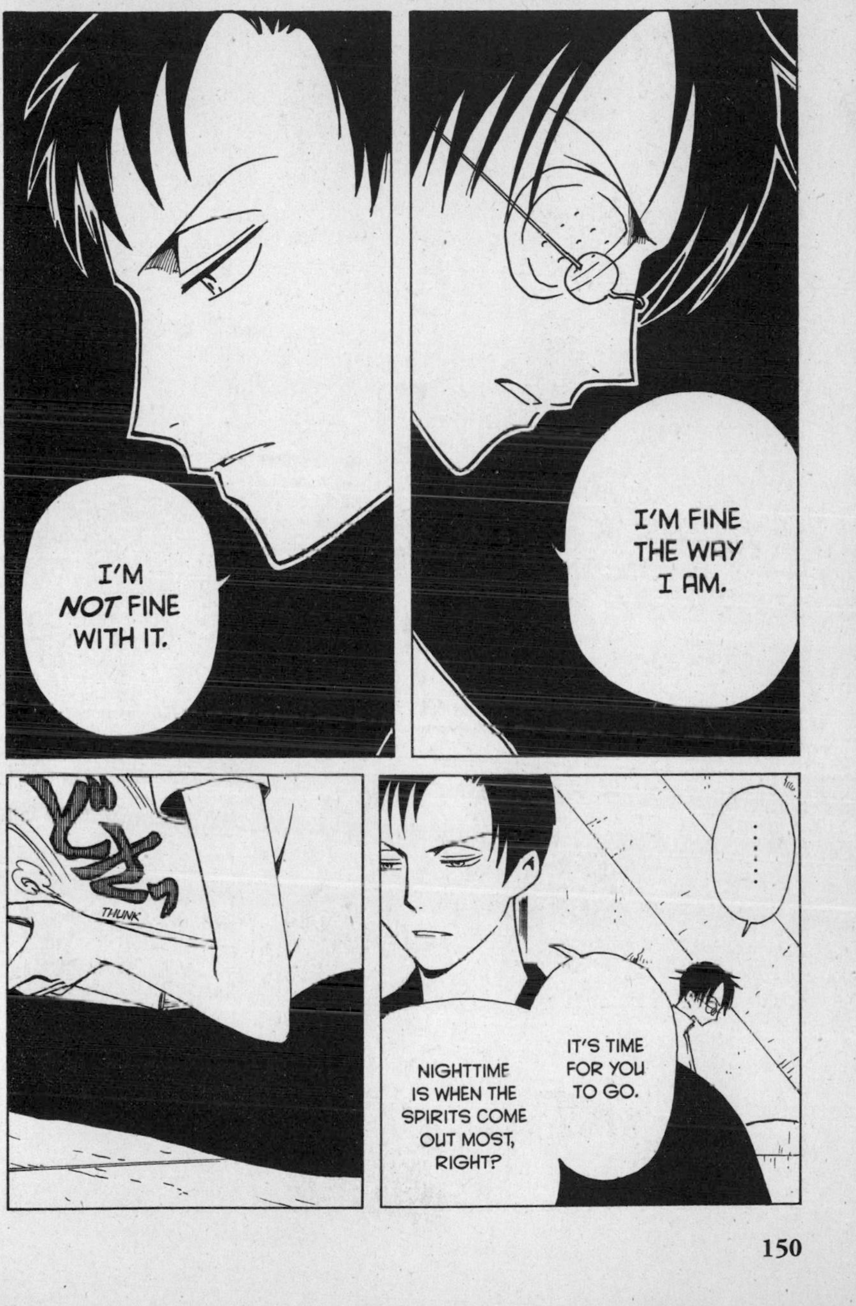
I'M FINE THE WAY I AM.
I'M *NOT* FINE WITH IT.
......
IT'S TIME FOR YOU TO GO.
NIGHTTIME IS WHEN THE SPIRITS COME OUT MOST, RIGHT?
THUNK

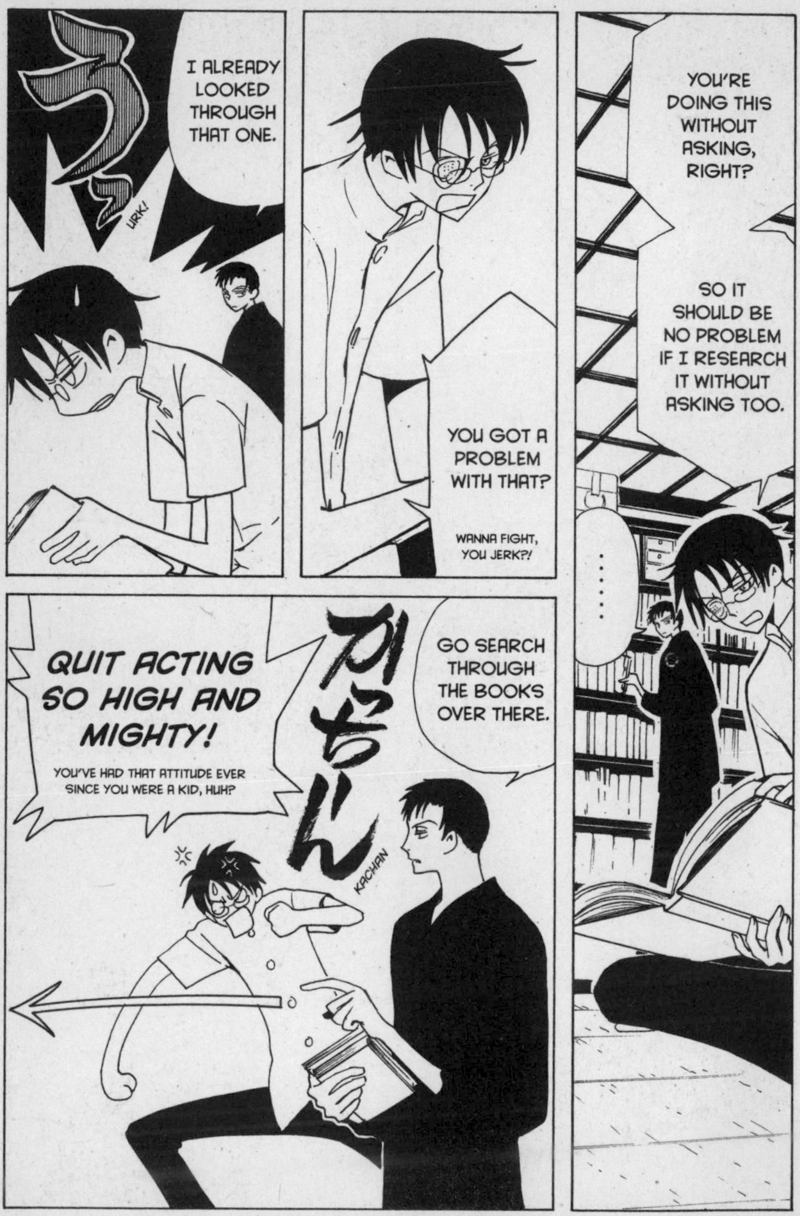
YOU'RE DOING THIS WITHOUT ASKING, RIGHT?
SO IT SHOULD BE NO PROBLEM IF I RESEARCH IT WITHOUT ASKING TOO.
......
YOU GOT A PROBLEM WITH THAT?
WANNA FIGHT, YOU JERK?!
I ALREADY LOOKED THROUGH THAT ONE.
う
URK!
GO SEARCH THROUGH THE BOOKS OVER THERE.
かっちん
KACHAN
QUIT ACTING SO HIGH AND MIGHTY!
YOU'VE HAD THAT ATTITUDE EVER SINCE YOU WERE A KID, HUH?

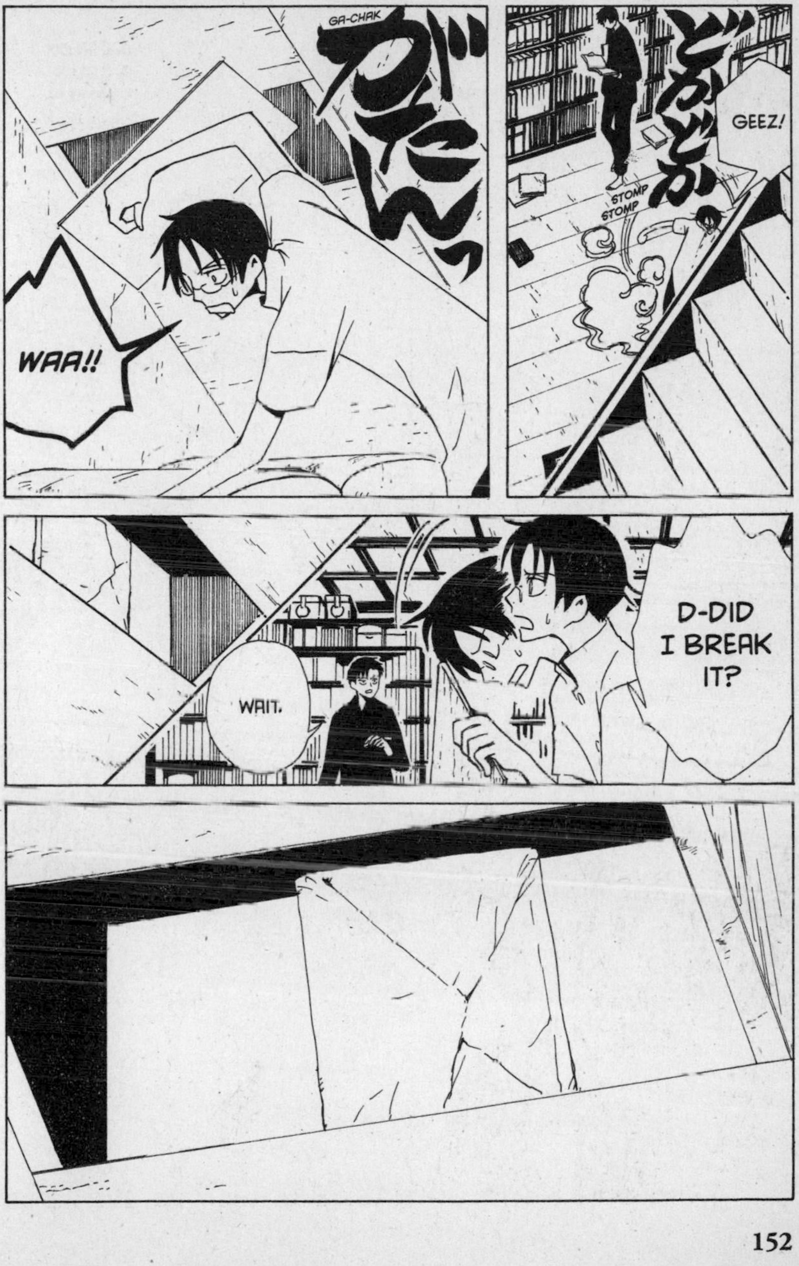
どかどか
GEEZ!
STOMP STOMP
GA-CHAK
がたんっ
WAA!!
D-DID I BREAK IT?
WAIT.

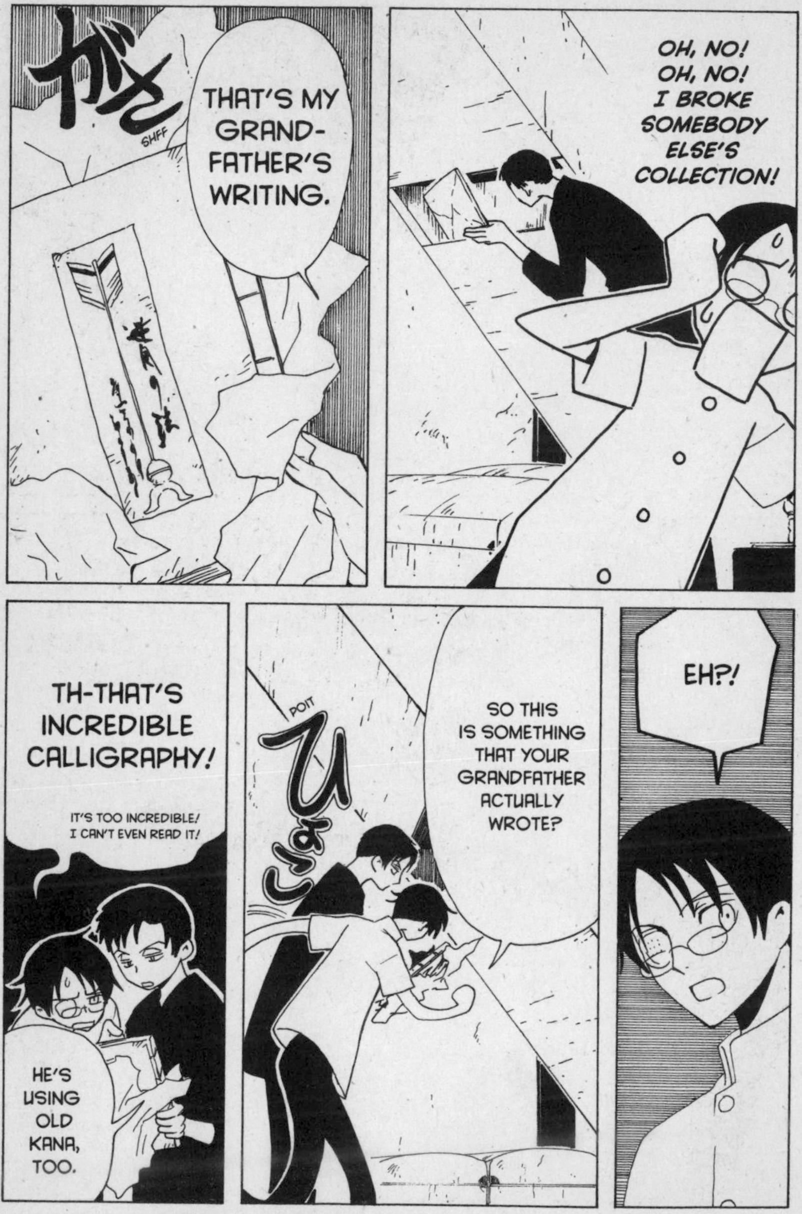
OH, NO! OH, NO! I BROKE SOMEBODY ELSE'S COLLECTION!
SHFF
THAT'S MY GRAND-FATHER'S WRITING.
EH?!
SO THIS IS SOMETHING THAT YOUR GRANDFATHER ACTUALLY WROTE?
POIT
TH-THAT'S INCREDIBLE CALLIGRAPHY!
IT'S TOO INCREDIBLE! I CAN'T EVEN READ IT!
HE'S USING OLD KANA, TOO.

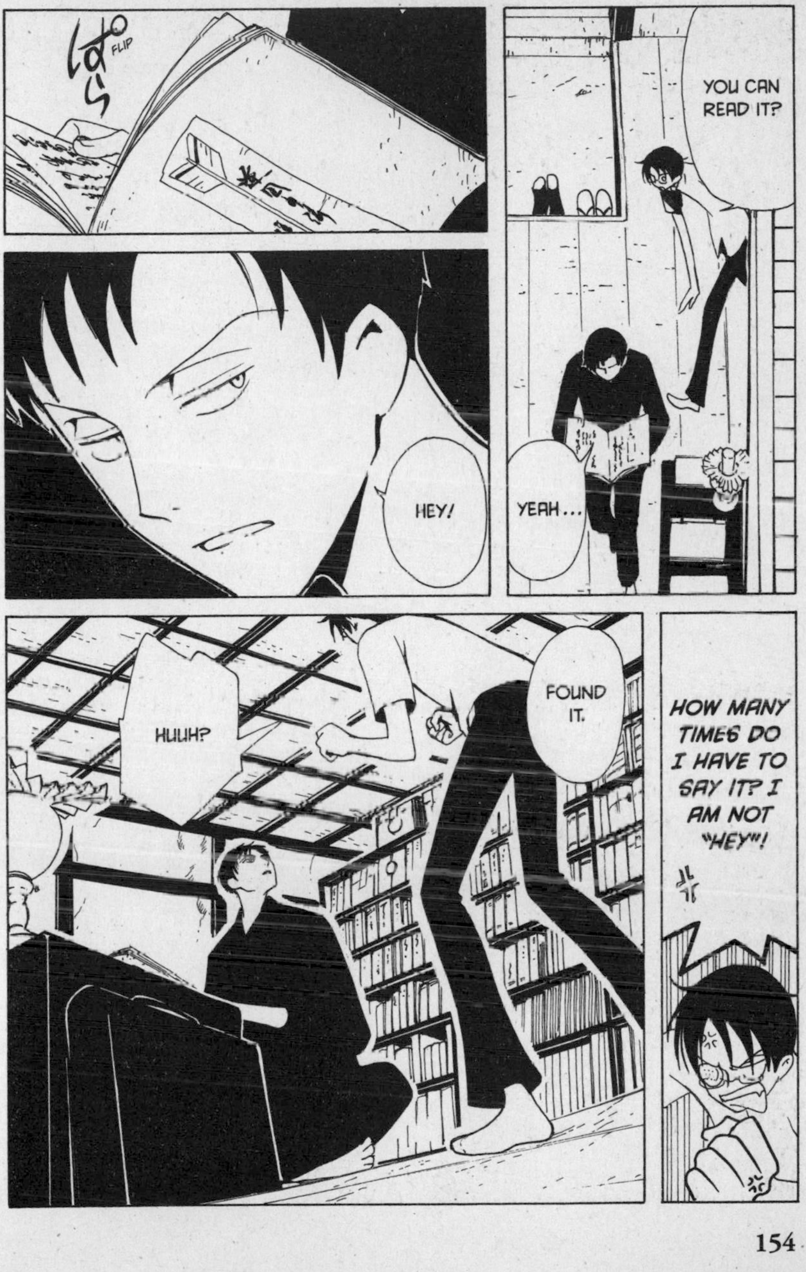
YOU CAN READ IT?
YEAH...
ぱら FLIP
HEY!
HOW MANY TIMES DO I HAVE TO SAY IT? I AM NOT "HEY"!
FOUND IT.
HUUH?

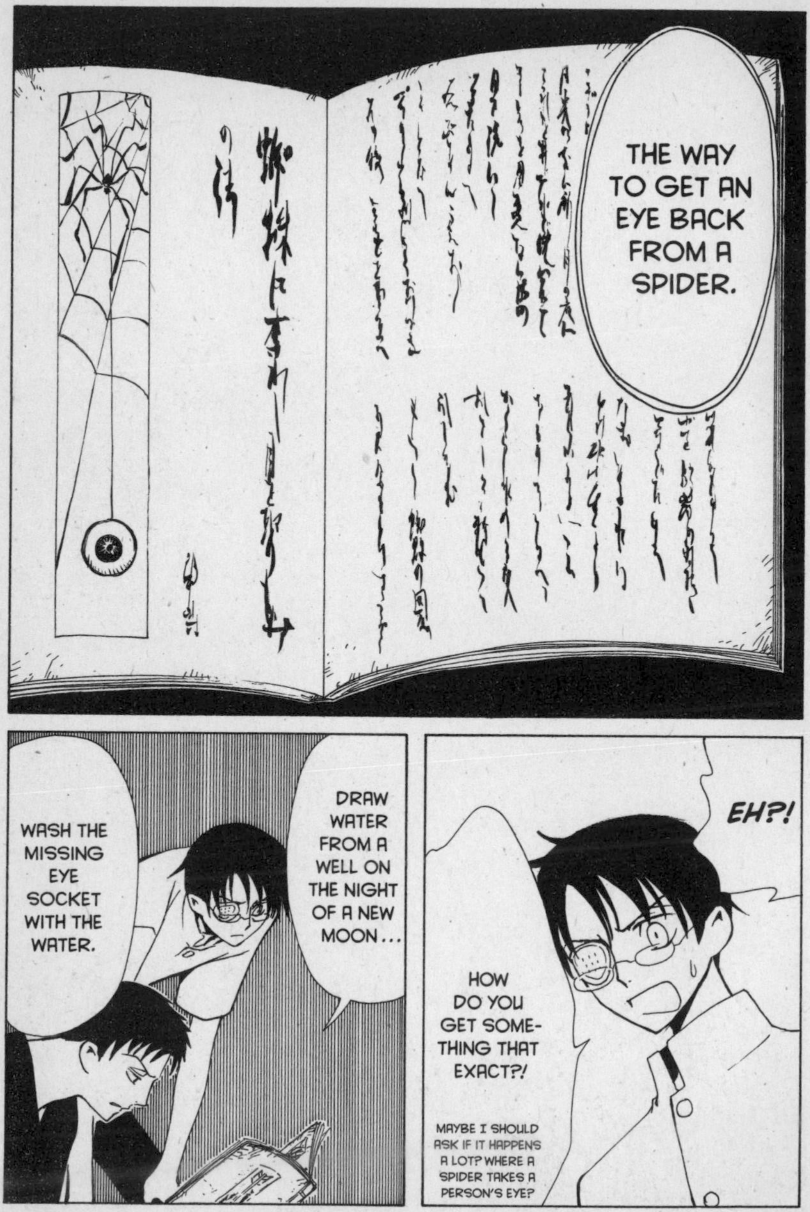
THE WAY TO GET AN EYE BACK FROM A SPIDER.
EH?!
HOW DO YOU GET SOME-THING THAT EXACT?!
MAYBE I SHOULD ASK IF IT HAPPENS A LOT? WHERE A SPIDER TAKES A PERSON'S EYE?
DRAW WATER FROM A WELL ON THE NIGHT OF A NEW MOON...
WASH THE MISSING EYE SOCKET WITH THE WATER.

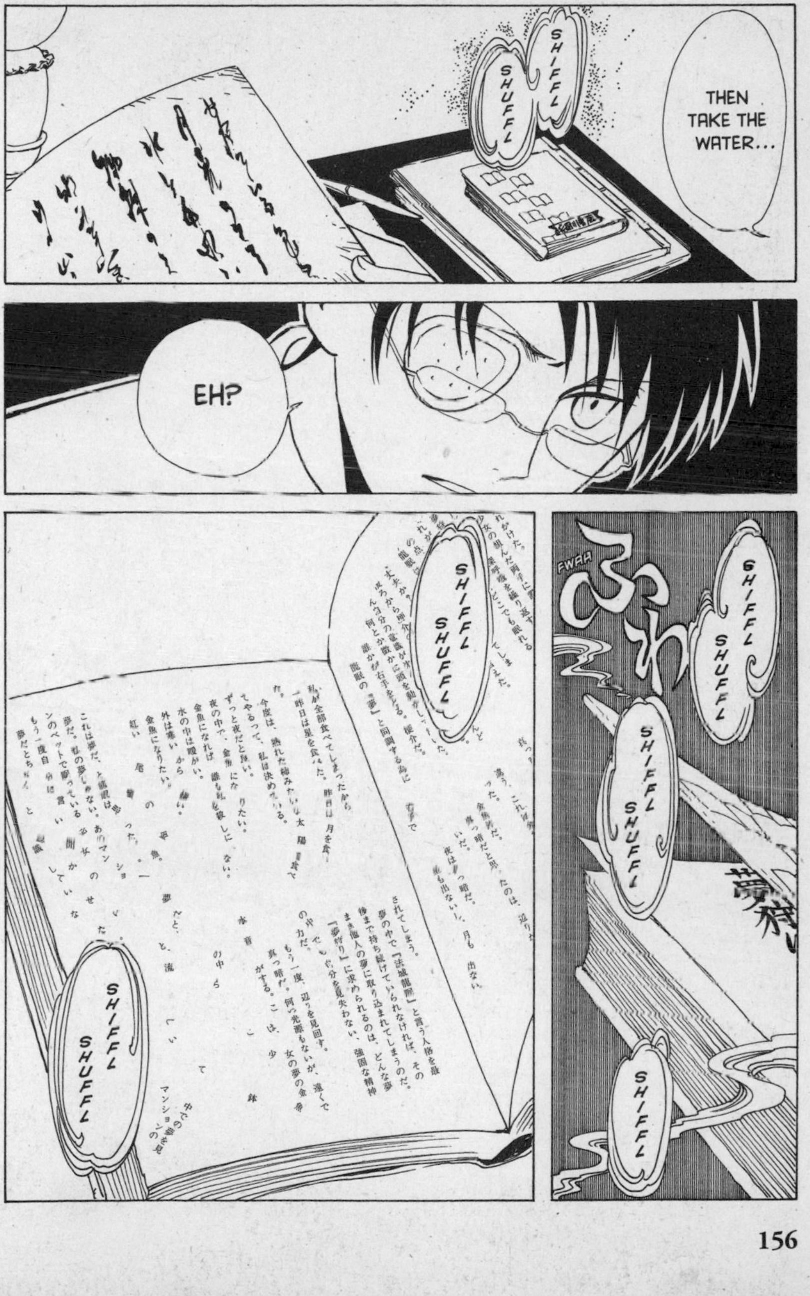
THEN TAKE THE WATER...
SHIFFL SHUFFL
EH?
FWAA
ふわ
SHIFFL SHUFFL
SHIFFL SHUFFL
SHIFFL
SHIFFL SHUFFL
SHIFFL SHUFFL

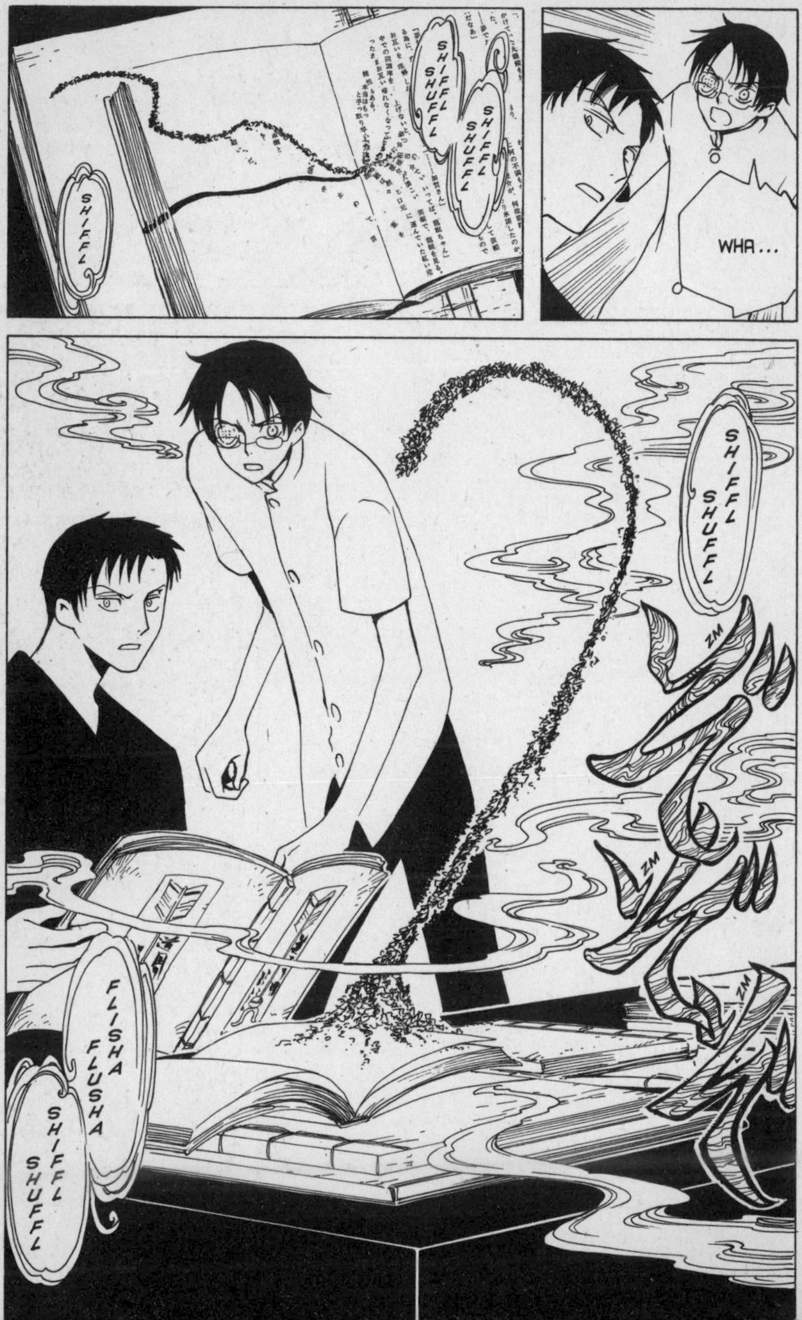
WHA...
SHIFFL SHUFFL
SHIFFL SHUFFL
SHIFFL
SHIFFL SHUFFL
ZM
ZM
ZM
FLISHA FLUSHA
SHIFFL SHUFFL

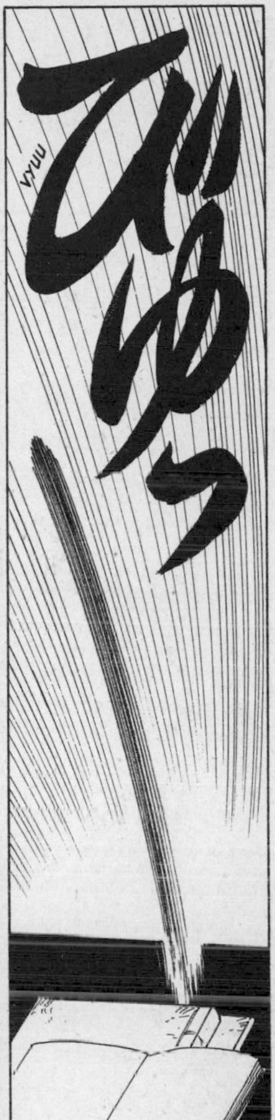
ぴゅう
VYUU

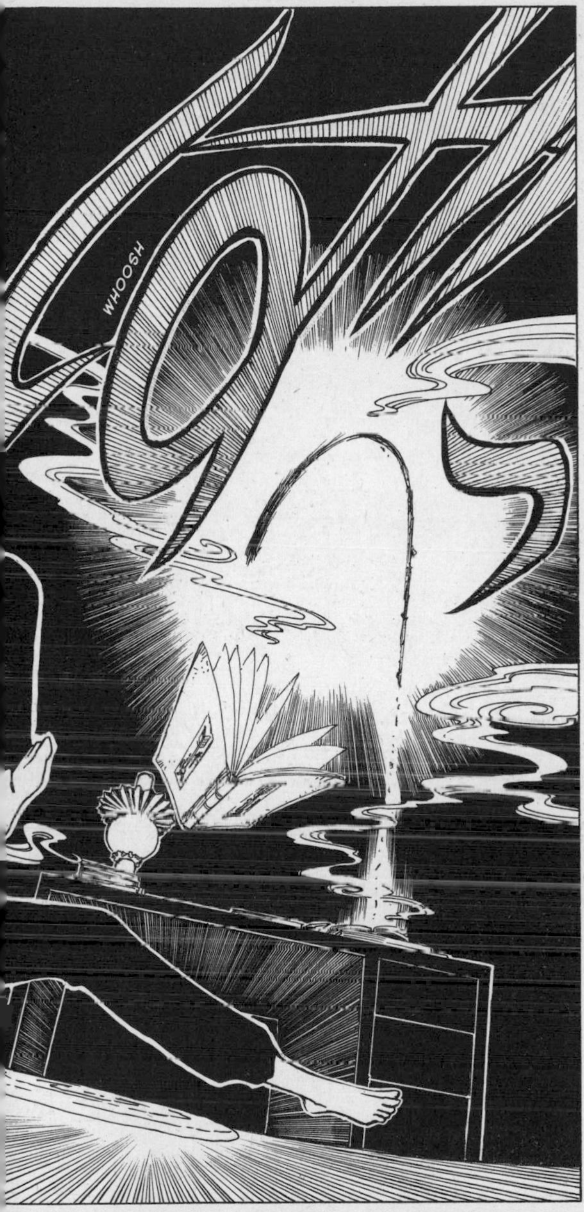
WHOOSH

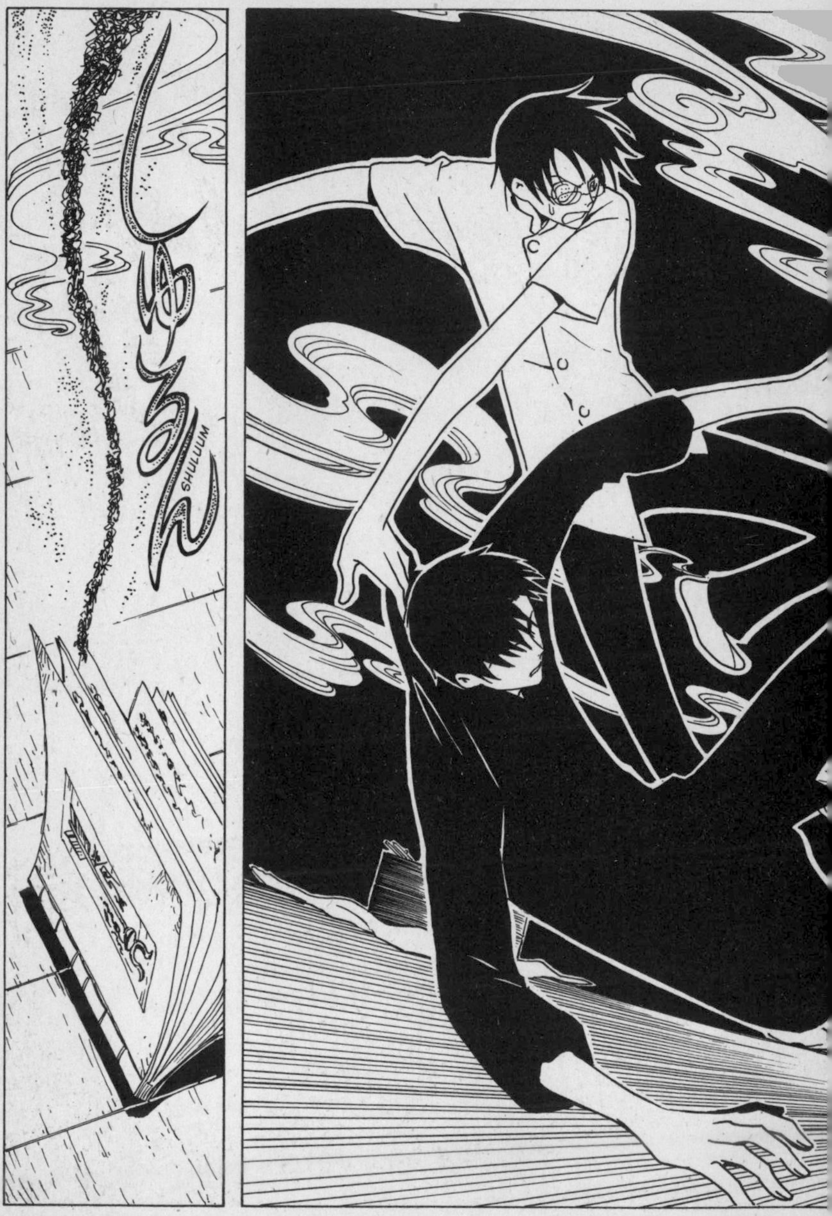
SHULUUM

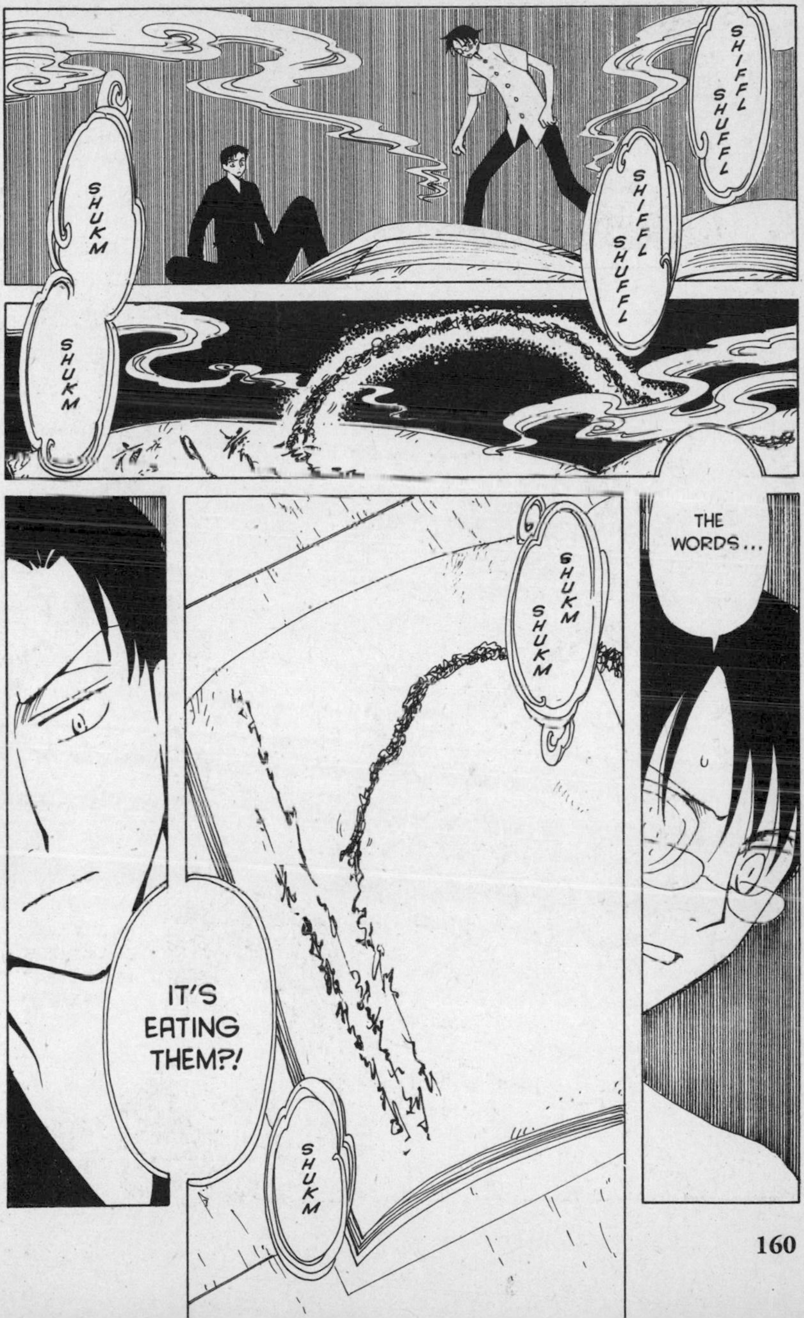
SHIFFL SHUFFL
SHIFFL SHUFFL
SHUKM
SHUKM
THE WORDS...
SHUKM SHUKM
SHUKM
IT'S EATING THEM?!

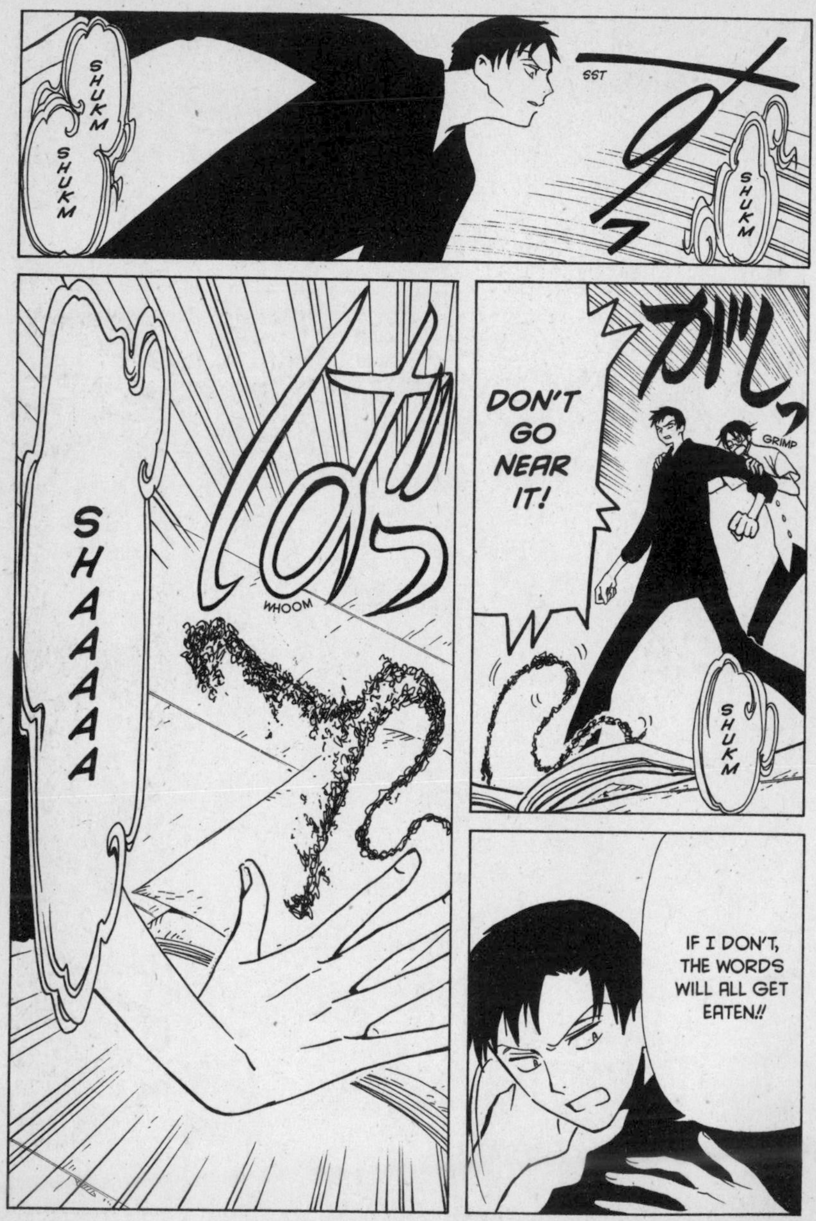

SST
SHUKM
SHUKM
SHUKM
DON'T GO NEAR IT!
GRIMP
SHUKM
IF I DON'T, THE WORDS WILL ALL GET EATEN!!
WHOOM
SHAAAAAA

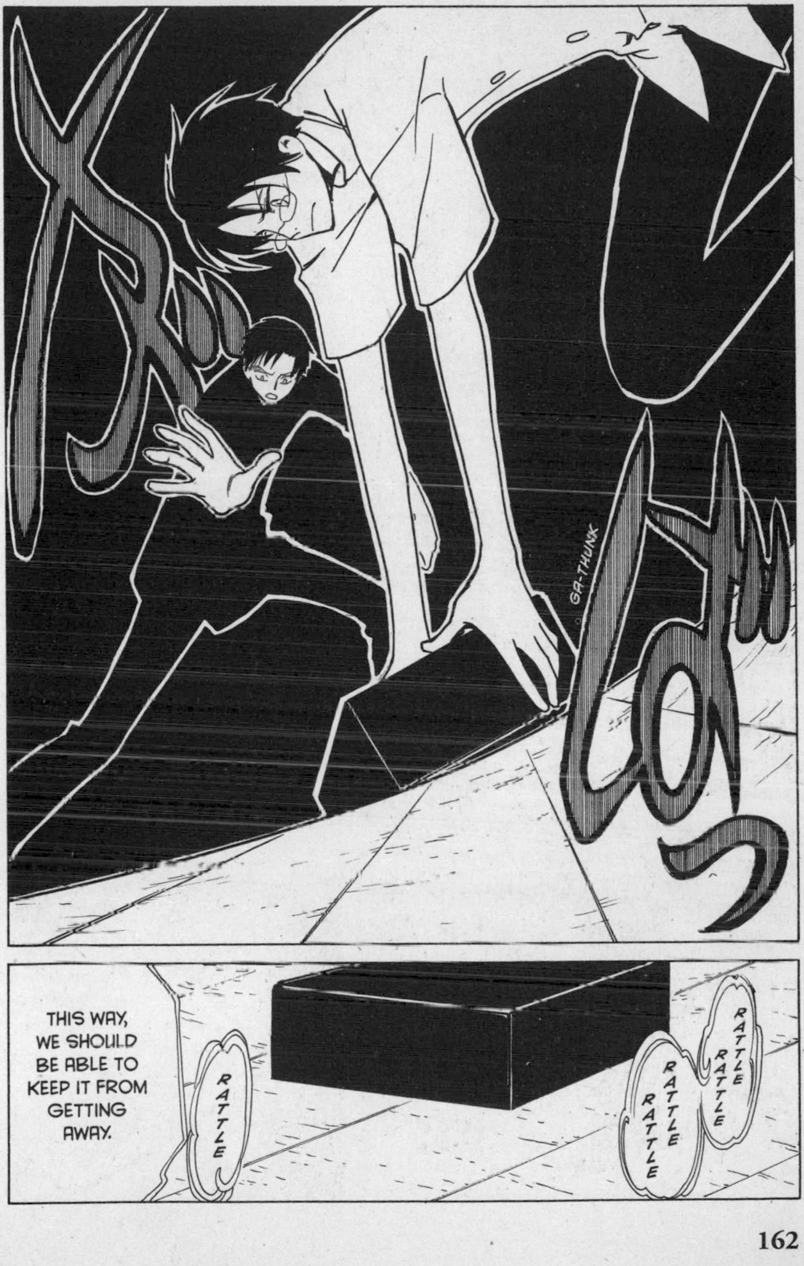
GA-THUNK
RATTLE RATTLE
RATTLE RATTLE
RATTLE
THIS WAY, WE SHOULD BE ABLE TO KEEP IT FROM GETTING AWAY.

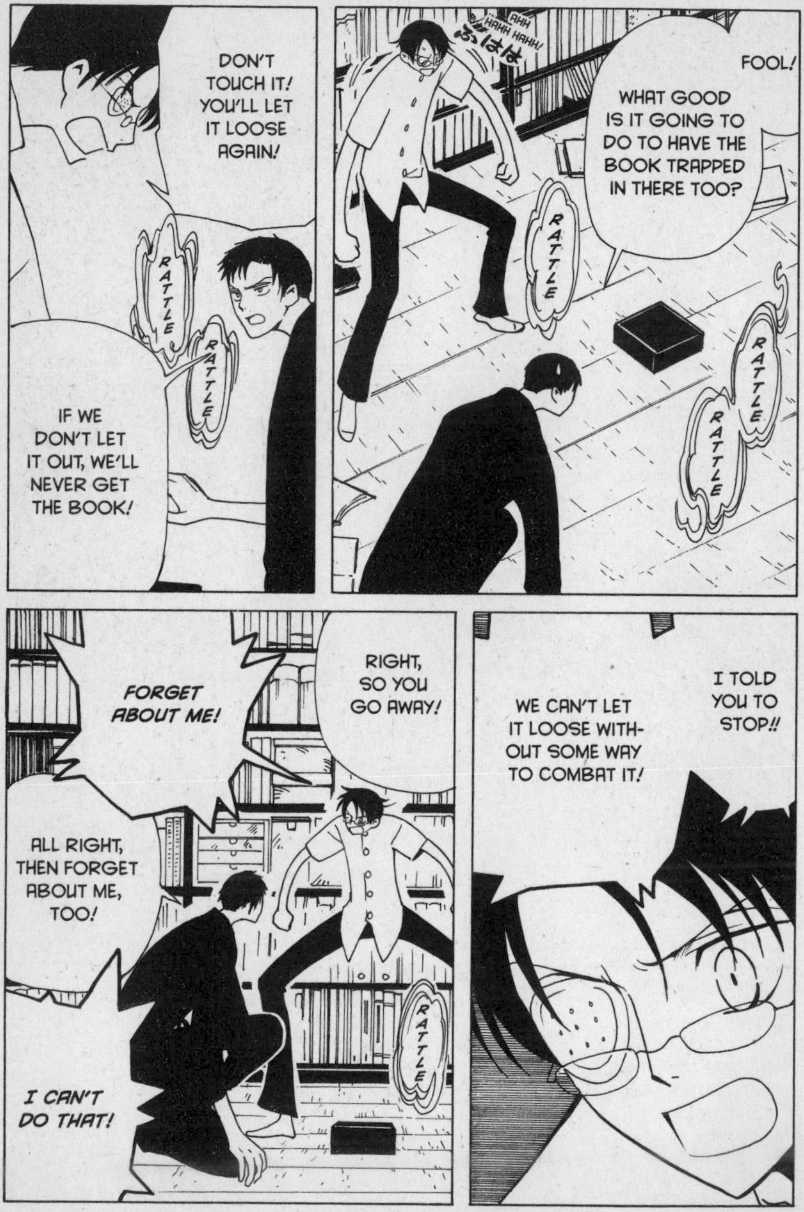
FOOL!
WHAT GOOD IS IT GOING TO DO TO HAVE THE BOOK TRAPPED IN THERE TOO?
AHH HAHH HAHH!
ふはは
RATTLE
RATTLE
RATTLE
DON'T TOUCH IT! YOU'LL LET IT LOOSE AGAIN!
RATTLE
RATTLE
IF WE DON'T LET IT OUT, WE'LL NEVER GET THE BOOK!
I TOLD YOU TO STOP!!
WE CAN'T LET IT LOOSE WITHOUT SOME WAY TO COMBAT IT!
RIGHT, SO YOU GO AWAY!
FORGET ABOUT ME!
ALL RIGHT, THEN FORGET ABOUT ME, TOO!
RATTLE
I CAN'T DO THAT!

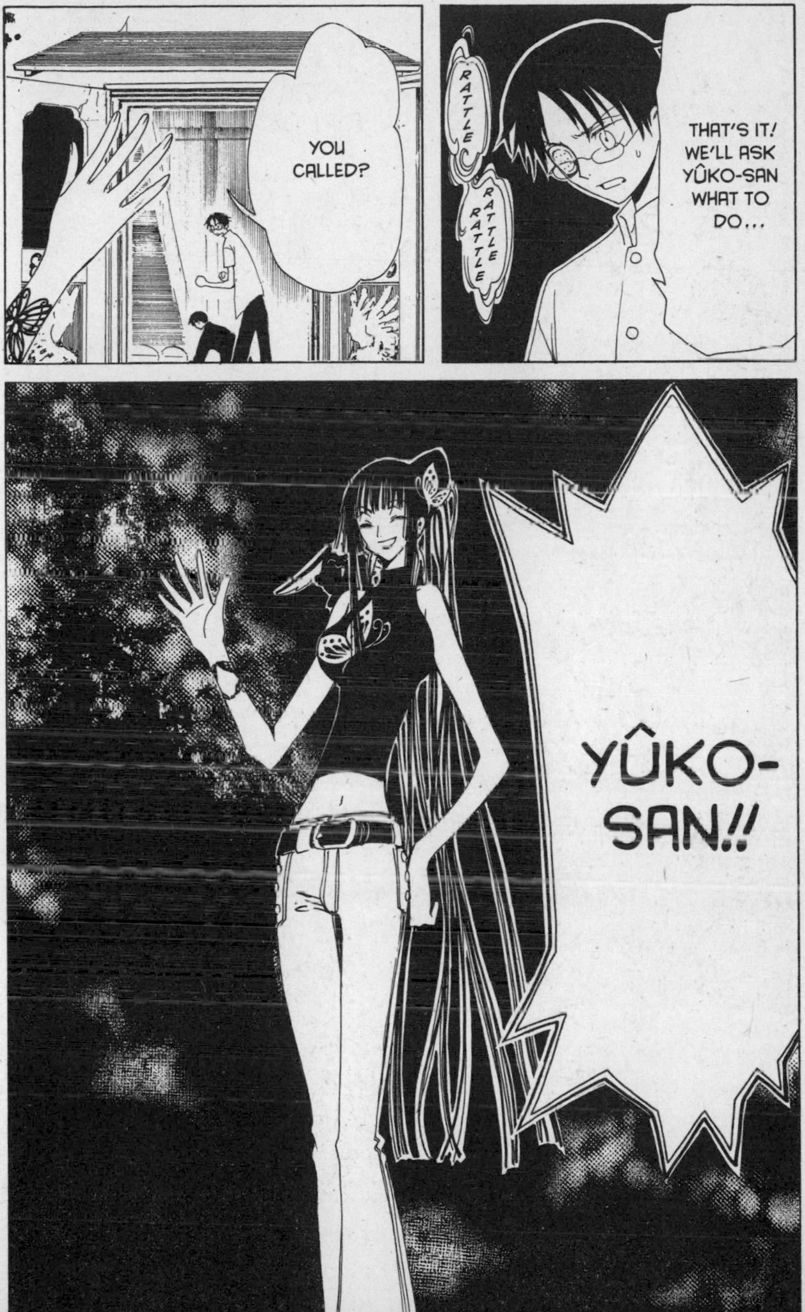
THAT'S IT! WE'LL ASK YÛKO-SAN WHAT TO DO...
RATTLE
RATTLE RATTLE
YOU CALLED?
YÛKO-SAN!!

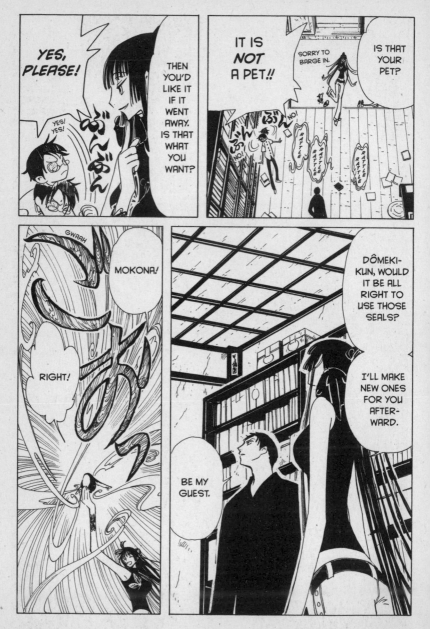

YES, PLEASE!

THEN YOU'D LIKE IT IF IT WENT AWAY. IS THAT WHAT YOU WANT?

YES! YES!

IT IS *NOT* A PET!!

SORRY TO BARGE IN.

IS THAT YOUR PET?

NO! NO!

GWAAH

MOKONA!

RIGHT!

DÔMEKI-KUN, WOULD IT BE ALL RIGHT TO USE THOSE SEALS?

I'LL MAKE NEW ONES FOR YOU AFTER-WARD.

BE MY GUEST.

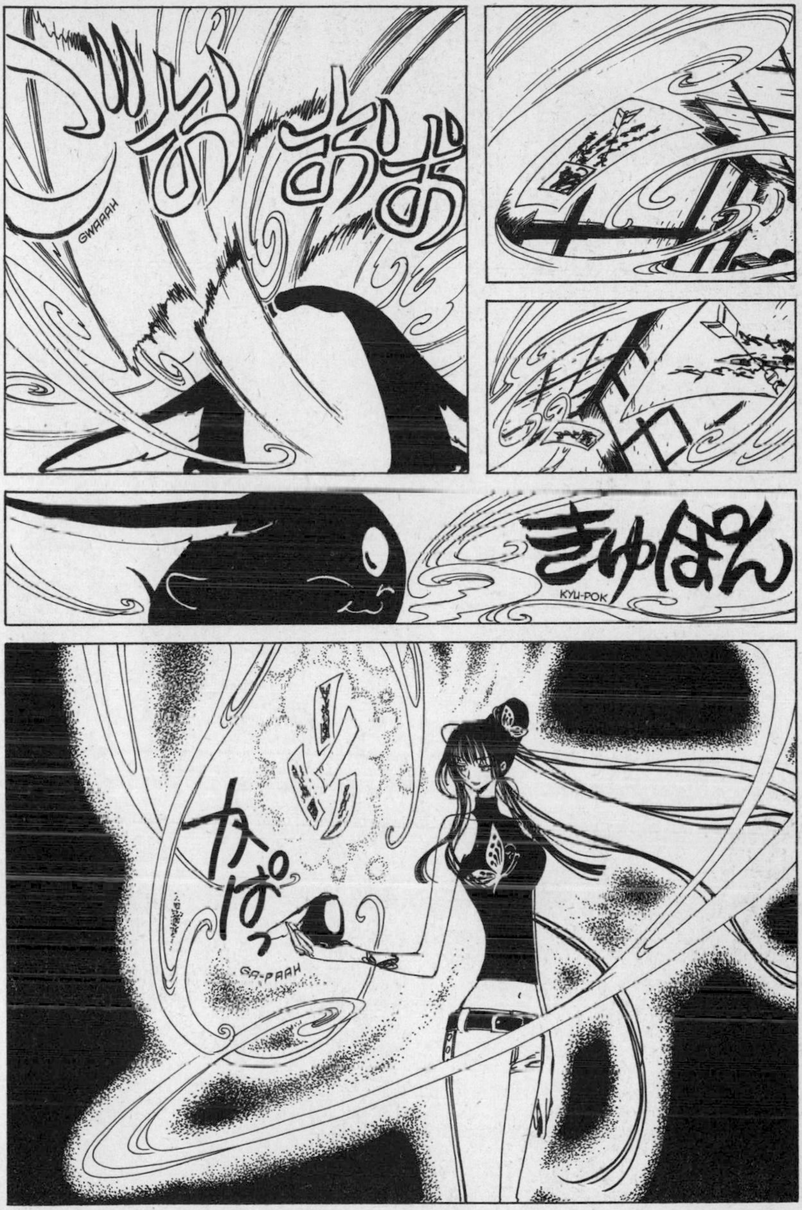
GWAAAH
きゅぽん
KYU-POK
かぱっ
GA-PAAH

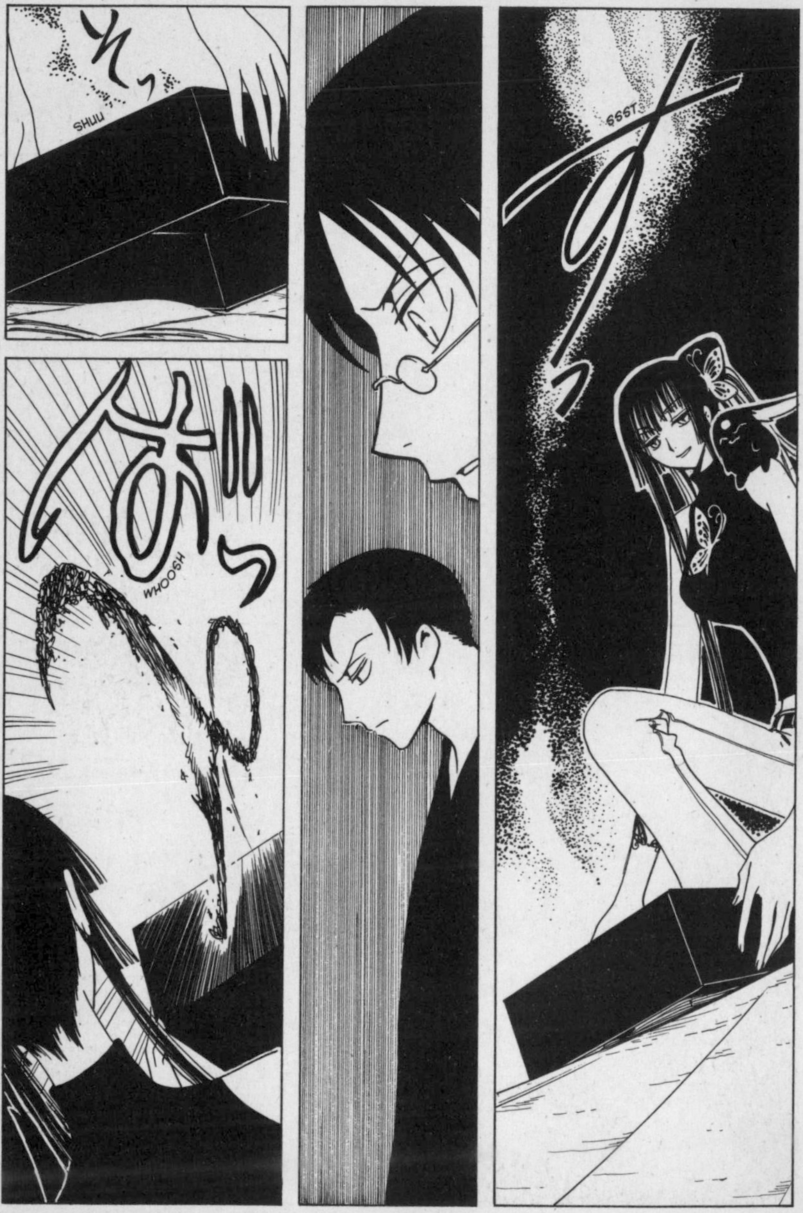
SSST
SHUU
WHOOSH

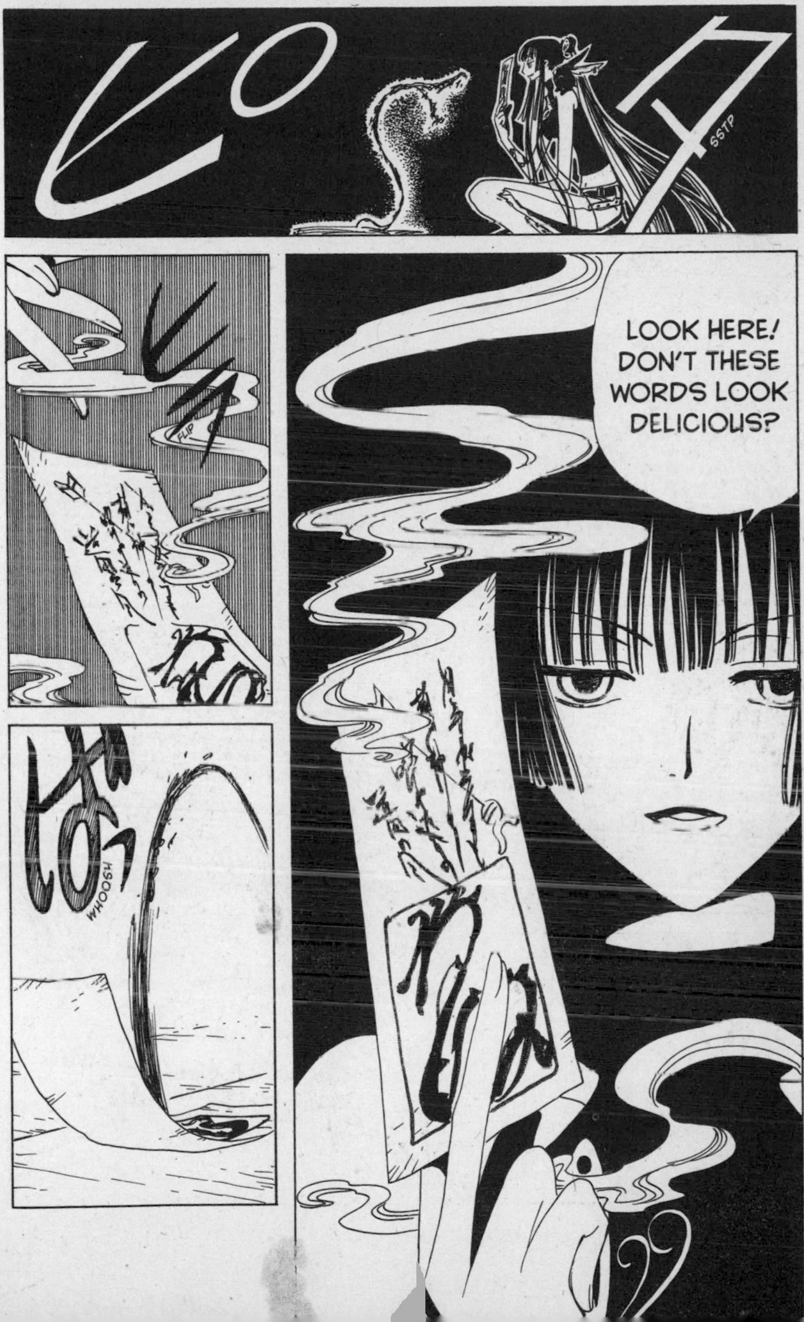
SSTP
LOOK HERE! DON'T THESE WORDS LOOK DELICIOUS?
FLIP
WHOOSH

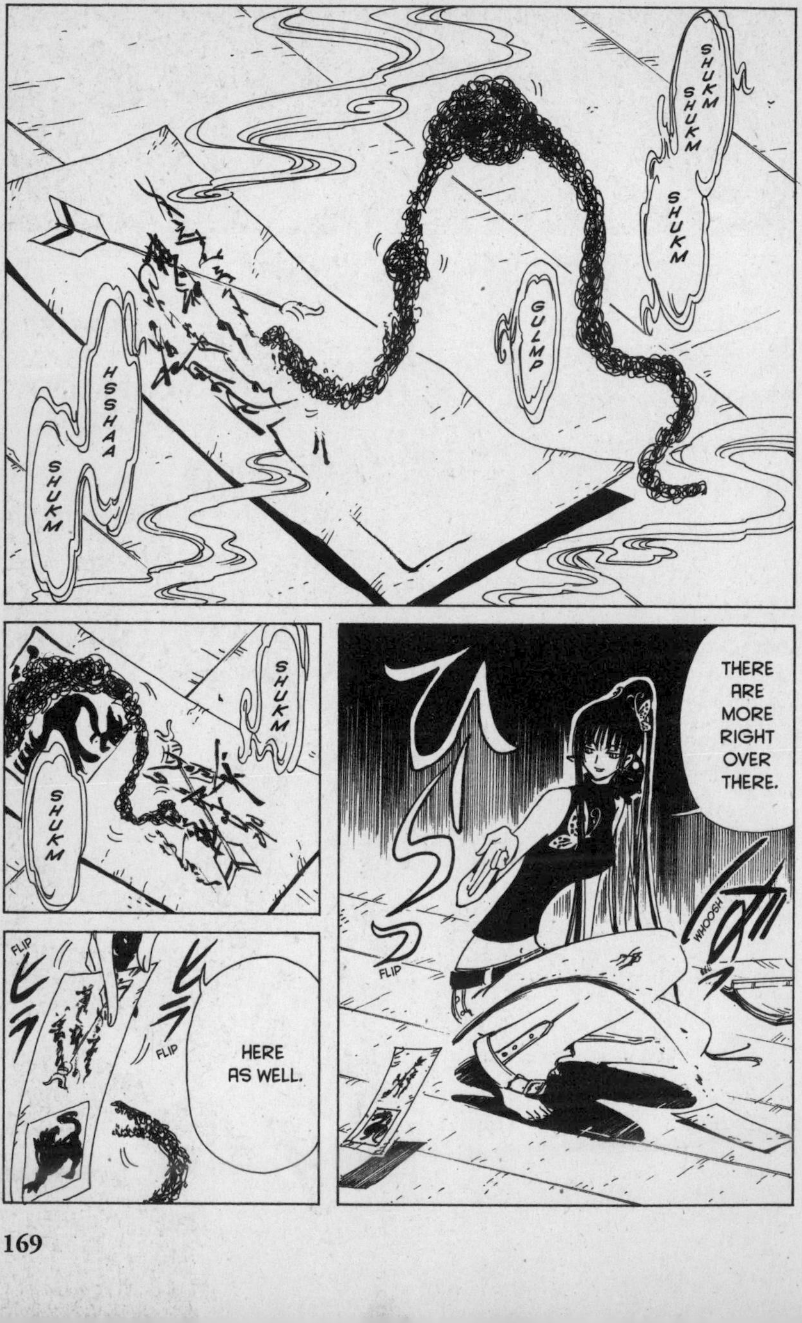
SHUKM
SHUKM
SHUKM
GULMP
HSSHAA
SHUKM
THERE ARE MORE RIGHT OVER THERE.
WHOOSH
FLIP
SHUKM
SHUKM
FLIP
FLIP
HERE AS WELL.

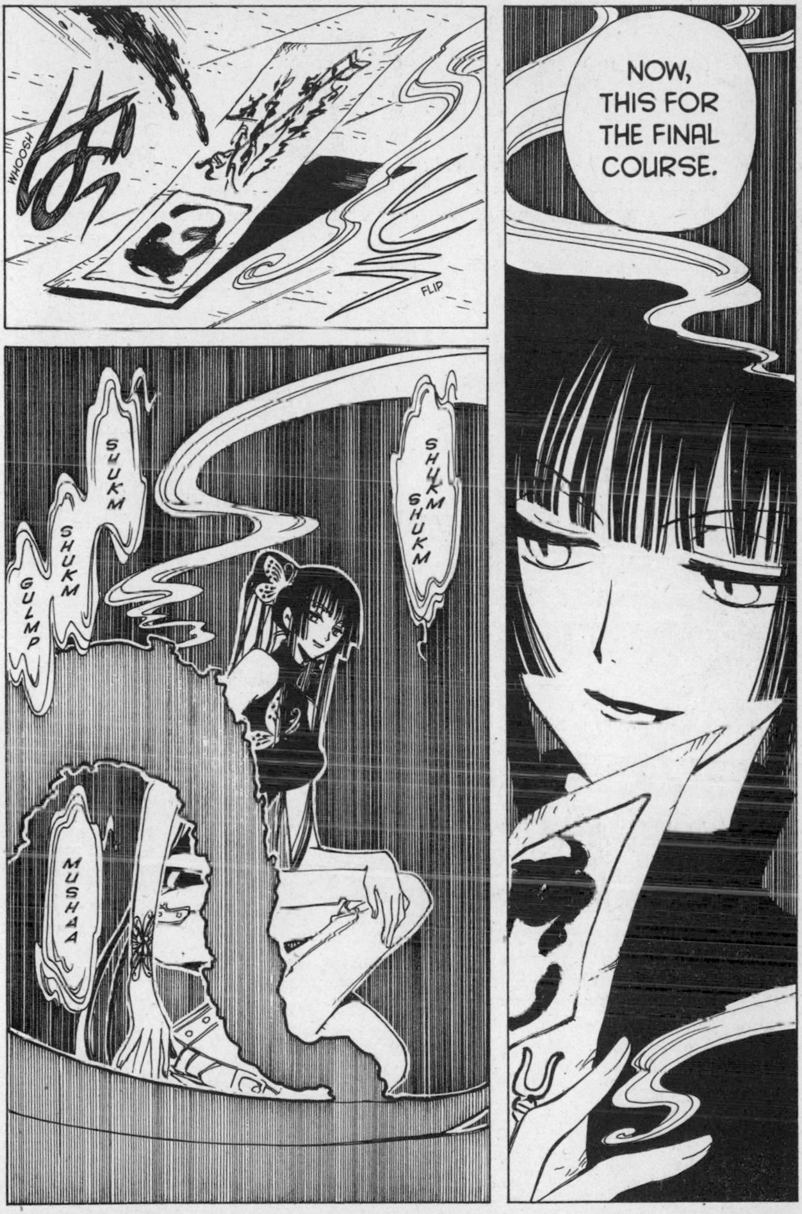
NOW, THIS FOR THE FINAL COURSE.
WHOOSH
FLIP
SHUKM SHUKM
SHUKM SHUKM GULMP
MUSHAA

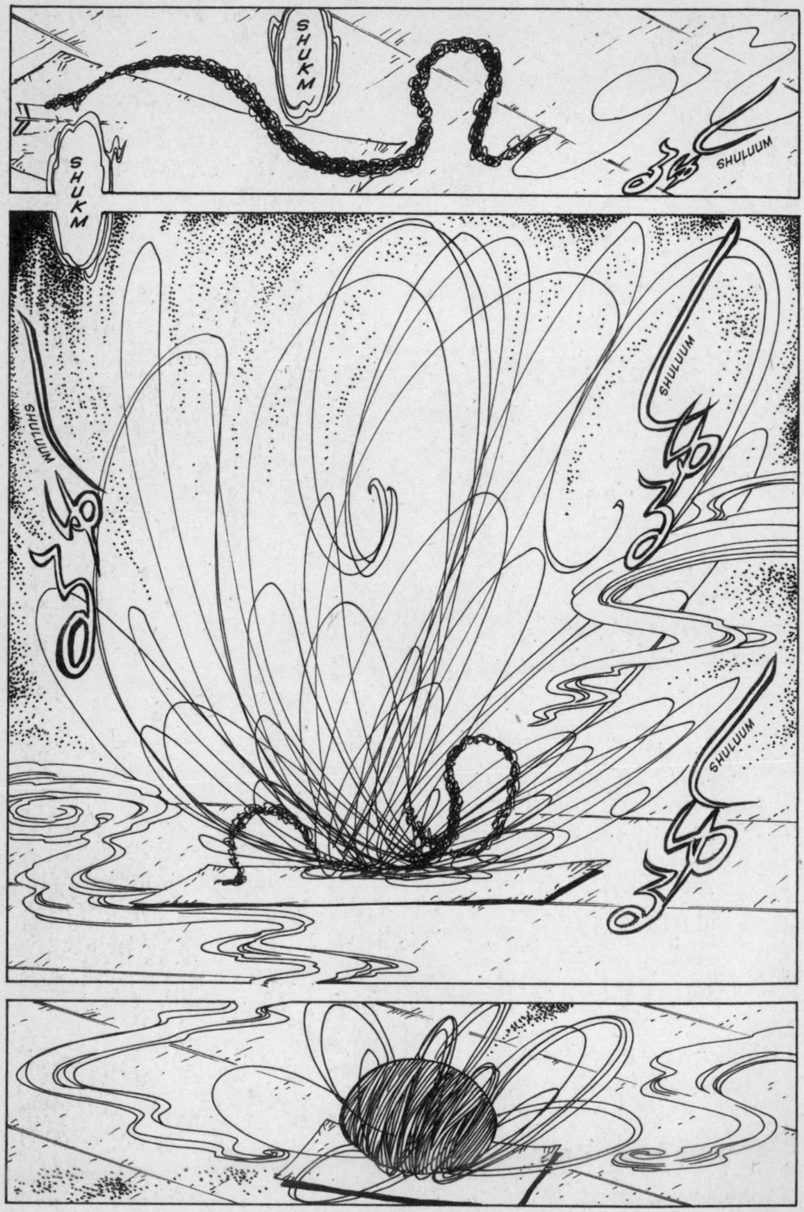
SHULUUM
SHUKM
SHUKM
SHULUUM
SHULUUM
SHULUUM

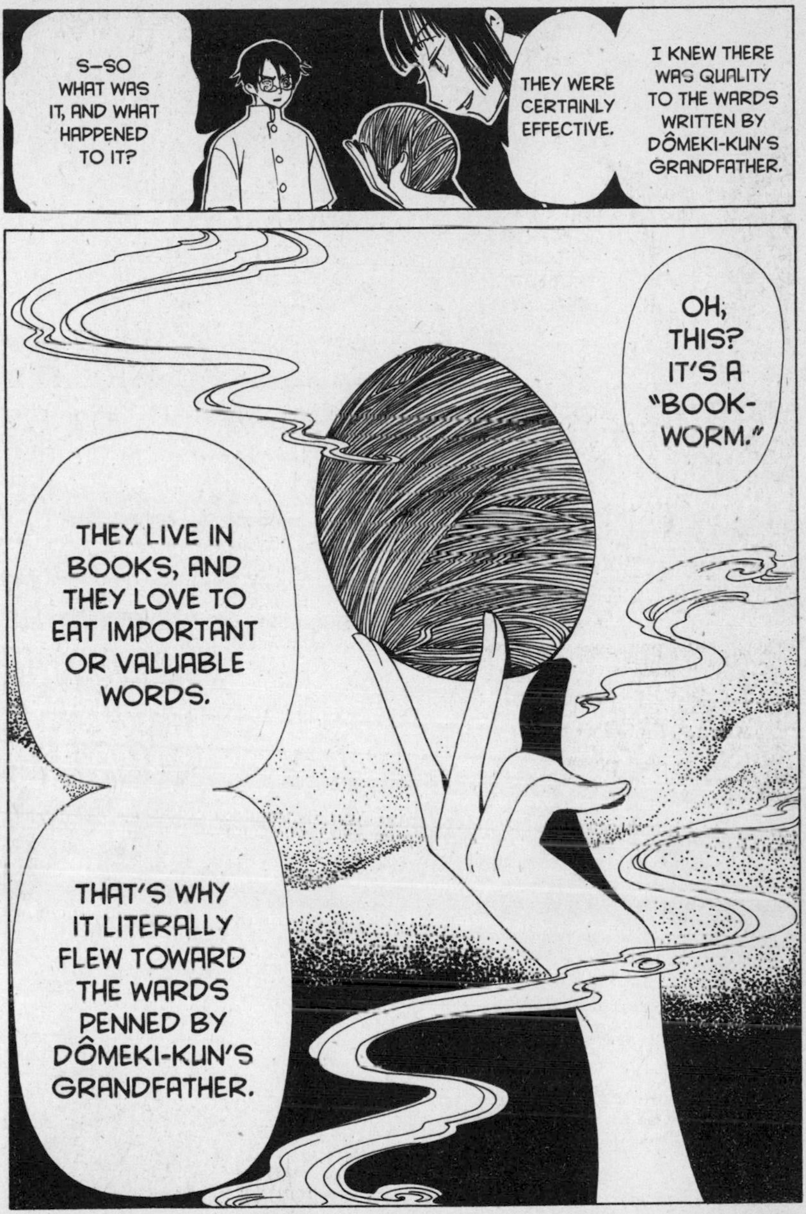
I KNEW THERE WAS QUALITY TO THE WARDS WRITTEN BY DÔMEKI-KUN'S GRANDFATHER.
THEY WERE CERTAINLY EFFECTIVE.
S-SO WHAT WAS IT, AND WHAT HAPPENED TO IT?
OH, THIS? IT'S A "BOOK-WORM."
THEY LIVE IN BOOKS, AND THEY LOVE TO EAT IMPORTANT OR VALUABLE WORDS.
THAT'S WHY IT LITERALLY FLEW TOWARD THE WARDS PENNED BY DÔMEKI-KUN'S GRANDFATHER.

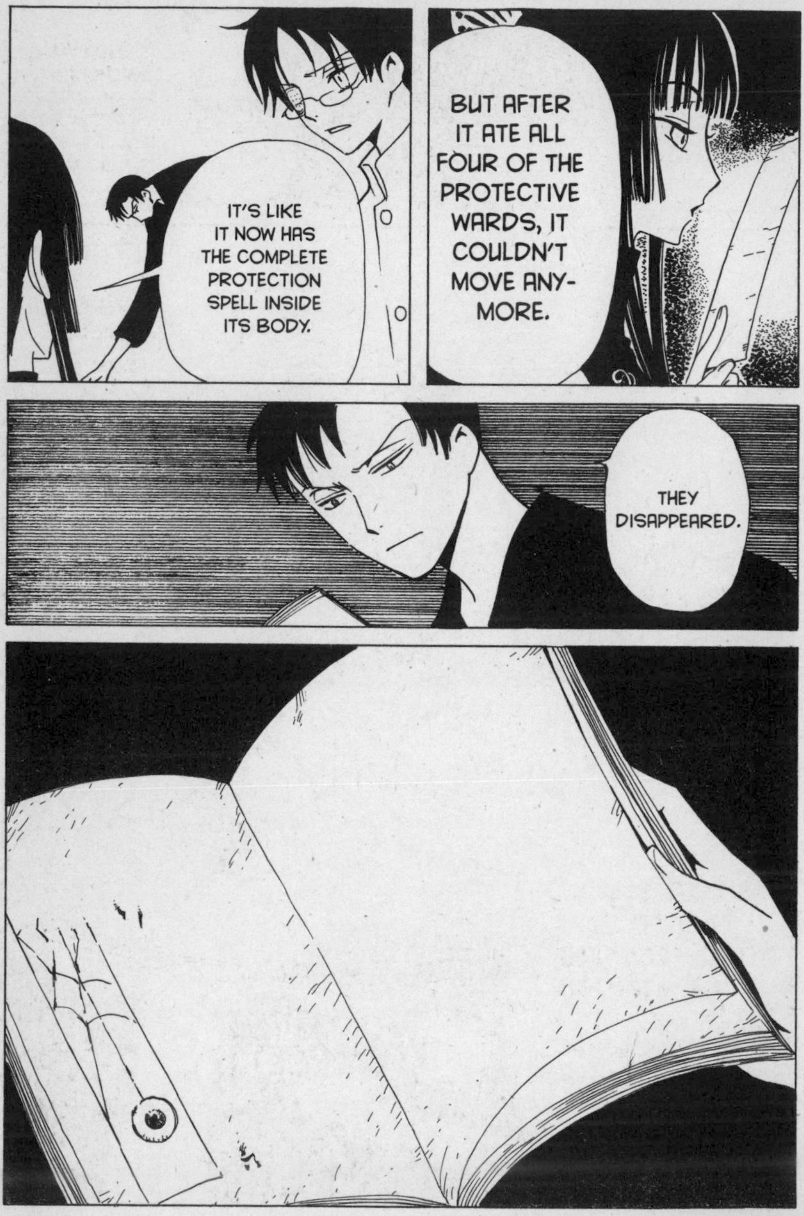
BUT AFTER IT ATE ALL FOUR OF THE PROTECTIVE WARDS, IT COULDN'T MOVE ANY-MORE.
IT'S LIKE IT NOW HAS THE COMPLETE PROTECTION SPELL INSIDE ITS BODY.
THEY DISAPPEARED.

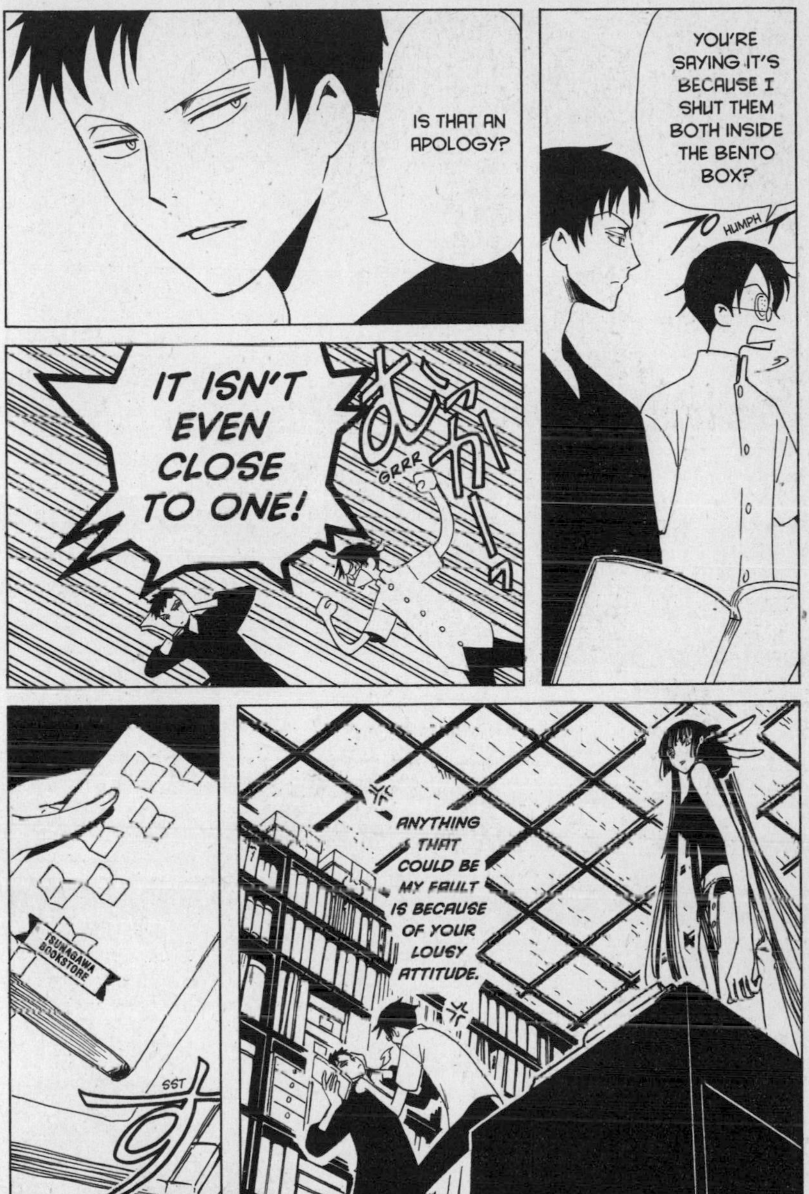
YOU'RE SAYING IT'S BECAUSE I SHUT THEM BOTH INSIDE THE BENTO BOX?
HUMPH
IS THAT AN APOLOGY?
IT ISN'T EVEN CLOSE TO ONE!
GRRR
ANYTHING THAT COULD BE MY FAULT IS BECAUSE OF YOUR LOUSY ATTITUDE.
TSUNAGAWA BOOKSTORE
SST

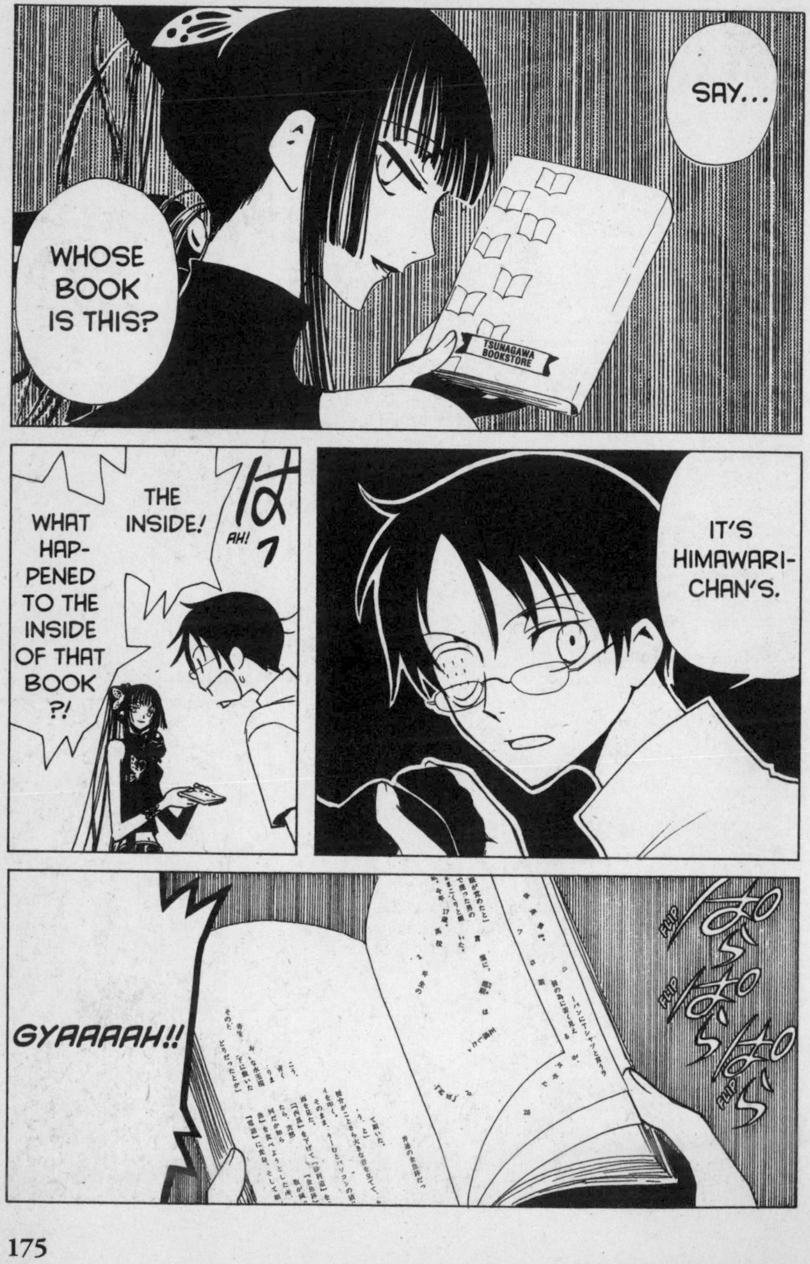
SAY...
TSUNAGAWA BOOKSTORE
WHOSE BOOK IS THIS?
IT'S HIMAWARI-CHAN'S.
はっ
AH!
THE INSIDE!
WHAT HAPPENED TO THE INSIDE OF THAT BOOK ?!
ぱらぱらぱら
FLIP FLIP FLIP
GYAAAAH!!

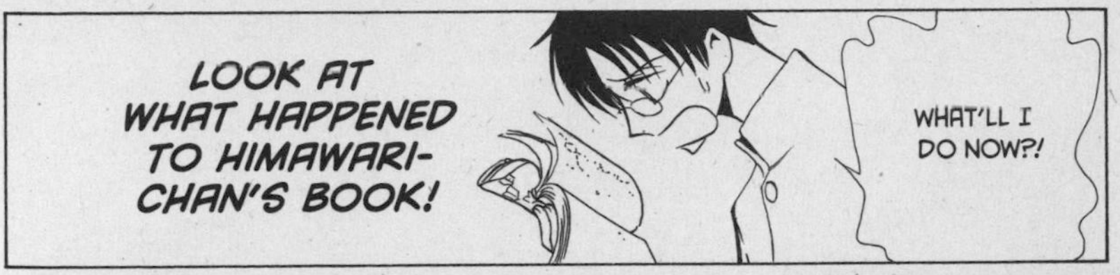
WHAT'LL I DO NOW?!
LOOK AT WHAT HAPPENED TO HIMAWARI-CHAN'S BOOK!

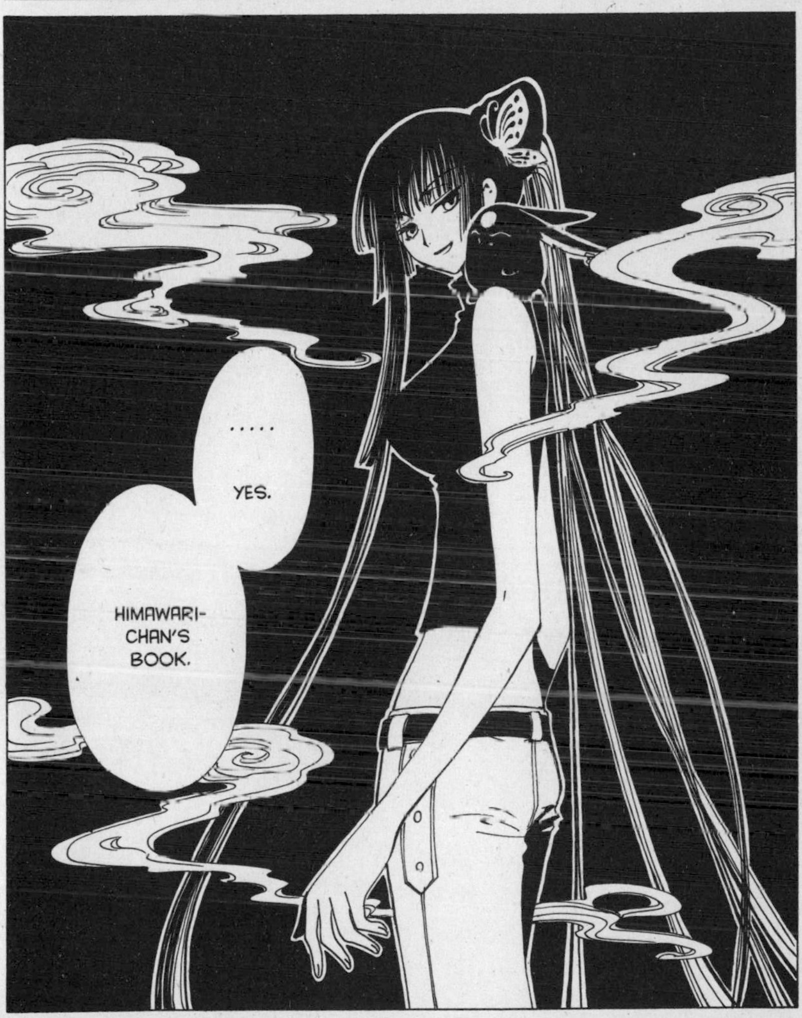
.....
YES.
HIMAWARI-CHAN'S BOOK.

≈ **Continued** ≈

in *xxxHOLiC* Volume 8

About the Creators

CLAMP is a group of four women who have become the most popular manga artists in America—Satsuki Igarashi, Tsubaki Nekoi, Mokona, and Ageha Ohkawa. They started out as *doujinshi* (fan comics) creators, but their skill and craft brought them to the attention of publishers very quickly. Their first work from a major publisher was *RG Veda*, but their first mass success was with *Magic Knight Rayearth*. From there, they went on to write many series, including *Cardcaptor Sakura* and *Chobits*, two of the most popular manga in the United States. Like many Japanese manga artists, they prefer to avoid the spotlight, and little is known about them personally.

CLAMP is currently publishing three series in Japan: *Tsubasa* and *xxxHOLiC* with Kodansha and *Gohou Drug* with Kadokawa.

Translation Notes

For your edification and reading pleasure, here are notes to help you understand some of the cultural and story references from our translation of *xxxHOLiC*.

Page 15, Time to dig in! (*Itadakimasu!*)

In a tradition that mirrors saying grace in Christian tradition, nearly all Japanese say the word "*itadakimasu*" before eating. "*Itadaku*" is the formal verb meaning "receive," combined with the formal verb ending "*masu*." The literal meaning would be "I shall receive," but now it is only something said by custom before eating.

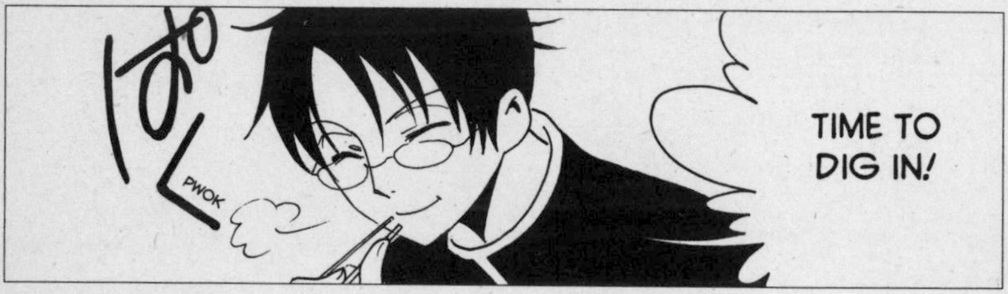
TIME TO DIG IN!
PWOK

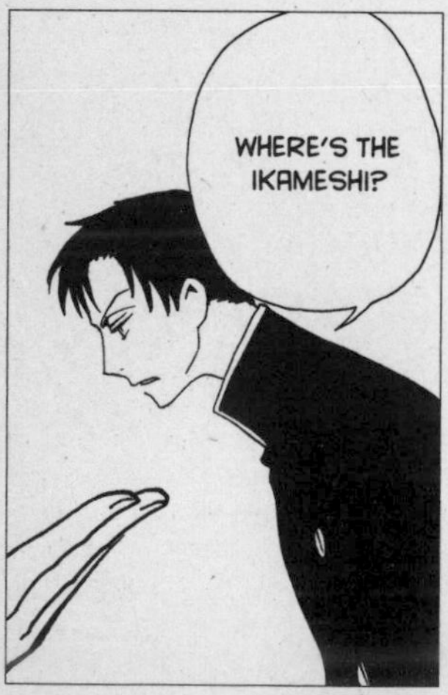
WHERE'S THE IKAMESHI?

Page 17, *Ikameshi*

In 1941, Japan was in the midst of a rice shortage due to the war, so an enterprising food vendor started to stuff what little rice he had into squid. Then he seasoned it with soy sauce and other ingredients, slow cooked it, and sold it at Mori Station near Hakodate on the Northern Island of Hokkaido. It was called "*ikameshi*" (squid-rice), and it became one of the most popular *ekiben* (train-station boxed lunches) in all of Japan.

Page 90, *Buridaikon*

Buridaikon is *buri*, a kind of yellowtail fish, simmered with *daikon* radish and ginger and served in a sauce made up of soy sauce, *mirin*, sugar, and saké. Rumor has it that the Emperor's chef invented it as a way to cook yellowtail, which the Americans brought when they arrived in the black boats in 1853.

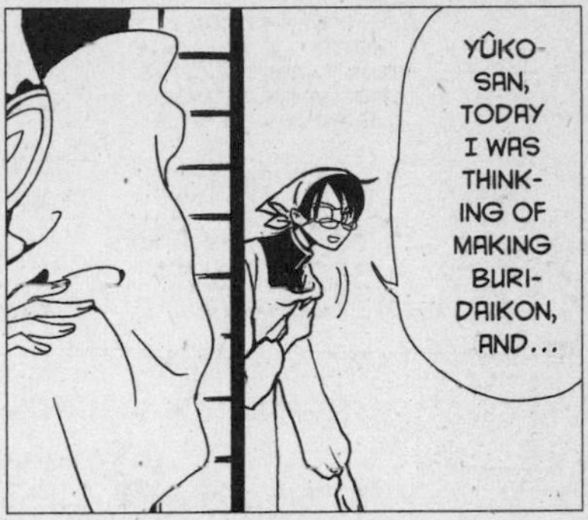
YÛKO-SAN, TODAY I WAS THINKING OF MAKING BURI-DAIKON, AND...

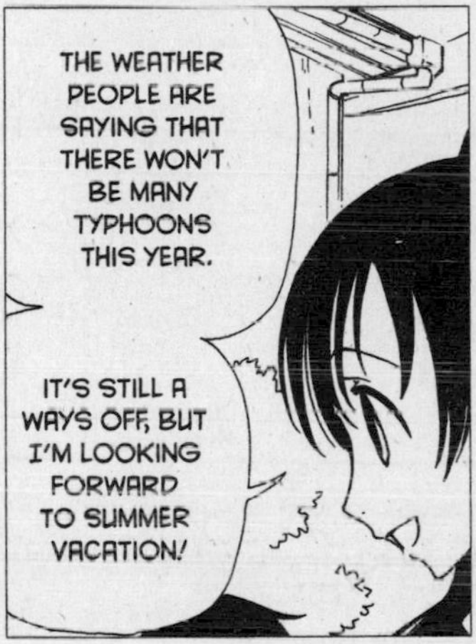
THE WEATHER PEOPLE ARE SAYING THAT THERE WON'T BE MANY TYPHOONS THIS YEAR.
IT'S STILL A WAYS OFF, BUT I'M LOOKING FORWARD TO SUMMER VACATION!

Page 123, Typhoons

The only difference between hurricanes and typhoons is the location where they have their effect. North America gets hits by hurricanes that have names. Japan and the other countries in northeast Asia get hit by typhoons that are numbered. Both are different names for the class of storms that are called (in general) tropical cyclones.

Page 125, Book Covers

Most bookstores in Japan will bag a purchase of several books, but if the customer buys only a single book, the bookstore may give the purchaser, in lieu of a bag, a book cover made of paper with the name of the bookstore printed on it.

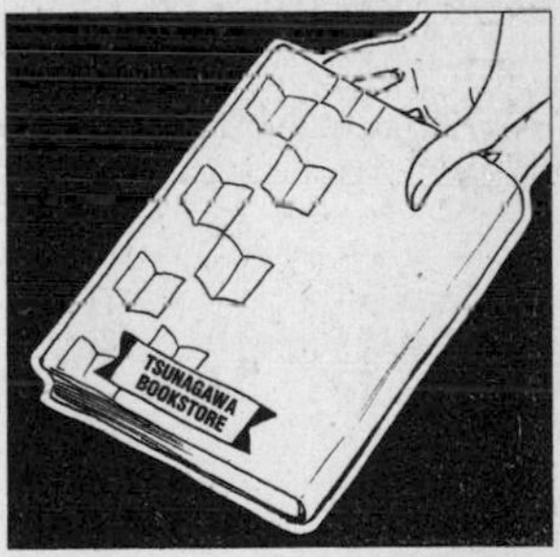
TSUNAGAWA BOOKSTORE

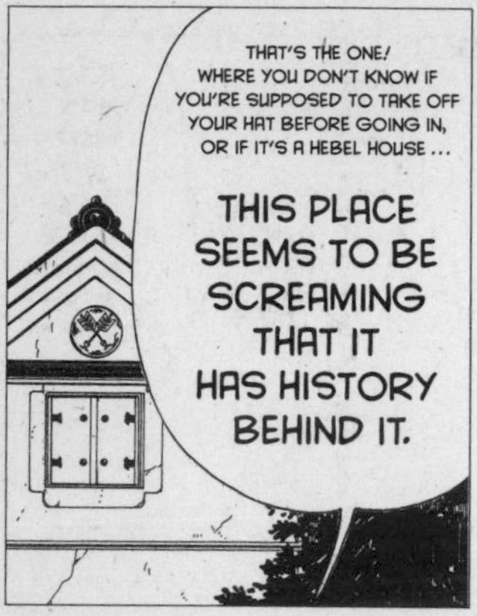
THAT'S THE ONE! WHERE YOU DON'T KNOW IF YOU'RE SUPPOSED TO TAKE OFF YOUR HAT BEFORE GOING IN, OR IF IT'S A HEBEL HOUSE...
THIS PLACE SEEMS TO BE SCREAMING THAT IT HAS HISTORY BEHIND IT.

Page 133, Hebel House

Within the first decade after World War II, a West German building contractor named Josef Hebel developed a new concrete-based building material. In 1961, he built his first Hebel House with it, and in 1967, signed his first manufacturing license with Asahi Chemical in Japan. Asahi is using Hebel's materials to create houses, apartments, and other buildings to this day.

Page 135, Tsuchimikado

Early in the Kamakura period (1185–1333), Emperor Tsuchimikado came to the throne and reigned for twelve years (1198–1210). But in this period as in the thousand years before it, it was the Shogun who wielded most of the power. During Tsuchimikado's reign, the Shogun was Yoritomo and his descendants.

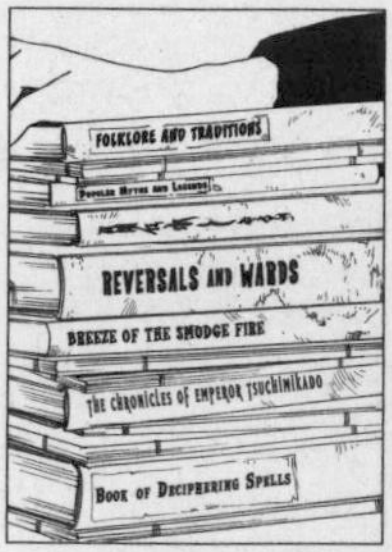
FOLKLORE AND TRADITIONS
REVERSALS AND WARDS
BREEZE OF THE SMODGE FIRE
THE CHRONICLES OF EMPEROR TSUCHIMIKADO
BOOK OF DECIPHERING SPELLS

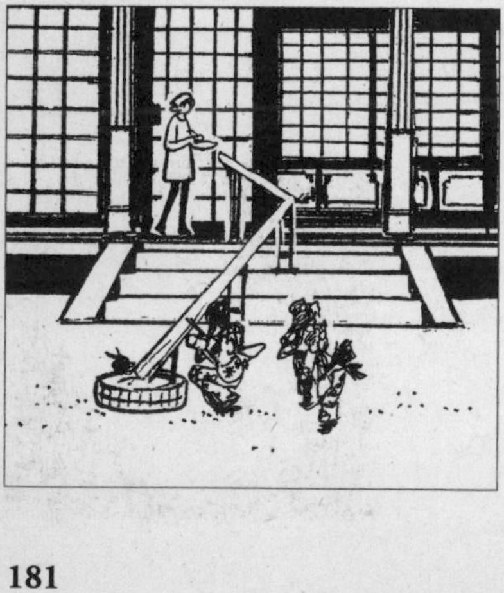

Page 136, Flowing Somen (*Somen Nagashi*)

This is a summer treat where boiled and then chilled wheat noodles (*somen*) are sent down a chute made of a bamboo pole sliced in half lengthwise. The diners are supposed to catch the noodles as they travel down the chute, then dip the noodles in a cup of chilled broth and eat them.

Page 140, Masumi Arabashiri

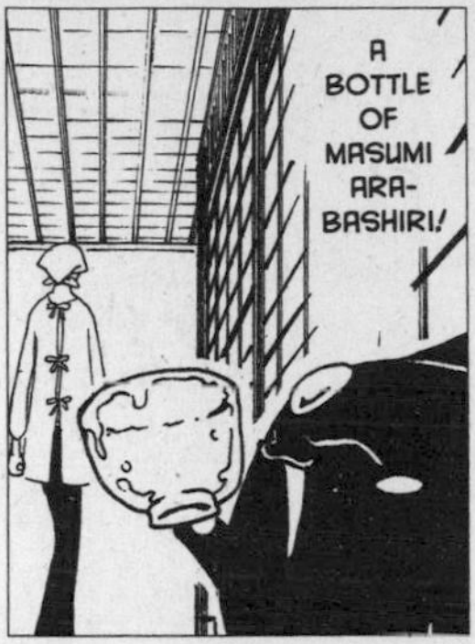
A BOTTLE OF MASUMI ARA-BASHIRI!

Arabashiri is a white, cloudy saké that is the first saké produced when the fermented *moromi* (final mash) is squeezed out from the cotton sacks used for filtration. It is unpasteurized, sold for only a few months in a year, and has a distinctly fresh taste and aroma. The saké company Masumi makes a well-regarded Arabashiri.

Page 148, Croquettes

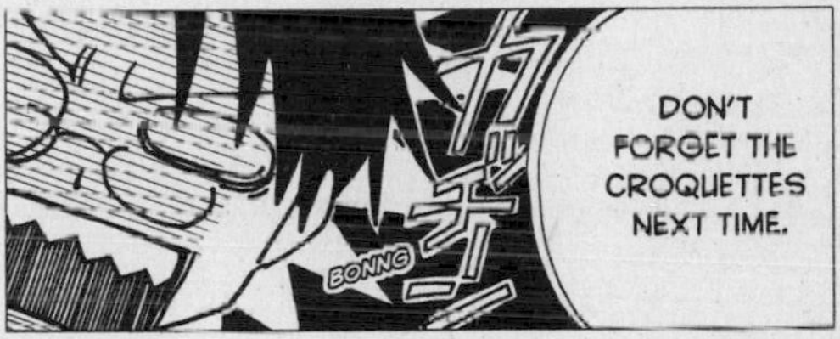
DON'T FORGET THE CROQUETTES NEXT TIME.
BONNG

Croquettes (*kurokke* in Japanese) are a European dish that has been adopted and changed to suit Japanese tastes. It is made mainly of mashed potatoes mixed with onion and bits of meats, then deep fried with a light breading.

Page 149, Thanks for the meal (*Gochisô-sama*)

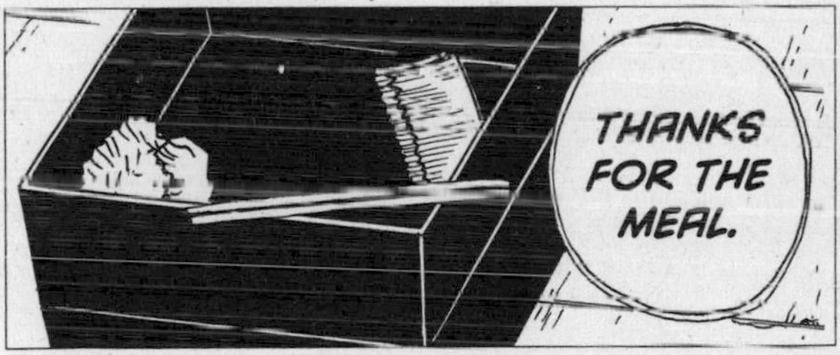
THANKS FOR THE MEAL.

Like the phrase "*itadakimasu*" (see the note on page 181) said at the beginning of a meal, the traditional thing to say at the end of the meal is *gochisô-sama deshita*, which means "thank you for the feast." However, the words have become so ingrained in the culture that it can be said when one dines alone, or when one has made the meal oneself. Now, it simply is something to say when one is finished eating.

Page 165, Sorry to barge in (*O-jama-shimasu*)

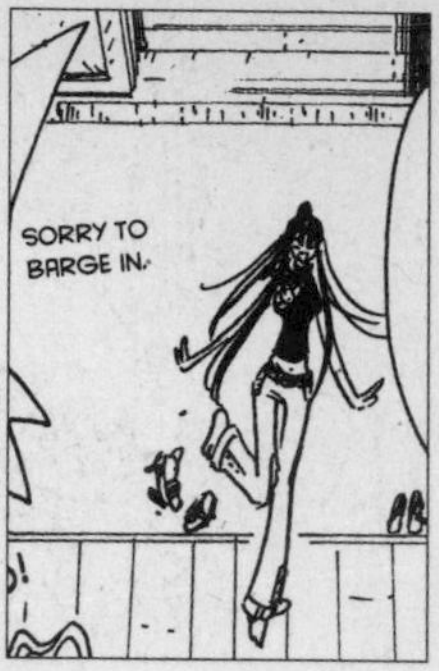
SORRY TO
BARGE IN.

Like other standard phrases like *itadakimasu* and *gochisô-sama* (see notes on pages 181 and 184), *o-jama-shimasu* is a standard phrase used when entering someone else's home. It literally means that one is getting in the way or barging in, but these days, it is just something polite to say upon entering a person's house.

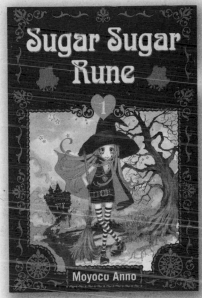

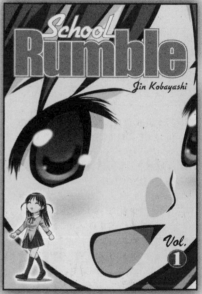

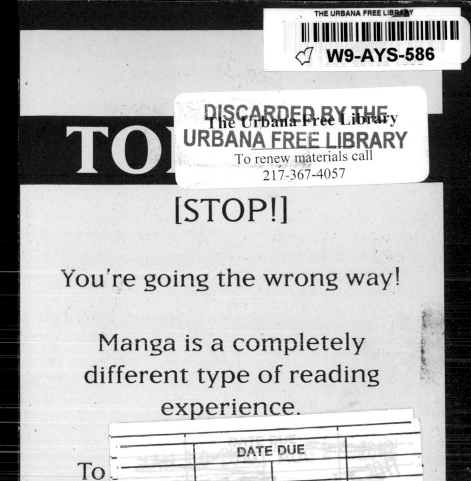

TOP

[STOP!]

You're going the wrong way!

Manga is a completely different type of reading experience.

To

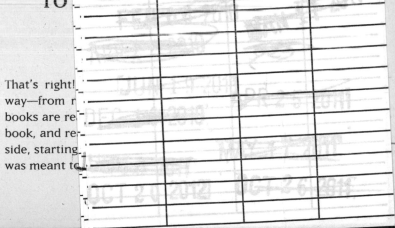

DATE DUE

That's right!
way—from r
books are re
book, and re
side, starting
was meant to